Regina Kuhne

Eternally Yours

Regina Künne

Eternally Yours

Challenge and Response

Contemporary US American Romance Novels
by Jayne Ann Krentz and Barbara Delinsky

LIT

Umschlagbild: Alexander Emka, „Lesende"
Rechte bei der Autorin

This book is printed on acid-free paper.

Bibliographic information published by the Deutsche Nationalbibliothek
The Deutsche Nationalbibliothek lists this publication in the Deutsche
Nationalbibliografie; detailed bibliographic data are available in the Internet at
http://dnb.d-nb.de.

ISBN 978-3-643-90604-5
Zugl.: Braunschweig, Univ., Diss., 2013

A catalogue record for this book is available from the British Library

©LIT VERLAG GmbH & Co. KG Wien,
Zweigniederlassung Zürich 2015
Klosbachstr. 107
CH-8032 Zürich
Tel. +41 (0) 44-251 75 05
Fax +41 (0) 44-251 75 06
E-Mail: zuerich@lit-verlag.ch
http://www.lit-verlag.ch

LIT VERLAG Dr. W. Hopf
Berlin 2015
Fresnostr. 2
D-48159 Münster
Tel. +49 (0) 2 51-62 03 20
Fax +49 (0) 2 51-23 19 72
E-Mail: lit@lit-verlag.de
http://www.lit-verlag.de

Distribution:

In the UK: Global Book Marketing, e-mail: mo@centralbooks.com
In North America: International Specialized Book Services, e-mail: orders@isbs.com
In Germany: LIT Verlag Fresnostr. 2, D-48159 Münster
Tel. +49 (0) 2 51-620 32 22, Fax +49 (0) 2 51-922 60 99,
E-mail: vertrieb@lit-verlag.de

In Austria: Medienlogistik Pichler-ÖBZ, e-mail: mlo@medien-logistik.at
e-books are available at www.litwebshop.de

ACKNOWLEDGEMENTS

This book on hand is the the printed dissertation which has been accepted by the Fakultät für Geistes-und Erziehungswissenschaften der Technischen Universität Carolo-Wilhelmina zu Braunschweig in the winter-semester 2013/14.

I would like to thank Professor Heinze, the dissertation supervisor, whose accompanying support and advice helped in such a friendly way, and to Professor Voigts, the second assessor.

I also owe a thankyou to my proofreaders Maggie Goring and Kenton E. Barnes.

And last I am very grateful to my husband, Michael, for his patience to listen throughout the entire process of bringing this study to life, and, to format the study.

ABSTRACT

This study explores the narrative and ideological development which unfolds in the contemporary popular romance novels of the American writers Jayne Ann Krentz and Barbara Delinsky over a period of time of twenty-five years. As in the first ten years of their writing careers, the chosen authors were writers for the restrictive uniformity of the romance genre predominantly published by Harlequin Enterprises, a Canadian publishing house, the study addresses the industry of romance writing that targets women as an audience and uses women writers for the task. I think that even this section of literature, represented partly in both authors' novels, mirrors specific contemporary American concerns and beliefs, transports social and ethical values in the narratives, and adapts to changes of taste and values in the American society, giving the *Zeitgeist* its due in order to stay marketable.

The study contains an in-depth analysis of three of the authors' novels: the first written at the beginning of their writing careers (1982), the second, ten years later (1992), and the third, another fifteen years later (2007). The structural analysis of each author's three novels is followed by a survey of the developmental, the narrative and ideological changes that transpire. Particular attention is directed to the presentation of gender behavior in the novels, to readership acceptance through narrative devices, and to specific American values. Against the background of romance scholarship, and the history of the romance genre, the novels are analyzed under the narrative aspects of plot, figural constellations, erotic scenes and the language used there, the writing style and the codes used to define the genre, followed by an analysis of American norms and values mirrored in the novels in order to identify changes.

Moreover, I maintain that by reading romance novels a reader reenacts a mythic rite: by identifying with anthropologically typical human needs and longings that are thematized in these novels, a reader becomes involved, and thus is integrated into the community of readers, of learners and of like-minded peers on the internet.

TABLE OF CONTENTS

INTRODUCTION

The title of this study refers to two different levels of meaning concerning US contemporary romance fiction: Eternally Yours relates to the aspect of romance novels' happy endings in order to satisfy reader expectations of a female audience. The terms Challenge and Response refer – differently and regardless of Toynbee's use of them – to the dichotomy between print market oriented production and romance authors subjected to the terms of the literary industry.

The fast diversification of the romance genre and its market along with the electronic expansion of publishing literature make reviewing exceedingly difficult. Therefore, it seems legitimate to single out, in a subjective way from the wealth of source material, the typical novels of romance fiction, as well as successfully marketed novels or authors. The objective of this study is to ascertain whether this kind of formula literature has changed over a period of twenty-five years and whether, despite the formula's parameters, whether an individual author's voice can be identified. Accordingly, this study explores the narrative and ideological changes which unfold in the American[1] contemporary popular romance novels of Jayne Ann Krentz and Barbara Delinsky over a period of twenty-five years. In order to introduce the genre these novels represent, I define the genre, which is followed by a report of the current situation of scholarship in the field of the romance genre. After having reflected on the theoretical principles and methodological strategies that will be adopted in this study, I will delineate the history of the genre and that of the publishing industry the authors are indebted to for being published at all. The guidelines they had to observe while writing the novels in order to be published are analyzed and juxtaposed with the novels. One part of this work is assigned to an in-depth formal and contentual analysis of three contemporary novels of each author (six novels altogether), one written in 1982[2] at the start of their writing careers, one in 1992[3], and one in 2007[4].

Each novel is analyzed first according to narratological methods (Nünning and Nünning 2008) under the following narratological decoding categories: Summary, Plot, Chapters, Setting, Time, Character Constellations, Conflicts, Relationship, Erotic Scenes, Writing Style, and Codes. The analysis of the three novels writ-

---

[1]   Unless otherwise stated 'American' refers to US America.
[2]   Jayne Ann Krentz: *Stormy Challenge*, Barbara Delinsky: *Sweet Ember*
[3]   Jayne Ann Krentz: *Perfect Partners*, Barbara Delinsky: *A Woman Betrayed*
[4]   Jayne Ann Krentz: *All Night Long*, Barbara Delinsky: *The Family Tree*

ten by one author is followed by a survey of the development and the narrative and ideological changes of each author that transpire. This way the reader of this study might obtain a better source of reference. Then I examine, by means of a synoptic survey, the structural narrative aspects in these novels as well as the ideology and behavioral norms, values and myths that emerge within the stories. I argue that each author has her own core theme she focuses on and her own narrative strategies. In a comparison, I delineate what the authors have in common, be they narratological aspects or ideological and/or differences resulting from their individual approach to writing romances.

As far as I can see, there are countless academic analyses of the romance genre on the market, but rarely one that endeavors to provide an in depth analysis of a novel, this way uncovering formulaic parts of the genre as well as a possible individual writing style. For, as in these analyses, the writers are generally seen as belonging to a group of genre writers and not as individuals with individual themes and 'voices'. They are only valued by their readers, and not the critics. There are many theoreticians who like to deny an author's individuality. Roland Barthes, for instance, negates the idea that a text can be attributed to a single author as also do, in part, Michel Foucault or Gérard Genette, and post-structuralist skepticism about the notion of the singular identity of the self has also been important for some academics working in feminist theories. Literature, seen from the perspective of deconstruction, questions concepts of personal identity, of individual and creative authorship, of gender, of linguistic and literary originality. These theories surely are the reason why many literary scholars analyze the genre and not the individual author's work. Whereas it is undeniable that authors are surrounded by the culture they are born into, and that their way of thinking, of speaking, and writing is intensely influenced by their culture, and the *zeitgeist* trends and styles, their individuality is their trademark, as long as they do not endeavor to write interchangeable novels. Readers do buy and read books by authors they appreciate and whose individual authorship they will never question because of the cultural palimpsests which linguists and literary scholars detect in the authors' works. To view authors as individuals and rightly so, I want to explore in this study by analyzing their novels if and how authors who are considered to write pure formula differ relevantly from each other.

I decided on these authors because, besides other criteria mentioned later in the text, as a reader, I noticed they seem to be different in the way that they have clear, distinguished narrative voices, they choose different themes to write about, and they are still writing successfully.

Furthermore, there is the question of why this genre is so exceptionally popular. In trying to examine the performativity of reading the romance novels, I aim to give one of many possible answers.

PART I

A PERSPECTIVE ON THE FIELD OF RESEARCH

1.1 DEFINING ROMANCE FICTION

Romance fiction is usually defined by what it is not: It is not 'literature'. It lacks the legitimating sanction of the dominant literary class. Most critics openly or implicitly adhere to the following negative convictions: whereas 'literature' should be indifferent, even contemptuous of the publishing trade in order to gain social and cultural recognition by being original and complex, romance fiction is simple, sensuous, exaggerated in every way and, most importantly because it is written for the lower classes[5], formulaic. Moreover, it is written almost exclusively by women. Romance authors produce one or even more paperbacks per year which are destined to be quickly discarded after reading. For John Cawelti formula literature is a kind of literary art that deserves to be analyzed and evaluated like any other kind of literature (Cawelti 8). With regards to the prolific writing of genre authors, he reasons:

> For creators the formula provides a means for the rapid and efficient production of new works. Once familiar with the outlines of the formula, the writer who devotes himself to this sort of creation does not have to make as many difficult artistic decisions as a novelist working without a formula. Thus, formulaic creators tend to be extremely prolific. (Cawelti 9)

Modern romance novels are usually defined by content and published form: they are mass-produced. Their success is measured by the public, the publishers are measured by their sales and the authors by the devotion of their fans. As early as

---

[5] The assumption that popular literature, especially romance novels are low-class literature is contradicted by Richard Hoggart: "the mass publications from which I draw most of my evidence affect far more than those working-class groups of which I have a close knowledge; in fact, in so far as they tend to be 'classless' publications, they affect all classes in society" (Hoggart 19). Umberto Eco also disclaims Virginia Woolf's terms of the three levels of culture (highbrow, middlebrow, lowbrow) by arguing against them: "I levelli non corrispondono a una livellazione classica ... Si sa che il gusto *high brow* non è necessariamente quello delle classi dominanti" (The levels do not correspond with the class stratification ... As is well known that as regards taste *highbrow* taste is not necessarily the taste of the ascendant class of society.) (Herlinghaus 876)

1944, Horkheimer and Adorno drew attention to the 'culture industry' perspective (Adorno 351). They saw the author as a person whose art is aesthetic, but also who transports ideology and has a social contract to fulfill. According to them, any artistic production resembles the production of other things. As such, the question arises whether an author is like an industrial worker who produces commodity fiction as specified by the market's stipulations. Strenuous efforts are made to distance art and literature from other commodities and by endowing literature with a certain aura, whatever this may mean, thus making it a more sophisticated commodity, buying this commodity causes readers to feel intellectually aware. Romance novel authors, however, regard themselves as 'workers' because they openly serve the demands of a mass-market. Their products are not endowed with an aura because as they are mass-marketed and formulaic, they cannot be regarded as elitist. As Horkheimer and Adorno would phrase it, as their writing standards are based on consumer's needs and they address millions of readers, they cannot be elitists. It seems, first and foremost, that they serve a human need, that of escape and relaxation.[6]

The story in a romance has to have the formulaic constants of an unmarried man and an unmarried woman who meet, are attracted to each other, but have to overcome some obstacle before they can marry. The required happy ending turns the story into a romance story. This is the conservative definition of a modern romance novel that, as a matter of fact, is no longer valid for most of the novels of this genre. Nowadays, the association of The Romance Writers of America (RWA) agrees with the following narrative ingredients that define a romance novel: "The main plot centers around two individuals falling in love and struggling to make the relationship work." Instead of 'man and woman', they speak of 'individuals' indicating that a romance story is no longer restricted to heterosexual couples, and the question of marriage is circumvented by the expression to 'make the relationship work'. In addition, now the romance novel has an 'emotionally satisfying and optimistic ending', which does not necessarily mean that the couple will find its happy end in marriage or, as the RWA put it: "In a romance, the lovers who risk and struggle for each other and their relationship are rewarded with emotional justice and unconditional love" (RWA 2012).

The genre is divided into two different types of publication and distribution: category romances and romance novels. Category romances are paperback novels, 190–250 pages in length that are published monthly and are sold alongside magazines. Romance novels are sold in bookshops and thus have a longer shelf-life. Both follow the same basic narrative form: that of a couple's meeting, and the

---

[6] The Oxford English Dictionary still connotes escapism negatively with the following definition: escapism is "the tendency to seek distraction and relief from unpleasant realities, especially by seeking entertainment or engaging in fantasy: virtual reality offers a form of escapism".

surmounting of conflicts which results in a happy ending. Depending on publishers' selling strategies, romance novels are also published within the genre categorization of 'Novel' or 'Women's Fiction', or no classification at all. Krentz and Delinsky began their literary careers writing category romances. Today, they no longer write for the category romance series. They have stayed with the genre, but have changed publishing houses and write longer romance novels. Delinsky claims to write Women's Fiction after her category romance writing phase. Why this is still fiction with a high percentage of romantic elements will be analyzed in this study.

Jennifer Crusie, scholar and romance writer, wrote in her plea for category romances:

> Category is an elegant, exacting form of fiction. It requires precise pacing, tight plotting, and exquisitely brief characterizations. It is truly as a fine form for fiction as the sonnet is for poetry. (Crusie 1998, 44)

Here, Crusie refers to the Shakespearian form of sonnets with their alternately rhymed iambic three quartets and the couplet at the end. The structured content of a romance novel could be seen analogously to the sonnet: in the sonnet's first two quartets a thesis is set out followed in the last quartet by the antithesis and the couplet by a kind of synthesis. Similarly a category romance presents the development of a love in the first two thirds of the novel, and the questioning of this love as the 'forever' kind in the last third, which is answered in the last chapter of the novel, the synthesis, as being the one both lovers were looking for. As not all sonnets written and published can be considered as artful, the same can be assumed of category romances. Seen from this perspective, the adherence to form and content indicates that these novels stay in the traditional field of literature, offering readers well established narrative forms, and because these forms are dated and not innovative, they are usually not valued by literary critics.

Cawelti, who examines the formulas that define a genre says,

> The concept of formula … is a means of generalizing the characteristics of large groups of individual works from certain combinations of cultural materials and archetypal stories. It is useful primarily as a means of making historical and cultural inferences about the collective fantasies shared by large groups of people and of identifying differences in these fantasies from one culture or period to another. When we turn from the cultural or historical use of the concept of the formula to a consideration of the artistic limitations and possibilities of particular formulaic patterns, we are treating these formulas as a basis for aesthetic judgments of various sorts. In these cases, we might say that our generalized definition of the formula has become a conception of a genre. Formula and genre might be best understood

> not as denoting two different things, but as reflecting two phases or aspects
> of a complex process of literary analysis. (Cawelti 7)

Cawelti defines the romance as the female equivalent of the adventure story generally understood as male directed and sees the crucial difference between these stories in the fact that the romance does not star a female character, "but that its organizing action is the development of a love relationship, usually between a man and a woman."[7] Therefore, analyses of romance novels cannot be restricted to one protagonist, but have two to contend with, a hero and a heroine, or vice versa, in order to be politically correct. According to Cawelti the romance's moral fantasy

> is that of love triumphant and permanent, overcoming all obstacles and difficulties. Though the usual outcome is a permanently happy marriage, more sophisticated types of love stories end in the death of one or both of the lovers, but always in such a way as to suggest that the love relation has been of lasting and permanent impact. This characteristic differentiates the mimetic form of the romantic tragedy from the formulaic romance. (Cawelti 41–42)

This characteristic not only differentiates the sophisticated mimetic form from the formula form, it is also the reason for critical denigration of the genre.

Another aspect of formula romances and the reason for their critical disparagement is their being considered as a means of a reader's temporary escape from the frustrations of life, and as popular entertainment which in itself can be regarded either as negative or as positive.[8] As these romances are shaped by the essential offerings of escape and entertainment, readers can experience the excitement of adventure, of a developing new love, of sexuality in the formulaic imaginary worlds, without being confronted with the insecurities and fears of their reality, especially because these readers are confirmed in their conviction that, in the imaginary world which is presented in romances, things always work out the way they expect them to and because the novels appeal to a bone-deep sense of optimism as a core world view.

---

[7] Not everybody will overcome dangerous adventures, but when they do their lives will continue the way they did before, whereas everybody's quest is love and once somebody has found it, s/he will hope his/her life will continue in the new state of bliss. Thus, the promise of a happy ending in a novel is different from that of the adventure story because here it is a promise of a secular blessedness.

[8] A Dear Author (web) contributor (Sunita) defines escapism less pejoratively than the OED and more formally: for her escapism is a cognitive activity that takes one's mind to a different place from its everyday life and provides different types of stimulation, comfort and/or cognitive stretching. She argues that scholarly research can even be seen as an escape from the modern world. (Sunita)

1.2 Objectives

For centuries, women have written love stories for women. Today, romance fiction written by women for women is produced under mass-market conditions, systematizing the satisfaction of readers' wishes, a *modus operandi* that in a way is comparable to industrial production. Supply is the response to demand or challenge. Thus I will consider differently the terms of Arnold J. Toynbee's theory of Challenge and Response by which he explained the rise and fall of civilizations in his *A Study of History* (1934–1961). I use these terms by defining Challenge as the publishers' requirements romance authors have to meet in order to be published and Response as the authors' executed individual answers. Therefore, Part II of this study concentrates on the industry of romance writing, targeting women as audience and using women writers for the task. (Today, in this genre, male authors have to assume female pseudonyms to become successful.)

I argue that this section of literature utilizes and mirrors contemporary American concerns and beliefs explicitly as well as implicitly because readers expect to see their society and their concerns depicted in these contemporary novels, a fact that challenges authors to respond accordingly. Assuming that these books are not only escapist readings but influence readers in constructing their moral attitudes, especially because the books are consumed by millions of women,[9] it seems justified to expound on the social and ethical values transported by their authors' narratives.

As the genre is not a monolithic block and each writer is allowed her individual writing style and individual themes within publishers' specifications, I want to explore the writers' difference within the genre, thus giving each writer her due. Today, as will be seen in the course of this study, readers have ample possibilities of choice and they clearly choose their favorite authors. There are various facets of the romance novel to consider that belie the assumption of their being 'formulaic scribble', despite their industrial mass market provenance. That romances are formula fiction is undisputed. But it is likely that through the formula of courtship and marriage, complex themes are portrayed. Furthermore, it can be assumed that the respective author decides what a romance is about, which setting and which language is used, and how ideology, values and attitudes are presented, and that values and attitudes featured in the novels, perhaps even ideologies, have changed over the years: in the case of my research, over twenty-five years. As these inferences can only be instanced on the basis of the authors' work the alterations

---

[9]   In the Harlequin 60th Anniversary Cover Shoot (2009) on You Tube, Donna Hayes explains that this publishing house prints 1,200 new books (she does not use the term 'titles'!) a year which means 130 million copies. According to the Océ Case Study of 2013 Harlequin issues 115 titles per month and close to 140 million books a year.

and shifts will be a testimony to the diversity and feasibility of modifications in romance novels.

The contemporary romance novels of two American women writers, Jayne Ann Krentz and Barbara Delinsky, will be analyzed. Both authors have succeeded in inscribing themselves into the top bestselling lists of 'light' fiction and have stayed there for over two decades, due to the interaction between production facilities, marketing strategies and, last but not least, to readers' responses, since their success is measured by the amount of copies sold.[10] Being best sellers on the 'light' fiction market for such a long time would not have been possible without adapting to the changes of taste and values, reflecting the changes women have undergone in society and giving the *Zeitgeist* its due if one wants to stay marketable. This study aims to emphasize the perceptiveness both these authors have maintained over the years, the different lines they have pursued, as well as the changes their writing has been subjected to in order to achieve a *Zeitgeist* kind of novel. It will show that the topics and the moral code presented in their writing is a reflection of American times and American notions of moral behavior and of the respective current concerns and challenges.

Therefore, the choice of authors was based on the fact that

1.) they started writing at about the same time and are still writing and that they are US Americans writing contemporary romances, set in the USA,
2.) that when they started out, they wrote category romances,
3.) that after nearly three decades, their books hit the bestselling lists regularly,
4.) that their novels are so successful that their present publishing houses regard their novels marketable enough to be issued as hard-covers first, and up to a year later, as paperbacks so that they might receive reviews in major newspapers like the New York Times,
5.) that their novels can also be found in public libraries which indicates a literary estimation, and
6.) that over thirty-five million copies of Krentz's novels are in print as are over thirty million copies of Delinsky's books.

As these authors are prolific writers, and Krentz has expanded her writing interests to different time eras and continents, her contemporary romance novels alone will be analyzed here because Delinsky has only written contemporary novels set in the USA. So to include Krentz's historical and futuristic romances in the analysis would make little sense.

Both authors are about the same age and began writing at the same time,

---

[10]   The number of the copies is never mentioned. Only the blurb of their category romances boasts millions of copies. But their days of writing category romances are over and now only their hard cover editions followed by paperback editions could be considered as indicators for a high amount if copies.

but they are deeply rooted in different parts of the USA, a fact that might also influence their way of writing: but this fact is not of importance for this study. Information about the biographies of Krentz and Delinsky can now be found on the internet because they are well known in the romance community as well as to readers of popular mainstream fiction. Considering their beginnings with category romances, it is obvious that, like their predecessors in the 19th century, Krentz and Delinsky write to entertain women and do so with professionalism, but do not aspire to write literary works of art. They have continued to entertain their readers. The purpose of this work is to find out what has become different within the fictional world of both these authors over the course of 25 years, or if it has altered at all regardless of the changes that occur in the real world.

The order of presentation of the authors follows an inherent logic. Krentz is still a stout advocate of romance, albeit of romantic suspense, while Delinsky has changed the genre in order to write women's relationship fiction with a strong psychological touch.

To be able to criticize, criteria are needed. Vilem Flusser recites the three traditional Platonic types of criteria we still tend to use as the first basis for our own standardized canon: the epistemological (true – false), the ethical (good – bad), and the aesthetic (beautiful – ugly) or the criteria which are generally known as The True, The Good, and The Beautiful. Flusser states that by criticizing a picture (or in this case a romance novel) we seem to be unable not to incriminate whatever we criticize.[11] This also accompanies our thinking processes like a 'basso con-tinuo' (Flusser 2010, 78–86) when we analyze romance novels, hence the debasement of the genre. Critics who only look at certain elements, thereby cutting the novel into pieces, give rise, Flusser believes, to incrimination because they rob the whole of its myth or its magic. But then this has always been part of what Bourdieu (*Die feinen Unterschiede*. 1987) describes as the function of classification. The literary field provides the different social classes with clearly distinguishing signs to enable them to position themselves culturally as well as semiotically. Bourdieu imputes the underprivileged classes with a cultural schism:

> Alles spricht dafür, dass 'populäre Ästhetik' sich darauf gründet, zwischen Kunst und Leben einen Zusammenhang zu behaupten (was die Unterordnung der Form unter die Funktion einschließt), oder, anders gesagt, auf der Weigerung, jene Verweigerungshaltung mitzuvollziehen, die aller theoretisch entfalteten Ästhetik zugrundeliegt, d.h. die schroffe Trennung zwischen gewöhnlicher Alltagseinstellung und genuin ästhetischer Einstellung. … Grund der Zurückhaltung und Ablehnung ist nicht allein fehlende Vertrautheit; es ist die tiefsitzende, von der experimentellen Form immer

---

[11] See also: Wayne C. Both. *The Company We Keep*. (33)

wieder enttäuschte Erwartung, einbezogen zu werden ... (Bourdieu 1984, 64)

As mentioned above, Hoggart and Eco deny Bourdieu's assumption that highbrow literature is only written for the upper classes because of their 'genuine aesthetic mindset', but nevertheless it will be reasonable to examine the connection between the form and its function in romance novels as part of the popular aesthetic.

Usually, an author does not look at a novel the way a literary critic does. The author might aspire to incorporate into her novel the aspects of *docere, movere et delectare*[12] and, in the case of romance novels, more *delectare* and *movere* than *docere* because the success of a romance novel depends on its audience's expectations of entertainment and encounters of 'magic', which need to be met, especially nowadays, when readers make use of many channels for feed-back and are not afraid to express their satisfaction or dissatisfaction with a novel, for example, via the internet. So the author, more the writer than the poet, who aspires to be successful, will prudently adapt to her readers' wishes as well as she uses reader connecting factors, thus respecting the author-reader contract.

This project will focus mainly on structural narrative aspects as well as time-related, ethical and psychological aspects. Whether twenty-five years of individual writing or a synopsis of both the authors' literary production are analyzed, it is essential to answer aspects concerning the development of the genre or to make historical references. In addition, romance fiction written by women for women is a focal point for scholars because of its historical development and political relevance in gender discourse. Accordingly, it is imperative to reflect on the possible emancipatory effect romance fiction could have on readers, or by contrast, to reflect on a stabilizing view of traditional gender relations. Regarding romance fiction as formula literature, as many scholars have claimed by researching only the genre is not enough. In this study I will examine whether the individual author's texts adhere strongly to the formula, or if they surmount it.

Therefore the objectives of this study are to find out a) what developments and variations emerge within the six novels, b) whether the authors have an individual voice within the parameters of the romance publishers' writing guidelines and the overarching formula and c) whether Fischer-Lichte's theory of performativity in connection with the myth of the 'Sacred Marriage' can give an answer of why this genre is so extremely popular. The leading questions are:

---

[12]   Usually Horace is allotted this citation, but he only states a poet's intentions being as follows: "aut prodesse volunt aut delectare poetae" (Ars poetica, verse 333f) whereas Quintilian in his Institutio Oratoria VIII, proemium 7 postulates: "Oratoris officium docendi, movendi, delectandi partibus contineri ... "

1.) How restrictive are the formulae and the writing guidelines for the authors? Do the authors clearly abide by them and/or do they transcend these restrictions and how do they do it?

2.) What narrative and ideological patterns of the modern industrial contemporary romance fiction are discerned in the six novels and do they change over the years?

3.) What are the authors' writing styles and core stories and do changes which they might have been subjected to twenty-five year period confirm a possible individual author's voice?

4.) Are there changing definitions of female and male roles in relationships in the authors' fictional society?

5.) As romantic novels are erotic stories, what sexual moral is presented in the narratives, which explicitness in the narrated sex scenes is there, which language is used, and are there changes?

6.) As reading the genre is exceptionally popular the question is how does the 'magic' of romances work for readers?

In order to obtain answers, the method and strategy I apply will be explained in the next chapter.

1.3 METHODOLOGY

The interdependence between literary theories and methods to analyze fictional texts is difficult to define since any theory describing and explaining literature is only partially applicable and no theory has reached a hegemonic position. As theories as such are always limited models that isolate or give preference to certain features of the studied object be they of the linguistic, the psychological, sociological or historical kind, they offer approaches to methodological *modi operandi*. Therefore, I will draw heuristically and commentarially on methodological terms and approaches of selected theories presupposing that they are open to scrutiny. In doing so I will refrain, for scientific economical reasons, from debating the respective discourses in depth and, therefore, will confine myself to aspects I consider to be relevant.

When the term narratology was popularized by structuralist critics like Roland Barthes in the 1970s, the definition of the term was restricted to the structuralist analysis of literature.[13] The post-structuralist reaction of the 1980s and 1990s against the scientific and taxonomic claims of the structuralist narratology resulted

---

[13]   Since Barthes equates the grammar of the sentence with the narrative structure in his paper "An Introduction to the Structural Analysis of Narrative". 1975 I will not use his theory to analyze the novels. One aspect, however needs to be referred to, the question of who is the the actant, or the hero, when "a great many narratives set up two opponents at odds with each other over a possession of a stake, and this opposition has the effect of 'equalizing' their action" (Barthes

in opening new lines of development for narratology in gender studies, psycho-analysis, reader-response criticism and ideological critique. Thus narratology has become a multi-disciplinary study of narratives, incorporating other critical discourses that involve narrative forms of representation. I understand narratology as the umbrella term, as the forum of multiple approaches to analyze romance fiction from the viewpoint of a variety of disciplines: history, psychology, ideological criticism, sociology. Vera and Ansgar Nünning's focus on the thematic and methodic differences between classical structuralist narratology and feminist literary theory and their integration will serve as a starting point for answering my questions. There, describing the attempt to integrate the 'how' of the structuralist narratology with the 'what' of the feminist literary theory results in placing greater importance on historization and contextualization in structuralist narratology and greater importance on form in the feminist theory (Nünning/Nünning 2004, 8). In the course of the study, each chapter will be connected with theoretical comments concerning the theme of the chapter in order to attribute them to their proper context.

I will focus on the genre of romance novels, the core of which is undoubtedly of a formulaic nature. Here I follow Andreotti's proposition of what constitutes the bourgeois trivial novel (Andreotti 2009, 236–240) because what constitutes the genre is that there, conservative or traditional narrative modi are applied. Even if narrative elements are used that transgress the genre, the text is bound to remain easily readable with inherent mimetic references. An audience of the genre that is used to a traditional logic of content and a teleological narration will accept only such kind of texts. This fact legitimizes a hypothetical pre-understanding of conceding mimetic approaches. Marie Laure Ryan's inference "that recipients tend to assume that a fictional world resembles the real world, unless explicitly stated otherwise" (Jannidis et al. 1999, 34), a process she terms as the 'principle of minimal departure', takes this mimetic fact into account. Also, considering characterizations when readers understand characters as real persons, the aspect of the mimetic takes on an important role. Henriette Heidbrink points to James Phelan's concept of characters:

> James Phelan was concerned with a double focus on character and progression (1989). He differentiated between *synthetic* (the artificial component), *mimetic* (characters as images of real people) and *thematic* (the implied significance) aspects of characters whereby these aspects can alternately be brought to front. He also separated 'dimensions' from 'functions' and stated that … "dimensions are converted into functions by the progression of the work." By emphasizing the dynamics of any narration he overcomes the

---

1975, 259). This duality of protagonists is one structural fact in romance novels.

> rather static structuralistic view and turns towards a kind of rethorical anal-
> ysis that aims at the text as communicative device. (Heidbrink 2010, 92)

Fictional characters, particularly those of romance novels in spite of their only being constructed verbally on paper, fulfill reader expectations when two of Phe-lan's criteria for characters are met: the mimetic and the thematic. That figures are only constructed verbally is one aspect that is never mentioned because it does not seem to be significant, if readers are aware of this at all.

The formulaic nature of the genre lets structuralist approaches to the texts seem a logical consequence: once a text is defined as being categorized to a spe-cific genre, this category cannot be innovative. In other words, Roland Barthes' reasoning that a writer's use of language in his/her text, although apparently unique, has always already been 'written', is supported by the one formula ro-mances are said to be subjected to. As texts are regarded as a plurality of other texts, of infinite and lost codes, the author is denied the chance of being an original creator (Barthes 1968/1977). This being the point of reference, many text-based analyses have been carried out with romance books picked at random, no author acknowledged, recording common themes and drawing conclusions about the ap-peal of the genre and the effects they have on readers. Romances have been studied the same way soap operas or Jerry Cotton serials are analyzed, which means, in the case of the Jerry Cotton serials, that six to seven writers produce stylistically identical texts, writers who are anonymous and appear to be one writer. In the case of soap operas the audience is not interested in the different script-writers but only in the story itself. With romance novels, however, it is different. There, au-thors are held in high esteem by their publishers and readers for their supposedly individual 'voices'. For them it holds true what Paisley Livingston demands in *Art and Intention*. He wants

> to elucidate a concept that is part of an important practical and theoretical
> framework of attribution and responsibility. It is important" he says "to in-
> sist on the latter motivation of the concept: behind the question of authorship
> lies the interest we take in knowing who, on a specific occasion, has been
> proximally responsible for the intentional production of a given utterance.
> And 'it matters who is speaking' not only because we want to know who to
> blame or praise, but also to whom our response to the utterance might be ad-
> dressed, should the circumstances permit; we might also want to know what
> else this same author has done, and in what specific sociocultural network
> the utterance was situated. (Livingston 2005, 68–69)

Notwithstanding, an author being understood by structuralists as only "a func-tional meeting point for a network of cultural codes and literary conventions" (Li-Fen Chen 2000, 14), real readers decide which category line they prefer, even if it is not the Harlequin brand, but a mainstream romance instead, and then they choose their favorite authors by trial and error reading. Once they have discovered them, they continue to read whatever the authors write because these special authors seem to touch them emotionally. Readers usually choose books by an author not by the brand. Seen from this viewpoint, readers recognize an individual as the originator of the product they enjoy, someone who seems to guarantee further enjoyable moments by providing them with her other books. For her readers, the author was and is never 'dead'. They are not only interested in her work but also in her personality. Currently, the internet is an appropriate source of information for them. Besides, legal implications such as the author's copyright of her work as her intellectual property or the author's legal responsibility for the effects of her work cannot be disregarded, along with other aspects, such as her dependency on her market and the media. An author's function as such is that of a producer of a material text. According to Foucault, s/he is regarded as the classifying principle that makes possible the grouping, restriction or comparison of the texts in this study.

The role an author plays for the reader is based on the product, the novel, a fact which requires consideration in which way the real author might be included in the analysis of this study. Simone Winko points out the discrepancies between the poststructuralist critical theory and the interpretational praxis that does not refrain from using the author construct (Winko 2002, 353–354). Given that the individual author of popular fiction whose name signifies a brand in her function as a marketing strategy promises future enjoyments to the reader and "the reader is the space on which all the quotations that make up a writing are inscribed" (Barthes 1968/ 1977), it is because of readers' reading choice that it should be considered a legitimate suggestion to fall back on the individual author's works in order to present in detail, distinct characteristics that emerge and focus attention on her writing individuality.[14] This does not mean that the intention attributed to the author to convey a particular understanding of her work will be focused on in this study. I accept that the author, as she is external to her work, can be ignored as a reference point for the ascription of authorial intentions. But as without her,

---

[14]   Michel Foucault, who, together with Barthes, is usually seen as the one who determined the 'death' of the author does not agree with this kind of attribution: In his discourse "Quest-ce qu'un auteur?" he says: "je n'ai pas dit que l'auteur n'existe pas; je ne l'ai pas dit et je suis étonné que mon discours ait pu prêter à un pareil contre-sens." (1969, 100) About ten years later he even proposes a little game in an interview with Christian Delacampagne in <Le Monde>in 1980 to stress the importance of an author: "Je proposerai un jeu: celui de l'<année sans nom>. Pendant un an, on éditerait des livres sans nom d'auteur. Les critiques devraient se débrouiller avec une production entièrement anonyme. Mais, j'y songe, peut-être n'auraient-ils rien à dire: tous les auteurs attendraient l'année suivante pour publier leurs livres ... " (Le philosophe masqué 104) (cited Konzal 3)

the novels would not exist, her function for this study is to be the authority or rather, the principle of classification that enables me to compare, to analogize, to group, and dissect her novels, to examine changes, and to ascribe these changes to this author if they are of an individualist nature. I will refer to the romance writer as the author or the writer, whereas the fictional person within the romance who might tell the story will be termed as 'narrator'.

To incorporate all structural and differentiating criteria of present theories of narratology would go beyond the scope in view of the fact that the subjects of this study are above all, mass-reader-friendly and not very complex.[15] In addition, part of the objectives are questions applied to cultural and feminist aspects.

In accordance with these conceptual deliberations, a basic element for the methodological *procedere* leads to a split analytical perspective that examines the following narratological aspects as well as the feminist gender related ones: the narratological aspects address the narrator, who, in romances, published under the tutelage of romance publishing houses and their writing guidelines, is presented as a covert heterodiegetic narrator who directs intradiegetic reflectors.[16] The narrator cannot be matched with a gender. S/he is only part of a third person perspective of one or more characters in the story that functions in the way of a first person narrative. The character as internal focalizer (Genette 1980, 185–194) seemingly transports all information necessary for the story but there is a very covert narrator behind this focalizer. Stanzel terms this narrative as a figural narrative situation in which a covert heterodiegetic narrator presents an internal focalizer's consciousness (Stanzel 1982).

To gain a positive reader reception is the main objective for romance authors and publishers. There are well established classical details and formulaic information that seem to be appreciated by romance readers and that authors do not fail to insert into their novels. These will be pointed out within the analysis of the romances.

Issues and methodological approaches would be less fathomable without information of previous studies on the subject of romances and specific analyses of the history of literature, and without information about the literary publishing houses, for example Harlequin Enterprises, as well as the information about the production and marketing modalities specifically applying to the category romance genre. Therefore, this study begins with a survey of scholarly works on

---

[15] Lotman (1993, 46–47) points to the relevance of considering the entropies of the text-code and the reader-code and their relative compatibility. The popular genre of romance novels aims at a one to one compatibility.

[16] It is difficult to decide on only one theory of narratology because some narratological aspects cannot be covered adequately with it. Therefore, I will use a hybrid of narratological theories (Stanzel and Genette and their followers).

romance novels and a brief glance at the history of romance fiction as a feminine genre. In order to understand the level of requirements the authors Krentz and Delinsky met when they began writing contemporary romances in the 1980s, a history of one romance publishing house is included, followed by a survey of the development of the modern romance genre that is partly defined by publishers' writing guidelines.

Part III presents an in-depth analysis of six contemporary romance novels: three novels by each author, the first published in 1982, the second in 1992 and the third in 2007. These novels are written in the form of the bourgeois novel of 19th century, the structure of which will be explained in more detail at the beginning of Part III. The novels are examined under the narratological decoding categories: Story, Discourse (Plot and Chapters, Presentation of Place and Time, Conflict, Character Constellations, Relationship and Erotic Scenes, Writing Style and Codes). The type of language used in the novels is expected to be primarily based on the romantically coded everyday language of the time. An examination of the writing style in these novels will be conducted in the way that descriptive texts of about 100 words are analyzed as well as the language used in sexual scenes.[17] In the subsequent chapter, Constants and Changes, the results of the analyses regarding the development and changes that may have taken place during twenty-five years are summarized.

Only a basic narrative analysis can be achieved when there are six novels to be dissected. But since the theme of this study is to disclose elements that reveal the narrative as well as ideological changes in these authors' novels over a twenty-five year period, an analysis of a smaller number of novels would not be sufficient for this study. Thus, it proceeds between the Scylla of the unparalleled (a singular romance analyzed as thoroughly as possible highlighting probable atypicalities of the genre) and the Charybdis of an approximate evaluation of the theme excluding the very detailed analyses.

Part IV examines, in a now synoptic (both authors and the six novels), analysis, some subtexts these works reveal. The in-depth study of the novels lays the foundation for analyzing facets of narrative discourse in Part IV: plots, focalization, content versus language, aspects of reader response criticism, tenses, and blanks which are inherent and relevant narrative aspects. Narrative modes like blanks (Iser) or the role dialogues and descriptions play within all the stories are part of defining the romance genre. The meaning of the use of one or several perspectives[18] for the romance fiction will be determined. Another narratological

---

[17]   Here I will not follow Nünning/Nünning (2004, 106) by including character constellations or plot segments and sequences into the summary of the story because these will be analyzed in their own chapters.

[18]   J. Hillis Miller distinguishes between the 'old-fashioned' term' point of view' as 'looking from a

aspect is the plot which will be examined under the facets of the Aristotelian three
act structure, with suspense curve and climaxes, as well as under the facets of its
construction regarding chapter divisions and subplots with their *topoi* linked to
the main plot, following a linear timeline within the stories connected with formula narratives.

Cultural aspects play a relevant role in order to get an idea about psychologic
and sociologic subtexts these novels reveal. Thus structural, psychological, and
sociological aspects are examined followed by an evaluation of the writers' possible individuality that is also uncovered in their dealing with writing guidelines,
as well as their different approaches documented in the other sections of this part.
Individuality of a romance writer or her individual voice can only be examined
with the understanding that the collected features which might justify a writer's
individuality will be distinctive within the genre, but not uniquely characteristic.
These collected features can be a distinctive writing style, a distinctive way of
character development, a distinctive way of emplotment across the three chosen
novels or distinctive themes. As these novels are not part of a series with constant
characters by whom an author might be identified, and both authors' works portray a variety of settings within the frame of popular fiction, literary characteristics
can be assigned to an author at best.

Romances are partly reader friendly formula literature where the main focus is
put on a love story that leads to 'a satisfying' happy ending and, therefore. it is not
realistic to expect too much structural, psychological and ideological complexity.
Although the stories might focus on everyday problems without profound perceptions of economical, societal and philosophical ideas, it might, nevertheless, be
revealing to analyze the degree of complexity readers of romances enjoy because
expectations and reader interests are understood as codes of norms and a system
of rules which are the underlying cornerstones for a text reception. Even though
the genre is supposed to be pure entertainment messages for readers can be uncovered. There still remains the question of why romances have such an enormous
appeal for so many readers which some scholars try to investigate and which is
hardly possible to answer satisfyingly. Despite of being aware of this, in Part V, I
also present a possible explanation by using the myth of the 'Sacred Marriage' to
lay emphasis on the performativity of the reading act of romance novels.

---

certain position', 'representation of consciousness' as 'the center of consciousness', and 'focalization' as 'drawn from optics and getting things in focus'. He concludes with saying that these
"distinctions are not useful in themselves. They are useful only if they lead to better readings or
better teachings of literary works" (2008, 124–125).

1.4 SCHOLARSHIP ON ROMANCE NOVELS

The following survey of literary criticism of modern American romances does not claim to be complete. It will only show the main directions literary criticism, combined with other academic fields, has taken to research this part of formulaic literature. Through this survey it will also become clear that my objectives have not yet been taken into consideration by others.

The opinion that romance novels are formulaic in every way, more so than other genre literature, in plot, in language, and in content, might also be deduced from the fact that romance novel publishing houses consider the most effective way of selling is to install the brand's name by issuing nearly identical book covers. Harlequin, the leading publishing house for category romances, is the initiator of this homogeneously looking product and controls not only the image, but also the length and the content of the books by presenting guidelines to the writers. From that standardized outward appearance, non-readers and critics seem to draw the conclusion of not only a uniformity of content and ideology in all romance fiction, but also the homogeneity of the readership. This marketing strategy of the romance book industry seems, and seemed, to backfire with academics as well as with non-academic readers because it leads to discriminatory reading[19] or to bias before the book is actually read. But over the last three decades this popular genre has become of increasing interest to scholarly analysis. Irrespective of whether the genre is discredited, it has its irrefutable, though mass-market, place within the literary culture and this is why it has begun to interest scholars, usually from the socio-cultural perspective. Scholars, especially the feminist ones, who studied romances during the 1980s had opposing and biased opinions regarding these romance novels. Crusie describes the opposing opinions as follows:

> Most critics of romance novels fall into one of two polarized camps that view these novels as conservative forms that uphold the existing patriarchal structure, or as subversive, resistant forms that challenge the existing structure. (Crusie 1997, n.p.)

Because of their growing awareness of the multi-million readership of these romances, feminists have become concerned about the effect these novels, which, they assume all contain patriarchal ideology, could have on the unsuspecting audience.

The formula of the romance novel, its essential standardization, is the negative basis on which feminist scholars usually base their arguments. "The first notable

---

[19] See Jennifer Crusie "Romancing Reality: The Power of Romance Fiction to Reinforce and Re-Vision the Real" where she accuses feminist scholars to believe that having read eight books is a solid basis to evaluate the genre.

publication was Germaine Greer's 1970 polemic *The Female Eunuch*, which argued that romance novels pacified, deceived, and manipulated their female readers and should be shunned by women" (Schneider-Mayerson 2010, 26). Carol Thurston describes feminist critics' literary criticism as follows:

> Though often disowned as 'literature' this popular fiction nonetheless has been relegated largely to literary analysis and criticism, where the focus has been on patterns in texts that demonstrate universality and continuity rather than diversity and change, and on consensus rather than pluralism. (Thurston 1987, 11)

This comment only emphasizes that scholars, as well as everybody else, want to criticize a genre according to their own literary and ideological norms, an attitude, in the case of romances, they, for their part, have often tried to accuse readers of whenever these readers want their convictions and beliefs represented in the romance novels. Because romance novels have thus been trivialized and stereotyped as a low form of fiction[20] that assumedly contains little complexity which is not worth examining, perhaps college teachers have not taken on literary research of this kind of literature for a long time. But then, the feminists' dawning realization and fears that romances' patriarchal content could have a detrimental effect on their readers have have forced feminists examine the genre more closely.

Moreover, along with a general blurring of the lines between high and low culture that is associated with postmodernism, literary scholars might also more easily accept the blurring of the lines between 'literature' and (popular) 'fiction' by acknowledging that sales figures and the ensuing popularity of that fiction needs to be examined. Or, as Cawelti observes, when so many people from all walks of life enjoy reading formula stories, these stories are "artistic and cultural phenomena of tremendous importance" (1977, 1).

There are about four groups of scholarship on romance: Empirical analyses of the readers trying to discover why readers read romances, if and how the readers are influenced by romances as regards their self-esteem, or if they nurture particular patterns of attitude towards relationships, or if they change their attitude towards relationships and in which way. These studies are an overlap between psychological and anthropological approaches. Then there is the historical and sociological approach, which attempts to analyze socio-cultural circumstances in

---

[20] Peter Wood is a typical example of an 'educated' reader who thinks he knows what highbrow literature should be about. Peter Wood, a professor of anthropology at Boston University, puts Harlequin romances at the lowest end of literature, calling it 'obvious dreck'. He knows what 'real literature' is like: First of all it is at least over a hundred years old. And then "it pushes us into a place where we have to make judgments and rely on discernment. And those are matters of deep concern to conservatives – at least those conservatives who believe that real human communities are built on traditions of moral striving in a world of imperfect individuals." (n.p.)

the times romances were written and the way they were marketed. The feminist perspective could really be included in the historical and social approach but here it is focused on patriarchal attitudes that are the main concern. The last approach is literary criticism that is centered around formal structures of romance. Not many of these approaches are so clearly divided into the listed category; most are a conglomerate of the four. In 1988, Angela Miles, the exception to the feminist rule, for quite early on she acknowledges that the Harlequin formula is not exclusively about patriarchal aspects that feminists of that time usually criticize, states:

> When a reader knows the Harlequin formula, she can identify her hero figure immediately, anticipate the pattern of events, and is involuntarily caught up in an extremely active and demanding psychological interaction with the text that has been called, without irony or exaggeration 'the Harlequin experience'. (Nathason/Young 2006, 375)

Miles explains this experience as a positive one that pleases her feminist ideas. She observes that "Harlequins are about not having to mother men" (ibid. 380) because the heroine expects the hero to show his nurturing side alongside his patriarchal one. In this way, Miles conveys that she believes in the female's superiority to the male and finds this belief mirrored in Harlequin novels. But then, she had already had the opportunity to read ideologically changed Harlequins which the scholars of the early 1980s had not come across.

Feminist scholars who analyzed romance novels at that time, often in short contributions in journals, were mostly more interested in the readers, their gender, their age, their social status, their level of education, the influence these books had on their sexual behavior, their patterns of behavior in relationships, and the reader expectations, while they usually considered themselves above being entertained by this kind of literature. They regarded the contents of the novels not worthy enough to be examined beyond their, as they read it, stereotyped ideological contents, formulaic plot, and language and thus, they outlined their own ideology which they superimposed on the novels. The ideological feminist interpretation, whether contemptuous or benign, often criticizes heterosexuality combined with a woman's happiness in a symbiotic heterosexual relationship, be it *expressis verbis* or in veiled arguments. Grescoe reports that Harlequin romances

> were spat upon by a whole school of feminists throughout the 1970s and beyond, with what now seems slightly outdated criticism. Typical of the time was a 1980 attack by Columbia University English professor Ann Douglas. She called Harlequins soft porn shaped to suit female emotionality and wrote that "the timing of the Harlequin's prodigious success has coincided exactly with the appearance and spread of the women's movement, and much of its increasingly anti-feminist content reflects this symbiotic relationship." In harsher language than most critics, she said the hero

and heroine of these books were emotional illiterates locked in a duel of sexual stupidity. If the statistics were true that middle-aged women read Harlequins, the professor was seriously concerned for them: "How can they tolerate or require so extraordinary a disjuncture between their lives and their fantasies?" (Grescoe 1996, 239)

Ann Snitow examines the role eroticism and sexuality play in Harlequin romances and concludes that the "Harlequin romances are essentially pornography for people ashamed to read pornography" (1979, 151) and she defends the sexually liberating and relaxing effects the romance fantasies have on the readers. Jeanne Dubino argues that all these novels contribute to reinforce the separation between the male i.e. the rational and public sphere and the female i.e. the emotional, domestic, and private sphere (1993, 105).

Modleski, 1982, Mussell, 1984, Radway, 1984, and Thurston, 1987, are scholars who react mostly positive to the reading experience of the genre they interpret from their feminist positions. Tania Modleski's study of three categories of women's popular narratives – Harlequin romances, gothic novels, and TV soap opera – 'tries' to avoid the elitist feminist position of condemning women who read these novels or watch these soap operas. She made this study

> out of concern that these narratives were not receiving the right kind of attention, I try to avoid expressing either hostility or ridicule, to get beneath the embarrassment, which I am convinced provokes both the anger and the mockery, and to explore the reasons for the deep-rooted and centuries old appeal of the narratives. Their enormous and continuing popularity, I assume, suggests that they speak to very real problems and tensions in women's lives. The narrative strategies that have evolved for smoothing over these tensions can tell us much about how women have managed not only to live in oppressive circumstances but to invest their situations with some degree of dignity. (Modleski 1982, 14–15)

The 'right kind of attention' according to her is to consider this kind of literature as escapist in a negative sense, just as she did in her earlier essay of 1980. There she gave her article the title "The Disappearing Act: A Study of Harlequin Romances" and interprets the reading act as a disappearing act because of its function of enabling an escape from the everyday life which she regards as an effect to depoliticize. In *Feminism Without Women* she maintains that "Romances provide women with a common fantasy structure to ensure their continued psychic investment in their oppression" (43).

Janice Radway is something like a prototype for feminist argumentation and, therefore, she is accorded more room. Radway's groundbreaking ethnographic study of romance readers, *Reading the Romance: Women, Patriarchy, and Popular Literature*, focuses on reader reception. She combines literary criticism with literary sociological approaches that represent an unprecedented attention to the reception of literature of not implied, but real readers, and a history of the political economy of publishing, with feminist psychoanalysis at its interpretive center. Schneider-Mayerson describes this study as "a fascinating amalgamation of approaches: a loose ethnography of viewers that represented an unprecedented attention to reception of literature and a thorough history of the political economy of publishing, with feminist psychoanalysis at its interpretive center" (24).

Each of these approaches has been joined and reflected on in later criticism in numerous studies, empiric and otherwise. Although they tend to ignore the socio-historical specificity of gender roles, Freud's theories provide the investigation of how adult emotions and sexuality are shaped by experience in infancy. According to Freud, a child's relationship with its parents forms the bedrock of emotional life for people of both sexes. Both genders, male and female, experience the same early feelings of sensual plenitude provided by their mother,

> but the need to recognize the difference between self and other, and to assert the self as separate from the mother, is lived out differently by each sex. For Freud, the boy child relinquishes the joy of maternal identification to gain the greater good of acquiring masculinity, through the Oedipal drama of rivalry and identification with the father. The girl, though, confronts the difficulty that her adult role model is the mother, the very figure from whom she must separate. Her achievement of selfhood will involve a contradictory play of rejection and internalization of the mother, and will demand a difficult repression of the wish to identify with the father ('penis-envy'). Thus male and female subjectivities are differently constituted. (A Feminine Genre 15)

Janice Radway draws on Nancy Chodorow's theory to read the romance as a pleasurable reenactment of the girl's Oedipal drama, but with a happy ending. She examines the romances her representative group of readers chose as the best and concludes that, as the heroine in these romances normally begins the story alone, separated from friends and family, the situation depicted echoes the child's attempts to seek individuation and emerge from the initial fusion of self and mother. In this situation of solitude, she tries to establish her autonomy through the 'masculine' ways of working and attempting independence, thus identifying with the father. However, this attempt at separation results not in the social success of power, but in the love of the ideal man who turns into the maternal figure which offers the nurturing warmth that adult women usually provide, rather than receive. The hero in the romances delivers "the reestablishment of that original, blissful symbiotic union between mother and child" which is really "the goal of all romances despite their apparent preoccupation with heterosexual love and marriage" (Radway 1984, 156). At the same time, the happy ending demands that its heroine accepts her own place within this gendered and inexorably heterosexual distribution of roles and foremost identifies with her role as wife and mother.

The reason these scholars of the second feminist movement expressed their anxiety that these novels seemed to stabilize existing traditional patriarchal ideology is that they usually examined historical genre romances, which were so persuasive in their content that to feminist understanding they had to be indicted for anti-feminist content. They argued that romance novels cannot challenge the existing patriarchal structure as any self-respecting literature should do because they confirm the establishment by the reunion of a heterosexual married couple which is an antithetical feminist concept of life for, for example, Radway and other feminist scholars. So Radway, for example, is convinced that "the romance continues to justify the social placement of women, that has led to the very discontent that is the source of their desire to read romance" (ibid 217). Accepting their 'social placement', women need ways to escape, and reading books is a kind of therapy, a way to meet psychological needs for travel and learning of which they are denied by their reduced existence as housewives (ibid 113). And so Radway concludes that the narrative structure of romances ultimately is antithetical to feminism because it serves to further indoctrinate women into an oppressive patriarchal system.

Today those assertions about the content, form and ideology in romance novels are decades out of date – and just how much feminist values have been incorporated into these novels since will be demonstrated in this study – but they are still often reviewed as contemporarily valid. The indictments are perpetuated by repeating the ideas of these scholars' works, published around the mid-1980s and earlier, as also being valid in the new millennium, although times and ideology in romances have changed just as they have in reality.

(When Donna Hayes, CEO of Harlequin, reports that the company publishes 1,200 new 'books' a year, she thus takes into account that many of these are backlist titles which the company owns and has a policy to republish only after five years of their last publication. This can mean that a category romance published in, for example, 1978 can have been reissued at least six times, always with conveying the impression to have been written quite recently. The implication of this fact will be discussed in a later section of this study.)

For my study, however, which is concerned with contemporary romance novels, these scholars, referred to above, require their rightful acknowledgement in this study, as the first novels of both authors I analyze were published in 1982. There is only one reservation to mention: these feminist studies apply well to late 1970s and early 1980s Harlequin romance novels. Radway and most scholars of her time mainly criticized historical romances, because this category romance line provided the most titles at the time and, as Dawn Heinecken points out,

readers often had no way of knowing, prior to reading it, if an individual
book would fit their model of the ideal romance. They read what was available to them, not necessarily what they would have preferred. (Heinecken
1999, 150)

While reading those feminist studies, I often asked myself why historical romances should display protagonists with feminist concepts of equality. Should
an author not depict the norms and values of the era she chose for her historical
romance in order to create a semblance of historical reality even if it is a romance with a happy ending?[21] Bruce Kuklick argues that interpreters who define
the central myths of the American past in terms of concerns of the present thereby
commit the historical fallacy of presentism (Cawelti 33). Presentism is one aspect
the feminist peremptory requests concerning historical romances and also the contemporary romances of their time should be examined more closely because there,
feminist argumentation often is not based on the historical legal reality. When they
accuse the author of portraying patriarchal behavior, they do not take into consideration an American husband's total legal power over his wife until the end of the
1970s.

Academic works on the subject of romance fiction published from the 1990s
onwards disclose different features from those of patriarchal ideology and de-
politicization as the main themes, but often these preconceptions are still the underlying basis. The year 1992 marks a turning point regarding scholarly feminist convictions which hitherto had regarded the genre as almost exclusively
disreputable: in 1992 Krentz edited twenty-one essays in *Dangerous Men and
Adventurous Women (DMAW)*. This collection is a mixture of academic and journalistic essays. The authors, all of them successful women romance novel writers,
present different aspects of the intentions they link with their work. They claim
that the initiated readers are aware of the novels as codes, whereas the uninitiated
are repelled, possibly by the book covers, as well as by the public 'knowledge'
about the romances as trash. They argue that they write fantasies, and their readers are cognizant of this. Their first argument is that their individual aim is not to
be known for their literary artistry, but for their skill to successfully create a compelling story that makes their fantasy accessible to their readers. The success is
not dependent on their conventional writing competence, but on how many readers can enjoy the fantasy. Their second argument tries to contradict the feminist
view of romance novels by asserting that the hero has no chance of instigating his

---

[21] Writer Robin Schone presented a sex scene of her historical erotica that did not render a correct
historical semblance: "Oh, God, yes, yes, that's it, let me hear you, moan for me, baby; moan,
I want to hear you," he groaned, nibbling, sucking, head wildly rooting from one breast to
another." She added her editor's comment: "'Baby' is twentieth century slang and does not
belong in a book that takes place in 1883". (ct. in Grescoe 216)

patriarchal ways. On the contrary, he is forced to acknowledge the heroine's equal power in the relationship. The authors call the heroine's gaining equal 'rights' in her relationship with a man, her 'female empowerment'. Thirdly, because of this imagined female empowerment, the authors invert the power structure of a patriarchal society within romance novels by endowing heroines with alleged male characteristics like honor, courage, and determination. This changes the hero's entitlement to have the exclusive right of power. A fourth argument is that there are neither mysogynistic nor misandrist tendencies to be found in the books. On the contrary, heroes are valued for their warrior qualities as well as their protective and nurturing qualities and women are valued for similar ones. Furthermore the book contains articles on reader identification, language and the structure of romance novels.

The articles on reader identification are the first hints at the theory of the shadow hero in romances. *Dangerous Men and Adventurous Women* is the first platform for a synoptic 1990s authors' view of their genre. The authors see themselves in a position of defense, thus often feeling pressured to write an apologia of the genre. Nevertheless, *Dangerous Men and Adventurous Women* is still regarded as a main source of reference for scholars because the articles acquaint scholars and readers with authors' insight into the genre that, up until then, had not been reflected on. In the analysis of Krentz's novels I will refer to these articles.

Seven years later, thirty romance writers outlined the various influences on their works, the way they deal with the romance conventions and their relationship with feminism and the feminist movement. Kay Mussel and Johanna Tunón edited these short biographic essays in *North American Romance Writers* (1999). Like the Krentz collection, it claims to be on an academic level because they both offer a bibliography which in Krentz's case is short.

Also in 1999, Anne Kalek and Rosemary Johnson-Kurek edited twelve critical articles in *Romantic Conventions*. They are not a continuation of *Dangerous Men and Adventurous Women* or *North American Romance Writers* because this time only two of the authors are scholars cum romance novel writers. In these articles, the authors portray historical ideological developments, the modifications in romances that have evolved at a pace consistent with changing feminist attitudes in society, psychoanalytic thoughts about archetypes, the reversal of fairy tales in romances, euphemist language of sex and other language facets, and conventions concerning different genres. Although many of the authors describe themselves as feminists, their feminism is more mellow than that of their belligerent 'fellow' feminists of the early days of the movement. They can let themselves discover other implications in the novels besides that of patriarchy.[22] Two essays will be

---

[22]   In an interview of 1997 (n.p.) Kay Mussell, asked if feminism and romance novels are mutually

referred to later in Part V: Abby Zidle's "From Bodice-Ripper to Baby-Sitter: The New Hero in Mass-Market Romance" and Amber Botts' "Cavewomen Impulses: The Jungian Shadow Archetype in Popular Romantic Fiction".

Abby Zidle points out that "several writers view the hero as the 'shadow self' of the heroine, complementing her characteristics – the union at the end of the book is not a marriage but a reintegration of the heroine's psyche" (Zidle 1999, 28).[23] There are two aspects in that theory, one psychologically oriented, the other reader oriented: they are based on C. G. Jung's Shadow-Construct on the one hand, and on the other hand, on Lacan's Mirror-Stage. The Shadow-Construct serves to clarify the ingredients that are necessary to explain the hero's personification as an integration of women's shadow impulses, which society frowns upon as inappropriate for women. Since the shadow represents denied anger, greed, envy, and sexual desire, the shadow heroes incorporate these characteristics in the following way according to Amber Botts:

> (They) have two socially forbidden parts to their sexuality: extensive sexual experience and clearly demonstrated sexual skill. The second characteristic, anger/aggression, is the characteristic most questioned by feminist critics. They object to the heroes' frequent displays of anger and aggression, which are oftentimes exhibited toward the heroines. The third characteristic of the shadow, danger, builds on anger and aggression. Danger goes beyond mere outburst of temper to actually threaten the heroine's well-being. Of the characteristics, it is the most extreme and difficult to integrate. (Botts 1999, 67)

Following this statement, the resulting argument is that for men, another man would be a greater threat for physical, social, and economic reasons. For women, a man would be a much greater threat than a woman since society gives greater power to men. For that reason, for women, the shadow figure is male. Thus,

> romances do not reinforce the patriarchy as a social institution as much as it fulfills a desire within a female reader's collective unconscious to observe a strong woman attracting, and more importantly, taming the shadow forces represented by the hero, which exist within the self. (Botts 1999, 72)

---

exclusive, answers as follows: "The newer romances incorporate feminist themes while still reaffirming more traditional notions about love and family. Moreover, many romance writers have openly claimed feminist values and, in the process, rejected easy stereotypes about themselves and their work. For example see the essays by romance writers collected in Jayne Ann Krentz's *Dangerous Men and Adventurous Women*. More difficult to illustrate, but I think equally important, is the change in feminist thinking itself. Twenty or so years ago, when academic feminists first became interested in the romance genre, there was a wider agreement among feminists themselves on what the feminist agenda would be – and conventual romantic relationships, widely assumed to be discriminatory toward women, were not part of it. Thus romances were seen as threatening female experience."

[23] I understand this as a continuation of Radway's reinactment of a girl's oedipal drama.

Lacan's Mirror-Stage is used to let the heroine recognize

> herself in the hero (as does the reader). This identification of herself as a
> cohesive psyche (her partnership with the hero) prepares her for maturity
> and provides her with a glimpse of the Imaginary, the mechanism for wish-
> fulfillment. (Zidle 1999, 28)

These psychological theories of meaning are obviously meant to upgrade the
relevance of research on romances and the genre itself by endowing the plot with
a depth through psychoanalytic explanations of emotional occurrences.

In 2003 Pamela Regis published *A Natural History of the Romance Novel* that
analyzes the formal structures of romance, beginning with an extended definition
of a romance novel and then following the genre from the time when women began writing novels until the present, using her formulaic contentual steps as the
basis to define novels as romances. She structures and defines eight rigid steps, not
necessarily in the presented order, that identify and distinguish romances from
other genres: Society Defined, The Meeting, The Barrier, The Attraction, The
Declaration, Point of Ritual Death, The Recognition, and The Betrothal. An important step is that of 'Society Defined' because it clarifies content and ideological changes and through this step it can be deduced why contemporary romances
follow a different ideological formula. Although Regis explains the effect the alterations of legal and social rights for women have on the content of the genre, she
seems to hesitate to pinpoint the phallocentric contemporary Harlequin romances
after about 1984. Regis calls her study *A Natural History*, because for her, the
romance novel is easily classified and formally static. In addition to the structural
aspect of the romance novel, she argues that scholars tend to regard readers as
passive consumers who are easily manipulated. In their analyses, these theorists
confine heroines to stories that ignore issues other than love and marriage. Regis
counterclaims that the romance novel does not enslave female readers, but empowers them by allowing them to read about intelligent, strong, and independent
heroines, albeit not particularly sexual and only heterosexual. Regis, herself, is
involved in the genre and is its stout defender. Her work is considered fundamental.[24] Her structural approach on the genre will be included in this study.

Also in 2003, Gabriele Linke published *Populärliteratur als kulturelles
Gedächtnis*, a comparative study of contemporary British and American popular romances of the publishing houses Harlequin/Mills&Boon. Her hypothesis is
that romances are texts which present an objectified culture and teach a realm
of knowledge that belongs to the collective knowledge of a group generating

---

[24] The paperback edition's dainty design reveals the female author but, in an academic world
where stringency and not playfulness is the rule, such a design seems counterproductive to the
seriousness of the work.

identity, that controls and directs actions and experiences and is passed on from generation to generation. But these normative and formative forces of the texts are restricted to a female readership of the societies' lower and middle middle classes (Linke 16). Linke points out in detail how much the different social developments in Great Britain and the USA influence the ideological content of the romances and national cultural details characterize the narrative structure. Contrary to many feminist approaches this study projects the author's impartiality which ensures a neutral orientation for the reader.

Lynne Pearce (*Romance Writing* 2007) describes the changing meaning of the term 'love' over centuries. She defines her romantic love model per the algebraic equation of $x + y$, (x and y standing for the love subjects heroine and hero and $+$ their connection) which love "radically, even irreversibly" transforms and redefines "the individuals concerned" (10). This transformation is identified in its positive form as $x' + y'$. She cites jay Dixon according to whom the Ur-Mills & Boon story-line depicts a heroine's "personal triumph" and the heroine also as "superficially self-fulfilled "while the hero is "ultimately disposable" (140), a fact, Pearce expresses as $x + y > x'(-y)$. "Whilst for some readers and critics this will be perceived as a positive – and possibly 'feminist' – outcome for the heroine, for others" she says, "– myself included – it will be seen as a failure of love in its more ideal form(s)" (141).

In her work *Historical Romance Fiction: Heterosexuality and Performativity* of 2008 which is based on J.L. Austin's speech act theory, Lisa Fletcher defines the historical romance as belonging to the genre by the 'performative' speech act "I love you", a phrase that is repeated in nearly every romance. This phrase is the deciding romantic speech act, "the narrative and ontological turning point of hetero-sexual romance fictions" (1). However, she criticizes this speech act because it installs heteronormativity as an unchallenged ideal in the Euro-American sexual ideology.

In 2008, Jajashree Kamble published her dissertation *Uncovering and Recovering the Popular Romance Novel* on the internet. She mainly analyses ideological contents. According to her, the commodity romance glorifies global capitalism, justifies unjustified wars, and worships heterosexual fantasies although the genre might also express some concerns. Thus, a black and white approach is excluded. For her the hero-construction in romances runs along the following line: There is the capitalistic hero whose sexual aggressiveness mirrors his excellent instincts for business, there is the soldier who believes firmly in capitalism, his democratic nation and his patriotism. These three convictions are his moral foundation. Virility, together with a strong sexual drive are the emanation of his patriotic being. Kamble identifies the aggressive heterosexual phallocentralization in the romances of the 1980s as a fear of homosexuality at a time when gays were fighting for their legal rights.

Sarah Wendell and Candy Tan's *Beyond Heaving Bosoms: The Smart Bitches' Guide to Romance Novels* (2009) is an amusing analysis of romance novels peppered with brash, often profane language. At the same time they provide astute descriptions of narrative and contentual elements of the genre. They acknowledge that the genre they like "vacillates" in quality like any other genre despite a shared structural foundation, "but because it gets discussed as universally and unilaterally bad by those who don't read it, there is a remarkable tendency to defend romance as if it were infallible" (129). They see that quality is dependent on the authors' creativity (122).

In 2010 Laura Vivanco and Kyra Kramer presented a different approach to interpreting romance novels with their article "There Are Six Bodies in This Relationship: An Anthropological Approach to the Romance Genre". In their abstract to the article they explain the 'six bodies' in their alchemical model of relationships as individual, social and political for each sex:

> In what we term the 'alchemical' model of romantic relationships, the heroine's socio-sexual body (her Glittery HooHa) attracts, and ensures the monogamy of, the hero's socio-sexual body (his Mighty Wang), allowing the heroine's socio-political body (her Prism) to focus, and benefit from, the attributes of the hero's socio-political body (his Phallus). (n.p.)

As at the beginning of the stories, both the Phallus and the Prism are incomplete. Their union, however, 'completes' them, and this can become complicated, as Vivanco/Kramer agree. They say: "The problem, however, arises when Prism and Phallus already are completed and only need a story to meet" (n.p.). Although at first glance this approach of giving a romance novel a seemingly new theory on the genre is tempting to follow if only to upgrade the estimation of the genre, but the use of ridiculous terms like the 'Mighty Wang', MW, or the 'Glittery HooHa', GHH, and their shortened versions discredits this otherwise interesting reading of the genre. Vivanco/Kramer adopted these terms from Wendell/Tan who wrote the popular scientific book mentioned above as they also adopted the term 'Prism' from Krentz's futuristic romance novels. Despite the phrasing, I do not think that their theory is meant to not be taken seriously.

Catherine Roach provides the happy ending with a different, religious quality in her article "Getting a Good Man to Love: Popular Fiction and the Problem of Patriarchy". She maintains that

> The romance story *is* narrative eschatology. A romance is a story about how to get to a healing end, an eschaton of love, commitment, completion, fulfillment, happiness, generational continuity, maturity, and hope. (2010, n.p.)

According to this citation, the romance embraces a multitude of aspects on a high level of meaning that will have to be evaluated and examined more closely. In addition, Roach sees the Happy Ever After ending construction as

> a foundational psychological component of human wish-fulfillment: we yearn for this ideal paradise where we are loved, where the quest for wholeness is granted, where wounds are made right, where pleasure and security reign guaranteed. (n.p.)

In Part V this approach of human wish-fulfillment will be included.

With these studies the scholars evidence the attractiveness of the genre and its large social range as well as its effect on the readers. The studies also indicate how feminist cultural and political viewpoints influence the topics of the research as well as the results. One can also observe that the epistemological interest in the scholarly occupation with romances is external to the material text or that subtexts are used for ideological-contentual constructions of interpretation. Once questions are raised about high or low literature, the equality of the sexes, or about 'justified' norms and values, they do not produce enough interest in examining narrative issues like constructions of plots or timelines within the novels or narrative codes or writing style. The topics in these studies predominantly consider the genre as a whole and often, novels seemingly containing common themes have been picked at random for a text-based analysis from which scholars draw conclusions about the appeal of romances, or the effect they have on readers. These studies touch my concept only marginally. I am interested in the two writers' novels as examples to illustrate the narratological patterns within publishers' guidelines and their transgressions in the course of time as well as possible ideological changes, and I am interested in a possible individual voice which is manifested in the texts. This has not yet been studied.

1.5 A BRIEF GLANCE AT THE HISTORY OF ROMANCE FICTION AS A FEMININE GENRE

There are some aspects of the history of the romance novel that need to be mentioned in order to understand why these novels have been disregarded as a feminine genre for centuries, why the way of life, ideas and values of the upper classes are the main ideological context in modern romances, and why there is a tradition of mass-producing literature. Although this study focuses on US American women authors, English women's novel writing influenced these romance writers more than the writings of their American predecessors. This explains the closer look at the history of the English novel.

One aspect of the history of the romance novel is its 'roman' beginnings, meaning that the language chosen for romances was that of the common people, *la lingua romana versus la lingua latina* which was exclusively used to address the clergy, erudite people and educated nobility. The oral tradition of narration was predominant at the time, but fictional romantic stories were written down and copied, and it is reported that women, rather than men, listened to these stories. Another aspect to consider is the invention of paper production and the invention of the printing press, which reduced the price of books enormously.[25] The invention of printing not only increased the readership, but also changed people's reading habits and with it altered the contents of available books. The transition from oral tradition to silent reading allowed people to read and enjoy books privately, a fact that helped to sidestep public control. To be able to enjoy silent reading and thereby indulge in one's private feelings by doing it was a great incentive to learn how to read. The reading material of that time displayed a high degree of morality. For centuries the content of the books continued to concentrate on the already existing prose of devotional literature, chivalric romances and chansons de gestes, all three often characterized as 'women's literature'. The most popular romances like *Tristan et Iseult* deal

> with the conflict between a personal will to absolute fulfillment, and the intractability of the real, which most often takes the form of social imperatives that frustrate the desire to be with the loved one … Marital dynastic, and chivalric duties will put an end to their idyll, and the story ends with their separation and death. (A Feminine Genre 7)

Whether happy or sad in its moral ending, written in verse or in prose, the romance of all times is structured as a quest for a union with the beloved. The romance of today retains this connection with medieval courtly romance because "Love, courtship, the possibility of reconciling the satisfaction of personal desire with social duty … were staple ingredients of the novel form from the outset" (ibid 8). Authors were of no importance in the Middle Ages.[26] Texts were produced, reproduced, and altered through transcriptions (vowel shift), additions, commentaries and compilations.

As literature originated in the class of those in power it was they who dictated the forms in which literature was acceptable.[27] Apart from the moral content, two aspects were of importance to the literary authorities until nearly the end of the

---

[25] see Elizabeth L. Eisenstein. *The Printing Revolution in Early Modern Europe*. Cambridge University Press, 1983.

[26] In his essay "Zum 'Autor' im mittelalterlichen Kulturbetrieb und im Diskurs der germanistischen Mediävistik" Thomas Bein clarifies that a concept of the author in the modern sense is different from the medieval one. Although some poets gained a reputation, the passing on of traditional literature was more important than the idea of originality (309).

[27] Heidi Brayman Hackel describes Renaissance women's reading habits. According to the patriarchal constructions of femininity, Henry VIII criminalized reading aloud by women with his 1543 Act for the Advancement of True Religion (102). Only "gentlewomen were permitted to

18th century: the allegedly truthful content of all literary genres, a requirement that had never had a chance with the chivalric romances.

The medieval and later literary section of histories, whether allegedly true, romantic or novel, was gradually subjected to a process of trivialization and commercialization. When romances were circulated in expensive and ornamented manuscripts, they were read out to audiences, family groups and others, in private surroundings, coffee-houses and such. The printed book, the alternative, comparatively inexpensive, did not only allow privacy when reading, but also made it possible to skip difficult paragraphs containing long reflections and descriptions. Chap books went one step further: they promised their readers easier texts, offering shorter sentences, more action and less reflection. Chap books, the lowest strata of books after the scientific books that addressed an academic audience and the 'belles lettres', the popular second market books, addressed to educated readers of both sexes, were cheap, small, paper covered booklets up to 24 pages long, containing pamphlets, political and religious tracts, nursery rhymes, poetry, folk tales, and almanacs.[28] They disappeared around the mid-19th century, being replaced by newspapers that are said to have adopted them, albeit in a new form. Today's shorter category romances have similar strategies for reaching their clientele. But the maxim to educate and delight persevered. One could be tempted to see modern popular literature, especially category romances, as the successor of the early modern chapbook. Both genres share a focus on readers in search of accessible quick reading satisfaction.

As late as 1747, Ch. Batteux still declared that 'romans' were of inferior quality when written in simple prose. In England, however, anticipating the marginal-

---

read the Bible to 'themselves alone' but, unlike their husbands, they were forbidden from Reading Scripture aloud to their families" (102). For a long time women were restricted to 'passive reading' that is listening to male loud readings. But women often circumvented these restrictions and read secular books on the sly. "... the bibliophile Christina of Sweden, who at one time commanded a royal library of 8,000 volumes reportedly found Tacitus 'as interesting as a game of chess' and read Plato before picnics and games of charades. For men, too, reading was, of course, sometimes a diversion. But reading as a diversion was generally cast as feminine, and books read in this way were characterized as 'trifles' and 'toyes'" (111). To read Plato and Tacitus was a rather decent occupation for a woman, but not to read books of love. E.g. Brathwait (1631) is alarmed "by the intensity of women readers' attention to love poetry, and he worries that they will read it as one should read a school text or Bible" (111).

[28] The Victoria and Albert Museum (London) holds the National Art Library chapbook collection. There the visitor is informed that "Chapbooks were produced from the 16th to the early 20th century and played a particularly important part in the spread of popular culture due to their very high print runs. Around 200,000 chapbooks were printed yearly in Scotland in the 18th century ... These high printing numbers also bear witness to the fact that literary levels in Britain were higher than one might suspect." (From the catalogue of the Victoria and Albert Museum, www.vam.ac.uk/content/articles/n/national-art-library-chapbooks-collection/)

ization of the 'romance' in favor of the middle-class oriented 'novel' William Congreve clarifies as early as 1692 that

> Romances are generally composed of the Constant Loves and invincible Courages of Hero's and Heroins, Kings and Queens, Mortals of the first Rank and so forth ... . Novels are of a more familiar nature; Come near us, and represent us Intrigues in practice, delight us with Accidents and odd Events, but not such as are wholly unusual or unpresidented, such which not being so distant from our Belief bring also the pleasure nearer us. (Knopf 1071)

These "constant loves and invincible courages of the mortals of the first rank" persevere in the plot constructions of modern romances, though modified and adapted to modern government systems. In the 18th century, the term 'romance' was used for explicitly grotesque and distant fictional settings and in the nineteenth century, was eventually restricted to love stories.

For centuries women have written dramas, novels, and poetry. According to Ina Schabert, literature written by female authors was taken seriously at times and at other times it was not only disregarded, but also treated with contempt (Schabert 1997). Although over the centuries, romance novels have been written by both sexes, most of those which have come down to us were produced by men focusing on male themes and attitudes. As long as female writers did not attempt to transgress the virtual borders of gender roles, but seemingly helped to educate other women with their fiction, at the same time confirming the existing political and patriarchal system, they had a chance of being approved as a female writer and of protecting their own social integrity.[29] Thus, these women wrote for women and women's entertainment as well as education.

Today, only a handful of pre-twentieth century women authors are acknowledged as worthy enough to be remembered in any history of literature written by men. More frequently, women authors are disregarded, and any feminist likes to enumerate reasons for the fact that this has nothing to do with quality, but with who has the power to set standards, to distribute and grant favors, and to ignore women.

Over time, authors were granted legal rights of authorship and copyrights. Female authors were regarded as mere writers because of the domestic topics they were expected to choose for their novels, and, therefore, these works were denied the acknowledgement of literary quality. Therefore, Schöbert refers mainly to the male author.

> As a result of varying national cultural developments in Europe, the author developed into a legal instance in the course of the eighteenth cen-

---

[29] See Sally Winkle. *Women as Bourgeois Ideal.*

tury, acquiring material entitlements vis-à-vis publishers, requiring protection against unauthorized reprints and plagiarism, and bearing personal responsibility for the content of his publications. With the development of the objective conditions linked to ... fictional texts for market-led public communication, the term author became a value-free collective name to which professional designations such as writer ... as well as evaluative classifications such as poet ... could be assigned. (Schöbert 2011, 31)

From the latter part of the eighteenth century, and increasingly in the nineteenth century the novel started to be identified as a feminine mode of writing. As at that time, a separation between male and female spheres was established more strongly, excluding women legally, economically, and politically from the public sphere which meant excluding them from wielding power and authority, women found their way by expressing themselves and their domestic concerns within the form of the novel, which became very successful because of their mainly female readers. Nevertheless, male publishers were more inclined to publish novels written by men. Knowing that they had no chance of being published and successfully acclaimed as women, some female novelists either wrote anonymously (Jane Austen: author's name: By a Lady) or under male pseudonyms like the Bronte Sisters: Currer (Charlotte, *Jane Eyre*), Ellis (Emily, *Wuthering Heights*), and Acton (Anne, *Agnes Grey*) Bell. This way they became successful and, today, still enjoy huge popularity.[30] By the 1850s, an estimated 20% of the literary English stage was occupied by women (Schabert 1997, 472). They often came from upper social ranks and wrote popular novels that reflected female views and perspectives. When school education became obligatory for all social classes as well as for girls, the female audience for such novels grew and the novels sold quickly and in large numbers. These books were genre stories that were often written not because the author, often of noble origin, wanted to establish her literary artistry, but because she needed the money for the upkeep of her family. Thus she used her talent to write stories for the masses, reflecting upper class women's way of life, ideas and values of that time, and simultaneously, educating while entertaining. As these novels attracted mainly female readers because of the themes that were discussed in them, male critics who often were writers themselves denigrated or ignored these novels. In *The Rise of the Novel*, Ian Watt sees a close parallel between the increase in women readers and the increase in the novel's popularity. In the eighteenth century, he claims, literature was "primarily a feminine pursuit" (Watt 1957, 43) and he lets Addison explain this fact in the Guardian of 1713:

> There are some reasons why learning is more adapted to the female world than to the male. As in the first place, they have more spare time on their

---

[30] Romance novelists claim these authors as their rightful predecessors in romance writing.

> hands and lead a sedentary life … There is another reason why those espe-
> cially who are women of quality, should apply themselves to letters, namely,
> because their husbands are generally strangers to them. (ibid 44)

In the Victorian age, the writing of novels as a genre was fully conceded as women's literary domain. Critics saw it as the female genre with regard to content, authorship, and audience. The writers of this popular literature, who were derided by male writers, were also secretly envied by them because of their financial success. As a result, male writers discovered the lucrative genre for themselves and enhanced it by adding male points of interest this way trying to oust women writers.

> … the enormous popularity of the novel made it ripe for revalorization
> from a somewhat despised new arrival on the literary scene, to a serious
> literary form: the novel needed the credentials of virility, and this entailed
> the deprecation of women novelists. (A Feminine Genre 8)

Thus, the female authors were restricted to writing so-called sensational or romance novels which, again, sold well because, in the novels, they presented typical female problems and female interests to their female audience. As these novels only attracted a female readership, critics, who were of course men, reviled them as the lowest form of literature (Schabert 1997, 475). They still tend to regard them as the most trivial form of literature, naturally with exceptions. This line of 'light' fiction for the masses was pushed into an industrial process of production that began with the publishing house Mills and Boons in London in 1908.

A hundred years later, women writers of every conceivable provenance are well represented in the literary market. But only a few women authors have gained literary recognition as a result of their complex and innovative ideas and writing styles. They do not hit the mass market, but on the other hand, more women authors than ever before receive the respect due to them. The 'gods' of the literary establishment, however, still remain predominantly male, whether as writers, critics or publishers.

In the course of the cultural democratization of the middle and lower classes of the Western world, a cultural assessment of positions through literature is disappearing, thus establishing a higher degree of acceptance for popular fiction and its authors, whether male or female. As seen in 1.4 of this study, this diverse new field has become more interesting for scholars as a valuable object for research. Thus, gender-oriented scholars have introduced a range of theoretical historical approaches that analyze the romance plot, typical for women-centered novels, versus the quest plot that for centuries was reserved for men, representing adventurous, cultural and educational ideals. Their research has resulted in finding 20th-century literature that thematizes the feminine quest plot which, however, centers on psycho-sociological patterns of development including the importance of the unconscious. They focus especially on the feminine Bildungsroman (Andrea Gutenberg 2004, 106). Gutenberg traces the romance back to the chivalric epics but reports that the first feminine character of narrative central interest is found in the eighteenth and nineteenth century novel. Here, she differentiates between various plots: the romance plot where the quest of the so-called ingénue is to find a suitable husband by waiting passively to be found by him, staying virtuously virginal until her wedding day. Feminine connoted romance plots usually manifest themselves in psychologizing and internal plotting. There is the new-love plot with its sophisticated courtship rituals, the comic-courtship plot, the seduction plot with its tragic ending, the wedlock plot which demonstrates the benefits of the partnership even after matrimonial misconduct, and around the mid-nineteenth century, cruel husbands or adultery that lead to a story's tragic ending. At the end of the nineteenth century, the ideology of romantic love as one that is not compatible with married life is presented in many feminine novels (Gutenberg 2004, 108–112). Gutenberg adds that the so-called trivial modern novels did not alter these Victorian plots.

To sum up, it can be concluded that romances were discredited as worthless literature written more for the common people, predominantly women, who either wanted to be included in the idealized way of living of the upper classes through stories read to them or printed for them in cheap, mass-market editions, or who wished to be informed about the right way to conduct their womanly lives. Many female authors down the centuries were well known and loved in their time and some have survived their male critics' undervaluation. It is interesting to note that the negative image of romance fiction and women writers originates in an estate-based society and that, gradually, popular fiction has received appreciation in democratic states that boast about equality, only, as Cawelti would observe, because everybody is aware of the human need for relaxation and imaginary escapism. But what makes the modern romances enjoyable is the happy ending, a fact that Jennifer Crusie, romance author, feminist, and critic, describes as the reason why this genre has not let her down. She says in her 1998 essay "Let Us Now Praise Scribbling Women":

> That's when I understood why romance owns 50% of mass market paperback fiction sales. Seventy per cent of book buyers and eighty percent of book readers are women, and like me, those readers are tired of serving and losing and waiting and dying in their fictional worlds. The romance heroine not only acts and wins, she discovers a new sense of self, a new sense of what it means to be female as she struggles through her story, and so does the romance reader as she reads it. (n.p.)

Western-European, and later, US American publishers' marketing strategies have been very effective since the invention of large-scale paper production and book printing. In particular romances that are based on genre expectations are spread far and wide in serializations and identifiable brand names. Technical changes and globalization have produced tremendous opportunities.

The outline of this chapter shows how much relationship plots of the various kinds attest to a persistent feminine need to read about male-female relationships. The following section will demonstrate how great the opportunities are, particularly for this kind of literature.

PART II

INDUSTRIAL LITERATURE

2.1 THE INDUSTRY OF PUBLISHING MODERN ROMANCE FICTION

As both Krentz and Delinsky first produced their novels under the harsh conditions of industrial writing, an outline of the history of Harlequin Enterprises (THE romance novel publishing house) to understand these conditions is required. North America, especially the USA, has a different attitude than Europe towards literature and writing literature. For decades, its universities have offered courses and degrees in novel writing. On the internet one can find a vast amount of scholarly advice on how to write a good novel or film script, and, in addition, vast numbers of books about writing novels, especially romances. This might elicit the impression that writing a romance novel is as easy to learn as dressmaking. Like dresses, romance novels are a consumer-oriented commodity. They are mass-marketed toward a pre-identified and carefully analyzed audience. Like dresses, they are based on patterns which are a little bit altered here and there, but always include all essential parts to create a special effect in order to maintain a consistent buying appeal to an established audience. The design of the fabric, however, and its texture make the difference. This marketing attitude seems to be the basis for some publishing houses which concentrate on genre fiction and which prosper because of it. As they need a large number of writing talents, they also offer advice on how to write a successful romance novel. The authors they contract write to make money and the texts they produce are a certain form of literature that meets their customers' expectations. Serving customers' expectations is taken seriously because being part of that large industry, authors and their products need to sell well.

2.2 THE HISTORY OF THE PUBLISHING HOUSE HARLEQUIN ENTERPRISE

Along with other mass-produced literary genres, this aspect of industrial literary production also applies to the production of romance fiction, especially if one considers the fact that readers of romances are said to buy and read more than 50%

of the paperbacks sold in the USA. One of these publishing houses is Harlequin Enterprises in Toronto.[31] Its history shows how this commercial way of thinking about literature has resulted in an overwhelming success. Today, Harlequin Enterprises, a Canadian company, is the world's largest publisher of series romances and Women's Fiction. In 1981, it became a wholly owned subsidiary of Torstar Corporation, Canada's largest newspaper publisher. Harlequin issues approximately 120 titles each month in 26 different languages, for sale on 109 international markets. These books are written by about 1300 writers worldwide who are said to share English as first language. They offer a broad range of fiction from romance to psychological thrillers, to relationship novels. In the year 2006, 131 million romances were sold, half of them overseas and 96% outside of Canada. Even in cultures that are very different from the Western European culture that is reflected in the novels, such as Japan or China, Harlequin Romances are received with few changes other than translation (Gianoulis 2002, n.p.). In these countries they owe their success to the happy endings. Peter Hühn and Wulf Künne showed in their empiric analysis on transcultural reception of popular literature that specific cultural peculiarities are not usually registered by a foreign reader because, being so subtly positioned, they are not revealed on a conscious level (Hühn/Künne 1978, 471).

Harlequin Enterprises began as a small paperback reprint house in Winnipeg, Manitoba, Canada in 1949. At that time, the operation was struggling and continued to struggle to stay solvent for years. In the mid-1950s, Richard Bonnycastle acquired the company on the death of his partner Jack Palmer. At the same time, his other partner, Doug Weld, gave up his stake and offered Bonnycastle his stock. Mary Bonnycastle, the owner's wife and chief editor, an avid romance reader, noticed the popularity of their reprints of romance novels from the British publisher Mills & Boon. Together with Ruth Palmer, Richard's secretary and stockowner, she persuaded her husband to acquire the North American distribution rights to the category romance novels which had been published by Mills & Boon in the Commonwealth nations. She and Ruth Palmer had noticed that novels with romantic sounding titles significantly outsold murder mysteries and crime novels. Mary eventually managed to persuade her husband to focus solely on reprinting romances, mainly English historical ones.

When Richard Bonnycastle died in 1968, over 78% of their book sales was in Canada although Harlequin had the rights to distribute Mills & Boon books throughout North America. All this changed when his son, Richard Bonnycastle Jr., took over the company. He relocated the company to Toronto, Canada, and

---

[31] Here I mainly refer to Paul Grescoe's history of the publishing house Harlequin, *The Merchants of Venus* (1996).

in 1970 he signed a contract with Pocket Books and Simon and Schuster to distribute Mills & Boon novels in the United States (Hemmings-Wirten 1998, 64). One year later Harlequin acquired Mills & Boon, with John Boon, the founder's son, remaining with the company and overseeing the British part of the operations. In addition Harlequin began to contract their own writers, who had to be of British origin, and whose novels were only printed when the stories were situated in a historical English setting. In 1971 Harlequin was publishing only one line of category romances, *Harlequin Romance*. Within this line, six novels were released per month. John Boon urged Richard Bonnycastle to introduce a second line, *Harlequin Presents*. The novels of this line were slightly more sensual than those of *Harlequin Romance*, and Mary Bonnycastle felt they overstepped her 'decency code', but they sold so well that, after only two years, they were outselling *Harlequin Romance*. Sales were and are all that matter.

A substantial reason for Harlequin's success was, and still is, its marketing strategy. As these novels were short-lived products, like monthly magazines, book sellers were not interested in filling their shelf space with them. So in the 1970s, former marketing strategist for Proctor and Gamble, Larry Heisey, created Harlequin's most innovative marketing strategy. He developed *Harlequin Presents* series with uniform trademark covers, distinguished only by the particular title, author and cover art. Thus, the company focused on selling the line of books rather than individual authors and titles, although the name of the author appeared in larger letters than the title. The books were marketed in places where women, Harlequin's traditional audience, already shopped: the supermarket or similar stores. The company also forewent traditional advertising and instead invested in giveaways. In order to seduce readers into buying Harlequins, free copies of *The Honey Is Bitter* were bundled with Ajax cleaning products and Kotex sanitary napkins.[32] Harlequin also established a mail-order service for subscribers which, today, is an important life-saver for the company.

In 1975, the company contracted their first American author, Janet Dailey. At that time Harlequin did not want to reduce their success by backing American themes and American settings in their romance novels, which at the time were untried and therefore risky. They even hesitated to contract more American authors, rejecting for example Nora Roberts, one of America's current top-selling romance authors. Around the same time, it terminated its distributions contract with Pocket Books and Simon and Schuster, leaving them with a large sales force

---

[32] It repeated this giveaway strategy spectacularly when the Iron Curtain came down, reasoning that Easter-Europe would want the same literary romantic escape they were already providing with the German-speaking Western European countries through the Cora Verlag. So, in 1990, the company gave away 720,000 books to East Germans at border checkpoints to introduce them to the Harlequin brand via Cora Verlag (Hemmings-Wirten 19).

and no product. Simon and Schuster and other publishing houses were aware of how Harlequin was not serving American readers' changing reading expectations. Along with other American publishers, they saw the potential benefit in hiring US-American authors and seized the opportunity to contract American writers Harlequin had rejected, a fact that also helped Krentz to start her writing career. In 1980, Simon and Schuster launched *Silhouette* Books with several lines of category romances, not only encouraging its writers to experiment with the genre, but also addressing contemporary social issues in an American setting and injecting more sensuality into the stories. It took five years for Harlequin to adapt and change its rigid attitude towards American authors, who then introduced the readers to American characters, reflecting American sensibilities, American courting traditions, and American assumptions in American settings. (Because of this conflict and the resulting publisher's concession the use of the terms values, morals, ethics, ideology in connection with American is justified and will be applied in the study, as the authors are US-Americans who write stories that are set in the USA, and also depict US-American life.)

In 1980, the company launched their own line of one plot America-focused romances, *Harlequin American Romances*, and the *Harlequin Superromance* line, featuring American characters in an American setting. At the same time, it extended the length of the novels of this line from 55,000 words to 100,000 words. These books are stand-alone novels, which means they are no longer monthly-published category romances and they have room for two or more subplots. Today, a high percentage of category and other romance writers are US Americans writing US-American romance novels set in USA.

It was also competition from publishing houses like Simon and Schuster or Dell that pushed Harlequin to reconsider its strict moral guidelines and to adapt to reader's changing preferences. When readers began appreciating novels with more explicit sex scenes, were waiving a virginal heroine, or wanted secret babies added to the story, the other publishing houses were quicker to evaluate their readers' changing preferences and responded accordingly. Harlequin failed to keep up with its readers because of the restricting Bonnycastle decency code and the rigidity of the heads of the company. Not even Alan Boon and the English company, who were able to adapt more quickly to changing reader reading preferences, could persuade them to become more flexible. Decreasing sales rates alone were the only language they could understand. So Harlequin launched new lines, too, only later than the other houses that had already placed their segments in the market. This sudden increase in category romance lines, however, meant an equally sudden increase in demand for quick writers to produce this new novel content. Naturally, that caused a proportionate decrease in the quality of the released novels. The ensuing redundancy in plots already associated with series romances added to the popular conviction that this brand of literature was 'trash', and it also became evident in the decreased number of titles being sold per month. Thus, Harlequin was no longer the primary provider of category romance. At times, it actually had to experience return rates of 70%. The 'war' between the publishing houses ended when Harlequin acquired Silhouette in 1984. Despite the acquisition, Silhouette continued to retain editorial control and to publish various lines under its own imprint. In 1992, Harlequin maintained an 85% share of the North American category romance market. But other mass-market publishing houses were, and still are, serious competition for the company because they offer their writers better royalties and the rights to their works.

In 1975, Torstar Corporation bought 52% of Harlequin and, by 1981, wholly owned the company, which retained the right to do its own line of business. Bonnycastle did not want to stay at the helm of the company. David Galloway, an executive at Torstar and later president held executive positions at Harlequin in the 1980s. Lawrence Heisey was named Harlequin's president by Richard Bonnycastle Jr. in 1971, and later, when Torstar acquired Harlequin, he was named chairman and retired in 1990. Donna Hayes became the first female Harlequin president and publisher in 2001. The company has now become so large that it can only be directed by a group of directors who are not referred to in a survey of the company's history.

Harlequin, as 'the happy ending publisher', began expanding into European markets as early as 1974. Here again, their American marketing strategies proved successful and profitable so that they now have offices in New York, London, Paris, Milan, Madrid, Hamburg, Stockholm, Amsterdam, Athens, Budapest, Warsaw, Tokyo, and Sydney as well as licensing agreements in nine other countries. Harlequin's principal subsidiaries are: Harlequin Australia; Harlequin France (50%); Harlequin Germany; Harlequin Greece; Harlequin Holland; Harlequin Hungary; Harlequin Italy; Harlequin Japan; Harlequin Mills & Boon U.K.; Harlequin Poland; Harlequin Scandinavia; Harlequin Spain. The editors in Harlequin's branch offices have a large amount of control over which novel will be translated and published in their market and they are allowed to choose from Harlequin's backlist.[33] With novels translated into the country's native tongue, the title is usually not translated literally, the names of the protagonists

---

[33] Harlequin has a large backlist. For example, it owns the category romances of Krentz, Linda Howard, and Delinsky. This means, how well or badly written these novels are, how ideologically acceptable or unacceptable to today's standards, does not matter for the editors or the publishing house. In 2010, for example, Howard's first novel *All That Glitters* written in 1982 was translated and published in Germany, although the author herself admitted that this book was a bad one. Krentz's *Stormy Challenge* also should not have been reissued in 2004 as a contemporary novel because it does not reflect her ethics of later years.

may be changed, and each novel is shortened by 10% to 15% compared with its American version. This is usually due to the removal of references to American pop culture, to the omission of puns and other wordplay that do not translate well and/or abbreviation of descriptive passages.

As Harlequin's audience wanted to read stories that reflected changes in women's roles caused by the second feminist movement's influences, thereby making society and women aware of the problematic nature of patriarchal attitudes, the company launched new lines to capture different segments of readers' evolving preferences. In 1984 the *Temptation* line, a more sexually explicit series, was started as the answer to 1980 Dell's Ecstasy line which "placed the reader firmly in the bedroom and reputedly were the first to offer straightforward sexual consummation without the usual bothersome interruptions" (Grescoe 1996, 162). More assertive, feisty heroines and more sensitive heroes were the order of the day. But nevertheless, the 1980s were still the decade where 'bodice-ripper' book covers of historical romances sold best, book covers that showed scantily clad embracing white couples that tended to depict male dominance. In fact, the book covers mirrored the content. The books pandered to the old-age male fantasy that women love to be raped. Jude Devereaux reports that her editor wanted her to include rape scenes in her story and when she refused, she lost her contract. Luckily she was able to move to a different publishing house and commence her career, now, as a bestselling author.[34] Today Harlequin has diversified its supply of romances into twelve romance category lines of 55,000–75,000 words that serve readers' expectations from chaste love stories to highly erotic ones, from African American love stories to same-sex romances. All these category lines have subseries that are linked either by themes, (maternity ward or Texas cowboys or men in uniform) or by family or friend connections. These series within the lines may be written by one or by various authors.

Currently the company contracts about 1,300 writers, almost exclusively female, who write mass market Women's Fiction for the female reading market. To ensure that writers keep within the category line, Harlequin hands out writing guidelines. These can be retrieved from the internet and do not seem to be so much restrictive as generic. The writing guideline for *Harlequin Presents*, 2009, serves as a good example:

> Length: 50,000–55,000 words …
>
> The Harlequin Presents line offers the ultimate in emotional and sensual excitement!

---

[34] Referring to the publishing industry as "a space of literary or artistic position-takings" in his essay "The Field of Cultural Production", Bourdieu claims that for authors their authorship in their work makes their work part of their identity. For him it is the editor who has "the power to impose the dominant definition of the writer" (42).

Although grounded in reality and reflective of contemporary, relevant trends, these fast-paced stories are essentially escapist romantic fantasies that take the reader on an emotional roller-coaster ride. Written in the third person, they can be from the male or female point of view, or seen through the eyes of both protagonists. All are set in sophisticated, glamorous, international locations.

With its focus on strong, wealthy, breathtaking charismatic alpha-heroes who are tamed by spirited, independent heroines, the central relationship in a Presents novel is a provocatively passionate, highly charged affair, driven by conflict, emotional intensity and overwhelming physical attraction, which may include explicit lovemaking. We advise keeping in touch with current reader preferences by reading the most recent titles available in the Harlequin Presents line.

However, we are looking for fresh voices ...

Staying within the category line, certain topics have to be avoided, for example sex and erotic descriptions of sensuality, and even the mention of nakedness are banned within the Inspirational (Christian) romance line, along with alcoholism, drug addiction, or terrorism. As times change, the last three may be part of the novel if the hero or heroine comes into contact with them by knowing someone who is or was an alcoholic or a drug-addict. Editors will see to it that the new writer observes the guidelines. (A review of guidelines for contemporary romances are given below (2.4) and the original texts of the guidelines are placed in the annex.) They will also help and push new aspiring writers to find their way into the category line that most suits them. New writers also find that other romance authors encourage their writing by giving hints and advice and by answering questions without fearing the budding competition, as far one can tell. This seems to be unique in the literary market.

Writing category romances under Harlequin's and other romance publishing houses' tutelage is similar to manufacturing a product that sells well because it is adapted to consumers' expectations. The authors are the designers for the special line. Regrettably for the authors, the copyrights on the books stay with Harlequin, especially those that are written under a pen name. Harlequin seems to demand from their writers that they write under given pen names (Rholetter 2002). Paul Grescoe points out how much writing romances can be something like working on an assembly line, churning out novel after novel:

If anybody kept track of the speed with which series romances were written, (Janet) Daily might have vied for that record (i.e. The Guinness Book of World Records), too: she claimed they never took her more than 20 days, although Heisey says "she never publicly said she could do one faster than five days because she felt that four days was obscene". In 1980 when she was 35 years old she had written 53 Harlequin books that sold 80 million copies, with reader subscriptions and the Harlequin book clubs being the reason for the success. (Grescoe, 119–120)

Barbara Cartland was another speedy writer. Of course, these writers are the exception to the rule, obviously using one sole formula as the backbone of their stories. But there are other writers, with a less rapid turnover, quick, but prolific enough to have gained their readers' love and respect. They are more gifted than others, they hit the right tone and develop their special 'voice' so that they can keep their readers interested in their novels for years. Once they have gained the respect and love of the romance readers' community, other publishing houses become interested in them and offer them better contracts, as well as the copyright ownership of their novels which Harlequin is reluctant to grant. Krentz and Delinsky belong to that exceptional group of writers. They started their writing careers under different pen names with a romance novel publishing house and belonged to Harlequin for a time. As the company owns the copyrights of most of their early books, many of them still are available in reprints.

During the Harlequin-Silhouette conflict, North American authors became increasingly prominent. They were given more autonomy in their writing and as such they created a more liberated heroine and a more sensitive hero who learned to express his feelings with his heroine's help. She held the power more firmly in the relationship and so needed no longer tolerate the rape-like and rape scenes that defined the hot historical romances of the 1970s. Both Krentz and Delinsky wrote category romances for some years until they changed to single titles that are longer stand alone novels, partly with different publishing houses. (Romance novels are divided into two sub-sets: category romances or series romances, mostly one-plots, and single-title romances that are almost popular mainstream romances.) To differentiate between single-title romances and mainstream romances is difficult because there are no real different categorizing characteristics for one or the other. Krentz and Delinsky have achieved success in both formats. Single-title romances generally fall into the 100,000 plus word count. The additional length of the novel allows the author more room for subplots and in-depth characterization. Thus, a more complex structure may often give the single titles a different tone. Today, both these writers are present with their more recent novels in hard cover editions, which therefore, might receive critical acclaim, followed by mass market editions, both American and English. Obviously, these novels do not appear in the romance category lines, but the authors' category romance novels, being on the Harlequin backlist, are reissued time and again.

2.3 THE DEVELOPMENT OF THE MODERN US-AMERICAN ROMANCE GENRE

In North America, romance novels (now almost always with a happy ending) are the most popular genre in modern literature. According to the Romance Writers of America (RWA) they comprise 55% of all paperback books sold in 2004.[35] (RWA offers market research studies on sales, subgenres, publishers, and on readership.) Why this genre is so popular has something to do with the writers' and the publishers' quick reaction to readers' changing reading preferences. According to Katherine Or, vice-president of Harlequin Mills&Boon and public relations director, trends concerning romance contents are modified every two years. She explains this adjustment by citing social changes and sees other media discourses as a sometimes influencing factor (Linke 2003, 76). I think the time span is actually somewhat longer. The need to adapt quickly to contentual adjustments, however, is taken account of by versatile writers. One characteristic in the romances beside the happy ending, which they are derided or loved for, is the important part that (explicit) sexuality plays in the American romances. Sometimes category romances are even referred to as female pornography. Carol Thurston explains why sexually explicit romance novels were not forbidden literature in the guise of a novel in the very conventional USA:

> The erotic hetero-sexual romance, with content that is sexually appealing and stimulating to a larger number of women, came into existence in the 1970s, when the social climate combined with a distribution strategy that put these romances into retail outlets that legitimized them for mass consumption by women – the American supermarket, discount store, and drugstore. Their legitimacy was further enhanced by the fact that stories were allowed to evolve as erotica without much notice and under the guise of a different label – romance. (1987, 9)

Cawelti wants to ignore the critics' accusations about romances being pornographic literature because he thinks that "the escape experience offered by pornography is really too immediately physical to be sustained for any substantial period of time", whereas "a more artful and ultimately satisfying form of escape is one that can sustain itself over a longer period of time and arrive at some sense of completion and fulfillment within itself" (1977, 14–15). Obviously, the written word is supposed not to be seen to threaten a reader's morality or to offend readers' sensibilities like a simple drawing in a children's book showing a small

---

[35]   see: Romance Writers of America/ industry statistics/ 2004 romstat report

naked boy's tiny penis could do so.[36] Thus it slips under the radar of the vigilant women's associations.

As early as the 1970s the romance publishing houses were able to gauge rather accurately what kind of romances would sell because they not only relied on their sales figures, but used other marketing devices like questionnaires to research their readers' reading preferences, ethics, morals, and convictions. Because, when the sales decrease, the reason for it must be found and so new guidelines are adapted to readers' preferences according to the changing values in the North American society. If possible, the developing partialities and tastes, dislikes and time-related themes are customized. Editors scrutinize an author's work and see to it that the contents of the novel follow the requirements of the guidelines for the different category lines in order to ensure that the novel is easy to sell because it contains generally accepted values of the time. Thus, in 1972, a publishing house 'allowed' Katherine Woodiwiss to write explicit (rape) sex scenes in her historical romance and because her novel sold so well, other authors followed in this line of writing, and their novels likewise sold well.

In 1972, when Avon published *The Flame and the Flower* by Kathleen Wood-iwiss, the first original single title paperback, the modern romance genre was born. This historical romance, more than twice the length of the average gothic one, features conventional elements of popular romance stories: a mature hero, a young virginal heroine, a forced marriage, and peril as conflict. As greater openness about female sexuality characterized the 1970s, Woodiwiss could also insert explicit sex in her story, a fact that helped to incorporate this new openness as part of the romance formula within the frame of a monogamous heterosexual relationship that culminates in marriage. At the same time, this plot is the short formula of a conventional romance novel: its core is the developing relationship between a hero and a heroine, usually both whites, and an emotionally satisfactory happy ending which generally means marriage or the promise of marriage. Short category romances (50,000 to 60,000 words) fit this formula. The story solely focuses on the couple playing out an initial lingering antagonism that turns rapidly into love, mainly with the heroine falling in love first. The hero has to be persuaded that what he feels as sexual attraction only is really everlasting love. An inserted conflict prolongs the process of his perception of love, so that the happy ending occurs at page 199 or 250, relative to the required length of the book, and not

---

[36] in 2007 it was reported in German papers that in preemptive obedience, an American pub-lisher did not want to print the above mentioned drawing, fearing public outraged actions from women's fundamentalist or conservative associations. In 2001, Susan Elizabeth Phillips ad-dressed the influence which conservative self-appointed guardians of the American people's sexual virtue exert over children's picture book publishers in her 2001 contemporary romance novel *This Heart of Mine*.

before. Love scenes range from chaste kisses to explicit sex scenes depending on the category line. In the early 1980s portraying explicit sex scenes was becoming the rule in certain contemporary category lines. The role sex was to play in a novel was upgraded to a leading one. Both writers, Krentz and Delinsky, started out in the more explicit sex lines.

Written for a female audience, the plot of these novels of the early 1980s was developed from a single perspective in free indirect discourse, mainly that of the heroine, and only in the third person singular because first person focalized stories did not and are supposed to not sell well: obviously, an omniscient author also went out of salable narrative style. Around the middle of the 1980s two or more perspectives were conceded, again responding to the challenge of reader preferences. Superficially featured local settings in these romances can be anywhere in the world and the story can be set from the Middle Ages into the future. But the cultural heritage of the USA alluded to in these romance novels is primarily the heritage drawn from Western European sources. This is the basis for the romance novel whose current form is almost purely of American provenance. When Krentz turned away from the pure romance category stories to the romantic suspense line she still had to follow her publishing houses' guidelines, only now those of the different category line.[37]

In single-titles, extended thriller or mystery elements, lengthened descriptions and in-depth characterizations of the protagonists as well as the surrounding characters alter the focus from the pure love story to a more complex plot. Sex scenes take on a new significance because other relevant events and circumstances take priority to explain the couple's developing relationship, commitment and love. Nowadays, the distinguishing line between single-title romance novels and mainstream Women's Fiction is blurred. Often it is only a question of sales figures which makes publishing houses put a novel in the respective genre.

Over the years, beginning in the 1980s, women writers started to gain an increasing foothold in the mainstream fiction market. It is scientifically substantiated that more women than men read fiction[38]. Is Addison's explanation of 1713 still valid? We can only speculate. Anyway, as female readership prevails, women's

---

[37] Silhouette Romantic Suspense guidelines of 2009 are the only ones available now. They are not as restrictive as they were in the 1980s. In parts they ask the following from their writers: "... The hero should be a force to contend with. He may be harsh and direct, but never cruel. Though formidable and heroic, he is capable of being saved, and it is up to the heroine to get him there. Our heroines should be complex strong and smart. As independent as the heroine may be, she is often in jeopardy and needs the hero's help to overcome obstacles. Because this is primarily the heroine's story, we ask that roughly 60% of the point of view be hers, and 40% the hero's ... " There is not anymore a requirement of the protagonists' belonging to, at least, he upper middle social class.

[38] See: Romance Writers of America/readership statistics retrieved 02.06.09

themes – and romances are at the top – written by women seem to strike the right chord and sell so well that mass market editions attain a large circulation. Mass market pocket book covers shout frankly: we love to entertain you! Choose the right genre and we promise emotional satisfaction! In order to emotionally satisfy a reader and also draw her attention to aspects outside her realm of experience, these novels require writers who not only enjoy regaling readers with well plotted stories, but also have the literary skill to keep the reader interested. These novelists' primary goal in writing is to offer the reader entertainment, giving her a few hours' respite from whatever challenges she happens to be facing. On the other hand, as the genre aspires to accessibility by the highest number of readers possible, the frequently expressed 'grade 6 reading level' notion is mentioned in a derogatory way, although this cannot be applied as a valid standard for an evaluation as highbrow literates sometimes write on even lower reading levels.

2.4 ROMANCE PUBLISHING HOUSES' WRITING GUIDELINES

It is difficult to obtain pre-internet writing guidelines offered by romance publishing houses to aspiring authors because, once the guidelines had served their purpose, when readers' reading choices had moved in different directions, they disappear. They do sometimes reemerge by chance and then they become interesting material for the purposes of comparison. Around the 1980s, guidelines were sent to prospective romance authors on request, courtesy of a stamped, self-addressed envelope. This shows the publishing houses' politics of not commissioning, but instead accepting unsolicited novels. Regrettably, these guidelines like the latest ones, are not dated. The earliest guidelines for contemporary romances I could find through *romancewiki* were those of *Gallen Books, Dell's Candlelight Ecstasy* line, and the *Silhouette Desire* line, all from around 1980. These guidelines are divided into the following titled paragraphs, indicating which narrative aspect an author should pay attention to when writing a book for this publisher's line: characters, setting, plot, writing, and love scenes. According to the guidelines, romances focus on the developing love story, which must not be overshadowed by other things like secondary characters, who should stay in the background, or adventure or problems that are only permitted when they heighten the emotional highs and lows of the developing relationship. *Gallen Books* are the most elaborate regarding characteristics. They expect the heroine, 18–30 years old, not necessarily a virgin, to be beautiful, well dressed, to be spirited and intelligent, aspiring to or having a career in a glamorous industry, whatever that may be: one of the preferable professions listed is working in an agency or being a computer expert. She needs to be liked by the reader because she starts with personal problems she recognizes and eventually overcomes. These personal problems are: selfishness, jealousy, sibling rivalry, difficulties with parents, stubbornness, imagined figure problems, and fear of handling money, which can only be a result of a patriarchal indoctrination. In addition, *Silhouette Desire* likes its heroine to be independent (in an economic sense?) and not too subservient, although after the wedding she is expected to work in her husband's business and for her, home and family will always come first. *Candlelight Ecstasy's* heroine, 25–35, is mostly established in an interesting career. No other traits are given.

The question of virginity of the heroine, which I was led to believe was so important in romance novels, is not raised often in guidelines for contemporary novels. I also guessed a heroine's age would change from around 20 to 35 or 40 in the later guidelines, but I was wrong. Either she is supposed to be 23 and older (*Temptation* 1991), in her early 20s (*Blaze, Temptation's* successor, 2004) or age does not appear to be of importance because it is not mentioned often in later guidelines. This makes sense. When a heroine is expected to be independent, mainly through working in a job or profession, she needs to be a little older to have an impressive salary, or if she started her own business it would take time to have reached the successful stage she has obtained in the story. Moreover, the age of a romance heroine whose marriage should be crowned by a child is restricted to around 40, which needs not be mentioned in a guideline.

A hero's age stays between 30 and 40 and 15 years of age difference between the couple is the maximum permitted. Always tall and muscular, he dresses well like the heroine, he is not necessarily handsome, but above all, he must be virile. He is rich and successful in a 'position of authority' (*Gallen Books*), which enables him to be self-confident, strong, passionate, tender, and understanding. *Gallen Books'* list of his character traits is augmented by *Silhouette Desire* who makes him into an arrogant, self-assured, masterful, hot-tempered and often mysterious man, capable of violence and passion, whose one trait of tenderness might have a redeeming quality. *Candlelight Ecstasy* proposes no hero traits at all for an author to work with.

Secondary characters are to be placed in the periphery, they are never allowed to overshadow the protagonists. The other woman or a male character who is interested in the heroine were still part of the romance plot in the 1980s. In these guidelines the permitted settings are located internationally, provided they are romanticized. Only after 1982, can they be American or 'foreign', which indicates an established North American readership.

Plot requirements are mostly contentual and less structural. Apart from the central theme, that of the developing love story which should be a convincing, full-dimensioned and mature love affair *(Candlelight Ecstasy), Gallen Books* provide the most detailed specifications: good plotting, good character development, fast paced action where no obvious 'padding' is permitted. The heroine's tension with the hero is a necessity, and the story can end with marriage or 'basic differences will be resolved if only to acknowledge they will always exist'. All incidents and characters must be important to the overall telling of the story. Even subplots are needed, be they parallel, contrasting, or otherwise connected to the major plot. *Candlelight Ecstasy* recommends avoiding formula plot devices such as marriage of convenience or amnesia. The conflicts introduced should arise out of the relationship such as career vs. marriage, or unresolved feelings regarding a prior relationship. *Silhouette Romance's* shorter list of requirements insist on the heroine's perspective, only allowing analepses in the heroine's head: otherwise they demand a sequential, straightforward narrative. Suspense or adventure augment the plot of *Silhouette Super Desire* to 'heighten the emotional heights and lows of the developing relationship', but they do not explicitly demand a sole perspective.

Gallen Books insists on descriptions of clothing, people, body language, of descriptions of nature and building interiors. If lengthy passages of background information are unavoidable, they should be broken up with demonstrations of character interactions. *Silhouette Romance* likes its authors to forego long-winded descriptions: instead they should offer sensuous descriptions that include the senses of taste, smell, and touch.

Love scenes are the final point in the guidelines. *Silhouette Romance* insists that premarital love-making should be followed by an immediate wedding. The tried and tested narrative device should be an interruption at the brink of consummation, be it a person, an incident or because one or both protagonists 'suffer from doubt or shame'. Even descriptions of nudity are mentioned: above the waist, the narrative tone is titillating, below the waist, veiled references to 'hidden' or 'secret' places are permitted, otherwise descriptions should not be too graphic. *Silhouette Desire* requests the love scenes to be conducted as a celebration of the physical pleasures of love. Tastefully handled premarital sexual encounters that include nudity and love-making should be dealt with by concentrating more on the highly erotic sensations aroused by the hero's kisses and caresses, rather than the mechanics of sex. For *Gallen Books*, rape scenes are out.

One last aspect in these guidelines is reader oriented: *Silhouette Romance* wants the reader transported out of her ordinary life when reading the book, which finally, in 2010, is termed as 'escapist' fiction. Ideally, the story should be so emotionally moving that a reader will shed some tears as well as rejoice at the happy ending (*Silhouette Super Desire* after 1982), and the hero should be so desirable that any woman could imagine herself falling in love with him (*Silhouette Desire*). For this reason, the stories, although fantasy, must be grounded in reality, so that readers encounter realistic, believable characters in realistic relationships, depicting fears, doubts, and problems familiar to them or, as *Silhouette Super Desire* demands, the heroine's actions and reactions must be familiar or believable to a reader.

Krentz and Delinsky are reported to have written novels for Harlequin's *Temptation* line, which depicts pure romantic fantasy and has been out of print since 2005 (60,000 words). The only guideline for that line I have been able to find was published in 1991. (This does not necessarily mean that this guideline was only recently issued. It may have been valid for years.) There, the woman of the Nineties should be involved in a career, and desires to meet a partner in order to achieve emotional and sexual fulfillment (!) and to make a lifetime commitment. (Obviously the hero is the tool for her to achieve this.) Written from a North-American viewpoint, a good blend of sparkling dialogue and minimal narrative are the narrative requests for the line as are secondary characters and minor sub-plots to enrich the plot. Love scenes should be highly erotic, but above all, emotional. These extensive guidelines could be regarded as the writing foundation for both authors being American and wanting to write stories set in a US-American locale and social milieu. Topics not to be mentioned are religion, moral attitudes, social backgrounds and politics in the broadest sense, the only restriction focused on seemingly is premarital sex without ensuing marriage. Even virginity is of so little importance that it is mentioned only once and then as not being a necessary virtue. Whether editors were and are the ones who have the power to accept or reject a book is not an accessible matter.[39]

The *Silhouette Desire* writing guideline, retrieved in 2010, again express what the line is about without separately treated headlined topics, although the guideline is presented in five paragraphs. According to the guideline this line offers sensual love stories that immediately involve the reader in the romantic conflict and its quest for a happy-ever-after resolution. Indicating how 'fast-paced' the stories should be, the guideline states that the exposition should be executed in the first chapter so that readers are informed about what to expect from the very beginning. If the heroine was the first character mentioned in the 1980 and 1982 guidelines, now it is the hero who comes first. Although he is given fewer scenes from his point of view, 'in many ways, he owns the story'. But the writer of the guideline quickly adds that the heroine is equally important. (In 1982, it was he, a romance reader should imagine falling in love with, according to publishers' guidelines, which also meant he was assumed to be the main character in the romance story.) The hero is now powerful and wealthy, the one in charge and not a simple employed worker. Remarkably, this difference is specifically explained which could

---

[39]   Jennifer Crusie is one of many authors who reports editors' interferences and errors of judgement (So Bill, …).

mean that in 2010 class differences are difficult for writers to understand, and, therefore, to characterize. Being an alpha male, arrogant he may be, harsh or direct, but never cruel. His traits require the heroine to discover his vulnerable self and thus, she can 'save' him. (This coded language of the 1990s means that the traditional romance heroine's part in the formula role play is now to save the hero with her love from whatever internal conflict and communicative solecism he is ailing from. Offering her (sexual) self to become the other half of his soul, she is able to heal him and make him whole again or play his interpreter. Her reward is his everlasting love.) Whereas, in 1982, marriages of convenience were used too often and, therefore, should not be employed in the plot of the 1990s. They are now once again en vogue as are secret pregnancies and reunion romances.

The heroine is endowed with fewer characteristics than the hero. She should be complex and smart but also 'flawed', which is not explained, but means that she is not the beautiful girl of the 1980s. According to the hero's importance explained above, she is the means by which a reader is expected to fall in love with the hero. Again it is emphasized that, because *Desire* novels are sensual reads, one love scene or more are required, but the sensuality must be appropriate to the storyline: no other qualifiers given. The main objective for these short novels of 50,000–55,000 words is to reach the fulfillment of 'the promise of a powerful, passionate and provocative read'.

The 2010 writing guidelines adhere to the narrative structural aspects of plot setting, characters, and narrative devices such as perspectives, descriptions, and characterizations, but they do it in an ordinary way without an expected strictness.

When analyzing these guidelines, it becomes clear that they lack parts, that in fact, should be contained within guidelines. In 2008, I asked editor Emily Ohanjanians via email if a writer is given more extended guidelines once she is seriously writing her novel. She replied that Harlequin does not commission stories, but authors propose stories to their editors who then accept them or not. As such, extended guidelines are not necessary. She said Harlequin authors are aware of what makes a good storyline because they familiarize themselves with the genre by reading published novels of the line they want to write for, and they are aware to which degree they may include sex scenes. She laid emphasis on the fact that Harlequin is a publisher of romance novels that by 'nature' include sex scenes with which vigilant women's associations seem to agree *nolens volens*. Ohanjanians explained that authors learn how to write successful romance novels in a number of different ways: by reading them, by working directly with editors who know the genre well, by writing experience, etc. The rules for writing a romance are short: all romance novels have to have a hero and a heroine with strong characters, internal and external conflicts, and a plot that involves romance as its central theme. Up to this point she did not give a surplus of information relevant to my question, but then she referred to the construction of any successful story, including romance novels: they all need the 'grid' of the story arc because in any story there should be an inciting incident, a turning point, a reward, a second turning point, a climax, a resolution and any number of steps between. This way a successful story is supposed to resemble a successful drama. Within these limits an author seems to have considerable freedom, were there not the unspecified limits an editor imposes on the author asking her to reconsider changes that may be contrary to her principles or to the contents of the story. These editorial interventions can be helpful or absurd[40] depending on the editor's own skill or personality and ethical disposition. What also needs to be negotiated internally are the ethical implications in the romances that are not discussed in the guidelines.

The guideline for *Harlequin Presents*, cited above (2.2), that could be retrieved from the internet in 2009, but no longer in 2011, still restricts the aspiring author to a third-person narrative, albeit with two permitted perspectives that offer the reader voyeuristic emotional and descriptive perceptions. The hero, still a 'strong, wealthy and breathtaking charismatic alpha-male' meets a 'spirited, independent' heroine. For the first time the guideline for *Harlequin Presents*, retrieved in 2011, equips the hero with 'depth and integrity', the first hint that he was supposed to display a moral quality, apart from being 'sexy, powerful, ruthless, and not being used to taking no for an answer', or beside his readiness to marry the heroine which had been his only moral requirement until then. In fact, however, the heroes of the 1980 or the 2010 novels display courage and integrity in droves, together with all the other conventional standards of goodness and rightness, of virtues that distinguish the good from the bad people without them having been solicited by guidelines. What Krentz and Delinsky choose to be their ideal hero's and heroine's characteristics will be analyzed below.

Krentz and Delinsky wrote romance novels within the category for about ten years, quite early on inserting some crime as the outer conflict their heroine has to overcome, thereby turning their writing to the romantic suspense that later became its own line within the short categories. Simon and Schuster's *Silhouette Super Desire* line of around 1984 required 80,000–85,000 words and allowed elements of adventure, suspense and melodrama to be incorporated into the stories. Thus, the authors, especially Krentz, were able to write longer stand alone novels. When Harlequin acquired Simon and Schuster it included the *Silhouette* type of suspense into its guidelines: this was more action-oriented than introspective and dealt with life and death situations, but foremost with the love story as the primary plot. As these writing guidelines provided a basis for the novels of both authors, their

---

[40] It is reported of an editor who wanted to force an author to put a defloration scene at the end of the novel although the story ran along the line of the 'virgin' having a secret child from her sexual encounter with the romance hero years before.

presence and relevance will be examined in the following analyses of their six novels.

Part III

Analysis of Six Romance Novels

Since these six novels were written by women for women it is impossible to block out feminist mimetic conceptions with reference to reality. I combine formal and structural aspects with feminist questions. This way I also include aspects of reader reception.[41] The results will be presented and evaluated in the chapters Constants and Changes.

Andreotti points out that traditional bourgeois novels, and romance novels can be termed as such if only seen from a formal point of view, are still predominantly written in the twenty-first century:

> "Innerhalb der Geschichte des Romans spielt der bürgerliche Roman, der im Realismus des 19. Jahrhunderts seine wichtigste Ausformung erfährt und in dessen Schlüsseltradition im 20./21. Jahrhundert zahlreiche Autoren fortschreiben, eine tragende Rolle." (237)

He sees the ideological basis for this bourgeois type of novel in a firm belief in the unity of the individual which means no fragmented identities, the unity of the language (mimesis), and the unity of the world which depicts a coherent reality.[42] According to him the following elements define this kind of bourgeois novel: a consistent fictional world rendered in a coherent, causal, spatial/chronological plot,

---

[41] Two issues of the fictional worlds theories seem to be relevant to me: the first is internal to a particular fictional world and relates to the problem of incompleteness and the second is external and relates to a reader's actualization of this fictional textual world. I understand incompleteness, that are gaps and indeterminacies within this constructed world, as the reason for narrative fiction to be instrumental in causing reflection upon ethical, existential, political and didactic value. Marie-Laure Ryan (1991) builds a typology based on various interpretations of accessibility, assuming a 'principle of minimal departure': "the principle of minimal departure dictates that the world of the text is to be understood complete, and identical to the actual world except for the respects in which it deviates from that model, either explicitly or implicitly, both in its own right and by virtue of any genre conventions it evokes (Ryan 1991, 51)" (Walsh 152). The reader fills the gaps with his/her knowledge of his/her actual world, a process which could be termed as a real world explanatory strategy. I subsume this reader actualization of a fictional textual world under the umbrella term reader reception.

[42] Richard Walsh states that "Fiction is usually understood to have a second-order relation to the real world, via the mimetic logic of fictional representation: it represents events, or imitates discourses, that we assimilate through non-fictional modes of narrative understanding" (150).

psychologically substantiated patterns of individual behavior, the protagonists' individual fate and development as the centrally assigned meaning, the teleological principle, where every occurrence leads to a (satisfying) end, symbolic representation of the protagonists' setting, and a consistent writing style. Andreotti reaches the conclusion that by means of structural analyses of this realistic type of novel it became obvious that popular literary texts, as for example romance novels, are based on the same narrative structures and *topoi* of the so-called highbrow literature (240).

Because of their conventional type of a closed teleological composition Crusie compares romances with the strict established form of the Shakespearian sonnet and others like Frye and Regis see them as a three act comedy translated into the form of the novel.[43] The plot of this closely defined genre with its introductory exposition, its tangled web of conflicts, and a solution in harmony becomes intriguing as it does with the romance story by way of its dramatically increasing suspense curve. Whether the chains of events in both authors' novels have dramatic effects will be seen in the analysis.

Narrative discourse criteria will be used in the following analysis, not only by paying attention to the elements which define the realistic novels according to Andreotti, but also by tacitly acknowledging the unity of the individual, the language, and the world.

In the section Plot, Chapters, Time and Settings the examination of the plot is followed by an analysis of the representation of time and geographical setting as well as the characters' social setting. Part of the plot is the division of scenes and situations into chapters. The way a novel is divided into chapters reflects the writing strategy of an author. Whether chapters separate two different scenes or situations and how this is presented in the six novels will be seen in the ana-lysis.

Character constellations, relations of contrast or correspondence, life in the universe of discourse whether complex or simple are focused on in the analysis of the characters. Character traits as being the cause for supporting and furthering the action or impede it will be examined. A characterization of the figures results in a concentration of semantic aspects. I understand fictive characters to be elements of their constructed narrative world and thus limited by their individual construction and the frame of their text world. This means that the arsenal at disposal is reduced to a system of contrasting relations versus correspondent relations which usually are already embedded in the other character. These differentiations are of-

---

[43] Theodor Fontane mentioned this, as he saw it, 'ideal' relation between drama and (bourgeois) novel in a closed composed form when, in 1855, he praised the structure of Gustav Freitag's novel *Soll und Haben* as follows: "… er hat dem Drama und seinen strengen Anforderungen und Gesetzen auch die Vorschriften für die Behandlung des Romans entnommen. Das dünkt uns ein Fortschritt … " (148–149).

ten identified as belonging to the criteria of gender, age, status, and background. And as such these character blanks have to be filled with character traits in order to become (centrally) significant. Sometimes, however, these different powers are not assigned to different characters but united in one.[44]

In the section Conflicts, Relationships, and Erotic Scenes the characters' text-internal worlds, their emotional relations and experiences are reviewed as well as their function within the overall structure of the novel. This raises the question of what experiences the authors ascribe to their characters and how close to reality these experiences in the fictional world are portrayed as being. If for example they are near to reality and they are so familiar to a reader they will not need an extensive description.

The section Writing Style focuses on the authors' typical writing strategy and the figural narrative situation which causes a dominance of an internal versus an external perspective.

Repeatedly I refer to a reader and her (fulfilled) expectations because the romance genre is constructed or composed according to empirically researched time-related reader preferences. Therefore, suggestive effects, certain writing strategies, and wordings have had to be taken into consideration as have the requirements of writing guidelines in order to keep the contract between author and reader going.

3.1 ANALYSIS OF THREE NOVELS BY JANE ANN KRENTZ

3.1.1 *Stormy Challenge*

Stormy Challenge (1982), was written under the pseudonym Stephanie James for Simon and Schuster's *Silhouette Desire* line. Up to that year Krentz seems to have published thirteen books, followed by another thirteen in 1982, *Stormy Challenge* being the only one reprinted. As far as I can see, like *Stormy Challenge,* all her category romances are contemporary ones.

SUMMARY

Twenty-seven-year old Leya Brandon, owner of a prosperous bookshop, inherited half of her late parents' firm, Brandon Security Systems, which is in deep financial trouble. Leya's younger brother, determined to save the firm, found himself a consultant from whom, he is sure, he will learn how to salvage the firm and make it profitable. He wants Leya to sign a contract, which would give Tremayne,

---

44 In their anthology *Characters in Fictional Worlds* Eder/Jannidis/Schneider refer to Phelan who "has proposed the description of characters as participating in a mimetic sphere (due to the character's traits), a thematic sphere (as a representative of an idea or a class of people) and a synthetic sphere (the material out of which the character is made)." (16) These aspects of characterization will be observed below.

the consultant, far more power than Leya thinks is good for her brother and the firm. So she goes on a short vacation, taking the contract with her. There, she meets Court Gannon, a man she is attracted to, and trustingly she shows him the contract to ask his opinion about it. Court manages to persuade her to sign the contract, but not yet to go to bed with him.

Having mailed the signed contract, she telephones her brother, and during the conversation it becomes clear that Gannon and Tremayne are the same person. Court explains he only wanted the contract out of the way to be able to concentrate on the relationship, but Leya does not believe him. It seems to her that first foremost he wants to take over her brother's firm. She asks him to leave her alone, but then they go to a party where they meet her ex-lover. She pretends to be engaged to Court, a deception Court happily agrees to. No sooner have they reached this fragile truce, than an offhand remark sets off the misunderstanding again.

Despite her misgivings, Leya knows that Court is 'Mr. Right' and, so, she tries to find a way to remove the one obstacle between them. She decides to give her brother her shares. Seeing her abdication of rights as an act of trust and knowing that up to now he has behaved clumsily, Court transfers the responsibility for the relationship to her. To ensure that he will not misunderstand her actions he gives her a pair of emerald earrings that are for pierced ears. Once she is ready for a commitment and really wants him in her life, she will be courageous enough to have her ears pierced. In addition she is allowed her terms. So when he sees the emeralds in her ears he readily agrees to her terms, namely marriage. The last chapter is dedicated to her wedding preparations which are overshadowed by her imaginary worry that he will not appear for the wedding, the wedding itself and their honeymoon beginning with their sexual blissful reunion after their mutual statements of love.

PLOT, CHAPTERS, TIME, AND SETTINGS

Stormy Challenge has 250 pages and 12 chapters which are only numbered without additional headlines. The beginning of the chapters is marked by a first letter in a bigger bold print. Otherwise the pages remain unadorned. The plot of the story following the formula of the three act drama is simple: deception followed by misconceptions and distrust, ending in trust, love, and marriage. In the first two chapters (9–52) the introductory exposition contains every part necessary to be on par with the expected content of the story: the lovers' ambivalent instant attraction, the hero's high-handed male arrogance and his deception, the heroine's past relationship and both their social status. There are no real highs and the turning point (giving away the shares and receiving the earrings) is nearly overlooked after all the sparring of the lovers-to-be. The ruse with the earrings used as a turning point is slightly different from other romance novels .[45]

The story is rendered in the epic preterite, which as a literary device allows the reader to participate as if it were happening in the present.[46] Moreover, stories narrated in the past tense give credence to its having really happened. Narrated in a linear, successive time line with one thought flashback at the beginning, the love story develops over a period of roughly four weeks in winter. The protagonists meet at an inn somewhere in Oregon, stay there for two nights (time to fall in love with each other), return to Santa Rosa where they go to a party together one day, go to work the next day, visit each other in their respective homes, and go on a winery tour together for one day. Then there is a time gap of several days. One Sunday night Court announces that he will be away for a few days, but will definitely return on Friday for the cocktail party, where she tells him she is ready to be engaged to be married to him. After that the time reference is vague. No more than a week seems to elapse between the engagement and the wedding. Returning to the inn on the Oregon coast where they fell for each other on their honeymoon the same day signals the end of the story. Everything solely focuses on the linear development of the love story, even if there are changes of places, but there are no exciting incidents or subplots.

The characters move between the Oregon coast and Santa Rosa, Northern California. Descriptions of the landscape (beach in Oregon) and the townscape (Santa Rosa) are not given profusely, more in an aside, mostly about three sentences long, vague, and more used to indicate the characters' moods, which is consistent with publishers writing guidelines:

> In silence, refusing his proffered arm, she stalked beside him down the path leading to the rocky, untamed beach. The aftermath of the previous evening's storm had left the usual calling cards of carelessly tossed driftwood and broken shells. The tide was out and the sea moved sleepily under a gray sky.
>
> Leya felt herself absorbed into the scene, her senses responding as they always did to the feel of the ocean environment. It appealed to her love of the tactile quality in life, and when she accidentally caught Court's shrewd glance, she knew he was aware of the effect. Grimly she closed her face … (60)

To help the reader become acquainted with the lay of the land, remarks about, for example, the house where the heroine lives do not extend beyond three sentences,

---

[45]   Typical solutions of the time are e.g. illness that makes the lover understand that she belongs to him, or an intrigue that ends in celebrating her innocence and his right to love her.

[46]   See Käte Hamburger. *Die Logik der Dichtung.* (39)

but the short elements of a place the writer selects for her description makes the reader draw associations of intended images from her own American experience.

> For a moment, he sat in silence surveying the old two-storey structure with its encircling porch, graceful windows, and gingerbread trim. The new wooden siding was painted in rich butterscotch and the trim was in white. Her home dated from a warmer, more inviting era of house design ... (81)

Using the phrase "warmer, more inviting" evokes the illusion of an equally warm and inviting person living in that house. The bedroom in the hero's apartment is described as follows. Here again, the bland color of the room decoration gives an insight to its occupier's character.

> The room was sleek and modern and neutrally colored as the rest of the condominium. Low-profile teak furniture and cream colored carpeting and drapes were relieved by a suitably modern abstract painting hanging over the bed. The quilt on which she lay was a fat, fluffy goosedown affair that had probably cost a fortune. Too bad it had been done in beige. (142)

The characters do not move around much. The heroine goes to her bookshop in a Santa Rosa mall area. In an aside it is mentioned that she runs quite a large business, and the new one she plans will be even larger. (61) The planning is not given a prominent place in the story and other than being mentioned, no insider knowledge is displayed. Other activities such as his hobby working with electronic gadgets (told, not shown) or her jewelry-making are also given with no intent of making them a crucial part of the story. They only serve to move the protagonists from one place to the next. It seems important to profess that the characters both have interests outside their jobs.

At one time, Court and Leya go together on a winery tour in Napa Valley. This trip is also reported in a generic way. The really important issue of this trip is their peaceful and pleasant conversations, referred to only, indicating a sense of connection. As there is no verbal battle going on and no dialogue inserted which might carry the action forward, this episode serves only as stopping point almost overlooked by the reader because of its descriptive brevity. Lengthened, this episode would perhaps have made it understandable for a reader why the protagonists want to belong together outside the bedroom. Another place they go to are cocktail parties, but again the places and the people there are insignificant except for a display of jealousy. All in all, the local setting of the story gives some orientation which has to be decorated with details in the reader's mind because of the indistinctly rendered pictures of the protagonists' surroundings.

The social setting is in accordance with the writing guidelines. In this American setting, the heroine, being of second generation wealth, is not allowed to lead the life of an idle person. Instead, she works hard and is a successful entrepreneur with a degree in business management. Court's family does not seem to be rich, but at least he has studied finance at UC Berkeley and is on his way to becoming wealthy. Social life seems to take place at parties that family or friends give in order to maintain their social standards.

This simple linear and short plot, the fairly generally described local settings and the social setting hinted at might make room for a reader's imagination to fill in, although she is not given time to do so because the high tension in the dialogues divert her.

CHARACTER CONSTELLATIONS

If, in the eyes of romance novelists, the man is "the most dangerous creature on earth" (*DMAW* 5) whom the heroine needs "to bring to his knees" and, as mentioned above, he in many ways owns the story. It is only right to analyze his character first.

THE MALE PROTAGONIST

Court, aged around 35, receives the standard romantic external outfit: he is "large and solidly built without being an ounce overweight" (12), has dark brown thick hair, well spaced deep-set brown-and-gold bedroom eyes, high cheekbones, and a strong chin. Nothing soft about him. He is well and expensively dressed, drives a "very sleek foreign car" (81), and knows how to conduct himself properly in different social spheres. His parents were understanding when he, their only child, as a youth enjoyed tinkering with his tools and electronics, preferring his own company to that of his peers. This explains why there are no friends around. He found for himself the right combination of work and hobby to make money as consultant for electronics on the solid basis of college education. For the story itself, a day to day account of his work is not intended. The reader assumes that he is working at Brandon Securities because he has his office there. He also seems to spend time in the well equipped workshop in his apartment, but these activities play no part in the story other than being mentioned in order to show dedication to whatever he is working on. Keith, Leya's brother, values him, considers him to be his mentor, and idolizes him. Court is said to be excellent at what he does and that means he has already become successful and rich, not financially independent yet, but being self-employed, he is able to neglect smaller projects in favor of the more lucrative ones. There actually is not much information about his finances, so the reader assumes that he, being chosen by Keith, must live on a solid financial basis or he would not have gained Keith's trust.

Court is perceived as a straight, honest guy, trying to state his intentions openly, with little sensitivity, dominant and not being used to taking 'no' for an answer. When they have just met, he makes it clear to Leya that he wants to bed her and in so doing, 'chain' her to him. Because he is hooked, he tries everything he can think of to get her into his bed, which for him is an act of binding possession. He is an experienced man with insignificant lovers in his past, a typical romance hero trait because ex-lovers are supposed to emphasize the readers' perception of his virility. But now his focus is exclusively set on Leya. Tricking her about his identity, which he reasons was intended as a shortcut to end the problem of the contract so that he could concentrate on his love life, is an understandable male ruse for him and he does not understand why this has backfired. In his helplessness to reestablish their relationship, the means he uses to achieve his ends border on the brutal. He forces himself on Leya, and when she wants to escape from his grasp, he yanks her back to him by her braid. When she refuses his advances he 'punishes' her with brutal kisses (67). It becomes clear that this dominant male strives for total surrender of his woman, and his jealous possessiveness shows signs of the unhealthy, or the utter feeling of insecurity:

> "What the hell did you think you were doing in that corner, anyway? Making comparisons? Or did you want to see what I'd do when I saw you? You once said something about being interested in genuine male jealousy, didn't you?"
> "That's ridiculous!" she grated, a little frightened now.
> "I agree. But since you're so interested, I'll be happy to show you what it's like to be standing under a ton of bricks when they come tumbling down!" (221)

He already considers Leya to be his 'private property' (221) and so he does not allow her want to choose someone else, a fact that only he takes into consideration. He lives in a patriarchal, macho world where he considers jealous possessiveness his male right and acts upon it, so that for a reader of the new millennium it is unimaginable that he can establish a satisfying relationship with his wife-to-be, a relationship where these two people live on equal terms. What is considered as a mellowing of this harsh man is that he allows Leya to propose. When she asks for marriage, he knows he has achieved his goal of chaining her to him.

Court is represented as a one-dimensional character who acts like man of the 1970s whose rights over his woman were at least partly patriarchal. To induce tension into the story his patriarchal traits are exaggerated. He is, however, a man full of insecurities who resorts to threats. Because of his insecurities his threats are bordering on the pathological when, for, example, he explains: "I'm in the mood to whale the daylights out of you. So you might want to exercise a bit of caution" (99).

THE FEMALE PROTAGONIST

Of average height, Leya Brandon, aged 27, thinks that she also is average in the looks department, but considers her intelligence above-average. (When Leya takes a critical look at her reflection in the mirror, the reader is given the opportunity to learn what she looks like. This narrative device is often used in a text featuring only one perspective.) Having a degree in business management and English from UC at Santa Barbara, she uses both studies to run a bookshop so well that she plans to open up a second branch. She does not need the shares in her parents' firm. Being successfully self-employed, she has a healthy self-confidence, which is also supported by her artistic jewelry-making at her professional workshop at home. She runs her businesses precisely, whereas her housekeeping is "delight-fully chaotic" (85). Her professional life plus the insinuated excellence in her hobby are quite appealing character traits that lead the reader to expect a level-headedness which she does not apply to her emotional life with Court because of a betrayal of a former lover and Court's deception. In her heart of hearts, she knows she can trust him and there is no counter-evidence as to why she should not, but she displays an obvious stubbornness and immaturity regarding personal af-fairs. Her verbally professed ideas of equality between the sexes become obsolete by her acceptance of Court's domineering behavior and by her cowering. Perhaps she really believes that "Shrews are never innocent victims". When Leya agrees to trust Court and to marry him, they, at last, have sex. The climax she experiences is that of being "at once tamed and untamed", but why she accepts the idea that she needs to be tamed, and to what purpose, does not become clear. A little later on, "the participants in the small war were unconcerned" about who had surrendered to whom (231). The picture of love as a constant war between them that is laid to rest with marriage is pleasant but not convincing. Marriage is the ultimate goal for Leya, but as the protagonists do not appear to have much in common, apart from physical attraction, this marriage does not bode a promising future. There is no indication for a need for each other outside the bedroom.

The protagonists are presented as flat characters. It is true, they are given some additional possible character traits, but those are reduced owing to the fact that they are 'told' not 'shown'.

SECONDARY CHARACTERS

In this fictional universe it seems as if the protagonists live in some kind of vacuum with almost silent people moving around. Only a few people talk to them briefly, like the host of the party, or a customer in the bookshop. Even Leya's brother emerges only for short moments to utter some misdirecting remarks and, in the end, to give his blessing to the union. Another character is Leya's former lover, Alex, whose short appearance causes her to lie by pretending to be engaged to Court, thus creating a turning point in the story. Leya's shop assistant Cynthia gives the impression of being a friend rather than an employee. The short remarks she is allowed to utter have no structural function for the story and do not advance the protagonists' characterization.

These people appear for a short time, no more than three pages each, and after having stirred up the lovers' emotions, vanish again into the crowd. Court is reported to be an only child, but even when the wedding takes place, his parents do not appear, although no alienation or quarrel is mentioned. Possibly, the construction of this restricted social surrounding could be ascribed to category romance writing guideline requirements because according to them, relatives, such as a brother, could be allowed to play a tiny role, but the 'stage' is reserved for the couple alone. Thus the absence of other more complex character constellations avoids external conflicts and focuses exclusively on the protagonists' sexuality and emotional world.

CONFLICT, RELATIONSHIP AND EROTIC SCENES

Publishers' writing guidelines insist on conflicts for the lovers as one important aspect of the plot. There is no conflict to speak of. The faint conflict which drags on and on in the book is the heroine's inability to trust Court after the deception about his identity, not his macho behavior. Leya's inner conflict is blown out of proportion: she likes and dislikes the fact that he wants to go to bed with her, but does not want to give in, before she knows for sure he is not interested in taking over her brother's firm, but is only interested in her. When she decides to take the firm out of the equation, the other feigned conflict that remains is that he will not come to his own wedding, which really does not make sense since he wants to be 'chained' from the beginning.

The protagonists' relationship develops along these lines: from the beginning, both protagonists feel attracted to each other. The second day of their acquaintance, Court states his intentions clearly: he wants to go to bed with Leya. Astonishingly for a romance novel of that time, she is not supposed to be a virgin and seems to have had sexual relationships before Court. This way she can focus on a different goal, marriage.

> She promised herself silently, she did not allow this man to treat her as prey. She was glad that he found her attractive because the feeling was mutual, but she had very definite ideas on equality in a relationship. She also had very definite ideas on the depressing nature of relationships based purely on sex. (17)

In the course of the evening they kiss, he feathers her face, throat, lashes, and ears with tiny kisses while she puts her arms around his neck and encourages him until he cups her breast, and when he proposes they go to his room to make love, she stops him because she "needs time to be sure" (49). Those kisses happen from page 33 to 51 in installments, interrupted by longer dialogues. He cajoles and she reacts in a shrewd way. When he says something, she decides it is not what she wants to hear or what she wants to hear, but does not want to admit to herself and him. So he 'disciplines' her or tries to 'tame' her by forcing her into his arms and replaying his seductive kissing. The following scene shows the possessive attitude that he develops from the moment he sees her.

> She knew she had to get away from Alan West. But even as she tried to dodge politely aside, Alain's hand fell protestingly on her shoulder. It did so just as Court emerged beside them.
>
> "Good evening, Leya." His voice was a dark and unbelievingly soft menace. "Say goodnight. We're leaving" His eyes went to the hand of her shoulder, and Leya stared at him unhappily.
>
> Alan, sensing the suddenly thick atmosphere, took one look at the strained faces of the other two and removed his hand with a small exclamation of apology. "Sorry," he murmured laconically to Court. "Didn't realize she was private property."
>
> "She is having a little trouble understanding that herself, apparently," Court shot back coolly, grasping Leya's wrist and starting back toward the door.
>
> "Take your hands off me!" Leya hissed waspishly as she was dragged forcefully through the crowd. "There is nothing for you to be upset about! I was merely chatting with Alan –"
>
> "Flirting is the word," he growled stonily … (220)

The protagonists continually play advance and retreat throughout the novel. There are six longer love scenes in *Stormy Challenge*. They continue for many pages because suggestive movements are dissected and interspersed in the dialogues. In the first erotic scene he only cups her breast (33–51). Then he manages to kiss her and touch her nipples (63–64). Later, he surprises her in her bedroom when she comes out of the bathroom and although he has her naked in his arms he only "forces his tongue deep into her mouth" (87–94).

At a party, he carries her over his shoulder out of the room and into his bedroom, a supposedly romantic act often used that focuses on his virility. This time, she actively participates in the seduction. He unbuttons his shirt and slips off his shoes and manages to undress her. She lets his kisses go as far as her stomach and thighs. Then she kisses his nipples, unclasps his belt buckle and toys with the opening of his slacks. They nearly have sex, but he suddenly decides he needs her to admit her absolute trust in him, which she is not ready to give and because of that she feels frightened that he might rape her. They redress and the play of advance and retreat begins anew (141–155). Later, he invites her to dinner at his home where again he gets as far as kissing her stomach before she calls off the action (177–186).

After he agrees to marry her, at last, they have uninterrupted sex, where "his fingers were arousing her to unbelievable heights" and later "he surged into a driving rhythm that carried her along in the way that a storm over the sea sweeps across the waves" (225–232). To repeat that experience she has to wait until they are married a week later. There again, their lovemaking is depicted with an ocean simile. "The pattern of their lovemaking soared, making them one with the night storm that was rolling in off the ocean" (245–49).

The advance and retreat pattern is one of the basic patterns of 1970s romance novels. Yet in many romance novels of that time the hero does not have to make himself so disagreeable by flaying the heroine with words although the relationship is one of dominance. Here the male wants to dominate 'his' woman relying on means he knows that have worked until now: to force his woman into submission if she does not meekly obey his wishes. Once he has decided he wants her, she becomes his property and is not allowed to compare him to her former lover. But as the old ways do not work so conveniently anymore, this hero has realized that he needs to consider a give-and-take part in the relationship.

One of Leya's reasons for denying herself to Court are her ideas of equality. To emphasize they are acting on equal terms in the bedroom, she should have initiated a successful seduction and not only responded to his moves. According to *Dangerous Men and Adventurous Women* this is important in a romance novel because it should be the woman who encourages the man of her choice to understand that his special woman is able to be on par in every way. Leya is proud to be able to propose. Otherwise, she is afraid of Court. Sentences like the following one demonstrate this: "Leya knew a surge of feminine triumph as she realized Court was past the point of being able *to punish her tonight*" (147 my italics).

This sentence, without its context, generates the idea of a battered woman. There are many of those sentences that stand in the way of making this novel enjoyable. By 1992, ten years later, Krentz had written many novels that had a different ideological basis, so that in *Dangerous Men and Adventurous Women* she could ignore the kind of books like *Stormy Challenge* that might have paved her way to an ideological reversal.

WRITING STYLE AND CODE

Through questionnaires and careful research of sales figures, publishers try to find out what the readers' preferences are and according to those, narrative perspectives play an important part for the stories readers want to consume. Up to 1990, category romance novels were to be written in the third person only, preferably from the heroine's perspective. The omniscient narrator of previous romance novels had to give way to the internal focalizer, the heroine. Only gradually did it become clear to the publishers that the third person heroine's perspective alone ceased to be of interest because of its inherent limitation and so they conceded perspectives of the hero and heroine and even other characters' perspectives within a book, but still giving preference to the third person. (First person perspective was not welcomed because this restricted the author even more in what was to be told.) When a single, third-person perspective was indicated in the guidelines, it was believed to encourage reader identification. Now it was believed to prevent it. One perspective only is not necessarily a disadvantage, but I assume, there were many, too many not so well plotted stories with dumb heroine imaginings, so that the demand for at least two perspectives increased.

Stormy Challenge, still bound by the patriarchal ideology of the 1970s, obeys the dictates of the time. Written entirely from Leya's third person perspective, although a covert narrator explains what a heroine would never think of noticing beside adding atmosphere through dialogue tags, the readers are allowed to look only into her head. Her convoluted reasonings have no counterpoint in the male ones. (His reasonings in the dialogues have to be taken at face value, something Leya often likes to ignore). So the story drags on, on the basis of her conflicting emotions. Leya is always debating in her mind whether she wants to believe him or not, love him or not, believe him or not; it is a constant up and down of highly charged emotions that culminate in bursts of love-hatred internal tirades:

> Her pride was at stake here. Did she really want to admit to him what a fool she had been? And then there was the fact that Keith sounded so happy to know she'd signed the contract. Did she really want to ruin his working relationship with Court before the partnership had had a fair chance? What if Court turned out to be the salvation of Brandon Security after all? … Why was it so difficult to take a hard stand against Court Tremayne? Why was she trying to find a reason to give him a chance? (84)

In *Stormy Challenge,* one of the negative effects of having only one perspective is that at least half of the book is dialogues, which, of course are not negative, *per se.* The covert narrator uses much explaining through dialogue tags, mirroring the emotional upheaval of the protagonists. Verbs like 'blaze, glaze, shriek, snarl, storm' etc. make clear how stormy this challenge is, and adverbs like 'scathingly, disgustedly, grimly, mockingly, belligerently, tartly, disdainfully, aggressively, wrathfully, furiously', etc. show the atmosphere in the novel. The heroine works herself up into an angry state, taunting the male protagonist, becoming astonished that he himself becomes annoyed and tries to end the sparring by using physical outlets. Comments of a covert narrator are especially displayed in the many adverbs of the dialogue tags and the reported texts in between them. Since the reader is only given Leya's perspective, it is too subjective to correctly judge other characters, but there is still an abundance of dialogues that reveal Court's character better than through Leya's mind.

There are ten whole pages without dialogue in the book.[47] In these pages, Leya ponders the whys and wherefores of her irrational behavior (86 or 186). One page is dedicated to a report of a winery tour where no battling of wills requires a dialogue (206). Once there is a descriptive part between the dialogues, usually not more than three to four sentences, it is not even overly detailed.

In the description of sexuality and sexual situations, the verb 'force' is used abundantly: he "forced his tongue deeply into her mouth" (91), or "he used his grip to force her into full awareness of his growing desire" (92). Although Court stops at the mere though "to force her into bed" (167), or "force himself on her" (167), rape still is an underlying theme (154). The narrative tone, set by adjectives, verbs, and nouns, expresses an aggressive undertone that later reveals as the helpless reaction of a man who does not get immediately what he wants. Only when nearing the denouement of the story, does a softer tone prevail although, in the end, their love-making is still labeled as a "love battle" (232). In three abortive sexual encounters, many adjectives, verbs, and nouns indicate male dominance: "And she never quite knew when the moment came that Court actually reversed the seductive assault making her the one under attack" (40), or "The unmistakable desire was a commanding aggressive pull on the very core of her femininity. It stirred her loins and weakened her knees ... " (92)

Male genitals are named as "his hardness", "his body", "himself" as in "he asserted himself against her" (231), or "losing himself in her softness ... " (249) The personal pronoun alludes to his being one with his penis, the action 'take' describes the male claiming possession of the female. The female primary genitals also are circumscribed as "her femininity", "the heat in her loins", "the dampening, fiery heart of her desire", and "the warm place between her legs". These wordings are considered as 'purple prose' that refers to florid writing in general and euphemisms to avoid sexual organs.

Sometimes it is possible to draw meanings from the names the characters of a novel are given. In this case, the name Court Gannon Tremayne seems to a.) relate to the noun 'courting' which he is trying to do albeit with a lack of finesse which b.) the Gannon = cannon alludes to. Leya, on her part, might be the Latin lioness (leo – lea) who behaves in a typical female way until she is 'ready' to mate. Another, the status of a relationship revealing aspect, are the endearments the lovers heap on each other. Leya does not indulge in endearments. She always calls Court by his given name. Only once does she furiously addresses him as "you egotistical, overbearing, arrogant creature" – the adjectives in this combination are stereotypes in the Krentz romance novels of that time – and she also calls him

---

[47] Mario Andreotti sees the prevalence of dialogues in popular literature as an indication for this genre (242).

you "beast". After the wedding they address each other proudly as Mr. and Mrs.
Tremayne. Court, however, finds many endearments for Leya: Honey, my little,
my sweet Leya, darling, sweetheart, my maddening little, my sweet shrew, little
witch, you vicious little thing, little wanton, and, at last, my dearly beloved wife.
Seen like this, it becomes obvious that these more condescending endearments
clearly show who feels superior to whom:

> I've known all along that part of the problem is your pride," he said sooth-
> ingly. "I've known it because you are a lot like me. Given the same set of
> circumstances, I'd have had a few problems along that line myself."
>
> Leya felt like a pet rabbit being stroked by a wolf. "Very generous of
> you," she told him dryly.
>
> "But I think you were trying to accomplish something important today
> by giving your stock to Keith. I think you were asking me to show you that
> my interest in you extends beyond business. And I'm quite prepared to do
> that."
>
> "You are going to be understanding about my pride problem?" she
> mocked warily.
>
> "Definitely." He smiled, eyes crinkling beguilingly. "I've got a way to
> get around all the words."
>
> "Ah! You're going to try and get me into bed without them after all!"
> she nodded wisely.
>
> "It may come to that, but I'm going to try something else first." Leya
> licked her lower lip with a short, quick stab of her tongue as she considered
> him cautiously. "Now what are you up to, Court Tremayne?"
>
> "Intrigued, are you?" he chuckled, half-turning in his chair to dig into a
> coat pocket. "That gives me a decided advantage, you realize." He removed
> a small jeweler's box from his coat and swiveled back around to face her.
> The green velvet box rested on the palm of his hand as he held it out to her.
>
> "A ring?" she asked disbelievingly, her untrusting eye going from the
> proffered gift to his glittering gaze. (198)

A text filled with adjectives and adverbs is what is expected of a romantic novel,
(*DMAW* 25) but this text where there is no plot to speak of, no other possibilities
given to turn away from the recounting of endless repetitions of the same contrary
feelings, is narrated in a overwrought style because of the dialogue tags.

The sentences in the dialogue are clearly written middle class speech. Although they are short simple sentences, where necessary even consisting of one or
two words only, when the situation needs more than those, the language becomes
elaborate in wording and subordinate clauses are added. As mentioned before,
longer narrative parts, not interrupted by dialogue, are rarely found in this novel.
The following text of five sentences is even a little longer than usual. It is typical
for the short way Leya's professional work is described. If examined closely, only
one and a half sentence make the 'description':

> The morning wore on, with Leya deliberately refusing to think about the previous evening. She buried herself in plans for the new branch of Brandon Books, going over sketches, estimating order quantities, and discussing hours of operation with Cynthia. She was involved with a shelving plan, working at the back of the shop while Cynthia handled the customer traffic, when a shadow fell on the paper in front of her. She looked up to find Court standing beside the small table on which she was sketching. She started, not having heard him enter the shop. (159)

Four times the author uses the same subject for each beginning of these five sentences. A hypotactic sentence construction deflects from the same sentence beginnings, although participles again are abundantly used. The words within the sentences range from nine to thirty-one and the word lengths are of the two syllable variety. (105 words, 5 words with three syllables and one with six syllables)

One assumption about romance novels is that mostly Anglo-Saxon language is used rather than the Latinate language, thus depicting everyday life and being easier to understand than the more educated Latinate language level. But this assumption is easily countered:

> "It's one of the things we have in common," he grinned and she felt his teeth on her skin. "Don't worry. This little flare-up between us is a temporary thing. Once the dust has settled, we'll both be able to lapse happily back in our normal, serene lifestyles." He sounded pleased at the prospect.
>
> Leya froze in sudden anguish. My God! she thought helplessly, he sees me as some sort of temporary toy to relieve a small stretch of boredom he's passing through! It was either that or he was convinced she would undermine his influence with Keith. Those were the only two reasons Leya's agile mind could come up with Court's apparent interest in her as a lover. She had been an idiot during the past two days to think he was genuinely attracted to her! (71–72)

In these paragraphs, which were chosen at random, the language is more elaborate than everyday language. From my German point of view it can only be assumed that words like 'temporary, serene, agile, apparent, and genuine' do not belong to an everyday vocabulary. But they do not seem to stand out noticeably as being too sophisticated.

The story of *Stormy Challenge* is a rather mangled reversed version of the Shakespearian *The Taming of the Shrew*. Readers, especially readers of romance novels, want to identify with one of the main characters. It is disputable whether the female character in *Stormy Challenge* can be used as a model for identification, as she lacks traits for the reader to identify with.[48] From beginning to end

---

[48]   One trait, for example, which is seen as indispensable for a romance novel heroine is her ability to nurture. Leya does not show any such traits.

the male character is set in his ways and he is asked to undergo a change in his personality to become worthy of the heroine, something which should be a necessity according to the romance writers' own set standards of the 1990's romance novels. Court seems to change in part but revokes it when he is feeling insecure. Nevertheless, the readers of the early 1980s still seemed to have kept asking for stories containing such patriarchal attitudes. The expectation of a love story with a happy, satisfying ending alone made them buy the books. Doreen Owens Malik explains why:

> We can put up with inadequate plotting; dithering, petulant, even childish heroines; and numerous flaws as long as the essential element is there – that fantasy, the compelling relationship with an indomitable hero who becomes so fascinated by and enthralled with the heroine that by the end of the book he will do anything to possess her. (75)

Moreover, there are other elements in play. According to Krentz and other romance novel writers, there are codes a romance novel reader will automatically look for in a book, be they plot-, setting-, or language-related. In their article "Beneath the Surface. The hidden codes of romance", Linda Barlow and Krentz reveal those codes that are hidden in the language. They maintain that

> Outsiders tend to be unable to interpret the conventional language of the genre or to recognize in that language the symbols, images, and allusions that are the fundamental stuff of romance. (15)

The text of the back-cover gives the reader the first code phrases to which she responds 'with lively interest and anticipation' as she looks forward to the pleasurable reading experience the novel promises. I think that in *Stormy Challenge* the phrases "her heart clearly wasn't at risk" or "aching for the fulfillment only he could give" might be an incentive for the reader to buy this book. What the novel promises in satisfactory fantasies are texts like the one taken from *Stormy Challenge*:

> She knew herself helpless to continue fighting the effect he had on her for long. It enveloped her, absorbed her, seduced her sense of touch in the same way that the isolated beach did. The heat of his body was a delicious counterpoint to the crisp, chilled breeze. The earthy, tantalizing scent of him filled her nostrils like the smell of the sea, and the feel of his hands was as alluring as the sight of a storm on the waves. (69)

This text has all the necessary ingredients for a romance novel code: code words or phrases like 'helpless', 'heat of his body', and 'the earthy, tantalizing scent of him', literary comparisons, and a suggestive situation. This, Krentz and Barlow say, is the language that works for romance novels. They believe that stock phrases and words like 'he went on wryly', 'she sighed', 'golden eyes pinning her', 'eyes shimmering with an enigmatic expression', 'affecting a casualness she was far from feeling', let the readers associate certain emotions with such language. So they expect to feel "the same responses each time they come upon such phrases" (*DMAW* 21).

Another "detail about romantic description is the use of paradoxical elements, echoing the heavy use of paradoxical plot devices" (*DMAW* 26). In *Stormy Challenge,* the heroine's feelings are often torn between hate and love: "I've never admitted that!" she almost screeched, nails digging into the quilt. At least not out loud, she added in silent justification (142). These paradoxical feelings show that the hero cannot be the insensitive man he is presented as being through his speech. The heroine understands (and so does the reader) that engaging in verbal sparring will win her the respect and the love she most desires. So "the duel of wits" is "her most potent weapon" (*DMAW* 23). All this arguing leads to 'real' communication: in the end, the heroine enables the hero to express his love, not only physically (which comes first), but also verbally (which is the culmination of all). Krentz and Barlow place great emphasis in their essay on romances on this fact by saying that this is the prime message a romance hero must learn to convey, and that the reader expects him to do it in style.

Answering the question of why even a weak story still draws women to buy and read such a book, Krentz and Barlow think that it may well be that the use of romance codes are more important to the success of a particular romance (*DMAW* 28) than other elements like plot or the development of characters or the originality of the author's voice. According to the requirements of a romance novel, *Stormy Challenge* is completely conformist, especially for the early 1980s where the narrative battle-of-the-sexes-style was still in vogue, but changes in reading expectations took place, and ten years later, because of them, heroes and heroines were forced to undergo changes, too. In the blurb on the back cover that refers to the romance novel's story code, wording is used to motivate the reader to buy the book. In the case of *Stormy Challenge* the story promises sensual reading. Key words like 'heart at risk', or 'all-consuming desire' or 'he'd left her hungering for his lean strength' or 'aching for the fulfillment only he could give' are the coded incentives to buy and read.[49] Inside the book, on the first page before the title,

---

[49]   The full blurb text is as follows: New York Times bestselling author Krentz writing as Stephanie James delivers sizzling and compelling characters in a classic romance! Leya Brandon didn't know what – if anything – she could believe of all Court Tremayne told her. He'd already lied about his name. And while she thought her heart clearly wasn't at risk, she'd clearly underestimated his all consuming desire to win her for his own. Little did she know that Court had no intention of stopping. Not until he left her hungering for his lean strength, shivering at his gaze and aching for the fulfillment only he could give ... Krentz is "one of the hottest writers in romance today" – USA Today. (Back cover from the Harlequin reprint 2004)

the reader, looking to find further code allusions, is offered this excerpt from the novel:

> "Stop fighting me," Court whispered.
> "All I ask from you tonight is the truth, or at least a portion of it."
> "What portion?" Leya asked, already aware of the warmth of him as he overwhelmed her senses.
> "At least admit that you want me. Just stop fighting me long enough to let me show you how good it will be between us." Court held her wrists in one hand over her head, letting his fingertips trail sensuously down the length of her throat.
> "After tonight," he muttered, "you will play your games with no one else. I told you once I will be a very possessive lover, my sweet Leya. And I meant it. I'm going to make sure you know the limits" ...

From this excerpt, a reader can already see the tenor the book is written in. Whether it is an incentive to buy the book is not recorded on the internet. It is interesting to note that the two reviews of the reissue in 2004 by fans of Krentz on Amazon comment on the datedness, but do not mention the strong patriarchal tenor of the novel. So, Harlequin is right to count on fan readers and expects to sell these reprints well.

3.1.2 *Perfect Partners*

Having previously only read Krentz's post 1990 romance novels, I would not have recognized *Stormy Challenge* as one of hers. Since *Stormy Challenge,* Krentz's heroes have gradually overcome the possessiveness that bordered on the pathological, and eventually have become a different kind of man (*The Gambler's Woman* 1984, *Legacy* 1985, *The Ties That Bind* 1986, *Test of Time* 1987, *Lady's Choice* 1989).

In 1992 Krentz published her last category romance, two historical and two contemporary single-titles. As *Perfect Partners* is the first contemporary romance novel by her I read and as it marks her transition to single-titles, I decided to analyze it for this study. *Perfect Partners* meets four of my premises: First, it is a contemporary novel, second, it was written 10 years after *Stormy Challenge*, third, its characters are very different from those in *Stormy Challenge*, and fourth, it is typical of Krentz's novels of that time. She inserted a little crime in her category romances early on. All her subsequent single-titles, be they historical, contemporary, or futuristic, are romantic suspense novels.

SUMMARY

Letitia (Letty) Thornquist, a 29 year old librarian at an Indiana college, inherits Thornquist Gear, a large sporting goods company in Seattle, from her uncle Charly. This company was single-handedly turned into a large business by Joel

Blackstone while Charlie went fishing and only came back to sign whatever Joel gave him to sign. At the age of eighty-one Charlie had agreed to sell Joel the company, but he died before Joel could buy him out.

Shortly before Charly's death, Letty broke off her engagement and later, in order to take over the reins of Thornquist Gear, she quits her job at the college. When Joel tries to convince her to sell him the company on the grounds that she does not know anything about running such a big business she refuses to do so because she has already done a great deal of research and thinks she will be successful at the head of the operation: but only if she has a mentor to guide her. As there already is an underlying strong attraction they both feel intensely, Letty chooses Joel to be the one. Consequently, she moves to Seattle where Morgan, her father, a professor of medieval philosophy, and Stephanie, her stepmother, a professor of linguistics, had moved some time before. Letty assumes the position of president at the firm while Joel, as her chief executive officer (CEO), sees to the-day-to-day running of the company. Becoming more and more competent in her new business field, Letty sometimes questions Joel's decisions, never for the sake of a power struggle, but always when she thinks there are valid reasons, and in the end, Joel agrees admiring her sound business instincts.

Some time before his death, Charly had given Joel permission to buy 51% of a failing company in Echo Cove, Copeland Marine Industries, which specializes in boat outfitting and repair. This purchase has everything to do with Joel's carefully planned revenge on Victor Copeland. In Echo Cove, Joel's hometown, Victor practically reigns over the town, being its sole employer. At the age of 21 Joel wanted to marry Diana, Victor's daughter. One day, when Victor caught them together he lost his temper, nearly killed Joel, fired him from his job at the yard and ran him out of town, not quickly enough for Joel to witness his father's despair over being fired as well which then resulted in his father's getting drunk and driving off a cliff into the sea on his way home. Now that Joel has set his revenge in motion and is at a point where he can actually start to destroy the company, Letty discovers Thornquist Gears' ownership of Copeland Marines. Sensing there is something not quite kosher about this, she decides to have a look into the matter. Together with Joel she drives to Echo Cove, meets with Victor, Diana and her husband Keith, spends a sexually satisfying night with Joel, inspects the business, manages to have Joel released from jail where he was taken to after a brawl with jealous Keith, and receives a five-year-plan from Keith to save Copeland Marines.

When they return to Seattle they learn that Letty's ex-fiancé Dixon, a professor of finances, has decided he wants Letty back so that he can take charge of Thornquist Gear. He has taken hold of Letty's office and gone through the important financial documents. Getting rid of him is difficult.

Letty manages to persuade Joel to read Keith's salvage plan. She also convinces him to focus his revenge on Victor alone, this way hoping to possibly salvage the yard with Keith in charge, thereby securing the yard as the town's lifeline. Joel succeeds in exacting his vengeance by personally firing Victor, who, in return, attacks Joel and destroys his apartment. Now that everybody is aware of Victor's innate violence, Joel and Keith organize security at the yard, send the women (Letty, Diana, and the very pregnant Stephanie) to a family cabin in the mountains to hide while Morgan and Joel keep vigil over Thornquist Gear. Victor is prevented from burning down the yard in Echo Cove, but manages to escape and then he telephones Joel pretending that he knows where Letty is. In order to protect their women, Morgan and Joel drive to the cabin thus unwittingly showing Victor the way. Victor tries to ram their jeep over a cliff into the river, but does not succeed. He fights with Joel and because of particularly bad visibility caused by a blizzard, he falls over the protecting rails into the river, not before having confessed to Joel that it was he who had killed his father. Meanwhile, Stephanie goes into labor. Because of the blizzard, there is no way to take her to the hospital. So Letty and Diana act as midwives, and when Morgan and Joel arrive at the cabin, the child, a boy, is born. Joel has intended all along to marry Letty, but her ownership of Thornquist Gear prevents him from proposing because he does not want everyone to say he is marrying her to take possession of the company. After the incident in the blizzard, their attitudes change and they can agree to split the ownership in half and so be able to marry without loss of face. The story ends when two months later Letty announces her pregnancy to a very happy Joel.

CHAPTERS, PLOT, TIME, AND SETTINGS

Perfect Partners is 372 pages long and consists of 20 chapters which are only numbered and without headlines, but with a small graphic ornament underneath the number. The beginnings of the chapters are marked by a first letter in a bigger bold print. Otherwise the pages remain unadorned. The plot is a love and revenge story where revenge is not directed at the other protagonist but at an outside character. Subplots related to the plot are the pregnancy and birthing difficulties of the heroine's stepmother, the extended display of the heroine's ex-fiancé's stubbornness, and the hero's ex-lover's and her husband's actions. In the first two chapters (1–40), the introductory exposition contains every part necessary for the reader to grasp the complexity of the following story: the lovers' instant, not ambivalent, but trusting, attraction, their different ways of approaching issues caused by their different social upbringing, the importance family has for a relationship, and the hinting at the crime part. The suspense curve is increased by the retarding effects of the subplots, particularly by the birth scene at the final crisis.

The story of the novel which develops over a period of four weeks is rendered in the epic preterite, but the reader is given the illusion of its happening in the present, especially because more than half of the book is composed of dialogues. The story begins one day in September with the memorial service for Charlie, held when the evenings in Washington State become cooler and wintery weather approaches. Just four weeks later a blizzard in the Cascades, where the Thornquist cabin is located, covers the land. For the story this blizzard is a crucial plot device for, as a consequence of it, Joel's revenge finds a redeeming end and Stephanie has to give birth to her son at the cabin. This way, life and death are reconciled. The story is told on a chronological timeline. Not every day is accounted for and when it is, only the important hours for the story are related. The two weeks when Letty accustoms herself to her new position at the company are left out, but from day nineteen onward, the chain of events thickens the plot and crisis after crisis comes rapidly so that from then on, each day is accounted for in different lengths. To recount three days – this is the time Letty and Joel spend in Echo Cove – takes 138 of the 372 pages or six chapters (98–235). The day before the blizzard is presented on another fifty pages or three and two half chapters of reporting. There, the events follow each other quickly (297–351). The beginning of a new day rarely coincides with a new chapter. Even the epilogue, which is not labeled as such, is only a new paragraph within the last chapter, although there is a reported time-lapse of two months. Events that happened in the past of the story are recounted in the dialogues. This means that the chronological timeline as such is not interrupted.

Perfect Partners is a contemporary story, set in the USA of the 1990's. Joel Blackstone, Letty and her family live in Seattle where Thornquist Gear and Letty's parents' faculty is located. Seventy miles away in the mountains the family owns a weekend cabin where they go after Charlie's funeral, and which later is used as hideout, which the three women are sent to.

The descriptions of places serve to typify the characters. Everything in Letty's parents' two homes, at the cabin and at their house in Seattle is state of the art in a cold way, while Letty's apartment seems to be so cosy and inviting that Joel quickly feels at home there. Joel's apartment, the essential furniture of it consisting of sports equipment and a large TV, is only mentioned when everything of value in it has been destroyed, which shows it does not function as 'home'. Thornquist Gear, the firm, becomes the playing field and the backdrop to the protagonists aligning their forces.

At Echo Cove, on the coast, 100 miles from Seattle, Letty and Joel book two rooms with a connecting door. This connecting door serves as a plot device to move the action on. Nearly every place they go to is within walking distance of the motel: the restaurant where they meet the Copelands, the bar where a jealous Keith attacks Joel, the police station, and the library where Letty learns something about Joel's youth and his father's death, and at the same time, about the town's economic circumstances. The library is the room that symbolizes Letty's inquisitive mind. Joel shows Letty his parents' house from the outside and his secret former retreat, a rather dilapidated barn. The happenings that took and take place in that barn lead to climaxes of the plot. Victor's boat yard, as his business, is only briefly mentioned.

As the genre of romance novels focuses on the love story, descriptions of locations are strictly background information when they do not reflect the mood of the characters, or are used for characterization. Thornquist Gear is presented with more than three sentences of description for it is information about the successful enterprise of a self-made man, seen in the size of the business and in Joel's pride:

> Four stories below Joel the sales floor of the downtown branch of Thornquist Gear hummed with activity. The summer camping season was over and the ski season was about to begin. The annual run on ski boots was already starting.
>
> Ten years ago Thornquist Gear had occupied one tiny shop on First Avenue. Today the company leased half a block of office space and had retail outlets on the east side and down in Portland.
>
> The first two floors of the downtown store were retail, and the two upper floors housed Accounting, Marketing and other operations. Joel still got a surge of pride and deep satisfaction every time he walked through the front door of Thornquist Gear. (54)

When the characters move from one place to the next, the reader needs to receive some imaginary visual clues. She is given those in the shortest possible form and so descriptions of place rarely exceed three sentences, a typical example being the following ideating a maritime surrounding when Letty and Joel meet Victor for dinner at the restaurant in Echo Cove.

> Five minutes later Joel opened the door of the Echo Cove Sea Grill. The restaurant sported a huge neon fish on the roof and boasted a marina view. A large roaring fire blazed on the stone hearth that dominated the entrance area. Letty smiled at the hostess. (104)

So, similar to *Stormy Challenge,* these rooms and places are semantically charged. They are used for characterization as well as for turning points in the story.

The social setting also differs from *Stormy Challenge*: With Letty and Joel, two different social cultures meet, but do not clash. Although Letty, her father and his new wife belong to the academic social circle, they are rich and successful because they know how to make money using the knowledge acquired in their ivory tower. Joel, however, is the legendary American self-made man with no academic background, who is intelligent and now, a successful man, confident enough not to be intimidated by these academics. In terms of the traditional upward mobility of the heroine in romances here, the hero's humble origin marks a reversal of the order, but his social recognition by way of monetary success minimizes class differences.

CHARACTER CONSTELLATIONS

THE MALE PROTAGONIST

When Joel Blackstone drives Letty to her father's cabin after the memorial service, she takes her time to have a close look at him. The description of him combines a reflection of his outward appearance with the tension in him which puzzles Letty:

> There was a restless impatience in Joel Blackstone. Letty could feel it. It burned in his tawny gold eyes and vibrated along every line of his lean, hard body.
>
> He seethed with it, although he was masking it well beneath a layer of cool self-control. There was anger burning in him, too. Letty could feel it, and it sent a shiver down her spine.
>
> Angry men were dangerous.
>
> The sense of potentially explosive power in Joel was underlined by the fiercely moulded planes and angles of his face. It was a savage face, Letty thought, a face that reflected the ancient hunting instincts that by rights should have lain deeply buried in a modern, civilized man. They were clearly much too close to the surface in Joel Blackstone. She guessed he was in his mid-thirties, thirty-six or thirty-seven, perhaps. Something about him looked far older, however. (10–11)

The description already contains *in nuce* what makes a romantic hero, especially a Krentz one: a man with eyes that burn, a savage face, a lean, hard body, ancient hunting instincts, and cool self-control, a man who radiates rough charisma. Underneath, his civil veneer stripped away, one will find a rough, dangerous man. Joel's past has formed his life and values. When his mother was dying of cancer, he had two places where he could retreat into himself to cope with his grief: the town-library and a deserted barn outside the town. Being a private person he did not and does not have friends, only acquaintances. This and his revenge plan are the reason for his spending all his time expanding the business. Like Court in *Stormy Challenge* he is the lone wolf in his function as the leader of the pack. Until Letty appears, his social life is non-existent, but Letty gives him a new family – her family – and together they acquire friends.

Even after fifteen years he still has nightmares because he feels responsible for his father's death. Putting the blame on himself is a trait that gives his character more depth. To work off the adrenaline from these nightmares, he uses the sports equipment in his apartment or he goes running, a fact that explains his superb physical condition. He has a healthy self-confidence resulting from his ability to build up such a successful business which means he does not feel intimidated by Charlie's academic relatives. For him they simply do their jobs and he does his:

> "I didn't know professors got paid enough to afford Porsches and weekend cabins like this."
>
>   "My father is one of the country's leading experts on medieval philosophy. By temperament and training, he is himself a fine logician. My stepmother has written some of the most important papers being published today on syntactic and semantic analysis."
>
>   "So?"
>
>   Letty was amused. "So they are both brilliant analytical thinkers. It gives them an edge when it comes to making financial investments."
>
>   "I'll keep that in mind the next time I want some advice on the stock market," Joel said. (15)

He is sure Letty will not agree to his revenge plans, but self-discipline and his survival instinct cannot prevent his overwhelming wish to love Letty and act upon it:

> This was insane, he told himself. The last thing he needed. Where the hell was his common sense? He had to keep his mind on the big picture. He was going to be juggling a lot of firecrackers during the next couple of months. He could not afford to let himself get distracted. (29)

Later on, after he has gone to bed with her, he settles in her home and is determined to marry her because he begins to understand that he really needs her around:

> Joel's restlessness grew. He usually felt this way only in the middle of the night when he was unable to sleep. He thought about changing into his sweats and going for a run along the waterfront. Then he realized that what he really needed was to talk to Letty.

Letty had a way of helping him see things more clearly at times. She would understand the new elements in the equation, the emotional and human elements that he sometimes misunderstood or simply ignored. (306)

Letty particularly values one character trait of his. He is open to her different way of thinking and often finds she makes valid suggestions regarding problems he had not realized were there. This openness of acknowledging other people's opinions extends, though a little forcedly, to the examination of Keith's five-year-salvage-plan. His sound business instincts as well as his innate honor allow him to give up his plan to destroy a whole town in retribution for one man's misdeeds.

When the need arises to protect what he loves, he is levelheaded and a good strategist. He knows how to take charge of the situation from signing up a security firm to keeping watch over the firm himself, armed, of course, and to think of removing the women from the danger zones. All in all, he is the ideal husband and son-in-law: mature, reliable, strong, determined, intelligent, and honorable. When he feels appreciated he is able to return the appreciation. Having a loving wife and children are his dreams of happiness.

THE FEMALE PROTAGONIST

Through Joel's eyes, the reader is accorded a first impression of 29-year-old Letty and her impact on him. Here again, with this first description of her, the reader is given the relevant facets of her *in nuce*. She appears to be short, rumpled, with a thick wild mane of honeyed brown hair in a topknot. Large and curious eyes peer at him through a pair of round tortoiseshell frames.

> He realized with a small shock of interest that she had a nice full mouth. He also noticed that the jacket of her suit appeared to be rumpled, at least in part, due to a certain roundness of her figure. She was not the least bit heavy, he saw, just pleasantly curved in all the right places. There was a certain sensuality about her. This was the kind of woman men secretly pictured in their minds when they thought of home and hearth and babies.
>
> Joel groaned inwardly. As if he did not have enough problems on his hands. (6)

Before, Letty seemed to have found satisfaction in her life being an intellectual and valuable librarian at her college somewhere in Indiana. But inheriting her uncle's company causes her to reconsider her life, particularly since she has broken off her engagement to a professor. Raised in academic circles, she is interested in most everything she chances upon. One repeated phrase attributed to her is that she has read "a couple or so articles on a subject". Thus she has done "a great deal of research" (35) before she endeavors to run the company. One relevant piece of advice she was given through this research is that she needs a mentor. Combining levelheaded consideration and love, she chooses Joel. She tries to become familiar with the operation of the business and, feeling responsible, it becomes important to her to represent the corporate image and do it irreproachably. She is beginning to show leadership qualities:

> He had never known anyone quite like Letty. Joel shook his head in amazement as he recalled the events of the night. Little Letty Thornquist, respected member of the staff of Vellacott College, professional librarian and ex-fiancée of some turkey professor, had single-handedly strong-armed the forces of law and order in Echo Cove, Washington.
>
> Translated, that meant Letty had gone up against the Copeland power and won. She had gotten her chief executive officer out of jail. All charges had been dropped.
>
> She was turning out to be an okay executive, Joel decided. As a mentor he must be doing one hell of a good job. The thought made him grin briefly. (175)

Letty is a born problem solver. Like her dead mother, she is a very good judge of people, understanding their underlying emotionality and idiosyncrasies. Quickly she figures out what makes Joel 'tick', just as she does with her pregnant step-mother and her ex-fiancé. She knows when to leave Joel in peace and when to 'nag'. From the business point of view, she could agree with Joel's decision to liquidate Copeland Marines, but she has a noteworthy reason to disagree.

> "Do you mind telling me why you are so determined to save that rinky-dink town?" Letty released him and took a step back. She was surprised at the question. "I'm doing it for your sake, of course."
> "My sake?" Joel swung round to confront her. His face was rigid and his eyes were harsh. "What the hell is that supposed to mean?"
> Letty cocked her head, uncertain how to explain it to him in terms he would accept. "Destroying the entire town would be too much for you to carry around on your conscience," she said gently. (273)

After her experiences with her ex-fiancé's self-centeredness, she feels that Joel appreciates her for herself. She exudes an emotional warmth that is reflected in her home-making activities, like preparing dinner or baking biscuits while he is reading financial papers. Taking on this nurturing role does not mean she will be giving up her new profession as president of the company, with all the accompa-nying responsibilities. It only emphasizes her inclination to make a home not for, but with Joel.

At the beginning of *Perfect Partners,* Letty thinks of herself as being unable to sexually respond to a man in a satisfying way, a fear that is confirmed by her ex-fiancé who blames her for his unfaithfulness. This is her one personal problem, particularly because she has fallen in love with Joel and fears her sexual inabil-ity to respond will destroy their attraction. But soon she is allowed to sexually experience with Joel whatever she has dreamed of. She knows now why nothing was right in this department until Joel came along. So her intelligence becomes reconciled with her sexual and caring emotions. The combination of these traits make her the ideal wife for Joel.

Thus the character constellation of the 'lone wolf', the man with a superb physicality and ability to protect his own, and his partner, a woman with the ability to seduce his emotionality in the way it pleases her is ample material for extensive descriptions of emotions and actions that lead to a socially satisfying traditional ending.

SECONDARY CHARACTERS

Letty's parents play an essential role within the novel. They each are given more than three sentences describing their outward appearance and they play their dif-ferent roles of father and pregnant stepmother well. Morgan, a professor with a professorial distant attitude, acts as adviser to Letty and he also assumes the role as future father-in-law by using his rights as a father to ask Joel about his honor-able intentions with Letty and by being a partner to Joel in danger. Men protecting their women. Stephanie, Letty's new stepmother, plays the sophisticated professorial partner who is always very effective, cool and controlled until Letty helps her to confess her fears, and persuades her to let her husband share them with her. In order to bring two plots to climax at the same time, she gives birth to a healthy boy. Moreover, her character serves once again to demonstrate Letty's character trait of intuitiveness.

The other couple which plays an essential role in the plot is Diana and Keith Escott. Keith loves his wife and this is why he does not move away from Echo Cove. He continues to work for Victor Copeland and puts up with his father-in-law's temper and humiliations. Meanwhile, he has worked out a strategy to salvage the yard and when he glimpses a possibility, he seizes the opportunity to show his salvage plans to Letty. His determination impresses Letty along with the perfect plan that provides a way for Joel to focus his revenge on Victor Copeland alone. At the end of the novel, Keith becomes the prince in shining armor riding to his wife's rescue. Diana is a daddy's girl who married the man her father approved of. She fears her father's violent behavior, although he has never touched her in that way. But she had witnessed his rage when he nearly killed Joel in the barn years ago, and, therefore, does not dare to leave Echo Cove with Keith because she fears Victor's brutal retributions. Diana serves as a contrast to Letty's active and courageous nature. Victor Copeland is the villain required for the suspense in the story. In addition, this character is responsible for Joel's inner conflict. He is a violent, possessive man. He beat his late wife and idolizes his daughter so much that, for him, nobody is really good enough for her. With age, his business instincts deteriorate while at the same time he overestimates his abilities. The most important employer in town, he has learned from experience that he can get away with almost everything, including his increasingly violent rages. In his self-deception, he thinks he has a right to these outbursts, even the right to go so far as to kill. His fictionally convenient death is a relief to everybody.

A problem-instilling character on Letty's side is her ex-fiancé, Philip Dixon, a professor and business consultant and a patronizing, insensitive man. Since finding out that Letty has inherited a large business he pretends they have not separated and wants to run the business for Letty. He serves as a contrast to Joel, being patronizing and misogynistic:

> (Letty) pushed open the door of her office. Philip was sitting behind her desk. Letty was stunned by the gall of the man. He was sitting behind her desk just as if he owned the place. She was vaguely surprised how territorial she had become about Thornquist Gear ...
>
> Letty struggled for breath. "Philip, I don't think you are seeing the picture here. Thornquist is my company. I don't need anyone to help me run it."

"Now, darling, I know it seems like great fun at the moment, but the fact is, running a firm this size takes considerable experience and training. If you want to dabble in it for a while, I don't see why we can't create a special title for you. Even let you have an office of your own."

"I have an office of my own ... and you are in it. I would like you to get out. Now."

"Letty, you're becoming emotional, darling." Philip said soothingly. "That's not like you." (209)

Thus the character constellation is extended by more secondary characters than in *Stormy Challenge*. These characters play supporting roles as antagonists, contrasting educational differences (Joel-Dixon) and revealing the evil concealed by the power wielded by a man for a long time. Moreover, the protagonists, until then fairly solitary people, enter into relations of friendship beside becoming part of a family.

CONFLICTS, RELATIONSHIP, AND EROTIC SCENES

Two different kinds of conflict move the story forward. In a romantic story internal conflicts between the protagonists should prevail, but romantic suspense novels, and *Perfect Partners* is one of these, contain external conflicts which overshadow the internal ones, or alternatively, internal conflicts trigger off external ones, such as Joel's in this story. Joel knows that his revenge plan to destroy Copeland Marines will meet with Letty's interference, but he accepts this because he knows he needs her balanced way of approaching problems, which thus, establishes a part of the foundation of their relationship. On the one hand the conflict is solved by Victor's death, and on the other hand the yard is salvaged and thus the town.

Another external conflict – this time between the protagonists – that seems to be unsolvable at first, is Letty's inheritance of the company. In the end Joel finds a solution for this dilemma: he will buy out 50% of the company and work as her CEO, and she will remain its president. So both can live without losing face while at the same time a balance of equality is established between them. Letty's personal problem, that of her sexual inability to respond, is solved by experiencing the love of the 'right' man. Joel's personal problem, that of his revenge, is solved satisfactorily by Letty.

Morgan and Stephanie, Diana and Keith, the couples in the two subplots, have issues of trust, which Letty helps them overcome. The relationship between Letty and Joel, however, is based on trust from the beginning. As a result, they can enjoy becoming intimate sexually and emotionally, in that order.

From the beginning, Joel and Letty imagine each other in erotic ways. To him, she is sexy as well as "the kind of woman men secretly pictured in their minds when they thought of home and hearth and babies" (6), and this reveals his dream about his future. To her, he seems to be dangerous, and, therefore, attractive because he seethes with emotions she cannot fathom yet, but will eventually. In addition, her awareness of him lets her consider first whether she will be able to satisfy him in bed. Whenever he is in Letty's vicinity, his personal fascination with her grows, along with a feeling of possessiveness (64). Invited to have dinner at her new apartment, he kisses her with a raw sexual energy so that her glasses fog up. He then slides his leg between hers in such a way that she practically rides his muscled thighs. As this happens too quickly for her, she stops him, but they agree that now they know for sure that each is interested in the other (82–84).

Late at night Letty, prevents Joel from running off his frustrations of the evening spent at the Echo Cove restaurant. So he channels his energies into seducing Letty by asking her to control him with sex: she is to give the orders and he is to follow them "like a good, respectful, well-trained employee." At first she is rather shy, but with his encouragement, she asks him to do whatever she has read or dreamed about. As well as what he did at her apartment, he undresses her and, complimenting her breasts, he licks the nipples, and then she orders him to go on touching her:

> "Lower", she ordered in a desperate, tiny voice.
> His fingers slipped through the triangle of honey brown curls until they found the dampening folds of flesh between her legs. "Here?"
> "Yes." Letty lay stunned under the sensual impact of his touch. Her fingers dug into the sheet beneath her. Her toes flexed and pointed, and then her knees lifted. She could barely speak when she tried her next command ...
> For long, glorious minutes Letty gave herself up to the incredible sensations that were budding swiftly within her. Occasionally Joel asked for further instructions. She gave them eagerly, trying different patterns until she found the ones that seemed to have been designed precisely for her body. (124)

When a little later "his mouth was on her in the most intimate, the most exotic, the most passionate caress" (126), Letty experiences her first orgasm and for him this scene is equally exciting: "I'll admit the last time I came in my jeans was when I was sixteen, but what the hell. I'm only a man and you are pure dynamite" (127).

This seduction scene is the longest in *Perfect Partners* comprising thirteen pages (115–128). When, in a romance novel of the Harlequin brand the heroine is no longer a virgin, the first sexual intercourse between the protagonists has to end in something equally mind shattering as a defloration would be, only nicer, something that makes this relationship special. In this novel it is Letty's first orgasm which annihilates all her sexual worries up to then. The following morning each protagonist replays in his/her mind the night before, he praying that this kind of fulfilling intimacy will work with him only, she feeling rescued from her fears of not being able to respond satisfactorily to a man. There follow two other longer erotic scenes. In the barn Joel is stirred to the depth of his soul and Letty offers him comfort which turns into a desire that is "not so much physical as emotional ... He pounded into her, unable to slow down or exert an ounce of finesse. He had to fill her with himself. He needed to lose himself in her forever" (190). This scene establishes for the reader Joel's dependence on Letty and his need for her. He already regards her as a part of himself and being self-confident, he is manly enough to acknowledge it. She becomes his other half.

The game they play is not one of advance and retreat as it is in *Stormy Challenge,* but more one of give and take. Both feel respected and loved and plan a future together. "He was not certain when he had started thinking of Letty as his woman, but the feeling was entrenched somewhere deep inside him now" (176). She knows "the day she started sleeping with Joel Blackstone, a part of her had begun planning on marriage ... Back where she came from, people got married when they fell in love" (288). Some reticent erotic scenes follow, where, between the paragraphs, the reader can imagine for herself what happens sexually.

At the beginning of their acquaintance Letty tells Joel why she ended her engagement: she had surprised Dixon while he was getting oral sex in his office. Letty stage-manages something like a reenactment of this scene, the last longer erotic incident of this novel. When she finds out that personnel is talking about her affair with Joel, although they both behave discreetly, she goes to his office to tell him. Taking this news calmly, Joel begins to cuddle her which inspires her on her part to "fumbl(e) with his belt buckle", "lower his zipper", "cradl(e) him in her palm", "touch him with the tip of her tongue", "tast(e) his essence", "determined to give him the kind of pleasure he had so often given her" (321–323). To Joel's "deep regret" they are interrupted by Dixon who understands this scene as his definite kiss-off.

After all these intimate scenes and the ones that give testimony to their belonging together in every other way, even discussing marriage, they are ready to confess their love to each other. Seen from the narrative composing perspective, however, they have to wait almost until the end of the novel when he goes on the warpath and she, removed from the danger zone by his insistence, waits for his safe return.

Publishers' guidelines for romance novels in the 1990s are also evident in *Perfect Partners*: preferably from the first pages or the first two chapters the reader will know who the protagonists are, what they look like, that they are attracted to each other, even when the time for a relationship does not feel right. Each protagonist becomes aware in his/her thoughts, and speech, that going to bed with each other is inevitable. For the reader this is the hint that the story will end with vows of everlasting love. In this way, Krentz follows the publishers' instructions as

well as the advice for all light literature, to let the reader know from the exposition
what to expect in the end. So the first erotic, not necessarily sexual, encounter
should not happen too late within the story. From then, it is free-handed, which
means there can be many sex scenes, not more than three explicit or longer ones,
or only one at the end, but erotic or sexual teasing in one way or the other is a
must.

A declaration of love during the narrated time of the novel is usually one-
sided while the other party has to be convinced that what he/she feels amounts to
love. Explicitly declaring his or her love becomes one of the culmination points
near the end of the novel. Krentz's heroines usually know earlier than their heroes
that they love their men and want to marry them. The intention of marrying or
marriage itself, a premise of heterosexual romance novels, is fulfilled in the end.

Usually an epilogue rounds the story off when the wedding is not part of the
plot, especially in the longer romance novels. Readers seem keen to know that
this couple will become a family. This is why pregnancies or small children often appear in an epilogue. Here, however, there is no epilogue to be found. But
since romance novels with hints of a growing family sell better than those without, Krentz at least inserts the announcement of a pregnancy, this way confirming
readers' hopes and convictions that marriage and children are the ultimate way of
life to be aspired to.

WRITING STYLE AND CODE

In *Perfect Partners* a covert heterodiegetic narrator tells the story from the perspectives of hero and heroine, split equally between the two. This means the free
indirect discourse allows the reader to enter the minds of both protagonists and
decide if the respective character is understood or misunderstood and what his or
her plans are. Here, dialogue and thoughts coincide perfectly. There is no misunderstanding between the protagonists of the type, which happens continually
in *Stormy Challenge,* because once a hidden plan or problem comes out into the
open, the protagonists can talk about it or act on it, and the reader is able to perceive that there will be no foul play. When, instead, of a dialogue a descriptive
narrative paragraph is necessary, short protagonist perspectives are inserted (usually not more than four sentences), and mostly they consist of a kind of report of
what the particular person does or why she moves to a different place. Phrases
like s/he thought occur sometimes in the narrated parts, making evident a covert
narrator from the outside, while at the same time distancing the reader from the
protagonist. But this does not happen often. Overall, the impression is conveyed
to the reader that she perceives actions and emotions from the inner perspective
of one of the protagonists. In dialogues, past events are recounted by one of the
characters, sometimes with delaying narrative tactics, so that an incident is re-

ported several times, showing different aspects due to the speaker's perception and intention, thereby putting off complete information until the dialogical information puzzle is finished. (The time when Victor had nearly killed Joel and the ensuing death of Joel's father may serve as example: hint (110), vague answer to the hint (113), Victor's side (133), Joel's insistence that Victor's report of the incident is full of gaps (145), a longer recounting of the whole event (182), the bartender's false testimony of Joel's father's state of drunkenness (244), report how Joel escaped Victor's murderous attacks, ending (293), when Victor proudly affirms having killed Joel's father (357).)

The main narrative characteristic in *Perfect Partners* is that more than half of the text is rendered in dialogues: the other half is made up of short insertions of narrated text, mostly not more than four sentences. Dialogue tags are used very differently from those in *Stormy Challenge*. Tags formed of verb and adverb exist, but are applied more in common language as there is no need to agitatedly over-emphasize as a result of a more rounded plot. Usually, instead of tags, a full narrative sentence follows, or more full sentences, or no insertion at all:

> Victor Copeland was definitely an important man in Echo Cove. "I reckon you've probably figured out by now that me and Joel Blackstone go back a long way," Victor said gruffly.
> "Yes, I got that impression." Letty noticed that Victor's color did not appear any better in the morning light than it had last night. She wondered if he had recently been ill or if his obvious weight problem was the cause of his florid skin.
> "I'll be the first to admit that our association ain't exactly been what you'd call pleasant," Victor allowed with a deep sigh. "He used to work for me in the yard, you know."
> "No, I didn't know."
> "Him and his pa, both." Victor shook his head at some old memory. "Hank Blackstone worked for me his entire adult life, until he got drunk one night and drove off a cliff just outside of town."
> Letty absorbed that information.
> "Joel's father is dead?"
> "Yeah. Been gone some fifteen years."
> "I see." (131)

The texts between the dialogues elaborate on the setting and, for example, offer the reader more insight into a person's character. Here Victor is presented as a parvenu who did not deem it necessary to refine his speech and behavior.

The story is told in the past tense. The epic preterite allows the reader to participate in the story as if it were happening in the present, according to Käte Hamburger. This is also a method narrators use to emphasize that this story happened in the past (like a fairy tale), and so it subconsciously conveys its fictitious character to the reader. It is necessary to point out this detail because so many critics of the romance novel insist on the reader's inability to perceive the romance novel's fictitious character. The hints are there, but whether a reader is able to notice them or not depends on her common sense as well as on her formal education.

In *Stormy Challenge,* the language is overly florid, but not only are different kinds of dialogues used in *Perfect Partners*, there are also longer narrated parts throughout the text, more from Joel's than from Letty's perspective:

> He loped down the steps without a backward glance. The crisp, clean night called to him, offering to blow away some of the anger and frustration that had been threatening to consume him all day.
>
> He looked back once as he moved out in a long, easy stride. He could just barely make her out behind the sliding door. Her nose seemed pressed anxiously to the glass. For some reason she did not look like a prim little mid-western librarian in that moment. Instead, with her ghostly pale night-gown and her wild, tangled mane she seemed more like some fey creature of the night. There was an intriguing, sweet, rather innocent sexuality about her that Joel was finding increasingly disturbing.
>
> Hell of a time to be thinking about sex.
>
> He jerked his attention back to his running. What was the matter with him? he wondered grimly. Letty Thornquist was a major thorn in his side at the moment. He did not need to complicate an already difficult situation with sex.
>
> Ms Thornquist probably did not approve of sex, anyway. She had un-doubtedly read an article that detailed the myriad dangers involved these days.
>
> Hell, even he had read a few of those articles.
>
> Joel ran easily on the edge of the blacktop road that paralleled the twist-ing river. When he looked down the steep embankment of the small gorge he could just barely make out the sheen of moving water. Charly Thornquist had come up here often to fish in that river.
>
> Joel gave himself over to the running, channeling his frustration into energy with a directed purpose. He could handle it as long as he did that. It was an old tactic, one he used whenever restlessness deep within him reached the boiling point. Nights were always the worst times. (25–26)

Joel goes running for the length two and a half pages before returning to the cabin. While he runs, the reader learns about his thought processes, which vary between his physical reaction to Letty, a description on where he is running, the reason for his running, his revenge plans, Letty's supposed reaction to it, his premeditated answers, and again his attraction to Letty. (In *Stormy Challenge* there is not one such long narrative part to be found.)

Half of this text is like an inner monologue reflecting a more informal style of speaking, while the other part is descriptive. The free, indirect discourse, or psycho-narration, does not demand very complex sentences, especially when the thinking person is a business man and not a poet. So his thought processes are not literary, but straight. Seventeen of the twenty-three sentences begin with a subject. Most of the simple sentences have modifiers, often only prepositional ones. About half of the sentences are complex ones with relative (6), participial (2) conjunctional (3) and infinitive (4) clauses. All these sentences show a common sentence pattern with an everyday vocabulary and tend to be on the short side with an average of twelve words per sentence. Only three sentences comprise twenty or more words.

Letty's thoughts are more complex, vocabulary-wise.

> Letty was the first one up the next morning. She awoke shortly before dawn and emerged from the bathroom with some vague notion of making pancakes. She realized the wind was still shrieking through the trees.
>
> Then she looked out the window and saw the grey and white world that had engulfed the cabin overnight. Letty could see only a yard or two beyond the window because of the thick swirling snow. She had no difficulty ascertaining that the blanket of white on the ground was already very thick and growing thicker by the minute. (351)

(From my German point of view, language like "emerging from the bathroom with some vague notion" or "having no difficulty ascertaining" seems to be stilted.) Letty's thought processes are also a little more complex than Joel's, sentence-wise and some sentences are much longer.

> The following morning, ensconced behind her own desk and deep into a description of the new ad campaign for Pack Up and Go tents, Letty realized she was still stewing over what Joel had said after Diana left the office the previous day. Or, rather, over his startled surprise when she mentioned marriage and a family.
>
> Okay, so he had obviously not been thinking a whole lot lately about getting married and starting a family.
>
> One could attribute that to general male obtuseness. Maybe he just needed a little prodding in the right direction. Letty brightened briefly at the thought that she had at least planted the notion in his brain. Now all she could do was wait and see if it took root.
>
> On a more positive note, she felt reasonably secure now about his lack of romantic interest in Diana Escott. They definitely shared a past, and both were carrying scars from that past, but Letty was almost certain Joel was no longer attracted to the other woman.
>
> Letty turned the page in the report on the ad campaign and frowned over a photo of a male model in he process of pitching one of the new tents. (278–279)

Four of the ten sentences begin with a subject, well placed in the text. There are only two shorter simple sentences and all the others show a more complex sentence pattern, be they participle or prepositional clauses, or clauses with coordinating or subordinating conjunctions sometimes both in one sentence. This means that Letty is given the more articulate expressiveness of a librarian, while Joel is the typical man who does not like to talk a lot and who, *qua* education, is not eloquent.

One recurring phrase in *Perfect Partners* is that of Letty's having read articles about a subject. Sometimes this lightens a tense situation in a humorous way, at other times it makes some items of the story seem convincing when, for example, Letty is able to read financial papers or know enough to play midwife. It also stresses that Letty will always be a curious and avid intelligent reader. This phrase is like an often amusing Boccaccian 'falcon' (Paul Heyse V-XXII) placed strategically throughout the book, and after the third hint, the reader will expect this phrase at the appropriate places and, not being disappointed, she is hooked.

The sexual encounters of the two protagonists are still told in a euphemistic language that seems to be the expected narrative style in romances, albeit here more concrete. The female side of the sexual act is more closely considered than the male side. Terms like orgasm or climax are used, the female genitals now are located "between her legs" and circumscribed as "dampening folds of flesh", "the plump folds that guarded her softness", "a part of her", "inside her", "the wet heat", and "tight warmth". His genitals are conveyed in terms like "dick", deliberately used to shock a sensitive female, "male member", "that part of him", "the heavy bulge in his jeans", "his engorged shaft" or "the broad tip of his shaft", "the fierce, hard length of him", and then the personal pronouns equating the whole person for a part: "he was getting hard", "he wanted to bury himself in her", "she closed around him like a small clinging glove", "he had to fill her with himself" whereas she "touched him, cradled him in her gentle palm, stroked him, touched him with the tip of her tongue".

Both protagonists take an active part in the sexual game. The use of the male personal pronoun 'him' and 'himself' portraying the male genitals allows to assume that the male human being is reduced to that bodily function of sexual activity, projecting the image that he is his penis or the penis constitutes him, particularly at moments when he is making love 'to' not 'with' his woman. It also could imply that at moments when he experiences being "complete and whole for one single instant in time. He was at last the man he was supposed to be" (190) it connotes the essential nature of being male as a sexual one.

Names, especially the family names in *Perfect Partners*, are significantly meaningful, but their meanings are the reverse of what they might suggest to a reader. "Thornquist" indicates an inquisitive mind that irritates, a fact that does not ensue, "Blackstock" implies that Joel's family might not know decency, and this does not coincide with what the reader learns about Joel and his family. Keith

Escott seems to be reduced to the role of escort, but behind the stage he is planning to rescue Diana, and Victor Copeland is neither victorious in the end nor does he cope efficiently with what he owns. Endearments that are abundantly used in *Stormy Challenge*, which always come from the man and are more on the belittling side, are not found in *Perfect Partners*. Here, the protagonists address each other by their given names and, in the end, proudly as Mr. and Mrs. Blackstock. In order to tease Letty a little – her full name, Letitia, mirrors her cheerful and vivacious disposition – Joel sometimes brings her inheritance into play, calling her 'Boss' or 'Madam President'.

What also should be mentioned is the reader-friendly printing of the text. There are many paragraphs dividing a page, on an average eight or more, for each direct speech apiece begins with one. This way a reader is not confronted with a too densely printed text.

In *Perfect Partners* the romantic code is not as easily found as in *Stormy Challenge*. It is not so much in the florid language, although there are still remnant phrases like "tawny gold eyes" or "sea green eyes" or "eyes brilliant with curiosity". The code lies hidden in the protagonists' behavior and in their given characteristics. He exudes a "sense of potentially explosive power", an air "of cool self-control" that makes it possible for the heroine to enjoy his dangerous side. She knows instinctively he would never harm her. Once interested in this heroine, the reader expects to settle down with a book that will satisfy her fantasies, telling of dangers that will be taken care of by an honorable, able man with good "hunting instincts" (11). The heroine, on her part, becomes her warrior's recreation by being a nurturing woman and one who offers him all the sexual passion he needs. The reader will discover that the love-hate paradoxes are missing. She must have enjoyed this change because Krentz's subsequent successful novels show the same paradoxical omission.

The text on the back-cover attracting a reader's attention does not contain much code, but the potential reader still finds an intriguing phrase in the last sentence: "And when Joel finds himself longing for a more personal kind of merger, the term 'perfect partners' takes on a whole new meaning altogether … "[50] This sentence and the name of the author guarantee a happy ending to this romantic suspense story. As in *Stormy Challenge*, an excerpt from the story is offered on

---

[50]   The full text is as follows: "She has just inherited his company. He wants it to get back. Letitia Thornquist, a midwestern librarian, doesn't have the right stuff to run Thornquist Gear, Inc. That is the bottom-line opinion of Joel Blackstone, the tough, ambitious CEO who built the small Seattle sporting-goods store into an industry giant. Now that she's just inherited the company from her rich Uncle Charlie, she's dying to have Joel, a perfect mentor, show her the ropes. But teaching business is not the only item on the agenda. And when Joel finds himself longing for a more personal kind of merger, the term "perfect partners" takes on a whole new meaning … " (Krentz. *Perfect Partners*. Mandarin Paperbacks 1995, backcover)

the page before the title in order to captivate a prospective reader. It shows a male attitude different from that in *Stormy Challenge:*

> Letty knew she was out of her league. A man like this would expect so much more from a woman than she could give. It was time for a dose of good old-fashioned midwestern common sense.
>
> "You're right. Things are complicated," she said breathlessly. "If you think it would be best for us not to get involved in a social friendship outside of business hours, I'll certainly understand. I know it probably isn't a very good idea. I wasn't sure if you would even come here tonight."
>
> "Letty ... "
>
> "I hope you didn't accept the invitation because you thought you had to, what with me being the boss and all. I mean, I consider you a friend as well as a co-worker, but I wouldn't want you to feel compelled to socialize with the boss."
>
> He silenced her by the simple expedient of putting his fingers against her lips. "Letty, have you ever done any juggling?"
>
> "No."
>
> "Then we're both going to have to hope I know what I'm doing." He took his fingers away from her mouth and kissed her again.
>
> Hard. (also 83)

3.1.3 *All Night Long*

About twenty-five years after *Stormy Challenge,* the contemporary novel, *All Night Long,* was published[51]. Since *Stormy Challenge,* Krentz has written about 140 novels with around a hundred still in print, and twenty New York Times best-sellers to her name. She wrote category romances (250 pages) until 1992, but began writing longer single titles as early as 1986. These longer novels never exceed four hundred pages and tend to be around 120,000 words, the number of pages depends on the printing conditions. *All Night Long* contains 321 narrowly printed pages. This contemporary story is the most complex one, plot- and point-of-view-wise, which Krentz has written to date.

SUMMARY

Fifteen year old Irene Stenson, a police officer's daughter, and wild, privileged Pamela Webb had been best of friends for one short high school summer. Their friendship ended the night Pamela dropped Irene off at her home, where Irene discovered her parents' bloodied bodies on the kitchen floor. It was ruled a murder-suicide, a fact Irene never could make herself believe to be true, and she is still dealing with the traumatic effects of this tragedy even as an adult.

Seventeen years later, Irene, now a journalist for a small daily newspaper, receives an e-mail from her ex-best-friend Pamela, summoning her to come back

---

[51] Actually it was published in a hardcover edition already in 2006

home through the code word they had used as teenagers intimating urgency and secrecy. Renting a cabin in Dunsley, she meets Luke Danner, the owner of Sunrise on the Lake Lodge, who is as attracted to her at first sight, as she to him. From her cabin she rings Pamela, but does not get an answer to her many calls. So at night, she decides to drive her car unobtrusively out of the lodge to the Webb's summer place, followed there by Luke who has a 'hunch' that she needs some backup in the darkness. They discover Pamela, apparently having committed suicide with an overdose of pills and alcohol. Irene does not believe in the suicide verdict, but there is no autopsy because Ryland Webb, Pamela's father and senator running for presidency, wants to hush up her death. Irene is convinced that Pamela's death is linked to the murders of her parents seventeen years before. Remembering where Pamela used to hide secret things, Irene goes back to the summer house breaking and entering, once again followed by Luke. In Pamela's hiding place she discovers a key. Then she hears another intruder coming up the stairs. She hides in the shadow of the master bedroom's balcony, from where Luke helps her to escape at the last moment before the house goes up in flames. The kisses they exchange after this climactic incident are a moving experience for both.

Wherever Luke and Irene go, they discover that many inhabitants of Dunsley are indebted to the rich Webb family, especially to Victor Webb, Pamela's grandfather. Only Tess Carpenter, Irene's former teacher, and her husband Phil can offer help in their investigation. The couple become the confidants Irene and Luke depend on. All four are convinced the house was torched by a Webb to destroy whatever evidence there was. When Luke and Irene come back from a dinner, Tucker Mills, maintenance man and gardener for Luke and the Webb's garden, tells them that he saw Hoyt Egan, Ryland's aide, at the summer house the day before Pamela died. Still being scared by Tucker's unexpected appearance, Irene asks Luke to spend the night in her cabin. They have sex, a cathartic experience for both. This establishes the new basis for their relationship, which entitles Irene to support Luke against his family's well-meaning interference when they go to Santa Elena, where Luke's family runs Elena Creek Vineyards.

Two days later, Irene discovers the reason for Pamela's email, a video hid in Irene's parents' former house, while Luke finds a murdered Hoyt. Pamela wanted Irene to publicize her senatorial father's inclination to sexually abuse little girls, in order to stop him running for presidency as well as protect his fiancée's daughter. At last Irene learns the truth about why her parents were murdered: that night, seventeen years ago, a desperate Pamela had given Irene's father, the integer chief of police in Dunsley, a video confirming evidence of her being abused by her father, at the same time confiding this to the wrong person, who then killed Irene's parents to silence them. Having thus learned the truth, Irene feels she will now be able to adjust and find closure. At a fund-raiser, Irene, together with her newspaper team and Luke, publicly confront Ryland about his ongoing abuse of small girls, and there, Alexa, Ryland's fiancée, realizes that her daughter is the next intended victim. But Ryland is not his wife's and his daughter's villainous murderer, neither is he Irene's parents', Hoyt's, and Bob Thornhill's, the former chief of police, murderer. It is Victor who killed for his son's senatorial career. He regards committing these crimes as his lawful right. Victor also tries to kill Irene. She is saved by Luke and Sam, the current chief of police. Victor dies of a gun shot wound shortly after.

Now that Irene feels reconciled with her traumatic past, the couple is free to plan their future. Luke sells his lodge and moves to the town where Irene lives. In an epilogue Irene and Kate, Luke's former fiancée and now his brother's wife, both women pregnant, enjoy being surrounded by a loving family.

PLOT, CHAPTERS, TIME, AND SETTINGS

All Night Long consists of 321 pages divided into 50 chapters plus a prologue and an epilogue. The chapters, prologue, and epilogue are numbered (the numbers written in letters in italics) without additional headlines but with a black and white thick line above the numbers. The beginning of each chapter is marked by a first letter in a bigger, bold print comprising three lines. Otherwise the pages remain unadorned. These chapters, with an average length of six pages, indicate a fast-paced action. The main plot in *All Night Long* is concerned with the solving of both Pamela's and Irene's parents' murders, as well as providing a strong suspense curve, while Luke and Irene's love story seems to be relegated to a subplot. Another, small subplot spotlights Luke's family dynamics: this does not increase the suspense curve, but instead serves to insert characterization of the protagonists and the state of their relationship with an amusing scene. Despite their love story being relegated to a subplot, the introductory exposition of the first two chapters (8–21), preceded by the prologue and Pamela's email, deals with the protagonists, thereby informing a reader about their different personalities, their trust in their instant attraction for each other, and their social status. From chapter three onward the crime takes precedence, but it draws the protagonists closer together, thus supporting the characterization of the protagonists.

Set in the USA of the early 21st century, *All Night Long* is a contemporary romance novel written in the epic preterite. In 2006, computers are a tool everybody knows how to use and their is inscribed into the story.

Not counting the time of prologue (the night Irene found her parents murdered in the kitchen seventeen years before) and of epilogue (Luke's family gathered around a pregnant Irene), the chronologically told story in *All Night Long* occurs within fourteen fast-paced days: on the first day, Irene rents a cabin at Luke's lodge and that same night she discovers a dead Pamela. The next night she nearly dies in the fire. Frightened, when she comes back to the cabin the following evening, she spends the night with Luke. On the fourth day, Irene is presented to Luke's family and the morning after, they both confront Hoyt Egan. The sixth day is action packed: Irene learns who the key, she found in Pamela's hiding place, belongs to, is nearly chased into a ravine, and finds out what Pamela was so concerned about, while Luke discovers a murdered Hoyt. The next evening they make sure that Ryland Webb terminates his candidacy for president. Luke and Irene spend one restful day together, but just the following day it dawns on them that not Ryland, but Victor is the murderer: his 'luck' runs out when he tries to murder Irene. The ninth day ends with Luke's marriage proposal. Actually, the love story and the crime story end on the ninth day, but one person still has to be reconciled with his guilty consciousness: Sam McPherson. On the twelfth day, Irene helps Sam by reminding him of her father's high regard for him, thus enabling him to forgive himself. Luke, in turn, helps his former fiancée and his brother to finally admit their love for each other on the fourteenth day.

The chronologically narrated time line is never interrupted by analepses. If past events need to be inserted, the author uses dialogues in which different characters relate these events, or else she uses Pamela's video. The growing complexity of the story's structure as well as an accumulation of actions are manifested by the application of a prologue, an epilogue and the division of the novel into many chapters. Although the story itself evolves over a short time interval of fourteen days, the promising happy ending of the love story is already decided earlier on, which could indicate its delegation to the subplot. Moreover, after the literary sleight of hand on the seventh day and the romantic ending on the ninth day, it takes another three days for a denouement of the story. The romance itself is ended satisfyingly via the epilog. It restores a reader's impression that she has been reading a romance novel, albeit a hybrid one.

One local setting is Luke's Sunrise on Lake Lodge in Dunsley, situated in the Ventana Lake resort region in the mountains of Northern California, not far from Luke's parental home in the wine country. Dunsley, a small community where everyone knows everyone, but not necessarily their secrets, is also small enough to give the richest family the chance to influence and manipulate people by obligation, an ideal setting for the rich villains of the story to go unpunished for whichever crime they commit, until Pamela's intervention. Pamela's summer home and Irene's former parental home are both situated, like the lodge, at the lake that later is revealed as a convenient getaway route for Victor's murderous activities. The lodge itself is depicted as a derelict place, comprising twelve cabins, one of which is inhabited by Luke himself. Being the only motel in town, it is inevitable that Irene and Luke meet there. It also serves to display the two lovers' flaws, such as her fear of darkness and his military way of dealing with paying guests. The third place, the vineyards at Santa Elena, represents no real significance to the story, other than being the place where Luke's family lives and where the reader meets the different family members. The same insignificance holds for the description of wherever the fundraiser takes place in San Francisco, or the location of Hoyt's apartment.

The semantics of rooms and other locations are not as clearly used as they are in *Perfect Partners*. The hero's living on and running the run-down lodge hints at the discrepancy between his marine persona and his academic one, a discrepancy not reconciled within his personality. Otherwise places do not characterize the protagonists so much, yet they present dramatically charged incidents, like the burning villa or the houses situated at the lake which provide different views, and thus, the key to solve the crime.

The social setting is more complicated than in *Perfect Partners*. Here, the differences of education between the protagonists are counterbalanced by the hero's dichotomized life: the hero's parents, rich and sophisticated, offer a contrast to the run-down motel managed by their son, the ex-marine with a Ph.D. in philosophy. His family leads a social life filled with big parties and other events, they need to invest in because of their business, whereas the hero has withdrawn from this social circle in order to not to be hindered in the writing of his book. This explains his living in the rundown lodge. Irene, the daughter of the town's well-respected police officer, has no friends in her hometown anymore. She grew up elsewhere and there she works as a valued journalist for a small newspaper. She and the hero meet on the same social level. The corrupt and rich people in the story wield political power and do not associate with anybody in town other than buying themselves a kind of immunity by obliging some of the townspeople.

CHARACTER CONSTELLATIONS

THE MALE PROTAGONIST

Luke Danner is nearly forty years old. A description of his outward appearance is that of an ex-Marine's fit body combined with "stark and fiercely hewn" features, hazel-green eyes of an "alchemist who has stared too long and too deeply into the refiner's searing fire" (7). This description of his face insinuates a more than one-dimensional character.

Most of his life and career is reported by Jason, Luke's youngest stepbrother. When Luke was six years old, his mother committed suicide and since then, his family, his father John with his second wife and their two sons, Hackett and Jason, have been deeply concerned that Luke, too, is suicide-prone because he is a self-contained person. Unlike all the other members of the family, he does not have the wine business in his blood, and so they assume that he does not have a real goal in his life, which, of course he does have, only it is very different from his family's objectives. He studied classical philosophy, graduated, decided to join the Marines and, while in the Corps, he finished his Ph.D. This formal education makes him a good investigator. During his time in the army, he was married to a woman who adored his uniform, but not the circumstances of his military life. Six months before the story of *All Night Long* begins, he left the Marines, tried for a short time to be a part of the family business, decided to marry and became engaged to Katy Foote, his father's friend's and business partner's daughter. He ended the engagement because he considered himself too old for the much younger girl, left the firm, and, having made solid investments over the years, bought the lodge at the lake. More used to giving orders than treating paying guests diplomatically, running a lodge is not in his blood either. When he bought it he wanted to use only one cabin to write his book in peace, but then he discovered that three people were financially dependent on the lodge and so he decided to keep it open, like a good officer who "takes care of his people" (225). He is portrayed as an intelligent, decent and honorable man although nobody, except Irene, seems to understand the reasons for his actions.

As a former Marine, he has learned the hard way not to show his emotions. He is not a talkative man and he communicates abrasively. Writing a book on philosophical and military strategies is, as Irene puts it, his "private version of therapy" (224) because, like Irene, he is plagued by nightmares which mirror the horrors, merely alluded to, which he had endured while doing his military service overseas.

Luke falls in love with Irene at first sight. He regards the first two nights of their acquaintance – coping with the police after finding Pamela and then, nearly being burnt alive and giving testimony – as having "spent more serious quality time together in the past couple of days than many married couples do in a year. Let's just say I've learned a few things about you" (106). Inviting her to the family party on the fourth day of their acquaintance means admission of his already serious intentions about Irene. With him actions speak louder than words. For the reader his personality comes across as introverted and withdrawn into himself, and although she is admitted access to his mind by way of free indirect discourse, he remains a stranger, the enigmatic 'alchemist'.

The Female Protagonist

From the first, Irene's outer appearance intrigues Luke:

> Spectacular, haunting, amber-brown eyes lit with intelligence and shadowed with secrets; gleaming dark hair cut with precision to follow the line of the jaw; a sleek, vital, delightfully feminine shape; sexy high heeled boots and a dashing black trench coat ...
> Right now his instincts were telling him that Irene Stenson wore the

boots and the trench and the attitude the way a man might wear a Kevlar vest as battle armor. (19)

As with Luke's description of his outward appearance, the reader is given an idea of what a person looks like together with hints of a characterization, so here, she is also given a suggestive pointer that looks are not all there is to Irene. Irene, aged 32, has become a journalist because of her investigative mind and also because she is obsessed with finding out what really happened seventeen years before. As an adult she still remembers many occasions with her parents that belie the verdict that her father first killed his wife and then himself. She remembers her father as a decent and reliable man and her parents being in love with each other. When, in the supermarket, customers recognize and speak to her, it becomes evident that her positive memories of her decent parents are correct.

Like Luke, Irene's father served with the Marines. So she recalls quite well what makes those men tick, how to handle them and what to realistically expect from them. From her father she has inherited her levelheadedness in dangerous situations, as, for example, when Victor forbids her to answer her cell phone she pretends to fumble in her shoulder bag to switch it off, but in fact pushes the button to record the conversation. A little later, she drops the bag on the dock before she lets herself fall backwards off the dock into the water to avoid being killed (301). Irene is also convinced that Pamela did not commit suicide, and she determinedly puts her logical and investigative mind to work, a fact that Luke can appreciate and admire.

Over the years, Irene has tried to wrestle her demons with the help of six therapists and a short marriage right after college. She still has nightmares – it was she who found her parents murdered in the kitchen – and to help her cope she has developed rituals like leaving the lights on in every room all night long or wearing black clothes. Learning the truth "made it possible for her to give the past a proper burial" (307). Because she and Luke have the same background with traumatic experiences, from now on she can commit herself to a relationship in a way she was not able to before. They both can henceforward allow themselves intimacy and commitment.

SECONDARY CHARACTERS

Dead or alive on a computer screen, Pamela is the pivot around which the story evolves. When she made friends with Irene all those years before, it was part of a search for the secure and caring family she longed for. Irene's mother knew this, and, therefore, she and her husband permitted this friendship, although it was clear that Pamela was already a disturbed young girl. Pamela trusted Irene's decent parents so much that she gave them a video, showing her father when he was abusing her. She sought help and, thinking that her step-uncle Sam was a decent man, who could be trusted, she told him who she was going to show the video to. Sam in turn told his father, Victor, not in the least suspecting that to silence them, Victor would kill the Stensons as soon as he was informed. Pamela grew from troubled teen into a troubled woman with commitment issues and a penchant for drugs and alcohol. She let herself be abused by her father and grandfather in different ways.

> Pamela was a whore at heart, but she was our whore and she was damned good at what she did. She was willing to sleep with Ryland's rivals, enemies, and anyone else, male or female, who had information we could use. She enjoyed her role as spy. It made her feel powerful to know that she was a critical part of the campaign strategy and that Ryland had come to depend on her. I think it gave her a sense of vengeance. (297)

Pamela regains control over her drug addiction and, she believes, over her father. But when she discovers he is about to abuse his fiancée's daughter, she contacts Irene. She has followed Irene's journalistic career and is convinced that news printed in even her small newspaper will stop Ryland's political aspirations. Her second attempt to reveal her father's sick addiction also ends with a murder, her murder, because, once again, she confides in the wrong person, this time her grandfather, who kills her as soon as he is informed.

Ryland Webb who, personally, appears on the scene only once, serves as a red herring. Until the end, the reader is led to believe that he murdered Pamela's mother, Pamela, Irene's parents, and two other people. Ryland is so far gone in his addiction that he has no feelings of guilt. In this he resembles his father, Victor, who considers it his right to murder anyone who crosses his purposes. Had Luke and Sam not intervened, Irene would have been his seventh victim.

When he was twenty-three years old, Sam McPherson, Victor's illegitimate son, did not know what to do with Pamela's revelation, and, therefore, went to his father to ask for advice. Since then, he has felt responsible for the Stensons' murder. His guilt is an almost unbearable burden, even seventeen years after his ill-fated call to Victor. In order to redeem himself, he tries his best to become as decent a cop as Hugh Stenson was. But Sam needs Irene's forgiveness to forgive himself and allow himself to begin a relationship. These four characters display four different kinds of guilt, two who are burdened with a deep sense of guilt, but actually are victims, and the other two are the real culprits who consider themselves blameless. Corruptness of the politically powerful often appears in Krentz's futuristic romances. Her contemporary romances have not so far used this topic as a theme.

Luke's family members are little more than place holders in the novel. They serve to slow down the action, they play their parts in the courting section, in the information section and in the welcoming section of the future member of the family. There are other non-descript characters who sparsely populate the scenes and give them some color.

Thus, the connecting link of the secondary characters' constellations on the heroine's side is the dead Pamela, who became, and is, the catalyst for the novel's chain of events. The secondary characters' constellation on the hero's side, his family and the family dynamics, are given the role of character interpreters.

CONFLICT, RELATIONSHIP, AND EROTIC SCENES

Irene is still shattered by her parents' vicious murder and only learning the truth will bring her peace. Luke also has his own demons to fight, which make an appearance in nightmares. So he and Irene have a common basis as each knows how difficult it is to overcome phobias and nightmares, aware that their causes cannot be annihilated, but that their power can be reduced.

Just as in *Perfect Partners,* an external conflict unites the couple, here the inner conflict of each protagonist gives them a basis for their mutual understanding. Hero and heroine do not fight each other and their attraction. On the contrary, they give in to it, so they can act together, supporting each other. When Luke and Irene meet, they are attracted to each other instantly, with one of them, in this case Irene, experiencing the (Harlequin) stereotype romance first feeling of "the last thing she wanted to do was get involved with him" (17). But on the second evening of their acquaintance, after a hot and enthusiastic kiss (111), getting involved is very much what she does want and so she acts accordingly. Because they spend so much 'quality time' investigating while he and she are thinking of making love all along the way, he admonishes himself that this would be too early. Asked to stay the night at her cabin, he chooses the couch to sleep on, but when she awakes him late at night, neither wants to or can resist their attraction.

There are two longer sex scenes in the novel, the first being the longest comprising six pages (171–176). Seen and felt from her perspective, he displays a sexual skillfulness to her astonished and delighted inexperience. It begins with "a meltingly slow, breathtakingly sexy utterly masculine look of appreciation" and when she winds her arms around his neck he kisses her, she him and they touch each other through their clothes. From the kitchen he carries her to the bedroom, sheds his clothes and frees her of her nightgown. (Carrying the woman to an (in)appropriate place and undressing her is one task for the man in a romance novel that is hardly ever omitted.) He takes her nipples between his teeth while she encloses "him with her fingers exploring the length and breadth of him" (174). When she is not yet wet enough, although "one long finger slid slowly, deeply into her, stroking, prodding, stretching" and "she could feel the slick dampness gathering between her legs", he stimulates her with cunnilingus which ends in her climax. Shortly after, when he "had pushed himself into her" she experiences another one. This intimate moment gives her the feeling that "for a few rare, glittering moments she was not alone" (176).

After the sexual act she is able to explain to him why, until now, she was able to achieve a climax only with the help of a vibrator and not with a man, thus making clear to him and the reader that he is the right and only man to facilitate her capability to not only sexually love. "One of my therapists told me ... I had intimacy issues. Something to do with a fear of letting myself get too close emotionally" (176). The use of a vibrator versus the real man indicates that a woman is a sexual being who is aware of her sexual needs and acts upon them. To a woman of the new millennium this is the alternative to having indiscriminate sex with whoever, and for the romance heroine it testifies her independence from a man and moreover her 'chaste' way of living.[52]

To make a relationship the special one in a romance novel, sexual satisfaction, symbolized in a 'wonderful' climax of both partners, is important. Here, it results in their both being able to soundly sleep afterwards without being woken by nightmares. They bring each other peace, a fact that also is hinted at in Irene's name. (Irene means 'peace'.)

From then onwards, whenever the protagonists make love, it is mentioned only briefly because this part of the relationship has been established, but other relationship issues do have to be cleared up. Irene is the only one to whom Luke can disclose why his family is way out of line slapping him with a diagnosis of erectile dysfunction because he did not initiate sexual intercourse with his much younger, now ex-fiancée.

After their first night together in bed, Luke concedes Irene rights in the relationship. "Like it or not, while we are together, you're involved with my family. That gives you a license to comment ... " (195). She moves into his cabin, for they do not need more time than these initial three days to behave like a married couple. So naturally assuming his role as protector as his given right, he gets angry because he is worried when he learns she went unprotected to her old home. "That's how men deal with emotions, didn't you know? We either get mad or we have sex ... " (265). But then he has to reassure himself of his assumption to see himself as her protector. "'... but I thought we were involved in a relationship. This isn't just a fling or a one-night stand.' He stopped in front of her. 'Or is it?'" (265).

Control is one of the keywords in a romance novel and Krentz's novels are no exception, in particular the sexual control the male protagonist exerts over himself. (Premature ejaculation for example is prevented by such self-control.)

---

[52] That women go into sex-shops to buy vibrators and other stimulating gadgets is already thematized in Krentz's *Trust Me* of 1995. Man versus vibrator is a byplay in many romances.

Luke decides Irene will not be in the mood for sex after what she has learned that day and he has enough self-control not to bother her. Then she decides to become active while he "delights" in her activity. She "encircles him with her fingers", "finds him with her mouth", "her tongue tips lightly along the length of his erection"; he "watches, riveted, as she settles herself astride and takes him deep inside". When "he is not going to be able to last much longer" she says "you don't have to be in control every time. Just let go" (266). In romance novels, her taking an active role in their erotic play and his enjoying it displays the subtext meaning of: they act on equal terms in bed and outside it. After his marriage proposal (305) they again make love, but this is a scene for the reader to imagine between paragraphs because now the relationship is established. Beside the protagonists' intellectual ability, their different traumata and how they overcome these form the essence of the novel. They are at the heart of the course of action, in particular on the level of their sexuality.

WRITING STYLE AND CODE

Most of the story develops in the hybrid form of free indirect discourse and psycho-narration in the third person of the two protagonists' perspectives. Often a covert narrator inserts tags like "Irene thought" or "Luke thought" into the thinking process of his characters. This covert narrator's subterfuge undermines the reader's illusion of having a really intimate look into the protagonist's head because she is made aware, although subconsciously, that there is always narrator behind inventing a character's thoughts. A reader might not notice at that moment that a different personality from that of the respective character's shines through because there are no omniscient narrator's remarks to be found, such as a foreboding one.

Some parts of *All Night Long* are inner monologue and some of these are printed in Italics:

> *Get a grip. It's an old cabin. Old wirings. Old bulbs (154),* or
>
> *Problem is, lady, I'm too old to play games. The next time we get close it's going to be all or nothing, and we both know that tonight is too soon for you (155),* or
>
> *How do you conduct a search when you have no idea what you are looking for? she wondered. Think about this. If Pamela did intend for you to find the key and if she wanted you to use it, she probably would have made certain that you would recognize whatever it was she wanted you to discover here (242).*

Even here a covert narrator inserted a "she wondered" tag, although a print in italics already emphasizes this as an inner monologue that really does not need a narrator's guidance anymore. It is rather absurd, as are the italics themselves because if the story is narrated from the perspective of the particular character, his or her thoughts do not need an extra attracting printing contrivance, especially when the covert narrator squeezes this tag into it.

Six short insertions of other persons' perspectives interrupt the ongoing alternate use of those of hero and heroine. Sometimes they are three pages long, mostly, however, only one to even one-half page long. First there is Sam McPherson, Victor's illegitimate son, whose thoughts hint at his participation in the Stanson's murder and his guilty conscience (81). While Ryland Webb is preparing and being prepared by Hoyt for Pamela's funeral, his thoughts turn to a blackmail problem he is facing and also his fear of his father (178). Victor Webb's thoughts reflect his disappointment in Ryland and his mistake of having bestowed everything on the wrong son. Who this son is, is revealed near the end of *All Night Long*. Then there is another interruption in the way of perspectives. This time it is a short conversation between Luke's father and Gordon, his friend and business partner. It takes place somewhere in the Danner mansion. From whose perspective this dialogue is reported is not at all clear. As far as I can see, this is the only part of the novel where the author lets the covert narrator be discovered as omniscient because s/he is not 'hiding' behind a personal perspective. This scene emphasizes the family's ongoing concerns about Luke's potential depression (187). Sam is awarded a second opportunity to reveal his thoughts. Through Irene's forgiving remarks, he feels freed to begin a new life (312). The last change of perspective is that of Hackett, Luke's step-brother, who is secretly in love with Katy. Now that Luke has assured him that Katy never was really in love with him, Hackett can finally act and make Katy his (316).

All Night Long's most characteristic device in the language department is the use of dialogues – again. They make up nearly half of the book. The characters speak in full, refined sentences and their style does not differ greatly from one person to the other. Sometimes, however, and this is Krentz's subtle humor, abbreviated questions or answers make the story more lively. Luke is assigned opportunities to give military short orders that create amusing situations, and Luke's brother, Jason, likes to comment on something with a "Howdy" which shows his juvenile attitude.

The narrative parts between dialogues are presented in short, mostly paratactic sentences. Depending on the situation, and most scenes are related to the crime, there are no overly ornate adjectives and adverbs. Actions push the story forward. There are no delaying tactics in the guise of description. When, for example, a room or a location is described, it serves to orientate the reader rather than to let her linger to savor the atmosphere. As in Krentz's other novels, it is difficult to find a text in *All Night Long* that contains more than ten sentences without dialogue interruption like the following one written in an educated style displaying long sentences with thirty words and more:

Irene tossed the pen onto the table and studied the latest version of the time line. Frustration churned in her stomach. No matter how she tried to connect the dots, she could not come up with a reasonable way to put Ryland Webb anywhere near Dunsley on the day of Pamela's death.

She had been so certain that when she sat down with all the facts she would find something in addition to a motive that she could give to the police to tie Webb to the murder. But thus far she had come up empty-handed.

There had to be a connection, she thought. It was inconceivable that Pamela had died because of an accidental overdose.

She got up and went into Luke's small, orderly kitchen to pour herself more tea. It was the fourth time she had gotten out of the chair in the past forty minutes. She had already wandered into the kitchen area three times, twice to refill her mug, once to check the refrigerator to see what she needed to buy for dinner.

Mug in hand, she went out the back door of the cabin, propped one hip against the porch railing and contemplated the placid surface of the lake. The view from this cabin was slightly different from the one she'd had while residing in Cabin Number Five. From here she could see more of the lake. (284–285)

Most of the thirteen sentences are main clauses with modifiers or one coordinating or subordinating conjunction, once enumerating main clauses. Only sentence number four is more complex, with two subordinate conjunctions and one infinitive clause. As Luke is reported to have achieved a Ph.D. in philosophy, the reader might expect a complex sentence pattern reflecting complex thoughts, but military life alters thought and speech tendencies. The following text can be seen partly as a covert narrator's description of what Luke's parental home is like, but it is clearly intended as a part of his perspective.

Luke came to a halt in front of the hearth and rested one arm on the carved oak mantel. He looked at the shelves full of heavy tomes and scientific papers that surrounded him. Every volume, journal and article in the extensive collection concerned the subject of wine making. Viticulture and enology were matters of great passion for everyone in the family except him.

It wasn't that he had not tried to follow in his father's footsteps. At various times in his life, including six months ago, he had made serious attempts to develop the kind of enthusiasm and all-consuming interest in wine making that drove his father and Gordon Foote and the others. But he had failed. In the end, he had always followed his own path, first into academia, then into the Marines and now into The Project.

He had known from the moment he and Irene had arrived at the sprawling complex that housed the Elena Creek Vineyards cellars, wine-tasting facilities and reception rooms that sooner or later his father was going to corner him and raise the subject of Dr. Van Dyke. (183–184)

Again, as with Irene's narrative perspective, the structure of the sentences is plain but longer in the number of words, up to forty-seven. Three simple sentences, then ones with one coordinating or subordinating conjunction. Two sentences show a more complex pattern, one beginning with a longer adverbial phrase and added to the main clause, it has a subordinate clause followed by an infinitive one. The last sentence is longer with a relative clause, two subordinate ones and one coordinate clause. In this text there are also enumerations, first three enumerations of things, then of times and at last of places.

In Luke's dialogues, his questions and answers are on the short side, reflecting a military life of a commanding concise nature and, at the same time, showing limited interpersonal skills when it comes to, for example, the task of checking in guests which is a necessary part of his new profession as owner of the lodge. When Luke's thoughts are otherwise occupied he subconsciously returns to the military way of communication:

> "Name, address and driver's license, number, Addison", he said.
> "Full signature at the bottom. Initial the department date." ...
> "All finished, sir." Addison pushed the form back across the counter with obvious relief.
> Luke gave the paper a cursory glance, checking to make sure each section had been filled in. "Checkout time is twelve hundred."
> Across the room Irene closed her eyes in a rather pained way.
> Addison went blank. "Uh, twelve hundred what, sir?"
> "Hours. High noon."
> "Yes, sir," Addison said quickly. "Don't worry, we'll leave before noon."
> Luke swiped a key off a hook and handed it to Addison. "CabinNumber Ten. There's a list of regs posted on the back of the door. Read 'em."
> Addison blinked uneasily. "Regs?" (118)

This kind of subtle humor in the quotation above is Krentz's speciality. Krentz also likes to put a 'falcon' into her story that leads the reader through a story. Here there are even two: Luke and Irene try to find 'connecting dots' to solve the murder and Irene's dead father's inherent decency is confirmed about her in different ways by different people throughout the story.

The protagonists' sexual intercourse, still a significant, though not so dominant part of this novel, happens without a prior emotional battle. As consenting adults they look forward to physical intimacy. Sexual awareness of each other is not constantly mentioned, but is subliminally there. Luke's initial sexual interest in Irene is related as follows: "His brain was consumed with the puzzle that was Irene Stenson. Other portions of his anatomy seemed to be equally interested in investigating the matter" (20). The other portions of his anatomy are: his "arousal", "the bulge in his jeans", "the length and breadth of him", "the fierceness of his erection" and the use of personal pronouns equating the whole person for one part. As a pendant to his arousal, she is "wet" but, once, not wet enough for his penetration. Her genitals are not explicitly identified, but as transpires with the male, they also are treated as equivalent to the whole person by the use of personal pronouns as in "he put his tongue in her", "stretching her", "filling her completely". In *All Night Long* this use of personal pronouns for both protagonists indicates the involvement of both, the whole person and the sexual being that is inseparable from all his/her other beings. Consequently, an orgasm takes on a deeper significance. Krentz underlines this by letting her characters experience climaxes that make them feel "exultant", "triumphant" and "for a few, rare, glittering moments … not alone" (175). Hence, sexual intimacy brings a kind of peace that lets these tortured souls sleep soundly through the night.

Only one of the family names in *All Night Long* can be fit with meaning: Webb. This family acts like a spider in its web. Like in *Perfect Partners* Krentz endows the murderer of six people with the name Victor whose punishment is also his death. As mentioned before, the name Irene means 'peace' and that is what she craves, an inner peace, and what she helps Luke to find, his inner peace. An endearment name between the protagonists happens only once: after Luke's marriage proposal Irene becomes his "sweetheart". Otherwise they address each other with their names and his other names for her, "lady" or "woman" shows him to be a man without a male superiority complex. This emphasizes that acceptance of equality is a fact.

As in both, *Stormy Challenge* and *Perfect Partners*, the printed pages, again, are reader-friendly. Usually there are no more than six sentences to a paragraph and owing to the fact that each speech act is provided with its own paragraph, the text in a page is cut up into at least eight parts. The blurb on the back cover of *All Night Long* that aims to captivate the potential romance novel reader talks about it being a a crime story, but not a romantic one, which is consistent with the love story ranging as subplot. Nevertheless, a prospective buyer will form the idea that this book will offer the much looked-for happy ending as she is also informed that this is a novel of romantic suspense with a mixture of 'desire and danger'.[53] The avid romance reader knows that Krentz delivers 'satisfying' romances. This time, there is no excerpt to be found on the pre-title page. Instead, there are the latest Krentz titles with newspaper reviews indicating that the novel belongs to popular mainstream fiction. Within the novel itself there are still paragraphs that let the romance reader's heart beat faster, serving the code she longs for, like: "His smile

---

[53]   The full back cover text: "After seventeen years, Irene Stenson goes home to investigate her parents' deaths – and encounters a nightmare more terrifying than she could have imagined …" "In her signature sharp and witty fashion, Krentz mixes desire and danger to create a riveting novel of romantic suspense."-Chicago Tribune Krentz: *All Night Long* 2007, Jove mass-market edition.

was so slow and so wickedly inviting that she was amazed she did not dissolve into a puddle right there in the entranceway of the cabin" (153), or the erotic scenes, in which, for example, the 'alpha male' carries his woman to the bedroom and undresses her, that also belong to the romance novel code.

The narrative style in *All Night Long,* similar to the one in *Perfect Partners,* creates the illusion for the reader of having access to the characters' inner beings: despite being told in the third-person, there are various perspectives, and a covert narrator directs the understanding of the story by way of dialogue tags and descriptions seemingly belonging to the particular perspective. The dialogues and descriptions display a tendency to be an elaborate, but not too elaborate language which can be described as unobtrusive American English with no false steps in the direction of pretentiousness. Despite fairy tale allusions, like the axiomatic eternal love, sufficient references to reality can be pinpointed for the reader to identify with, not least because of the more ordinary wordings the reader can connect with her own linguistic and world experience, thus factoring in the fulfillment of potential female longings.

3.1.4 Constants and Changes

Taking the three novels, *Stormy Challenge* (1982), *Perfect Partners* (1992) and *All Night Long* (2007), as terms of reference for possible changes in Krentz's work over the course of a time period of twenty-five years, the following constants and changes emerge.

According to Pamela Regis' eight criteria (1. Society Defined, 2. The Meeting, 3. The Barrier, 4. The Attraction, 5. The Declaration, 6. Point of Ritual Death, 7. The Recognition, 8. The Betrothal, not necessarily in that order) that define a love story as a romance, all three novels could be classified as romances, although in *All Night Long,* the Barrier and the Point of Ritual Death are only hinted at because the protagonists are so sure of their attraction to each other that no internal doubts about the relationship materialize.

All of Krentz's three novels are set in the west of the USA: the Oregon coast, Northern California and the state of Washington. These are places that Krentz is familiar with as she used to live in Northern California and currently lives in Seattle which, incidentally, is a stronghold of the Romance Writers Association of America (RWA). In all three novels Krentz describes, briefly, locations: landscapes, streets, towns, rural areas, houses. Landscapes are there to drive through, to reach a destination, towns and places serve as means to arrive at a house. Krentz uses these descriptions to ensconce her characters in a basic background against which the emotional side of the story can evolve, and this is a specification of the writing guidelines. In *Stormy Challenge,* a stormy ocean and an empty beach become a metaphor for the female protagonist's troubled feelings, but this is the only time Krentz uses a setting simile to reflect her character's feelings. Descriptions of settings nearly always remain basic, for example, a bar is like any bar of the same category, a restaurant like any restaurant of the same category, a third rate lodge like any third rate lodge. The reader forms a fleeting mental image from the brief informative descriptions because the plots move the story toward characters' actions, pushing the setting into the background and to the back of the reader's mind. She is not supposed to put in emotional and imaginative work to fill in a picture of the background because the characters' actions and emotions are of greater significance. Even so, this general depiction of a setting enables the reader, even a non-American one, to visualize her own brand of environment.

Although these descriptions of localities are on the short side, in Krentz's later novels they are semiotically charged, partly to portray characters, like in *Perfect Partners,* the building housing Thornquist Gear, Inc., which is a metaphor for the male protagonist's success in life, as well as developing into a significant tool in a decision hero and heroine have to make in order to meet their personal requirements. Or, the descriptions are semiotically charged, being set apart for decisive incidents, as in the case with the lake in *All Night Long,* offering the murderer unnoticed access to carry out his murders.

The timeline in all three novels stays chronological, a device that lets a reader enjoy the story without having to deal with the convolution of a disrupted one. Harlequin's or other romance publishing houses' guidelines dictate chronological timelines in their books. Novels told in a linear timeline offer easier reading, and therefore, are the preferred narrative method with genre fiction. Krentz has used the linear timeline from the beginning of her writing career. Over the years, she has taken to dedicating a prolog to events that have taken place before the actual story, or uses a character to report them: or, as she does in *All Night Long*, she uses a video document together with a prologue to report past events.

As readers prefer two perspectives in their love stories, and Krentz is not one to ignore mass market book readers' expectations, she stays within the appreciated two perspectives. Later, when her plots become more complex, she even adds other short perspectives in order to give more depth to a character other than the protagonists' characters, thereby moving from stock-characterization of secondary characters to making them at least two-dimensional as well as blending some mystery into the narrative (*All Night Long*). The complexity in *All Night Long* not only results from more subplots, but also from eight perspectives that introduce the reader to, sometimes cryptic, insights into different characters together with that of a third though deceased main character. *All Night Long*, timeline-wise and perspective-wise, seems to be of the highest degree of complexity a 'normal' romance reader is willing to go along with. As far as I can see, this novel is an exception among Krentz's novels, which tend to be less complex. Entertainment and 'easy reading' are a romance writer's goal, not literary complexity. Most of the 66 Amazon readers' reviews regard this novel as worth its hard-cover price: others would like less complexity or the crime part shortened, and a more centered love interest instead.[54] This might explain why Krentz returned to simpler novel constructions with her paranormal Arcane Society series from 2007 onward.

Although she always presents a well constructed, coherent plot, Krentz once admitted in an interview that plots are not her strong point. This is obvious in her first pure romance novels, where the only plot is the bone of contention between the protagonists of whether to have sex or not (e.g. *Stormy Challenge)*. There, the plot is not structured in the way that lets the tension build up to a climax. When Krentz changed her writing to the (category) romantic suspense, her plots improved, even if they were not unique: you can often guess who the culprit is, even though the suspense part guarantees suspense and a climax alongside the love story. Whatever flaws the story might reveal, Krentz always presents an intelligible, inherently consistent plot. In addition, she mostly creates a varied and interesting setting.[55] It is always a romance novel she is writing, where the suspense part rarely takes precedence over the romance one.

The later plots mostly contain only one or two subplots, which is not a complex pattern because the main theme is and continues to be the love story, even though, as happens in *All Night Long*, it seems to be relegated to a subplot. In *Perfect Partners,* the story is centered on the love story, and crime and family dynamics are supporting subplots. As the suspense in the plot eliminates the necessity of turning emotional ups and downs disproportionately into word battles, her narrative style also changes to a moderate one that no longer hints at being a romance story with the typical overinflated phraseology. Her writing style continues to be dialogical rather than narrative, but without the abundant use of dialogue tags of *Stormy Challenge*. Now, the dialogues no longer need overstated explanatory tags because the artificially set tempers of emotional outbursts, necessary to at least infuse a kind of tension, are taken over by the crime part in order to construct the storyline.

Moving from the category line to the romantic suspense line heralded an improvement in Krentz's plot-structures because now the crime provided the plot structure, and the lovers had a crime to contend with, therefore, not needing a love-hate pattern anymore. Krentz still writes romantic suspense novels, be they historical, contemporary, or futuristic albeit centered around her protagonists' various paranormal gifts. After all these years, the plot structures have become familiar to

---

[54] see Amazon's reader's 66 reviews on Krentz's *All Night Long*

[55] When an author has written over 150 books in the space of twenty-eight years not every one can be a masterpiece within the genre's criteria, but judging by the comments in readers' blogs she has written many that are considered as 'keepers'.

the readers, but they are still interesting because of the different settings. This does not mean that the stories are interchangeable, but that each story is given a subtle twist that is purely Krentz, as well as a criminal action that creates a convincing, often intriguing committing bond between the protagonists, beside their physical attraction. Thus, her novels remain romances.

As early as *Stormy Challenge*, even when bound to publishers' guidelines or editors' strict censorship, Krentz made her heroines fight their way into professional, personal, and sexual equality with their male partners. In 1992, when she stopped writing category romances, her heroines and heroes had for some years been acting on the level of equal terms, a fact that is essential to a positive feminist reading of the genre.

Krentz's narrative differs from that of other writers thanks to a tongue in cheek humor that coincides with the ease of her couples' bonding without fighting from the beginning of the story, this way overriding the love-hate formula. Moreover, she likes to use similes or metaphors as 'falcons' in the Boccaccian sense. As early as *Stormy Challenge,* she uses repeated similes, here that of a 'chain' that binds the couple together. Although used in a positive sense, it connotes marriage negatively because chains, even if they are 'golden', are still too restricting in the circumstances depicted there. Another repeated figure of speech is the metaphor of the ocean that symbolizes the heroine's feelings of both, turmoil and happiness. Here, Krentz's playful dry humor of later novels is not yet in evidence. In *Perfect Partners* Letty, the former librarian, has the habit of having read 'a couple of articles' about different topics: this remark is used like the literary 'falcon' as a connecting narrative line. Its repetition creates amusing uplifting interjections. Moreover, they serve a second objective: having read these articles enables the heroine to act appropriately in precarious situations, such as her stepmother unexpectedly giving birth in a remote cabin. *All Night Long* also offers a 'falcon', the expression 'to connect the dots'. Both hero and heroine try to analyze facts they know of or hear about, or find out, in order to solve the murders. They 'connect the dots' and, in the end, the solution is clear. This 'falcon' is not used in an amusing way because of the grave circumstances, but there are other scenes in the novel where Krentz's narrative wit emerges, infusing some respite from the seriousness of the theme. In addition, there is a repeated emphasis in *All Night Long* on the heroine's father's decency, not really a 'falcon', but perhaps this is done to contrast the morally debatable undercurrents depicted in the small seemingly intact rural community.

Krentz, I suppose, is appreciated by her audience because of her admittedly straightforward but not too simple plots, the interesting diversity of her contemporary novels' universe and backdrop, and her more character driven narratives, which keep her readers buying her books regularly. These books, often injected with paranormal pure fantasy, are located in an enjoyable wide variety of settings that sometimes have the makings of fairy tales: *Joy* 1988, *Wildest Hearts* 1993, *Hidden Talents* 1993, *Grand Passion* 1994, *Absolutely, Positively* 1996, *Smoke in Mirrors* 2002 to name but a few.

In the first of the three novels analyzed, *Stormy Challenge* (1982), characterization also differs greatly from the following two novels. The protagonists have no residual childhood turmoil, no emotional obstacles to contend with, other than a failed relationship on the heroine's side which did not damage her self-respect or her self-confidence. (If a reader were supposed to understand this heroine's aggressiveness as an indication of her damaged self-confidence, it would be explained within a story of this genre.) To compensate for a lack of tension, the language within the dialogues and especially the dialogue tags soars into emotional verbal, adverbial and adjective heights, hence making the story reasonably interesting for a reader who is only interested in an ongoing love story. The heroine's refusing his advances and the hero's taking no for an answer which leads to an aggressive verbal behavior on both sides, ends in an unbelievably blissful union. There is the expected advance and retreat pattern of the time, and the heroine's single perspective which the publishers' guidelines requested and which is an ideal device for making up one misunderstanding after the other, particularly when the heroine does not listen to what her partner is saying.

In a way, the characters' behavior and emotional contours seem to reflect attitudes and values of the North American society of their time (1982). The female protagonist of *Stormy Challenge* has already escaped the traditional ideas of womanhood and 1950s virtues. She lacks the nurturing side which was, and still is seen as a woman's most important character trait. She has become a woman of the 1980s who is accepted as a sexual being in her own right, and who is also convinced of vague feminist ideas of equality between men and women. Autonomy is spelled out in her double financial independence, first from inheritance and second from successfully running a bookshop on her own, even planning on opening a second store, but this aspect of her personality is only fleetingly touched upon. Autonomy is also spelled out in her, assumed, sexual relationship with a man before Court. Astonishingly, Court, who regards the heroine as his property, does not seem to mind her not being a virgin. Thus Krentz already severs her heroine from the reported publisher's premise of the traditional heroine's virginal status. But letting her heroine act as a successful entrepreneur as one feminist side of her is as far as Krentz is prepared to narratively go because she makes her heroine's emotional dressing reflect a girl's irresoluteness that does not tie in with her alleged mature feminist confidence. She even prompts her to explain that she would have given anything to have Court as husband (242). Such behavior is more typical of a romance category novel's narrative pattern than it is that of an independent woman. This still subservient female response to the hero is part of Krentz's Harlequin era.

The male protagonist of *Stormy Challenge* represents a romance novel patriarchal alpha male of his time. He is given all the right paraphernalia (looks, money, dominant behavior and, for the sake of the romance story, an assumed honorable character). Being on the threshold of a new age where women claim rights of equality which the female protagonist already verbally demands, he can still ignore these because, once expressed, they are of no significance for the development of the story. He does not, however, ignore sexuality, and he is driven by his own needs. All his aggressiveness is caused by sexual frustration and personal insecurity. He does not rate as a 'charismatic' male. As for lack of a better plot, the trope, sexuality, is the main topic in this book, his courting is more a pestering for sex in an astonishingly high degree of aggressiveness and his reason for marriage is to have unchallenged sex. Explicit sex scenes, therefore, are necessary and, of course, part of the author-reader contract of the time. Sexual intercourse, culminating in the best orgasm ever, is now the genre replacement for the heroine's deflowering, and enjoying sex becomes the trope for love.

Up to the late 1970s, the prototype heroine of the romance novel, and in particular that of historical romances, simply had to start out as a virgin. As to how, when and where in the story the virginity was lost or, better, taken, and just how explicitly this was related, depended on the author's moral values, the reader's moral expectations and, therefore, the publisher's moral guidelines, which have been modified in line with altered moral attitudes in society since 1975. Publishers have responded to readers' challenges, albeit gradually, Harlequin later than the others. It takes time to convert one ideology into another, trying to gain a new audience, while at the same time holding on to traditionally loyal readers. There are no virgins in Krentz's contemporary novels, not even in her early ones. There is just one exception, and here virginity plays a different role than the one expected in traditional romance novels (*Grand Passion* 1994). As far as I can see, virgins are part of Krentz's historical or futuristic romances. One fact, however, that has remained irrefutable for her protagonists is that sexual intercourse always led and leads to marriage. What already reflects a moral change of attitude in *Stormy Challenge* is that virginity or a demure sexual behavior before marriage being an essential characteristic of a respectable woman, is not picked out as central theme, although having or not having sex figures prominently in the story, but precisely not with the virginal or respectable womanly conduct demands of the 1960s in mind. The heroine resists the hero's sexual advances only because she does not trust him, an attitude that is chosen for the sake of the story's length, as is the love-hate pattern. But the trope trust, here thematized as part of the plot structure, is the underlying emotional premise for all of Krentz's protagonists' relationships.

The hero does not insist on his other right of having an untouched female, no matter what her age, as the moral expectation of his time. With regard to the way his behavior is presented this is not believable because, *expressis verbis*, he does not want his woman "making comparisons". Moreover, he is still a man deeply ingrained in his time, claiming his woman as his property, which he jealously guards and controls with a heavy hand. Thus, he assumes the unchallenged role as master in the relationship. Presumably, a 1982 reader found this coerced dependency of the female protagonist appealing. Even so, there is a hint of new times coming: the heroine is allowed to continue with her professional life for which, at least throughout the story, the hero does not contend with her. That fact, and that he does not insist on his wife being a virgin, shows a rift in his patriarchal attitude, along with his acquiescence in their both being "chained" to each other, a metaphor for marriage as a cage with not one, but two people inside.

Now that *Stormy Challenge* is available as a reprint, readers have posted their reactions to this book on the internet. Few are disconcerted by Court's macho behavior, but do not comment on his threatening the heroine with "I might find it more satisfying to beat you than to make love with you" or with "I'm in the mood to whale the daylights out of you, Leya, so you might want to exercise a bit of caution". (Most reviewers, however, seem to see only the happy ending.) Such a high degree of aggressiveness is not inscribed into the genre guidelines of the time, especially not in those for contemporary romances. The classic 'battle of the sexes' did not demand insinuated rape and threatened bodily punishment for a negligible misdemeanor. Surely the author did not want to construct her hero as a future wife-beater who cannot believably be turned into a peace-loving person just by marrying and having sex with the heroine. Why the Krentz novels of the early years contain this aggression is a mystery about which I can only speculate. Whether her change in hero characterization was caused by her own moral modification, the editors' advice to tone down her heroes' aggressiveness, or by readers' buying interventions, cannot be answered satisfactorily, but altered it is. She has never commented on it.

As Krentz did not seem to value the trope of virginity in her contemporary romances, she needed to create a convincingly matching partner for her non-virginal heroine, especially when publishers conceded two narrative perspectives. From about 1986 onwards she created and established her new hero, toning down overly patriarchal behavior and aggressiveness, but maintaining the heroic attributes. Although she was writing up to eight category romances a year, she seems to have found time to mentally reinvent both her protagonists, so that, in 1992, she was able to present a series of core characteristics which were to remain unchanged from that time onward.

In *Perfect Partners* and *All Night Long* there are repeated similarities that differ from *Stormy Challenge*. It seems that feminist influences have settled in people's minds and become commonplace during the last twenty years so that Krentz has been able to concentrate on her ideal relationships in variations (about 50 novels). The settings, characters, and plots change, but the recurring theme was, and is, an inherent world-view, displayed in the moral side of the characters. Her female characters are older, around thirty years of age, non-virgins, often divorced, but sexually not very experienced because even today this is an expected womanly virtue. They are average looking, which might be a modification issued by publishers' writing guidelines, and more on the slim and petite side. Their beauty and attractiveness is discovered in the eyes of their loving beholders. They are not vain, do not stand in front of their wardrobes endlessly wondering what to wear, their interests are not limited to shopping sprees or partying, which is often romance heroines' main interest, particularly in the so-called chick-lit where the tropes of shoe addicted or fashion addicted heroines are featured abundantly. Clothes, if they are mentioned at all, are semiotically charged. Whenever a protagonist's clothes are mentioned, it is usually done to indicate a unique character trait. In *Perfect Partners* the heroine wears glasses and usually looks a bit 'rumpled' in order to indicate her intelligence as well as her cosy emotionality. As such she is depicted in marked contrast to the hero's first lover, who is the elegantly dressed outward picture of perfection, and who thus, covers her insecurities. In *All Night Long* the female protagonist wears elegant black clothes, which are an expression of not yet having come to terms with her parents' death, not to mention her need to wear this 'uniform' "like a Kevlar vest". It is not so much their dress-codes, as the heroines' self-confident personalities that attract their lovers. They are professional women who do not need a man to support them and who are dedicated to their work and not to partying, something their men appreciate. Being of white middle to upper-class origin, they have college degrees that are not used to show off a knowledge of the beaux arts – unlike what is found in the novels of the English Queen of Romances Mary Stewart[56], an author who heavily influenced American writers of romantic suspense – but in their ability and skill to earn money. They are kind, active and courageous partners with good inter-communication skills, and an empathy that enables them to understand the psyche of their lovers. As such, they connect with their heroes as their soul-mates as well as sexually fulfilling lovers. They offer their male partners a home, nurturing them

---

[56]   In the 1980s, the Briton, Mary Stewart, was the writer an aspiring American romance writer was supposed to read – a Harlequin piece of advice – in order to see what the genre should be about.

on a diet of food and understanding. In Krentz's later single-title text worlds, this independent woman does not need to struggle for her feminist rights because they are already granted to her. She is never challenged in her right to think and act in whichever way she deems necessary, although, once she is in danger, the hero likes to remove her from the danger zone, albeit with her reluctant, but understanding consent. Whenever she displays her nurturing side as homemaker, it is her free decision to do this, but she is also responding to an ancient need to offer her alpha male, her 'warrior' – and in Krentz's romantic suspense, he really is that because he protects her from danger – a recreational homeport which is still the conservative idea of an American ideal family.

Authors of romance novels direct their narratives more on the aspect of *delectare* and *movere* than that of *docere*. The *delectare* part is ensured by a reader-friendly typography such as short chapters and usually more than three paragraphs on a page. Moreover, it is ensured by a reader friendly compliant to everyday language, by a *diegetic* tension curve, and by explaining the meaning of single action steps. But there still remains a small part dedicated to the aspect of *docere,* be it conscious or unconscious. One of Krentz's messages from the beginning of her writing career is that in the Land of Opportunity every (white) man or woman has the chance to take fate into his or her own hands, become successful and rich or at least financially secure, as long as they acquire the necessary educational background. At least since *Golden Chance* of 1990, she implies that the rules and conventions for a functional society are founded in well matched couples and strong positive family bonds that add stability to that frail institution of marriage because without family bonds and a well suited partner, life could become unsatisfactory and lonesome. That is in the background of her stories while the matching of a couple for a(n) (un)imaginable lifetime commitment stays in the foreground.

The novel's message to the readers about how the ideal female woman should be is as follows: she should be a mature, self-confident, educated, professional woman whose emphatic traits make her the counterpart to her man and who sticks to the notion of heaven ever after only when she puts some effort into the relationship. The reader might, unconsciously, realize and learn that what is important in a relationship is the intelligent use of her own womanly faculties, similar ethical goals and similar moral priorities to those of her partner, and, apart from that, a give and take by both partners, as well as an active participation in forming and maintaining a relationship, not a passive acceptance of fate and man. "With courage, intelligence, and gentleness she brings the most dangerous creature on earth, the human male, to his knees. More than that, she forces him to acknowledge her power as a woman". Thus, the woman always wins. Krentz and her fellow-writers refer to this undercurrent message as 'empowerment' of their female readers. I cannot agree with this statement because first it is misandrist and secondly Krentz's heroes are never "brought to their knees" (both citations DMAW 5). This viewpoint clashes with her protagonists' consensual bonding, and not only with their sexual bonding, at an early stage in the novel. One aspect, however, remains unalteredly patriarchal in Krentz's novels: the heroines obtain their worth as individuals by means of the subjective evaluation of their men who usually, with virtually no exceptions, take the initiative in the relationship and, who are protectors of their women and family, but never turn out to be abusive. There is no longer any question of their becoming abusive once they are married, unlike in *Stormy Challenge* where this is a development which is strongly hinted at.

Krentz creates a subliminal shaping of a womanly ideal by offering seemingly unreal, but strikingly personal fantasies to readers which, in fact, correspond with women's dreams which have been the subject of research on the part of the publishers. These ideals are paid regard to in Krentz's text worlds and thus serve as buying and reading incentives. A buyer of romance novels can choose according to her own predilection within the range of what millions of other women want to read. She, therefore, chooses to buy books that reinforce her already existing moral tendencies. Krentz's characters' characteristics seem to meet the specifications of her many readers. Reading about courageous, intelligent, college educated, loyal women appears to serve her audience's current personal ideas, moral convictions, and wishful thinking.

Romance novelists do not like to dwell on the lower classes because they construct their protagonists according to publishers' writing guidelines or because the fantasy is more effective when it is presented with rich protagonists. They do not present their readers with poverty, abuse, alcoholism, etc., at least they do not let these things happen to their protagonists at the time the story is told without a *deus ex machina* up their narrative sleeves. On the other hand, the high life of the rich and famous does not serve as a background against which success, upward-mobility and love are measured. In her novels, Krentz stays with the rich working people who find their meaning in life in working and in having a family, as well as taking an active part in idealized, fairy-tale-like family dynamics. This applies to all of Krentz's contemporary romantic suspense novels.

Preferably one or both protagonists have had disastrous childhoods or youths, or similar devastating episodes to overcome and escape, and are still struggling emotionally to get over them. At the time of the romance novel's story, the upwardly-mobile white hero has gained his financial independence, and in Krentz's novels he has reached the stage where his reputation as an overachiever in his chosen professional field precedes him: in *Stormy Challenge* he is a successful consultant with no family connections that could indicate the social class he comes from; in *Perfect Partners* his family was pure working class and he, himself, also worked in a boat yard before being forced to flee the town. Now he is a chief executive officer of the large company he built from scratch for himself and the heroine's uncle, and this company becomes the economically secure basis for both protagonists to appreciate each others' faculties. In *All Night Long* the hero's social background is upper class, but he chose not to join the family business. He was an excellent Marine and, added to this, he earned a Ph.D. in philosophy, his studies initially paid for by his family. Having inherited and saved enough money to live comfortably, he is able to pursue his goal of writing a book.

With the daily uncertainty of how to earn his living out of the way – although the Krentz hero still is deeply involved in his work and will never lead a life of leisure – now, the time has come to focus on the hero's emotional side. For this he needs the support of an equally financially secure – though not rich – emphatic, intelligent woman who is also able to understand and possibly discuss his professional problems, as well as being sexually attractive to him and in love with him. She will save him from the inner loneliness and emptiness he has just discovered now, at the beginning of the novel, having achieved his career goals. She introduces the new element of love he was subconsciously longing for by giving his life a new direction toward a satisfying togetherness (a little in *Stormy Challenge*, completely in *Perfect Partners* and *All Night Long*). Sometimes the heroine is a self-made woman, sometimes she struggles to make ends meet, and sometimes she inherited money and tries to build up her own business: the heroes, however, are always economically more highly rated.

Traditional romance novel heroes need washboard 'abs' and male butts to be physically attractive to their heroines. Krentz's male protagonists stay in superb physical condition, even when nearing forty, the reason for which she explains satisfyingly in *Perfect Partners* and *All Night Long*: Joel in *Perfect Partners* runs or works out to overcome his nightmares and Luke's working out in *All Night Long* is a habit that he has maintained from his former military life. Thus, it is not out of vanity that they stay trim and fit. This physical fitness, moreover, is required for the suspense part of her romances. In her romantic suspense novels, the male protagonists are characterized as follows: first, there are their professional abilities, which they utilize within their powers. Sometime in their past, they did a military stint – where and when is usually not divulged – which, secondly, enables them to defend their loved ones in danger. In many novels, the male characters practice martial arts.[57] The feeling of having the right to take the law into one's own hands seems to be part of an upright fictional contemporary American and, therefore, finds its way into that kind of romance. Krentz, however,

---

[57]   e.g. *Golden Chance*. 1990, *Family Man*. 1992, *Trust me*. 1995, etc.

differentiates: her heroes protect their own, but rarely with weapons. The acting out of the conviction of having the right to take the law into their own murdering hands is accorded to the powerful wealthy criminals. (*Perfect Partners, All Night Long*)

Krentz's ideal American from the late 1980s onward is a man who, in his heart of hearts, is integer (if he does not plainly show it from the beginning, his female partner will make him aware of it, as it happens in *Perfect Partners* and even more so in *Wildest Hearts* of 1993), decent, and honest. At the beginning of the romance, his emotional side is allowed to appear only in his sexual drive, which he shares with the heroine on a consensual basis. Once he has found his soul-mate, he yields to his deeper feeling that is love, but that also is expressed in the spectacular sex the couple enjoys. He initiates the beginning of their sexual relationship, and, because of his greater experience, he is the master on this playing field: she, however, learns quickly to become his equal partner in sexual matters which he, modern man that he is, enjoys vastly. With Krentz, sex, seen as part of an evolving process of a relationship, is a coming together that only further underscores an already satisfying unity. The physical aspect, the instant sexual attraction and surrendering to it on both sides, leads straight to marriage in a Krentz novel and the hero proves to be good husband material and a dedicated family man.

The kind of married life the protagonists of a Krentz romance will lead will be based on an ongoing professional career on both sides and on a continuous and very sexually oriented relationship, total mutual trust and honesty and the knowledge that one will always stand by the other. Whenever his male services are required, like physically protecting the woman the hero loves, he will take charge whereas, she will interfere in interpersonal situations he, being the stereotypical man, is not adept at handling, a fact he knows and gratefully cedes to her, which, in turn, empowers her part in the relationship. But when all is said and done, the power structure in Krentz's novels stays with the man at the centre while the woman surrounds him with her love, which he needs, her trust, which he needs, her loyalty, which he needs. She rescues him from the solitary life of a lone wolf. In return she receives his unconditional love and protection, satisfying sex and a baby. Readers agree with the opinion that America needs such able, intelligent men and women in reality as they are the backbone of a society.

Krentz's stories are formulaic in the sense that crime stories are also formulaic. They are stories with a twist. Her characters, both male and female, are whole, not fragmented individuals, are stereotypes in their moral attitudes of honesty, decency, courage and dependency, but different otherwise. Once she adds crime to her stories the suspense curve clearly follows that of a three act drama.

Krentz's text world is restricted, and, therefore, easy to comprehend. Local descriptions are of the generic kind because the stories could happen anywhere with a fairly mild climate. In her fictional world, everyone has a psychological problem of a varying degree of seriousness to surmount, but the problems are solved within the narrative and do not need further pondering, a fact that makes the novel an 'easy read'. As the reason for every action is satisfactorily explained from a psychological point of view, the reader does not have to fill any blanks that are left with her own musings. This way, complexity is reduced by explanation and by omission: omission of topics like political, economic or societal problems that would connect disturbingly with the nonfictional world. Krentz's contemporary characters are Americans without immigrant roots[58] and they do not care to leave the USA other than to serve their country in wars etc. (*All Night Long*). They personify the Land of Opportunity (*Stormy Challenge, Perfect Partners, All Night Long*). Societal and economic conflicts are understood as a personal history of success or failure which thus avoids criticism of real political states of affairs.[59]

Her characters, mostly self-employed, do not regard class distinctions or different levels of education as an obstacle for their love and married life. (In *Perfect Partners*: the heroine's academic education versus the hero's self-made man's ideology, and in *All Night Long*: the heroine's modest origins versus the hero's rich, academic upbringing.) What matters in this text world are character traits like innate intelligence, courage, integrity and fidelity.

There are also omissions of the possible role religion could play in this contemporary romance novel world, maybe in order to make the novel amenable to a pluralistic audience. Krentz's characters have no connection to any religious group. Yet, they are not atheists. By belonging to no religious group, they do not offend any believers. Religion simply is not important in their lives: they even live with the absence of a divine being. Happiness promised by the ideal marriage, replaces the promised happiness in the world to come.

Avoidance by omission plays into the hands of critics who argue that contemporary romance novels should not preserve conservative ideals and thinking. But it seems that Krentz's novels reflect the *Zeitgeist*, a mixture of political conservatism and of feminist demands, and, moreover, they are emotional fictive stories without references to the real world with its regard for pressing concerns and religious influences. However there are many links in her romance novels that connect with the readers' *zeitgeisty* emotionality and their fantasies of being and behaving like the heroine: the underlying humor in her single titles, the way the heroines solve problems for their heroes (*Perfect Partners, All Night Long*), the way the hero begins to appreciate the heroine in other ways than simply finding her attractive,

---

[58] See Nora Roberts' completely different fictional world in this respect.

[59] Aspects of politics and religion play a part in Krentz's futuristic novels: *Amaryllis, Zinnia, Orchid*.

the way he projects his own dependability, and the way he gives her exceptional sexual experiences. It is not a structural, politically correct investigation of life the reader is interested in a romance novel: she wants to be approached emotionally. In *Dangerous Men and Adventurous Women,* Krentz argues that the success of romance authors is based on how compellingly they can create their fantasy and on how "accessible they can make their fantasies" to the readers (Krentz 1992, 4). She seems to succeed in doing this continually as is borne out by her almost permanent presence on the NY Times bestseller lists.

To summarize what transpires as a constant in Krentz's novels is that

a) Krentz stays within the genre, romance novel, but changes to romantic suspense novels

b) her writing style remains dialogical, although she moderates it to a balance between dialogue without an overuse of explanatory dialogue tags and narrative parts

c) the plots stay consistent and the timeline linear

d) settings are in north-west or western USA and there, Seattle is the preferred town as starting point or reference point

e) the protagonists are not beautiful: the heroine is comely, the hero handsome, but then, beauty is in the eye of their loving beholder

f) the development of the love story takes place within a short space of time, no more than six weeks

g) heterosexual intercourse between white upper middle class people leads to marriage and having a family

h) sexuality plays a prominent part, although in the novels from 1992 onward, it becomes one of other expressions of the existing already emotional bonding between the protagonists. Moreover, there is the perpetual dilemma for the author to portray sexual equality while at the same time trying not to blur the distinctive traits between the sexes

i) the hero is as central to the story as the heroine

j) the stories often provide the illusion of fantasy tales; they come across as being fictional, even when their frame of reference seems to be grounded in reality

k) 'falcons' in the Boccaccian sense are used

What transpires as change is that

a) the romance novel pattern of love and hate between the protagonists is absent in her novels from 1986 onwards

b) the typical time-related genre romance novel ideation of the dominant heroes and malleable heroines changes to that of moderate heroes who are not deprived of their masculinity despite their moderate views concerning patriarchy, and who become aware of their own emotionality; and of heroines who use their intelligence, common sense, and typical feminine abilities. This is a monumental change

c) the plot is augmented by one or two subplots and the number of perspectives is increased

d) the language changes from florid to unobtrusive American English

e) Krentz develops a subtle humor in her narratives that emerges through some short remarks in certain situations

The question whether a typical voice can be determined, can be answered as follows: a novel by Krentz is recognizable from the 1990s onwards by her choice of her characters within often unorthodox settings and a consistent presentation of her protagonists' character traits which personify traditional moral values and the firm belief in families as the backbone of a society. Her subtle humor is another typical identifying feature, as is her placing of 'falcons' in the Boccaccian sense. Although these are identifying features they widen the scope of the genre slightly, but do not go beyond.

3.2 ANALYSIS OF THREE NOVELS WRITTEN BY BARBARA DELINSKY

3.2.1 *Sweet Ember*

In 1981 Delinsky published her first three novels with the romance novel publishing house Dell. This American publishing house together with other American publishers became aware of their readers' changing reading preferences more quickly than Harlequin and contracted US American writers. *Sweet Ember* was one of three category romance novels published that year and the only one available at the time I began my research.

SUMMARY

Stephanie Wright is asked to teach photography at a summer camp in Maine. Stephanie had spent ten summers there, first as a camper, later as a counselor. Eight years before, at this summer camp, Stephanie fell in love with and lost her virginity to the tennis instructor, Doug Weston, on the last night of the camp. The following morning she encountered Diana Weston at his cabin and, assuming she was Doug's wife, she fled back home to Cambridge. She burnt the many letters Doug wrote her without reading them. Now, eight years later, she allows herself to return to work there after she is assured she can take his and her daughter Melissa (Missy) as a camper with her. At the camp she discovers that Doug not only is there, but he also is head of the tennis department and head counselor. Doug is just as shocked as Stephanie to have her on the team. Stephanie evades his company.

They are not able to communicate openly because each seems to have been hurt by the other and their talks are evasive.

Having inherited her father's sportiness, Melissa attracts Doug's attention and soon they develop a special relationship. When he discovers that Stephanie is Melissa's mother he remarks nastily that by deflowering her he obviously had prepared her for many men after him. Once, they are forced to spend their day off together with a counselor couple who seem to be informed about Doug's life outside the camp of which Stephanie has no knowledge. Reluctantly, Doug reveals to her that he is a psychology teacher and the president of a college, but why he works at the summer camp remains a mystery.

At parents' weekend, Doug finally realizes that Melissa is his daughter. This new shock enables him to confess that more than anything else he wants Stephanie back, but she assumes he wants Melissa and not her. From then on Doug seeks out her company.

Two weeks before the end of camp, Stephanie's house in Cambridge is broken into and they both go there to talk to the police and put everything back to order. Being alone with no one to intrude, they spend a blissful night together. The next morning Stephanie agrees to marry Doug. Despite that, back at the camp, he behaves coldly, and is brusque and stand-offish toward her, an attitude she finds inexplicable.

On the last day of camp, Melissa breaks her foot and is taken to a hospital nearby by Doug who later berates Stephanie for neglecting her maternal duties. After the farewell banquet in the evening, Stephanie refuses to spend the night with Doug reasoning that he does not love her because she is hurt by his cold and aggressive behavior. The next morning, the day of departure, Doug asks her to talk things out when everyone has left camp. He pretends to take Melissa for a walk so that Stephanie can pack, when actually he takes her to meet his family. Since they have not arranged where to talk, Stephanie goes to his cabin and there, as she did eight years before, she meets Diana, Doug's sister, who is packing his things. Now her misconception about Diana's position in the family is cleared up. Overcome with remorse, she flees to 'their' clearing in the woods where Doug finds her. They talk at last and celebrate their reunion with a bout of ecstatic lovemaking. In the end they decide on a honeymoon somewhere in Vermont instead of Paris because this town would intrude too much on their getting to know each other.

PLOT, CHAPTERS, TIME, AND SETTING

The plot of *Sweet Ember* is a typical 1980s category romance novel plot. According to publishers' guidelines, the protagonists should be introduced early on in the story. Here, in the introductory exposition in the first chapter (1–32) the protagonists meet – and this is a moment of utter shock – right at the end of the second chapter. The reader, however, is already well informed about the protagonists' relational past that resulted in a child, unbeknownst to him, the heroine's (sexual) longing for the hero, and her professional achievements. As the story focuses on the development of a relationship, it needs to receive incentive incidents from the outside to structure the story. The first is to bring the former lovers together. The director of the camp sees to this. The second is initiated by a couple of co-workers who force the lovers to spend the day together in truce and so they relearn to appreciate each other. The third happens at the parents' weekend where an outsider causes Doug to realize that Melissa is his daughter. A break-in at Stephanie's house gives the lovers an opportunity to sleep with each other away from the camp. A fifth climactic incident typical of romance novels is illness, in this case Melissa's broken foot. Here this incident is used to allow the antagonism to flare up for the last time between the lovers. The love story is led to a denouement by Doug's sister. This way the story mirrors the structure of the three act drama with a slight suspense curve. (The story also contains the eight essential narrative elements that, according to Pamela Regis defines a romance.)

Sweet Ember consists of nine chapters and is 233 pages long. The chapters are numbered, written in letters, and the first letter of the chapters is marked as an oversized bold capital one. A kind of underlined garland above the chapter number adorns the first page of each chapter and the tops of the following pages have the author's name (pages with even numbers) and the novel's title (uneven numbers) both divided from the text by a line. The chapter length varies between thirty-three and nineteen pages. Only once does a chapter end in the evening and the following chapter beginning the next morning. Otherwise days change into weeks within the chapters. Even a structural highlight, like the day off, spent in Ogunquit, does not rate starting its own chapter. It is placed in the middle of chapter five and there it fills eighteen of the thirty-three pages. Moreover, at the end of the chapters, Stephanie nearly always deals in thoughts with her dilemma of loving Doug, but not wanting him to know it and telling herself she is her own mistress. This way there is a consistent ending to the chapters. Written in the epic preterite, *Sweet Ember* is a contemporary novel of the early 1980s.

The love story evolves within eight weeks of summer camp time. Two analepses in the heroine's mind take the reader eight years back in time, and in detail, inform her of the past love story and defloration, make her understand the implications of it, and expect 'nice' complications. Other than those two mental analepses at the beginning, the novel's story is told in chronological order. As there are no detailed accounts of those sixty days, large time gaps result and so, for the reader to have a clue of time, references of time are given in week intervals.

In one of her interviews, Delinsky says that she tries to put the local settings of her novels alternately in the six New England States. Here, the locations are a camp in Maine near Montpelier, [60] Cambridge, Stephanie's home, and Ogunquit, a town at the seaside. A location that is only mentioned, is Doug's property in the mountains and the houses on it in the north of Vermont. Delinsky's descriptions of local settings are usually more elaborate than is routine in category romance novels. Here, the surrounding area, e.g. that of the camp, is described more expansively than any landscape in novels by Krentz. The descriptions also are more likely to be anchored in reality:

> One by one, the old familiar landmarks appeared as Stephanie maintained a safe but steady speed on the country road. There was the movie house in which she had spent many an evening, both as an old camper and as a counselor. There was the fish house, where they had bought lobsters to boil on the beach. There was the ancient signpost, a veritable circus of pointing arrows which, when properly deciphered, directed the wanderer to this camp. There was the old and stately inn, somewhat more weathered but functional nonetheless, where her parents had stayed, year after year, on visitor's weekend.
>
> "Look, Missy. There is our lake!" she exclaimed, helplessly caught up in the nostalgia of the moment, the excitement increasing with their impending arrival. Melissa got up onto her knees to look out her mother's window for her first glimpse of Blue Willow Lake, its surface gently dappled by the soft breeze which ruffled it. Then it was gone, hidden once more behind the protective barrier of trees. Very gradually the road sloped upward, the lush greenery of the roadside giving way to amber hues of wild grasses. They drove past a small farm, or what had once been a farm, though even as a camper Stephanie had seen the dismantled plows and wagon wheels, now given over to rust and the elements, yet still suggestive of the once thriving enterprise that had been reduced to a nearby henhouse and a small herd of dairy cows.
>
> Just as the car reached the top of the climb, Stephanie made a sharp left on a minimally paved road, part tar, part gravel, as it had always been ...
> (23)

It takes another page of depicting this landscape before Stephanie and Melissa reach the main lodge of the camp. Descriptions of this length go on, be they of Stephanie's cabin or her darkroom, or of the town and the beach of Ogunquit, etc. This way the reader is given an opportunity to imagine the places and picture herself there as well. Wherever the characters move, the reader can follow them,

---

[60] Delinsky writes in "A Note from the Author" on the first page of the novel before the title: "*Sweet Ember* has a special place in my heart, in that the model I used for PineWinds was the summer camp I attended for seven years as a child. Those seven summers were the happiest and most carefree of my childhood. Writing *Sweet Ember* took me back there, just as rereading it does now." (Foreword to the reprint in 1997.)

possibly even find her way back without help. Description of places show no relations to correlate with distinctive character traits just as Krentz sometimes uses them. They only provide the opportunity to remember past feelings and experiences.

Work related text passages again inform the reader what Stephanie's tasks at the camp are about, and her use of analogous photography with its necessity for a well-equipped darkroom at the summer camp shows how dated the novel is. Considering the genre of the novel, however, there is ample information outside the love story which might delight a reader or disgruntle one who is not interested in extensive descriptions.

Social differences do not transpire clearly at a summer camp in the way they would in a text-intern everyday world. The camp hosts girls of affluent parents, and the instructors there seem to share their social background. In any case, the hero is well-off, and as a teacher and the president of a college, he is a respected member of his social group. The heroine's parents seemed to have been moneyed enough to afford to send their daughter to summer camp.

CHARACTER CONSTELLATIONS

MALE PROTAGONIST

As Doug Weston is only seen through Stephanie's eyes, the reader can imagine him by his actual words in direct speech or by what Stephanie notices about him. Thirty-eight years old, his dark hair already has some silver in it, he is of superb physique, tall, lean, with broad shoulders, narrow waist and hips, bronzed and sinewy legs, and "heart-throbbing good looks" (17), a typical romance hero model of the 1980s. Eight years before Stephanie was drawn to him by "the intensity of one-way gray eyes, seeing all, but letting no-one see within ... There had indeed been a quality of mystery about him" and, at the time, as "a superb and diligent tennis instructor during the day, he earned a reputation as the rogue of the night, indulging in the passing fling, then moving on" (16). When she found out that his reputation in no way approached reality "his gentle camaraderie, his subtle wit, his innate intelligence" (17) charmed her. Within the story, however, he only comes across as an incommunicative person.

Eight years later she meets this man who still is all she had noticed before and his career shows how much he is appreciated at the camp. It takes weeks for him to realize he has a daughter. Only then he, reluctantly, reveals to Stephanie details about his professional life outside the camp. He feels so strongly about his privacy – which is alluded to in the description at the beginning of he story (16) – that she virtually knows nothing about his social circumstances. He exhibits "a specter of the unfathomable anger that had possessed him at the start of the summer" (153) when asked to talk about his life in winter. His secretiveness is the basis on which the story is constructed. If he had told Stephanie about his family, she would not have jumped to the conclusion, based on his camp reputation, that his sister was his wife. Recurrently he "wants to talk this out", subconsciously, however, he postpones it to the following day when new situations will arise which need to be dealt with, so he remains unenlightened until the next time. This behavior indicates either an indifference to Stephanie's persona or an unwillingness to have to reciprocally provide information about himself, once she comes to mean more to him.

He is said to teach psychology at his school, but he does not seem to have internalized anything of what he teaches. Talking about his personal doubts and seeking answers by simply asking straight questions is not his way. At the very end of the novel it is revealed that, during the story, he fights an inner battle between his renewed love for Stephanie and the deep hurt caused by his lack of knowledge about why she ran away from him after their 'wonderful' night together. This hurt is shown in his unpredictable and contradictory behavior. Moreover, blinded by inner turmoil and jealousy when he learns she has a child he instantly assumes that Stephanie had turned into a loose woman after her initiation by him: this is a typical romance novel inference, a narrative device to erect the emotional barrier between the lovers. He bottles up his emotions or whatever concerns him privately and is not able to share or communicate this outside his family. Other than his extreme reticence with private information about himself, he is said to be popular with the campers, and is said to show extraordinary leadership qualities, neither of which a reader can witness in detail.

For a reader of the new millennium, it is astonishing to read about how uninhibitedly – and as if it were the most natural thing in the world – the tennis instructor Doug touches the children and young girls and e.g. lets someone else's daughter ride on his shoulders or sit on his lap: "Particularly when, after they'd finished eating, Melissa threw herself onto Doug's lap and lounged contentedly, her head against his chest, his arms encircling her small body" (119). This incident also shows the datedness of the novel, the shift in the moral assessment of politically correct conduct. Nowadays, allowing a child to do this, he would be in danger of being charged with child abuse. In 1981 this situation only emphasized a fictional unbiased way of expressing what a good relationship he is able to build up between himself as a teacher and his pupil although, even then, public opinion was alert to abusive behavior.

FEMALE PROTAGONIST

Like most category romance novel heroines of the 1980s, Stephanie Wright, 27 years old and eleven years younger than Doug, can "hold her own to any beauty" (26) with auburn curls, jade eyes and a slim body. She comes from an upper middle class family that cherished books and other cultural things and was wealthy enough to send the girl to the expensive summer camp for years and later, pay for Stephanie's and Melissa's keep until Stephanie was able to earn her own living. There is no mention of her having been ostracized for conceiving a child out of wedlock with no father on the scene.

Having been an overprotecting mother since Melissa's birth, Stephanie now has emotional difficulties separating from the child. As, fortunately, she is allowed to work in the camp at the same time, she will be nearby, should anything occur. To her relief, she finds out that Melissa is a happy camper. During Melissa's preschool years Stephanie taught herself photography and for three years prior to the novel's story, she had "taught photography part-time at two exclusive private schools, pioneering in the formation of a photography curriculum for children" (6). (This truly is a romance story, as at the time of Melissa's babyhood in the late 1970s, an unwed mother would not have been allowed to teach any subject without moral reservations of the parents. Here, holding the teaching position seems to be uncomplicated.) Her tasks at the camp are to document the entire camp season for a book on Pine Winds and to teach photography at every level. As she is not a confrontational person, she jumps to conclusions rather than ask for explanations. So, too insecure to face a conflict, she ran back home and burnt the letters Doug wrote without reading them, instead of confronting him. Like Doug, she also is said to be a private, well liked person. She is totally involved in her work and determined to excel at it and be successful. Determination to gain control of her life, as well as independence, does not extend to her feelings. Inwardly, she lets her emotions run away with her. The Doug who seemed to love her, and their one night together, is constantly on her mind and his daughter, who is his spitting image, is the perennial reminder of her love. At the age of nineteen

> it was a combination of pride and fear which kept her from prying, (into his life outside the camp) pride in her own strength and that of their relationship, yet fear of delving into another life in which she might never belong. (18)

At the age of twenty-seven, it still is pride and fear that keeps her from forcing him to reveal his circumstances. Doug, their relationship and the many implications, their love and his enigmatic behavior, disturb and intimidate her. As speaking in explicit terms is not the way they converse, neither knows where they stand in their relationship. She always muses that she loves him, no matter what his feelings for her are, daydreams and is unable to act. Their inability to share feelings erodes Stephanie's self-confidence, especially after their night in Cambridge when Doug's mood worsens and she has no idea why. Again, she distrusts her ability to judge people correctly. Her self-confidence at rock-bottom, she can only ask 'timidly' at the hospital what happened to Melissa and is berated by Doug for her irresponsibility, again. She accepts some responsibility for Doug's behavior, although what the cause might be eludes her, a typical trait instilled into women in romance novels of the patriarchal category and in real life.

> Grounded by heavy silence, a current of tension staticked through the air.
>
> "Look, Stephanie." Doug finally broke the stillness, his face a closed mask of steel confronting her. "I know you're not terribly pleased that I'm here, or, for that matter, that I exerted my own authority to have Melissa treated by my friend, but I have only done what I believe best for my child."
>
> "She's mine, too, Doug, or are the last seven years suddenly worth nothing?" Again she was shocked at the vengeful pitch of her own words, puzzled as much by it as by Doug's entire manner toward her. Had he tired of her so quickly after but one night of pleasure? Or did he simply despise her so much?
>
> Thunderous sparks grated against gray flint. "You'd better make up your mind, Steph. You can't have it both ways. Either you trust my instincts and accept me as the rightful father of your child or you stay the hell away!" Her gasp of disbelief was met by a fast receding expanse of back, as Doug returned to the less explosive atmosphere of the waiting room.
>
> What did he want? her senses screamed. Was he saying that he didn't want to marry her? Was he saying that he would live without Melissa after all? Or – and her stomach lurched at the sudden thought – was he telling her to leave Melissa with him and desert them both? Was that at the crux of his earlier accusation? (206–207)

Pondering over the underlying subtext of his words, rather than inquiring what he actually wants to say, has always been her way of interacting. Only after she discovers that not questioning impressions wrought, and continues to wreak havoc in her life, is she able to tell Doug why she really ran away all those years ago, and that she loves him. At last she can verbalize her emotions, but for how long, since she is so much in awe of Doug's overwhelming personality?

The figural constellation between the protagonists clearly displays an imbalance of power within the relationship. The man is given all the control to wield and to dispense feel-good factors.

SECONDARY CHARACTERS

Melissa, Stephanie's and Doug's daughter, plays an important role as part of the story's structure. She provides turning points, like Doug's discovery that Stephanie has a daughter, then, that she is his daughter, then, breaking her leg for the sake of bringing antagonistic feelings to explode or instigating a Point of Ritual Death in the relationship. Apart from that, she is given characteristics that behoove an adult, but are rendered only in words, not in actions. Being her father's image his genes also are prevalent:

> An athletic child, she was a fine little swimmer and a promising tennis
> player, even at her tender age.
>   Additionally, she never had trouble making friends, nor been bothered
> by the lack of them, all of her protestations to the contrary not withstand-
> ing. She was an independent soul, a loner, who went her own way whether
> in the company of friends or not. She was a self-motivator, a hard worker,
> and a hard player, whose instinct for superiority was threatened only by an
> underlying distrust of people, a characteristic which her mother recognized
> and for which she accepted the responsibility. (3)

Throughout the novel, however, she is only the little girl who needs and receives
her father's attention and his love.

All the other characters play a very small role in the story. Descriptions of their
looks and hints of characterizations are conveyed, e.g. Silvie's husband Sonny: he
is said to be a shy, quiet man and a surrogate grandfather (96), but is not allocated
one scene in the novel where he can act out his grandfatherly inclinations. The
other characters support the protagonists by giving them opportunities to reunite
(Silvie), to re-value each other (Elaine and Bob), and to give the story the much
needed climax (Diana), but they merely appear to carry out their task. These small
roles of the minor characters are congruous with publisher's writing guidelines.

CONFLICT, RELATIONSHIP, AND EROTIC SCENES

Stephanie requires a great deal of courage to return to the place where she loved,
felt humiliated and which ultimately she fled from. She wants to lay to rest the
ghost of a relationship that haunts her relentlessly. Her inner conflict is the love
for Doug she has never been able to get over, and her inability to communicate.
Doug seems to have an inner conflict, too, but as the novel is told completely from
Stephanie's perspective, his incomprehensible, irrational behavior just leaves the
characters to deal with it, willy-nilly, and the reader as well, unenlightened to a
high degree, so that they cannot comprehend his behavior. Only in the end does he
confess to having been confused and jealous, which seems to justify his behavior
to Stephanie. Since he is just as incapable of disclosing his feelings as she is,
their relationship cannot develop into something deeper. Like in Krentz's *Stormy
Challenge*, the following game of advance and retreat is played out, this time,
however, from the male protagonist's side and, naturally, in a different way: their
accidental or not so accidental meetings end in them both being frustrated. The
assumption of her having slept with other men allows him to sexually arouse them
both. He surprises her in the shower cabin to confront her in the way of the battle
of the sexes hinting at rape romance novels of that time:

> Angrily he put a hand to her hair, long strong fingers intertwining then
> pulling cruelly to tilt her head back. Her mouth opened in a cry of pain,
> only to be smothered further by the lips which reclaimed hers, the tongue

which launched a vicious invasion of her mouth's recesses. Frantically she
fought him, pushing against his chest and kicking his legs … "

He deftly unties the belt of her robe and takes it off and touches her
body, exploring her intimately and a little later, cupping her breasts to play
with the nipples. Fury changes to raw desire and turns to passionate tenderness so that the hint of a rape turns nonexistent …

As she gazed into that once-beloved and loving face, it lowered, and his
lips tasted her once more, now warmly, sweetly, full of the tenderness and
desire which welled within her own. (83–90)

Then he stops short of making love and disappears, leaving Stephanie worrying
about his whereabouts, but also devastated. Her sexual frustration increases. Cor-
nered by matchmaking co-counselors, they endure each others' company. He tries
to control his anger and frustration, and, to moderate the tension between them,
he negotiates a truce for the day. They go to a musical in the evening, in formal
clothes, which, for Stephanie, is something like an aphrodisiac and she spends the
ride back to the camp in his arms. Yet, the next few days pass as if the time at the
beach had never happened.

> She saw Doug daily, though he never stopped for more than a brief greeting.
> If he had felt anything special on that mutual day off, he certainly made no
> mention of it. Yet, she mused, following one quick run-in on the porch after
> dinner, there seemed to be a remnant of that same truce in effect, such that
> they could be friendly and amenable toward one another, with none of the
> simmering anger and open disdain shown in the past. (117)

Again, Doug leaves the camp site without a word when he discovers he is
Melissa's father. Stephanie manages to assure him that she has never been with
anyone but him, and, again, they are about to make love, only this time it is
Stephanie who stops them, remembering his imagined marital status. From now
on, whenever he has time, he is in Stephanie's vicinity. Stephanie tries to keep the
sexual tension between them at bay by evasion, always aware of how explosive
this is. At last they can give in to their sexual hunger during the night they spend in
Cambridge. The description of the seduction and love scene takes six pages. They
make love three times (185–191) which leads to his marriage proposal. During
that night she realizes that:

> she could not live without Doug. Whether he loved her or not, she knew that
> she needed and wanted him …   In those hours of exquisite lovemaking,
> her decision had been made for her …   And, whether he wanted her as
> mistress, lover, wife, or mother of his child, she knew she had no choice but
> to agree. (190)

The narrative climax on page 191 leaves forty-two pages to fill. So having agreed
to his proposal, Stephanie gets a brotherly kiss and from then onward, throughout

the last two weeks of camp time, or forty pages, Doug's behavior grows colder and more formal by the day. Just why he behaves like that he seems unable to articulate, teacher of psychology he is. He only vents whatever his frustrations are by accusing Stephanie of being irresponsible at trivial incidents, thus establishing his superior role in the relationship. Still feeling insulted by this, she refuses his sudden desire to go to bed with her. Since both are unable to express clearly what they think, they perpetually misunderstand each other:

> Whether the darkness was within or without, Stephanie no longer knew. She was amazed that she even heard his next words, so muddled were her very senses. "Now, tell me what's so disgusting about my wanting to make love to the woman I – the woman I'm going to marry?"
> Her only defense was anger. Where it originated, she knew not. Neither did she know from where it derived its strength. It shocked her as much as it did him, her final infuriated out burst. "It's disgusting when it's only physical! It's disgusting when it's filled with anger! It's disgusting when there is no love –" (212)

Again abruptly, he leaves her with his and her insecurities. The misunderstanding evoked by the neutral wording of Stephanie's retort "when there is no love" again is typical for the romance story because it creates a high point for the plot before everything dissolves into happiness. Thus, the advance and retreat pattern here is generated by the hero's repeated running away. In the end it is the heroine's turn to run away in order to be found by him, so that, balance restored, they can repeat their 'love making' in their secret clearing as a symbolic new beginning. The presentation of this lovemaking is more reticent than the other sex scenes, comprising only fourteen lines (227) while their declarations of why and how much they love each other takes ten pages and more dialogue space than anywhere else in the book (221–233).

WRITING STYLE AND CODE

The narrative situation is that of a heterodiegetic covert narrator who directs the homediegetic reflector, in this case the protagonist Stephanie. Sometimes the narrator emerges from behind Stephanie's perspective commenting on the ongoing occurrences. "It was on the Sunday of parents' weekend that the past finally caught up with the present, triggering a chain of events whose fallout threatened to permanently alter her own future" (118), or "The moment of decision was to come much sooner, than either of them had expected" (169), or "Mercifully she had no inkling beforehand of the situation, which was to ignite the explosion" (201).

The single perspective is restricting in the sense that perpetual misunderstandings and misconceptions become the name of the game. Then again, misunderstandings are pivotal for pure category romance novels so that they can qualify as becoming necessary for the plot they might have only partly to do with the use of a single perspective.

Dialogue can supply what is missing within the renderings through a single perspective. In *Sweet Ember,* it does not offer much supporting quality. Here, it makes up only about 20% of the novel. Mostly the direct speech does not consist of more than two or three sentences. Parts of a conversation are often interspersed in the narration, sometimes there is a span of nearly one page between one retort to the next. The speech part is short but evokes the notion of being longer because musings and explanations in thoughts between the speech parts imply a long conversation:

> *"Why didn't you answer any of my letters, Stephanie?"* His words jolted her, the last thing she had expected to hear, a pain tearing her at her insides as he waived the preliminaries and shot right to the core of his concern. She trembled as her mind made the dangerous journey back to those first, oppressive months following their affair.
>
> The letters had come for several months. At the time, her nerves were raw and exposed; she was angry, hurt, and desperately struggling to pick up the pieces of her shattered hopes. This was before she even knew that she was pregnant ... not that it would have altered the situation. She had wanted to wipe her life clean of Douglas Weston, and the best way had been to deny his existence. When she discovered she was carrying his child, she could no longer do that. Yet she refused, even then, to acknowledge him by reading any of the letters that continued to dribble in.
>
> There had been times, over the years, when she had rued her stubbornness, when she would have liked to have known what he had written, if only out of curiosity. But, by then, there were no more letters and she had presumably been forgotten. It was better that way, she had reasoned time and time again.
>
> Now, as her mind flipped into the present and this renewed agony, Stephanie felt driven to revenge, desirous of inflicting pain on its ultimate source. Turning angrily, her eyes narrowed as she lashed out with a venom of her own. *"I never read your letters, Doug. Not a one. They were never even opened. I burned each as it arrived."* A heavy silence fell between them. Strangely, she felt no satisfaction from the cruelty which she had inflicted. Indeed, she had hit her mark. It was as though he had been struck; visibly he flinched, his lips thinning to a hard line as he drew himself straighter.
>
> *"Why?"* His voice was cold and controlled, yet demanding.
>
> As his gaze pierced her very soul, she clutched the windowsill for support. *"There was no purpose in dragging on something that had no future. The summer was over. We each had our own lives to lead. You should never have written; there was no point."* Much as she believed the oft-repeated words, the sad truth they contained tore at her afresh, diluting her anger with a dose of pure unhappiness.

Slowly and pantherlike, Doug moved away from the door. Instinctively, she stiffened at his approach, knowing that she could no more escape him than its prey the panther. The key was to salvage her dignity, she told herself over and over, as each deliberate step brought him closer. When he was no more than a foot from her, he stopped, his eyes steellike, his jaw taut. His every muscle seemed poised for the kill. Desperately Stephanie fought the trembling that threatened to betray her fear. Anything, she could bear anything, she knew, but a repeat of that earlier violence. It was a sacrilege, that earlier kiss, when compared with the reverence with which he had once treated her. In a fleeting instant of shock, Stephanie realized that her body, traitor and wanton, craved that old, remembered touch, that adoration, that mind-boggling passion which once he had bestowed on her. A blush colored her cheeks, mercifully undetected in the dim light and its shadow, which his tall frame cast over her.

"*No point?*" His words brought her back to her senses … (61–63) (my italics)

The italics accentuate the speech parts and show the low percentage of speech within two pages. The paragraphs seem to convey a long discussion whereas the dialogue between the protagonists is on the short side, a fact, that reveals their communicational problems.

The language of *Sweet Ember* stands out as being rendered on an elaborate level, with many expressions that are not that often used in colloquial language. They originate from both sides of English, the Latinate as well as the Anglo-Saxon. The style seems to overdo the educated level with the long sentences on an average of twenty to forty words, which is typical for romance novels with high literary aspirations, even with category romances:

… Silvie proceeded to the looks of amused puzzlement to nimbly slide her wiry frame behind the steering wheel of the car, slamming the door behind her as she turned to greet Melissa, who, to Stephanie's heart-stopping notice, bore a look of round-eyed fear almost comical in its intensity. Instinctively, Stephanie trusted Sylvie to know how to handle the child, so she turned determinedly to the three awaiting women and introduced herself. Moments later, with the last of the preliminaries barely completed, all four turned in surprise as Sylvie opened the car door, sliding out as easily as she'd entered, though this time gently drawing Melissa with her. To Stephanie's instant relief and subsequent amazement, the child, who a brief hour before had been begging to return home, now seemed accepting of the situation, only her mother recognizing the veil of caution-tinged resignation which had befallen her expression. Trust Sylvie for her magical powers, Stephanie mused, and, for the first time in weeks, she genuinely felt convinced that, for Missy's sake alone, she had made the right decision in returning to Pine Winds. (26–27)

Multi-clause sentences of the subordinate variety are one of the narrative devices in *Sweet Ember.* Another predominant and prevailing device is listings of three or even four, be they clauses, nouns, adjectives or adverbial phrases:

> Compounding her grief, similar fates had befallen her father's coin collection, her mothers jewelry and several priceless etchings that had been in the family for years. Each torturous discovery brought a new wave of agony, the sorrow of memories and momentos now besmirched, tainted, and, in the last cases, gone.
>
> The police came and went, declaring that they would do everything possible to track down the culprits, though claiming that these cases were nearly impossible to crack. The insurance company was duly contacted and informed, requesting detailed lists of what had been taken – further prolonging the ordeal for Stephanie, whose stomach had already cramped over on itself, stricken as it was by each new realization of another long-cherished item gone ...
>
> By late afternoon Stephanie was fading steadily, exhausted to begin with by the schedule she'd set for herself during the past days at camp, crushed emotionally by the reality of the havoc surrounding her, overwhelmed by the hours of work which lay ahead, cleaning and putting things back in order. (177–178)

Often, this way of writing seems to be overplayed and results in stilted language. It is true that here the use of descriptive addenda, such as adverbs, adjectives, and nouns, is not as obviously clumsy as it is in other romances, but the use of expressions like "orbs" for eyes or "the ... searching of gray depths into green", or "Thunderous sparks grated against gray flint" kill the aspired efforts.

There are, unusually for a category romance novel, longer descriptions of rooms, landscapes and work, which give the reader a clearer picture of the protagonist's whereabouts than she is used to getting. However, what she is used to reading about are the heroine's thoughts and her inner life, displayed *in extenso.* The beginning of the novel recounts a twelve line long reminisced act of sexual intercourse between Stephanie and Doug where she recalls "her questing fingers", "the strength of his manhood, coupled with an exquisite tenderness" when he "took her" and then "carried her with him" "to the crest of passion" which exploded "in a thousand shimmering bursts". In her reminiscence she actively took part in the sexual game.

As the story is told solely from Stephanie's perspective, her emotions feature predominantly. Small hints, however, like "each" suggest the covert narrator behind her perspective who couples the protagonists' feelings to create mutuality: "Their kiss was new and electrical, charging each with a heady current, driving each to a pinnacle of desire", or the narrator lets "them" be catapulted "to a state of mutual elation". In fact, her imagined orgasmic mutuality of feelings is only

Stephanie's way of thinking because the character Doug is constructed in such a way that he is not given dialogical focus to complement.

There is only one area he is partly able to give voice to: their congruent sexual awareness of each other. Stephanie feels permanently sexually "aroused" when Doug is in her vicinity. An "omnipresent undertone of sexuality" as stimulus triggers "a tingling of long forgotten places", "a throbbing within her", "an arousal of stirrings which only he had ever awakened in her", "raw desire" and "a rebirth of a quiver deep within her". Mutuality, again, it is reported when Doug initiates physical contact: "Their kiss was new ... charging each with a heady current, driving each to a pinnacle of desire" and after she stops him a short time later, he declares accusingly: "you were as aroused just now as I was". That they share the same feelings in the sexual area is emphasized as soon as a likely situation occurs: "Could it be, my sweet, that you are vulnerable to the cravings of the flesh?" or: "His breathing was as labored as hers, small satisfaction that he had been as aroused". Shortly before they have sexual intercourse, their mutual involvement is stated, again: "If the tension within her, the coiled knot of desire tormented her, his state was no different" (186). So he "takes" her, and after this "frantic coupling which they'd demanded earlier" he "came to her again". Stephanie willingly and actively participates in the sexual act timing "her body to his thrusts". Instinctively she knows that when he teaches "her with mastered ease how to fondle and tease how to touch and knead" this will "heighten her own near explosive yearnings and his".

Genitals in his case are once "the strength of his manhood" and "his manly hardness", whereas she has breasts with "rosy buds" or lets him see "the rosy peaks" of her "breasts" or touch her "pebble-hard peaks". When he is allowed to see her naked "his eyes plundered the wealth of femininity" and later "lowered her bra to lay bare a host of further delights". Such exaggerations are displayed throughout the story. "Ecstasy" overwhelms Stephanie all the time. Doug only has to touch her breasts and she experiences "ecstasy", he kisses her and she is "floating in the passion induced delirium", but what a downhill turn when they only share "the explosive passion of the summit". The second coupling recaptures ecstasy: it "catapulted them, finally, through miles and miles of ecstasy". Unlike Krentz's heroine, this female protagonist is in a constant state of arousal. With Krentz the male of the couple usually parades a "hard-on" whenever the opportunity arises and acts accordingly, which in turn lets the female react in an ambivalent manner. This holds true for the novels of 1982. In *Sweet Ember* the female and her feelings, however exaggeratedly they are described, are congruent with the adopted single perspective. She becomes aroused herself and assumes, with the help of the covert narrator, that her partner shares her feelings.

Name giving in *Sweet Ember* is obvious for Stephanie's name: Wright seems to be a mixture between right and wrong. The name is the plot. Endearments are only used by Doug: she is "honey", "love", "my sweet". Obviously the man needs to express his affection in terms that evidence a little male superiority.

The code is the plot. Again, the back cover of the novel introduces the potential reader to emotions she will experience when reading the book. She is promised that she will read about terrible, unforgivable betrayal, heartbreak, and later, gentle love and sensuous passion will put her in the mood to buy the book to enjoy a satisfyingly happy ending.[61]

3.2.2 *A Woman Betrayed*

Ten years later, in 1991, Delinsky wrote *A Woman Betrayed,* a clear example of the transformation her writing had undergone since *Sweet Ember.*

SUMMARY

A Woman Betrayed tells the story of a woman whose husband disappears after twenty years of marriage and leaves her to cope with her liability for his tax fraud, with career disaster, family quandaries and disillusions on many levels.

One day Jeff Frye disappears, literally leaving everything behind. At first the family assumes there has been an accident, but soon it becomes clear that Jeff had to disappear because the Criminal Investigation Division of the IRS (Internal Revenue Service), in the person of Taylor (Tack) Jones is trying to track him down. The family reacts to his disappearance in the following ways: Laura, Jeff's wife and owner of a struggling new restaurant and a catering service, tries to adapt to the new situation by continually cooking and baking; Scott, their nineteen-year-old son, considers his father to be a man idolized by Laura, but also to be a coward; their daughter Debra, sixteen-years-old, blames her mother for not being a better wife for her father; Laura's mother, Maddie, a psychologist at a college, is only concerned about what the public knowledge of Jeff's fraud will do to her unblemished reputation; Lydia, mother to Jeff and Christian, believes that Jeff came to her place to say goodbye, only she did not realize it at the time. Laura's best friend, Daphne, a lawyer, helps Laura understand the arising legal implications and complications and represents her legally.

---

[61] The blurb on the backcover is as follows: "Always, the memory remains ... Stephanie Wright was just nineteen the first time she ran, heartbroken and angry, out of Douglas Weston's life. Stephie, a counselor at a girl's camp, and the older, devastatingly handsome tennis instructor, shared a summer by a gentle love, capped by one night of sensuous passion beneath the pines – followed by a terrible, unforgivable betrayal that sent her fleeing. Eight years later, when Stephie is confident enough to return to the camp, she is unexpectedly reunited with Doug. After despising him for years, Stephie is mystified to find herself fighting the same feelings that first drew her to him. But fight them she will, for there is more than pride at stake. There is Melissa, her beautiful seven-year-old daughter, who smiles up at her tennis teacher with gray eyes that mirror his own ... "

It transpires that Jeff has disappeared just in time and all Tack can do is to freeze Jeff's assets. Because Laura and Jeff have joint bank accounts, she has no money to pay the many liabilities. To pay them, she applies for a bank loan, which she does not receive because the owner of the local newspaper has maligned the family in many of its articles, thus discrediting the family's good reputation. This is also the reason why bookings for her restaurant and her catering service are canceled. As a result, Laura has to cut down on personnel. At the same time she is discovering who is loyal to her. In addition, because of the aggressive newspaper articles, Megan, Scott's former girlfriend sees an opportunity to take revenge by accusing him of rape. With Daphne's legal help he is acquitted.

Christian, Jeff's older half-brother and Laura's first lover, unbeknownst to Jeff, appears to help. Twenty years before, Christian did not want to commit, but age has changed him and he still loves Laura. He persuades her to take his money to pay her debts and he stands by her whenever he is needed. Christian takes Laura to his place in Vermont where they renew their love, and back in Northampton, she files for divorce in order to not lose her second chance with Christian.

Two months after the freezing of Jeff's assets, Laura's money is released thanks to Daphne's insistent efforts. Arriving at Daphne's place to thank her, Laura discovers that Daphne not only is having a love affair with Tack, but that she was also Jeff's mystery lover. Then Lydia has a heart attack and dies. At her funeral Christian notices a man standing well apart from the other mourners. He is Garrison Holmes III, the publisher of the local newspaper and, it turns out, Christian's father, a fact previously unknown to him. Now it becomes apparent to Christian why the family is so publicly maligned by the newspaper. Hence, Christian is in a position to threaten his father to make his paternity known to the 'world' should the newspaper continue to publish even hints at libel. After the police canceled the surveillance at Lydia's grave, Jeff meets Laura and Christian at the cemetery. They can talk things out. Three days later, Jeff fakes his death, letting his Porsche tumble into a gorge, together with his license, credit cards, and a little money. This way Laura can marry Christian and does not have to wait for her divorce.

The tale of Jeff's new life away from his family is interwoven into the main story. He had prepared his disappearance diligently. A year before he bought a fisherman's cottage somewhere along the Maine coast. Now, he has made friends with the owner of a diner and his retarded thirty-year-old daughter, Glorie. Here, at last, he is needed. When the owner is too sick to work and dies of cancer, Jeff happily takes care of the diner and looks after Glorie, whom he intends to marry some years later.

PLOT, CHAPTERS, TIME, AND SETTING

A Woman Betrayed is 471 pages long and contains 31 chapters ranging from ten to twenty pages of length. Like in *Sweet Ember,* the chapters are numbered, the numbers written in letters, and above the numbers there is a kind of underlined garland on the first page of the chapters whereas the following pages have the author's name (even numbers) and the novel's title (uneven numbers) at their tops. The author's name and the title are divided from the text by a thin line. This time, however, the first letter of each chapter is marked not by a capital but a small letter though in a bold print.

Each chapter ends with an incentive to go on reading. Here, the structure of a main plot with a pointed introductory exposition and small subplots of the typical romance novel falls short because the theme does not submit to those plot limitations and a three act suspension curve. The main plot focuses on Laura, the female protagonist, the gradual revelation of her character within the dynamics of her family, and her finding an equally strong partner in Christian. Then, there are four substantial subplots. The first is concerned with how Jeff fares in his self-chosen new life, the second tells the love story between Tack and Daphne, the third covers Scott's arraignment and dismissed charge of rape, and the fourth reveals Christian's family issues and his discovery of who his natural father is. Subplots one and two, being external ones, are loosely connected to the main plot whereas subplots three and four are closely woven into the main plot.

A Woman Betrayed is written in the epic preterite. Although it is a contemporary novel of the 1990s, there are no political or other time references to be found. One thing, however, becomes apparent: the digital age has not yet taken over. Darkrooms to develop films and print photographs are still necessary and people still use only telephone landlines, although accountants already work with computers. A heterodiegetic covert narrator directs the many homodiegetic reflectors. The story of the novel is given in a seemingly chronological order, maybe sometimes in a simultaneous one. As different characters, from whose perspectives episodes are narrated, live or stay in different parts of the USA or the world, incidents may coincide in time, but this is not significant to the linear storyline, and, therefore, not mentioned. Nearly four months of the Frye's family life are recounted in the novel, from facing disaster to regaining a normal life, albeit a different one with characters' altered attitudes towards life and behavior.

Due to the more complex plot, the range of local settings is more broadened. Most members of the Frye family live and work in Northampton, Hampshire, Christian somewhere in Vermont, and Jeff somewhere on the Maine coast. Christian is spending his vacation time in Tahiti where Tack visits him and stays there for a week. All these settings are given more than the usual four sentence descriptions of the category romance novels, as do the Tudor brick house where Laura and the children live, the restaurant and the catering service, Lydia's small house and Daphne's condo. Being a house-builder, Christian constructed and built a multilevel home for himself that 'breathes' culture. Delinsky gives narrative room to project descriptions of surroundings combined with the feelings of the person who dwells in them, as she does in the following text describing the library in the Tudor brick house. This and other descriptions of rooms and places serve manifold underlying meanings: they create a concrete world for the reader where she can move around in her imagination, and they mirror the characters of their owners. They also convey an upper middle class ambience which projects a kind of literate and classy atmosphere and which heightens a reader's self-esteem because she finds herself in the company of such educated characters:

> At the door to the den, she (Laura) stopped. This was Jeff's room, his retreat. Technically it was a library, lined top to bottom with books. The books were still there, but so were a new television and a VCR for fun. He also worked there, which was why the gleaming mahogany desk – which had originally sported a gold-edged blotter, several leather-bound volumes braced by brass bookends, and some scrimshaw – now bore a more functional pad, a computer linked to the office, and a rolodex filled with the names and addresses of anyone and everyone with whom Jeff had professional dealings.
>
> Should it come down to a search, Laura wouldn't know which names to call first. Jeff didn't discuss clients with her unless they bumped into one at a party. He put a high value on confidentiality, and she respected that. He was a decent person.
>
> Drawn into the room by the musty scent of Jeff's collection of old books, Laura let the atmosphere take the edge off her tension. Gently lit, as it had been all night, by the green clerk's lamp on the desk, the room had a feeling of history, and with good cause. On those shelves were an assortment of books, pictures, and mementos that documented their life together.
>
> Neatly arranged, as was Jeff's style, were books from their college days, Jeff's on such subjects as Financial Reporting, Advanced Federal Taxation, and Auditing, hers on American literature, Beginning Anthropology, and French. Jeff's shelves progressed to books on advanced accounting issues that he had read for graduate courses, as well as ever-growing collections of the Journal of Accountancy and the Massachusetts CPA Review. Laura's shelves, reflecting the fact that she had dropped out of college after a year, branched out into photography books, years of National Geographic, and diverse fiction. Those books bought used or in paperback early in their marriage were more weathered. The shelves filled more recently held handsomely packaged hardcover books. And, of course, there were the antique volumes, first editions that Laura had given Jeff over the years.
>
> Interspersed with the books were mementos from trips ... (10–11)

The characters belong to different social milieus. Laura was educated in academic circles where hypocrisy reigns like anywhere else, especially when non-academic people meet academic ones. Her mother constantly reminds her that she does not belong to this elite. Her catering service and new upscale restaurant guarantee she will receive high society as patrons, but she will never belong to that social class. Jeff's parents were lower middle class. Jeff had worked hard to climb socially and so was accepted in his social group. Now running a modest diner and living in an unassuming social neighborhood, he is more content than he has ever been, perhaps because he does not need to make a constant effort to remain socially acknowledged in the social circle Laura aspires to join. Christian cannot be placed in one specific social group because of his two professions. Diana, the lawyer, also has had to work hard to be accepted as a valued member of the male fraternity. Interactions between these characters and their friends show that they do not make social differences a subject of discussion because now they move within the same social setting.

CHARACTER CONSTELLATIONS

Actually there are three protagonists: Laura and her male counterparts Jeff (characterized personally as well as *in absentia*) and Christian, who takes on the hero's part for the love story.

THE FEMALE PROTAGONIST

Laura Frye is the pivot around whom everything and everybody rotates. Aged thirty-eight, still exuding a sexy charisma according to David, Jeff's business partner, and even her son's friends, she seems to be the personification of a perfect modern American woman: a successful entrepreneur and a 'super' wife and mother. To achieve all this, she draws on an overabundance of energy. At the beginning of the story she is the owner of an upscale restaurant, which has been financed by Jeff, and the catering service. Still involved in the daily course of events there, she also runs a perfect household and is her mother-in-law's primary care-giver. At the same time, she gets on picture perfectly well with her husband and her children. Or so she thinks. When Jeff disappears, however, she learns that she painted idealized pictures of her relationships. "The rosy world she'd known, where things went her way if she wished it and worked hard enough, didn't exist any more" (189). She is so competent that she overshadowed her husband. Being aware of her overpowering personality, she tried to involve him in the daily aspects of the family life, which was a recipe for disaster.

Facing reality is difficult for Laura. When they meet for the last time in their lives, Jeff explains to her why their marriage did not work. Jeff had understood the reason long ago, not so Laura:

> "You are who you are. If you had changed to accommodate me, you would
> have been the one diminished, and that wouldn't have been right either. The
> truth is, we were a bad match."

> "We had a solid marriage for twenty years," Laura argued. She had worked hard to make that so and wasn't ready to call her efforts a waste.
>
> "Solid doesn't mean healthy. I wasn't any better for you than you were for me. You needed someone stronger, someone like Christian." (455)

Only when Laura allows herself to give in to the attraction she still feels for Christian can she permit herself to take off the blinders she had put on for years.

> In all the years Christian had been coming to visit, she had never asked a single personal question. You were afraid of the answers, Maddie would have said, if she had known anything of what had gone on years before. You were afraid of finding him more interesting than Jeff. And she would have been right. (362)

Now Laura can also acknowledge the true reasons for marrying Jeff.

> "Did you love him?" Christian asked, needing to know that most of all.
>
> She dropped her chin to his chest. "I thought I did."
>
> "Did you love him when you married him?"
>
> "I wanted to. I told myself that I did."
>
> "Did you?"
>
> "Not the way I loved you," she said with sudden clarity. "What you and I did was hot and exciting and spontaneous. What I had with Jeff lacked that passion."
>
> "And you were prepared to live without it?"
>
> "I didn't know it was missing. I didn't make comparisons. I didn't allow myself to. Maybe I didn't dare. But Jeff was there, he loved me, and he wanted to get married, and that meant I could drop out of school and be free of my mother, and I wanted that above all else." (373)

Instinctively, Laura has taken over the role of the mover and doer in the family, which was never contested because, like her mother, she is equipped with the necessary stamina. Her dominant behavior, however, is a result of her attempts to show her mother that a daughter without an academic degree can still be a worthy, successful and respectable person. Yet, contrary to her mother's cold and analytical ways, she inherited her father's warmth and compassion. These traits make her a lovable, caring woman, and even when she learns that her husband has had an affair under her nose with her best friend she is hurt, but does not feel vengeful.

Her self-esteem is at rock-bottom because she has to fight on three levels: against her mother's constant display of superiority, her vanishing respectability and her self-betrayal over the years. It is Christian who helps her to rebuild her self-confidence as a woman and entrepreneur and who offers to take an active and de-cisive part in her life which she happily agrees to, knowing that from now on, she will have a shoulder to lean on.

Being the pivot around whom everybody and everything rotates, Laura plays the part of role model for reader identification. Because she is not infallible, but masters her problems of betraying herself and being betrayed and never thinks of conceding defeat.

THE FIRST MALE COUNTERPART

When Jeff Frye, Northampton's picture-book perfect male part of the couple, disappears, Laura, in order to report him missing, has to give a concise description of his outward appearance. According to it he, at the age of forty-two, is "a good-looking man, well-kept, in his prime," (46) with brown eyes, well cut brown hair and wire-rimmed glasses. People see him, as neat man who is punctual, predictable, steadfast, and successful, a man who seems devoted to his family. He often makes the papers, which report the tax seminars he gives, being one of the two partners of his Farro And Frye accounting firm. Being an uncommunicative person by nature, he never discusses clients because he puts a high value on confidentiality. This attitude served him well when he started the embezzlement.

Jeff does not have many friends from his past, if at all, does not drink, does not have buddies to paint the town red with. He likes to read a lot: his den, lined top to bottom with books, is the proof of it, as is the information that when he bought supplies for the cottage in Maine he included many books. As he is a private person he

> didn't see why friends had to bare their souls to each other, or, for that matter, why they had to share anything more than the simplest of thoughts. Who he was deep inside, what he was thinking – it wasn't anyone's business but his own, and it didn't matter, in the everyday run of things. (221)

When he saw an opportunity, although it was not legal, to obtain the money to finance Laura's biggest dream, an upscale restaurant, he took it, at the same time polishing his self-esteem. Even when he was a child, "he'd know exactly how to break a law if he wanted to do it" (154). Doing illegal things was also his way of getting an upper hand on Christian when they were young. For having been successful this way in his youth, he used his cleverness and expertise to commit tax fraud, going undetected for eight years. Astonishingly he is not hampered by any guilt in this respect, which could be explained by his upbringing. Although Jeff should come across as a spoilt man without scruples, he is portrayed as a reticent, nice person with faults that are made open to scrutiny, thus leading to the readers' positive understanding of his emotional problems. Lydia, his mother, whose pride and joy he is, tries to give Laura an inside view of Jeff, at the same time inspiring a reader to not judge him harshly. There was something in his eyes when he visited his mother for the last time:

"A look. Sadness. Discouragement. I knew that look. I used to see it when he was little, when something disappointed him in school, when he didn't do well in a test, or he wasn't elected to the student council, or he asked a girl to a prom and she turned him down." Her wrinkles shifted around the saddest of smiles … "He used to try his best, then come in second." She stopped talking. After a minute, more softly, she said, "That was the way he looked, as though he'd tried his best, but failed." (69)

In his family's opinion, Jeff seems to have chosen the cowardly way to resolve his problems, whereas he considers leaving Northampton to be "the bravest thing he had ever done in his life" (224). The reader does not have to guess what motivated Jeff to begin a new life without a past to contend with, as she is introduced to his perspective early in the story, on page 32, where, at his cottage in Maine, he has drunk himself into a stupor, which he considers as "a rite of passage long overdue. As if, six weeks before his forty-second birthday, he had finally become a man." What still bothers him is not having been able to face up to Laura. For him, disappearing is the only way to live a life where he could come to respect himself. So he took his first steps intelligently, thoroughly planning his disappearance one-and-a-half years before the beginning of the story.

He is not a very sexed person. Even his affair with Daphne seems to have consisted more in avoiding loneliness. His relationship with Glorie is not based on a sexual attraction, but on their mutual understanding of each other, albeit on different levels, and his being necessary for her welfare, and this is why he considers a marriage to her sometime in the distant future. What he craves in Maine at first is to do whatever he wants to and to be free from any responsibility, seeking for himself the independent life his brother seems to live. Not in vain has he been a reliable person for his family for twenty years, and so he finds people whom he wants to rely on him as well, but this time, he is really needed and being in charge he is given every chance to grow competent in many ways which before he was denied. Although his new life has become much more ordinary, he is content, perhaps for the first time in his life. His new name, Evan Walker, will be a reminder of his past, but he knows he will not have to 'walk' again in the future. He has become the man who now can respect himself, who is respected for the right things and is needed by others.

THE SECOND MALE COUNTERPART

Like his brother Jeff, Christian Frye is introduced early in the story where the reader learns about a part of the professional side of this man through his own short first perspective from page 35 onward. Aged forty-eight, he is the renegade of the family, and something like the family outcast. At the end of the third quarter of the novel, the reasons for his behavior are explained. Having been an unwanted child who was always blamed for things going wrong, these childhood experiences left their mark on him and shaped his adult life. When he was nineteen-years-old his mother told only him that Bill, the man they just had buried, was not his real father, but she had promised never to divulge his progenitor's name, a promise she takes to the grave. She assures him that the man is still living and is a very public person. Discovering at last who this man is, a man he has grown to dislike for his spite and hateful editorials on the Frye family, he is relieved to see that, for all his difficult youth, he has shaped himself into a decent man whose similarity with his biological father ends with the appealing outward appearance.

Being raised in a family where Bill, his stepfather, "needed a scapegoat for anything that went wrong" and chose Christian for that role, where his mother wore blinkers because she had made a deal with Bill and therefore "wouldn't allow herself to see or think evil of him", where Jeff was encouraged "to blame Christian for everything" (323–325), Christian's reaction to this unfair treatment was stubbornness and obstinate behavior. But one day it occurred to him that his brains could be used as revenge, and he started studying seriously to excel this way. Joining the Peace Corps was his way of escaping Northampton where he would always be prejudged because of his juvenile misdemeanors.

He did not tell his family about his having joined the Peace Corps or about his love affair with Laura, who never told anybody about it either. As he regretted deeply his decision not to marry Laura at the time, his visits at family gatherings were painful for everybody because he behaved abrasively, which was his way of dealing with his jealousy. This time, however, he comes home and for the first time in his life he has his mother's attention solely directed at him, albeit for a very short time. They can talk and he strives to show her the decent person he has made himself grow into, with good, long-standing friends and successful achievements in both his professions, photography and house-building. The self-centered hedonist of old times turns out to be a serious, helpful, responsible man who, like everybody else in the novel, craves love, trust, respect, and understanding. In turn, he readily gives what he would like to take. His dominant personality will not wither under strain when he lives with the dominant Laura. They will balance each other. Now that Christian has dealt with his anger of old times, he can look forward to a rewarding family life.

SECONDARY CHARACTERS

A Woman Betrayed is one of the many books Delinsky has written that portray a network of relationships to surround the protagonists. Each secondary character presents a facet of the novel's theme, betrayal. Here the secondary characters are thirty-two-year-old Taylor (Tack) Jones and forty-year-old Daphne Phillips whose love story could fill its own romance novel because it has all the trimmings of one, such as a secret that hinders a decent Daphne from marrying Tack, or the problem of the age difference that might prevent them from having children of their own, or Tack's boyish attitude, which changes and turns him into a maturing adult during the story. But as supporting characters in the novel, foremost, he is an investigator of a tax fraud and she is Laura's best friend and lawyer, who helps her with the legal problems of Jeff's disappearance, as well as with Scott's defense at court.

The Frye children, Scott, aged nineteen, and Debra, aged sixteen, are not allocated much narrative room and complex characterization, although each has to overcome a problem, he the charge of rape and she, going through a defiant phase, the offering of her virginity to someone unimportant. Otherwise, they both behave like cases in a textbook for psychologists, with denial, seeking the culprit for Jeff's disappearance within themselves and then outside themselves in their mother. Their role show how Laura is sometimes blind to their needs and tends to be an overprotecting mother.

Then there are the in-laws: Madeline McVey, a selfish professor of psychology. She constantly criticizes her daughter, Laura, to the point that her critiques fall flat because she does not give her any sort of encouragement. Being proud of her academic status, she does not respect Laura and her decision to make her life different from the academic one her mother had planned for her. Madeline's psychologically infused remarks let the reader understand Laura's behavior, but also, sometimes, parts of the story.

Lydia Frye, Jeff and Christian's mother, however, regards Laura as her daughter and respects her and therefore, Laura enjoys taking care of her. Moreover, being a weak woman, she seems to have idolized her husband, who had married her knowing that Christian was not his child. During his life, she never contradicted him, even when he clearly mistreated Christian. She also idolized their son Jeff so much that she ignored and neglected Christian's emotional welfare and rights, and continues to do so up to Jeff's disappearance, a fact the author uses to conjure up Christian as having grown into a self-respecting character in contrast to Jeff.

The last secondary character in this web of relationships is Glorie. She marks the starting point of the relational network that Jeff starts to weave in his new home in Maine. Glorie who after an accident was in a coma for three years, woke up mentally retarded. Although she is thirty-years-old she is like a trusting child who will never be able to fend for herself in life. When Jeff assumes responsibility for her this is seen as a redeeming act, and the reader becomes kindly disposed towards him and learns that he is on his way to being a self-respecting person. Delinsky endows each character with negative attributes, thus demonstrating aspects of the real world and showing that people can be lovable even if they are not perfect.

CONFLICTS, RELATIONSHIP, AND EROTIC SCENES

Many internal conflicts are woven into the novel. They have to do with aspects of betrayal, either the kind of self-betrayal or that of being the recipient of it, and secretiveness.

1.) Jeff's conflict: He craves to lead a life where he is valued and needed, not only a breadwinning addendum to his family. To achieve that he betrays his family.

2.) Laura's conflicts: a) trying to be perfect in every way other than academically, and not succeeding. b) being dominant, and as such, an excessively caring person who does not see other people's real needs. c) trying to win her mother's respect and failing.

3.) Christian's conflicts: a) acknowledging to himself that he can give in to his love and commitment to Laura and his family. b) trying to show his mother his matured self and make her declare her love for him and reveal his biological father's name.

4.) Debra's conflict: dealing with immaturity and precocious youthful sex.

5.) Scott does not have any internal conflicts, but the accusation of rape is sufficient for his characterization.

6.) Daphne's conflict: being successful but lonely, she had an affair with her best friend's husband (Jeff), who was also lonely, and feels guilty for her deceptive behavior. Her way to atone for it is to help the family in legal matters. She thinks of herself as a bad person with no redeeming qualities.

7.) Tack's not so big conflict is to grow into a mature adult and become a self-confident man. In that, he succeeds in the end, even being able to understand and pardon Daphne's deceptive behavior.

Those are the characters' inner conflicts. The outer conflicts are as follows:

1.) Jeff's disappearance and the resulting financial and social problems.

2.) The newspaper's malicious campaign.

3.) Scott's arraignment on rape charges because the newspaper articles have outlawed him.

Nearly every character in the novel explicitly has the sexual side of his nature revealed, be it an affair resulting in an illegitimate child (Lydia) or the juvenile sexual experiences of the Frye youngsters, or the innocent relationship between Glorie and Jeff which he intends to take further in time, but not before a marriage to her. They all are mentioned in a sexual way as in "getting hard", "using condoms", "doing it", but there are no explicit sexual scenes or interrupted ones. Those are given to the protagonists, Laura and Christian, and to Daphne and Tack. (In a romance novel sexual scenes are reserved for the main couple, but as Delinsky has already left the restricting category romance novel writing phase, she has more plotting freedom.)

While married to Jeff, Laura was his faithful wife, albeit one who did not let herself "dwell what might have been wrong in (her) relationship with Jeff" (388). Now that she is given a second chance with Christian, she defends it against whoever doubts her. Christian is the man who takes the initiative and invites her to his home in Vermont for a week, where they renew their love. Seeing the house he built for himself, the photographs that speak to her, she understands even better the man he had matured into, but also why she subconsciously chose her hobby, photography. It is a reminiscence of her time with him. In a typical romance novel, the protagonists would have sex from the moment they entered the house, as now they are undisturbed. Here they wait until after their much needed sleep. They make love on the carpet and he makes her come two times before he himself "erupts" into a powerful orgasm. A little later he

> carried her to his big bed, where he proceeded to show her that his desire for her wouldn't be sated by one coupling or even a second. He made love to her over and over again. He reacquainted himself with her body by inches, using his hands, his mouth, his body parts in ways that Jeff, for all the years he'd had with her, had never imagined doing. Christian made her feel worshiped, and she worshiped him in turn. Her passion ran without reserve, heightened by time and maturity and an awareness of the rarity of true love. (369)

This is the only explicit sex-related scene for these lovers told within four pages, the first coupling taking one page (366–369). She is carried by him to the bed which is a typical category romance procedure, but there are no constant reminders of how aroused one or the other lover is as it seems to be one of the requirements of a category novel.

The other couple, Tack and Daphne, begin a totally new relationship with stumbling-blocks to overcome, like age difference, career and secrecy. At the beginning of their relationship they have one thing in common: loneliness, no one to come home to, especially on New Year Eve. So Tack persuades Daphne to spend it with him and this leads to their first night with a good deal of sex (three pages), their first coupling taking one page from foreplay to end (210–212), and the beginning of a serious relationship where sex plays a role, but not a prominent, explicit one.

Writing Style and Code

Although Delinsky weaves a network of supporting secondary characters around the protagonists in *A Woman Betrayed*, she restricts the perspectives to four people: Laura, Jeff, Christian and Taylor. The chapters are not always dedicated to a single perspective: sometimes a chapter is separated by up to three. Often the stringency of a perspective is diluted by surrounding characters who mix their way of seeing things into it by dialogue which suggests to the reader that she also has access to their inner beings. Or, like in the following text, the emotions that should have belonged to Jeff's perspective, but are found in the conversation between Laura and Debra, give more insight in Jeff's feelings than the reader gets from the perspective assigned to him.

> Raising her eyes (Laura) said, "Okay. I suppose I did run things. I gave your father credit where credit was due and then some, but in the final analysis he didn't take the lead."
>
> If she had been hoping that the confession would calm Debra into a workable truce, she was wrong. Debra wasted no time in turning that confession against her. "He *couldn't* take the lead. You always did things your way. You wouldn't give him a chance."
>
> "I gave him plenty of chances. He just wouldn't take them."
>
> "Because he knew you'd be angry if things didn't go your way. Face it, Mom. You're a dictator."
>
> "Careful, Debra –"
>
> "That's what drove Dad away. He couldn't stand not being able to express himself, so he did it in a way that told you what he thought of you, then he took off." (328)

The narrator behind all the perspectives is vaguely spotted more in the narrative parts, i.e. not totally leaving the respective perspectives to the character. S/he rarely appears from behind the scenes e.g. to encourage the reader to continue reading. "On Monday morning, the current picked up" (89), or "And then Lydia took sick" (420). The over-all impression, with the exception of Jeff's parts, is that an omniscient narrator tells the story although it evolves around the different perspectives.

In comparison to *Sweet Ember*, the dialogues have increased, so that half to three quarters of the novel consist of dialogue. These dialogues are often followed by a paragraph of up to six sentences of narrative text. In addition there are still longer narrative passages without dialogue break, some longer than three pages. These passages deal with the recounting of events or occurrences that happen in between and therefore are needed for the reader's information. Most longer narrative passages, however, present inner prolonged thoughts and emotions, such as Jeff's, who craves human companionship after a week spent in solitude. The following paragraph explains Jeff's conflicting emotions along with a short characterization.

> There was another reason for going into town. He was in desperate need of the diversion. In between reading his books, listening to his radio, and cleaning up the cottage, he inevitably thought about those he had left behind, thought about Laura and David and Daphne and Lydia and how he had let them all down. He wondered how messy things were, whether the IRS had come out into the open, whether they were making life hard for

Laura. She would survive, he knew she would, she always had. She would make the most of the situation and carry on. But he wondered about Debra and Scott. They were the toughest part of all this. He worried about them – not about their daily well-being, because Laura would ensure that, but about their feelings for him. He knew they would come to hate him, and he supposed he deserved it; still, the more he dwelt on it, the more pain it caused. With no one to ease the isolation he felt, he was becoming an emotional wreck. Living in solitude meant living with a man he didn't particularly like. That was a punishment in and of itself.

So he was risking discovery by taking a walk into town. Not having dealt with any locals except the Bangor realtor from whom he'd bought the cottage, he wasn't sure what brand of humanity he would find. But he wasn't picky. Human contact was human contact. He wasn't any prize himself, after what he'd done. (139)

As Jeff's disappearance is the axis around which the story revolves, dialogues, musings, events are occupied constantly by this one occurrence, but not in a pleonastic way because the reader is offered many different aspects and a brisk plot that make repeats of a tedious kind unnecessary.

Seen from my German viewpoint, the language has the quality of an inconspicuously well written style with considerably shorter sentences than those in *Sweet Ember*. Which is only saying that the reader can concentrate on the plot and does not stumble across elaborate wordings. The plot and the story are complex enough in the way of emotional complexity to guarantee a challenging language which is shown in the following text-example of Christian's conjuring up childhood memories when he lets himself into his mother's house using the key he was given when Jeff was born.

After a week, his mother was home and the wondering ended. He was the big brother, which meant he went off to school with his key and had to be content to come home and watch his parents dote on the baby. He tried to understand when they explained that his little sister had died in her crib when she was just Jeff's age, so they had to watch Jeff all the time. But he didn't like it.

In his child's mind, the key was the culprit. He tried losing it, but his teacher found it in the wastebasket before the janitor could take it away. He tried flattening it under the tire of his father's Ford, but it wouldn't flatten. He tried flushing it down the toilet, but it stayed in the bowl like a dead weight until his mother fished it out.

The key had been all over the world with him, a good luck charm perhaps, since he had emerged from more than his share of adventures unscathed, but for years it was also the embodiment of his anger. It opened the door to the house from which he had been locked out for so long.

In time, the anger had faded. He built his own life, found his own pleasures. Still, there was something about that key. (295)

This text is clearly a composed one with sentences mostly more on the short side, five being simple ones. The sentences which emphasize Christian's efforts to lose the key in order to regain lost love, begin identically with "He tried … " only to be continued with a "but" that explains why he failed. The remaining complex sentences relate a complex situation and use not so common words like culprit, embodiment, emerge or unscathed.

Mostly, 'making love' is the wording sex is described in *A Woman Betrayed*, with the exception of what Megan does, the girl who accuses Scott of rape. She "practically gives it out on the street corner". Female feelings of sexual arousal in the past and in the present are expressed as follows. Lydia admits that "the sound of his voice made my heart pound" and "the sight of him made me quiver". For Laura the memories of her time with Christian are "exciting, poignant, sweet" though functioning as "aphrodisiac" they are "nowhere as potent as the man in the flesh". Thinking of Christian's love-making she feels "a warm current spread through her".

The women Gwen, Daphne, and Laura take an active part in arousing their lovers. Accepting that Taylor needs "a fix every few days or he was climbing the walls", Gwen, Taylor's lover who finishes their "purely physical arrangement" at the beginning of the story, knows how to manipulate him for another bout of sex by letting her hand doing "wonders between his legs" so that he is "lost". Mutual stimulating of sexual desire escalates at the first sexual intercourse between Daphne and Taylor. First "his body was heating at an alarming rate" when he lets Daphne touch him while his own "hands were busy on her ribs, her waist, her breasts". Then "buttons came undone, flesh met flesh, and breathing grew harder, but there was no stopping the hot and heavy need …   He felt her hands on the fastening of his trousers, then his zipper" and this activity of hers makes him "so full, he was ready to burst". And before he "enters" her, his thumb "basked in her heat". This use of terms connoting emotional states rather than explicit terms for the act is applied again in the sexual intercourse between Laura and Christian. Again reciprocal activity heightens the situation and mirrors emotions. Laura's hands "stuttered slightly over his nipples". Seeing that "he filled his boxer-shorts provocatively", feeling that "the headiness had help from that part of him pressing against her stomach", and that "he was fully aroused" she answers his confession "I have a fierce need" by slipping "her hands into his shorts" running them" to the hot, heavy swell of his erection. While she stroked him, she raised her mouth to his. He seized on like a starving man". A little later, "wherever he touched, she burned".

The final consummation of the sexual act is worded as "to enter her", "to thrust inside her" or, the female activity, "she (in this case, Daphne) straddled him and took him inside". The personal pronoun emphasizes the degree of intimacy.

But, as with all category romance novels, even if Delinsky distances herself from them, here again, it is the orgasm that makes the physical union important. Taylor desperately hopes that the quality of his orgasm will bind Daphne to him: "... the only thing he was thinking about was coming so hard and high and long in her that she would be his slave forever" (332). So it is not the orgasm he gives her, but his own orgasm that might make her proud as a woman to be able to arouse him that much. Obviously it is a female's craving that is referred to here because Laura, for her part, also needs the proof of Christian's desire for her. "Christian's pleasure more than repaired the damage" of Jeff's betrayal to her. "Christian made her feel worshiped, and she worshiped him in turn" (369). Worshiping includes his reacquainting "with her body by inches, using his hands, his mouth, his body parts". Laura needs to incite Christian's desire for her to restore her feminine self-assuredness.

An obvious meaningful name-giving in the novel is Jeff's alias. He is Evan Walker, the man who swiftly walked away forever. Frye could be interpreted as 'fried' by the newspaper as well as in people's minds and Laura's maiden name, McVey, 'make way' could allude to her mother's always finding a way to explain occurrences from a psychological point of view, or Laura's stubbornness in following her career. Even Tack's name could be regarded as noteworthy. By adding the letter r to his name it could refer to his inefficacy to track down Jeff.

Nobody in the novel uses any endearments to indicate personal involvement. The characters address each other with first names only.

As this novel was not published in the category romance novel, but under the heading of Women's Fiction, the reader won't necessarily expect pure romance, but the potential reader first sees the pink cover of the book and not its spine. The text on the backcover, however, promises a romance story and assures the reader that here she will read about a woman who discovers her strength and own worth. A wedding cake on the front cover is all a reader of romance novels needs to be attracted to to buy the book, even when at a closer look she discovers the missing bridegroom on top of the three tiered wedding cake.[62] Still, the parts telling about the different courtships, the description of sexual intercourse and the promising

---

[62] The complete text of the backcover is as follows: "THEY WERE THE PICTURE PERFECT FAMILY with a twenty-year marriage, two terrific kids, and a successful career, Laura Frye has everything she could ask for ... until her husband Jeff mysteriously disappears. Beside herself with worry, Laura maintains that the Jeff she knew would never leave her voluntarily. But what about the Jeff she didn't know? As her husband's many secrets come to light, Laura is left with a shocking picture of the man she married ... and a world is falling apart. Shaken to the very core, Laura looks for ways to hold her family together and rebuild her life. What she finds is a strength she never knew she had, and a love she thought she had lost forever." "When you care enough to read the very best, the name of Barbara Delinsky should come immediately to mind." – Rave Reviews –

'happy' endings for three couples create enough plot with the satisfying code, not so much in words than in meaning that life is worth living only with the right partner and within the institution of marriage.

3.2.3 *The Family Tree*

The Family Tree was written in 2007, twenty-six years after *Sweet Ember* with more than seventy-five longer and shorter novels in between. Since 1991 Delinsky has written novels that focus in parts on death, illnesses, physical handicaps and personal secrets. Family always plays an important part in them. In *The Family Tree,* she returns to psychological and moral deficiencies, which provide part of the background for the story.

Summary

The ardently awaited daughter of Hugh and Dana Clarke, née Joseph, is not what her white parents expected: Elizabeth Ames Clarke, Lizzie, has bronze African-American skin. Her child's skin color does not matter at all to interior decorator Dana whose heritage is unknown, but it does to Hugh. Hugh, a lawyer, was born into a pedigreed American, Anglo-Saxon, rich, upper-class family with a family line that is accounted for in detail in his father's newest book "One Man's Line" that is to be released in six weeks. So Hugh cannot be responsible for his child's skin color. The Clarke side of the young family accuses Dana, whom they have always regarded as a misfit in their social circle, of having had an affair with David, their black, divorced friend and neighbor. To clear her of this suspicion and a little of his own, too, Hugh demands a paternity test, which confirms Hugh as Lizzie's biological father.

Then Hugh urges Dana to start digging for answers. Dana is illegitimate and her mother died when she was a child. She does not know her father's name, nor does her grandmother who raised her and whose yarn shop is Dana's emotional home beside the one she built with Hugh over a period of five years. Never really having wanted to know about her father, Dana feels pressured by Hugh to locate him. By chance, she discovers the name of one of her mother's college friends who remembers her father's name. Jack Jones Kettyle turns out to be a Catholic priest. At another stage of his life he was married and had six children, one of whom resembles Dana so much that he instantly and happily acknowledges her as his daughter, although he had never known of her existence. Dana's feelings for him are ambivalent. Jack's family line is of white, also accounted for, descent. So Dana tries to look into her grandparents' family history. No African-American ancestor can be singled out.

When Hugh and Dana bring Lizzie in for a checkup, the pediatrician informs them that Lizzie is a carrier of the sickle-cell trait, a trait that one in twelve

African-Americans carry and Caucasian people do not. Dana's blood test is negative whereas Hugh's turns out to be positive.

Eaton, Hugh's father, now has to admit he had heard rumors that his mother had had an affair with a light skinned African-American lawyer, but as Eaton turned out to be white and so did his children and grandchildren, he supposed that the rumors had just been that: rumors – until Lizzie. After she was born, he was in so much denial that he really believed in an affair on Dana's side. Now everybody in the Clarke family has to reconsider their respective utter convictions regarding certified origins, and, therefore, granted rights and supercilious behavior: Eaton, his white upper-class conviction of superiority, and also his wife's changing attitude towards him; Hugh his never questioned rights to belong to that class which was the secure basis for his profession and his championing minorities; Hugh's brother who is in denial, but will have to acknowledge the truth some day. In the end, Dana and Hugh begin to start over, but on a different level, that of equality with regard to their social classification.

PLOT, CHAPTERS, TIME, AND SETTING

The main plot is outlined in the summary above. But there are four subplots that are closely connected with the issues of the main plot of pretense, secretiveness, selective prejudice, social acknowledgment, and respectability.

1.) There is Dana's grandmother's attempt to put her late husband on a pedestal although he was a bigamist.

2.) There is Corinne, a customer of the yarn shop, who tries to project wealth in order to be accepted into her aspired social circle. In the end her husband is accused of fraud and she is stripped of money and a home.

3.) There is Eaton whose social, high-handedness crumbles with the forced acceptance of his African-American heritage, and, who, moreover, tries to decide on how to deal in a decent and honest way with the upcoming book signing tour and his appearance on national television. His new book is all about his pride in being a member of such an upstanding, old illustrious family, the Clarkes, to whom, technically, he cannot claim to belong anymore.

4.) A fourth subplot, not interwoven into the personal lives of the families, is the case Hugh takes on *pro bono* and wins. At the hospital he meets the mother of a seriously injured illegitimate four-year-old boy who needs expensive medical treatment. So Hugh legally helps his mother to receive the needed money for the treatment and more for the boy's education from the senatorial father of the child.

The Family Tree is 329 pages long and consists of 30 chapters, the longest one extending to fifteen pages. The chapters are numbered without an additional headline and there is no first letter of the chapters in bigger bold print. The pages remain unadorned. Nineteen of these chapters begin with a name, more with Hugh's than with Dana's, and five with a date, mostly a day of the week, so that the impression of a kind of report is emphasized. The chapters are not dedicated to any one person. From chapter twelve onward, the perspectives often shift to different people within chapters, a fact that implies a covert, omniscient narrator. Tension is not so much created by the chain of events and their climaxes of a low order, but by the novel's explosive theme itself.

This contemporary novel of 2007 is told in the epic preterite. One real time reference, September 11, a milestone in American history, is made in connection with Hugh's detective, Yunus El-Sabwi, a former cop, who was born in Iraq which had been fact enough for Americans to link him with illegal groups. Hugh defended him and Yunus was reinstated to the force, but his life there was made so unpleasant that he resigned and now works for the private security force of a company owned by Hugh's family. This reported part of Yunus' life emphasizes Hugh's excellence as a lawyer, the wealth and political power the Clarke's clan wields in their world, and Hugh's unbiased attitude.

The story is told in meticulous chronological order comprising one month of story time. Nearly every day is accounted for, be it by mentioning the baby's age in days or weeks or by giving the day of the week. The events of the day when Hugh discovers he is the carrier of the sickle cell trait are extended over five chapters or fifty-six pages.

Principally, the novel is set in Newport, Rhode Island, where Dana and Hugh live in a so-called Newport cottage and where Ellie Jo's yarn shop, the hospital and the courthouse are located. Then, there is the unnamed community near the sea, forty minutes south of Boston in which the elder Clarkes reside in a Georgian Colonial house with five bedrooms, six bathrooms, and a salt-water pool. (To an American reader the style of these houses seem to be possible to imagine.) Dana and Hugh drive to Albany, New York, to Jack Jones Kettyle's rectory, but stay there only for about an hour.

Rooms, or locations as such, do not play the significant role they do in *A Woman Betrayed*. True, the reader is informed about the heroine's in-laws' impressive estate or the house she decorated herself, giving it a welcoming feeling. But one semantically charged location is the yarn shop. This is the place that offers, above all, emotional comfort and warmth, even for Dana's husband. Membership of a social class is one of the matters of concern around which the story revolves.

CHARACTER CONSTELLATIONS

FEMALE PROTAGONIST

Thirty-four-year-old Dana Clarke, née Joseph, born out of wedlock, is a designer by training, but knitting and designing knitting patterns is in her blood. Wherever she is, she takes her knitting with her because this is her way to obtain emotional balance. Dana's mother drowned when she was five years old. Her mother, whom she idolizes, had told her next to nothing about her father. Unconsciously, Dana is angry that he has neglected her. She grew up with her grandparents. Although she lives with Hugh in their Newport cottage, a large house whose interior she designed, too, her grandmother's yarn shop is still her safe haven, her grandmother her anchor, and some of the customers her surrogate family. This is the place where love is given unconditionally. Dana is convinced she has found her soul mate in Hugh and their opposing character traits make their union even more intimate.

> Hugh loved his wife. He truly did. He loved her for many things, not the least being that she was genuinely laid-back. She didn't get mired down in details the way he did. She didn't have his compulsive need for order and logic or precedent. She went with the flow, could adapt to change with a smile and move on. He admired her for that.
>
> At least he always had. Now, as he looked at the baby again, Dana's nonchalance suddenly seemed irresponsible. She should have made it her business to know who her father was. (34–35)

For Dana the fact that her child's skin color is different from that of her parents is astonishing, but nothing to worry about other than what Lizzie will face growing up, a problem Dana partly witnesses in David's, her black neighbor biracial daughter. Dana who needs unconditional love and security feels her love for Hugh and the baby rejected because now she has been accused of infidelity by her husband and, in addition to that, when the DNA test shows that Hugh is the father, she is forced to do what she had forbidden herself to ever do: to find out about her father. It becomes obvious that there is a deep angst of rejection that prevented her from looking for her father. Her world has gone awry. Whatever she believed was true or could never happen turns out to be different: her husband distrusts her, her mother has lied about her father, and her father turns out to be a caring man who would have loved her had he been able to be a parent for her. But she still has a place of refuge: the yarn shop, her grandmother and her friends at the shop.

To Dana it is not important that some people will cut them dead for reasons of racial bigotry, as two of her clients have already done. With the exception of her naive mother-in-law, who gradually breaks away from the family's disdainfulness, the Clarke family continues to reject her. Her friends, however, prove to be real friends and when she is given the opportunity to take over her grandmother's yarn shop, she is happy she can stay in her much needed haven.

From the beginning of their acquaintance Dana found that Hugh is different:

> "What we had before all this was special. Before I met you, I never dated super-rich guys, because I didn't trust them not to use and then discard me."
> He made a dismissive sound. "No guy would do that."
> "I grew up in this town," she argued. "I saw it happen more than once. There were the super-rich, and then there were the rest of us. We were playthings of the super-rich. Take Richie Baker. We called him The Spoiler, because his goal was to deflower virgins. As soon as he'd slept with one, he dumped her, and who's he married to now? One of the super-rich. I learned to avoid guys like you. And then suddenly all that caution didn't make sense, because everything – *everything* – spoke of decency and trust. Did I ever ask about women you'd dated before me? No, because they were irrelevant, because I knew you felt differently about me." (169)

Dana's trust in Hugh is absolute, as is her love. Despite the fact that the forced paternity test hurts her feelings, she is able to accept, though only to a certain degree, his inherent need to know, and this later helps the couple to start over. It is not one of Dana's character traits to exact retribution. Finding out that Hugh is the one with a black ancestor does not instill feelings of revenge in her, but feelings of relief: "I felt relieved. This makes you more human. It makes me feel less inferior" (263). For her, it is important that Hugh will love their child as much as that he needs her to love him. She is convinced that from now on they will shoulder the difficult task of raising their biracial child together.

MALE PROTAGONIST

Hugh Clarke, forty years old, independently wealthy, comes from a family that "had come to America on the MAYFLOWER and been prominent players ever since. Four centuries of success had bred stability. Hugh might downplay the connection, but he was a direct beneficiary of it" (4). Having grown up in this white privileged bastion and taking his heritage for granted, his self-confidence and his professional confident excellence is rooted in the knowledge of his family's social importance. Dana once says to him: "First and foremost, you think of yourself as a Clarke" (137). Hugh has already documented his professional, social and racially unbiased worth by becoming a partner in a mixed race law firm whose clients are largely minorities and by taking *pro bono* cases for underprivileged people. He understands himself to be an advocate of racial equality and a liberal. Against his parents' wishes he married a woman who has no family heritage to show for and who, on top of it, is illegitimate, but whom he loves. When he is criticized about his choice of wife from an inferior social class, he tries to explain it:

"Why do you think I waited so long? Why do you think I refused to marry those girls *you* two loved? Because *then* there would have been affairs, and on my side. They were boring women with boring lifestyles. Dana is different." (22)

Hugh is fully aware of the power of money. Knowing what is important for people of his social milieu helps him to legally strong-arm them when necessary. He not only looks like his father, he also has similar character traits. Other than that they both value decency, honor and fairness, they also give the same meticulous attention to detail which is essential for the historian father's writing and for the son to be a successful lawyer. Dana judges him accurately when she says: "He'll want answers … Hugh is dogged that way. He won't rest until he finds the source of Lizzie's looks, and that means going over *every inch* of our family tree" (28). This compulsive need to know leads Hugh to stubbornly examine each possibility, be it a paternity test insinuating infidelity on Dana's side, a search for Dana's unknown father or her grandparents' family tree, or even his own blood test, all as a means to find out where Lizzie's skin color comes from. His compulsive need to know becomes pivotal for the story. If he were not such a stickler for the truth, he simply would have accepted without further ado that someone in Dana's ancestry was of African-American origin: in doing so he would not have hurt his wife's feelings so deeply, and in addition he would have spared himself and his family this emotional upheaval. (And the book would not have been written.)

Having learned about his African-American grandfather, the first thing Hugh does is to tell the truth about his checkered ancestry to his black friend David, whom he had accused of having an affair with Dana, a fact, that now shames him twofold. Hugh feels confused and helpless and wonders how he will be able to deal with his new knowledge about his family in an honest and decent way. Belonging now to a group of people, he, until now, has defended from a standpoint of superiority, makes him question himself whether he is a hidden bigot, although, seen from the outside, he was "already doing everything right where race was concerned" (286). He loves his wife and his daughter, but Lizzie's different skin color throws him so much that he overreacts. When Dana asks him if they can find a way to go back to where they were, Hugh only sees a possibility for it after he knows for sure where the baby's skin color comes from. To undo the inflicted hurt is difficult, but the couple has enough love left to overcome hurts. From the moment his need to know is satisfied, Hugh finds a way to show Dana how much he loves her and their child.

OTHER CHARACTERS

Combining the rounding out of the protagonists' characterization with exhibiting the different facets of her matter of concern in the subplots is one of Delinsky's idiosyncrasies in many of her Women's Fiction novels. In *The Family Tree*, the secondary characters support the protagonists' characterization, that of unconditional love, which Dana craves, and that of Hugh's need to know, which nearly destroys his bonds of love and friendship. Furthermore, they present different aspects of deception the upper class needs to uphold their power and relevance, which is the second matter of concern in the novel. Here they are:

Ellie-Jo, Dana's grandmother is the key to understanding Dana's obsession with wool and knitting, along with her indifference towards her illegitimacy. She gave Dana a sheltered upbringing as well as unconditional love, and continues to offer the latter after Lizzie turned out to be biracial. Moreover, Ellie-Jo has, up to now, successfully concealed her husband's bigamy and tries to keep up pretenses and respectability.

Dana's refusal to search for her father before her child's birth is important for the plot construction to incorporate because of her inner preoccupation with feelings of abandonment that result in her need for unconditional love. Jack Jones Kettyle's readiness to acknowledge her as his daughter causes Dana to reluctantly recognize that her mother, whom she had previously worshiped, had denied her a childhood with a caring father.

Eaton Clarke is not able to give his children unconditional love. He is too pedigree-proud to accept a daughter-in-law who not only does not come from his social class but is also illegitimate, a fact he regards as so unacceptable that he treats Dana like a second-class citizen. Apart from this, his values of decency, honor, and fairness are mirrored in his considerations of how and when to go public about his biracial origin. Dorothy, Hugh's mother, represents womanly decency. She is also presented as a typical upper class 'ditz' who, obviously for the first time in her life, is becoming aware of her social class' arrogance.

Crystal Kostas, whose case Hugh takes *pro bono,* is merely the means to show Hugh's compassionate character beside his legal excellence. The child's father, a hypocritical senator, personifies the arrogance of his social class thinking that he can get away with corruption because of the power his wealth supplies him with.

A different kind of deception is shown in Corinne's yearning to belong to a respectable social circle. An additional kind of hide and seek comes to light when a good customer at Ellie's shop reveals herself as Lizzie's black great-great aunt.

CONFLICTS, RELATIONSHIP, AND EROTIC SCENES

The main conflict in *The Family Tree* is the characters' attitude toward racial and class equality in US society. Each character's attitude casts a different light on the matter, be it seeing no difference of skin color in your friends, or simply a loving acceptance of your child's racial origin; be it going into hiding, or publicly acknowledging your newly learned knowledge; be it bigotry, or reactions in between. Then, there is the conflict of self-deception and other kinds of pretense, as mentioned above.

Besides this main conflict, the characters have other inner battles to fight. Dana who, at the beginning, seems to have found what she yearns for, discovers that she has not yet overcome her childhood insecurities. Subconsciously, she has made her unknown father responsible for her orphaned childhood and has to learn now that her anger about his indifference has been misplaced. To resolve this conflict is her part in the novel. In addition, the Clarke clan's humiliating behavior makes her feel inferior. Dealing with this problem, as well as Hugh's mistrusting demands, is her other conflict.

Hugh's conflict arises when he, who has always been an advocate of racial equality, learns that he has been acting with feelings of racial superiority typical of a white man. Now he has to tackle inner insecurities he never dreamed he would have. But they emerge at the end of the novel, not at the beginning and so leave room for readers' interpretive thoughts. Another issue of the novel, shown in nearly every secondary character, is the conflict people have between the persona they project to the world and the persona underneath, which are quite different. (Eaton, Ellie-Jo, Corinne, Hutchinson).

The character constellations in *The Family Tree* are complex and asexual, and only deal with family dynamics. The yarn shop is one center where friendships have been forged into a somewhat surrogate family over the years by way of the interest in knitting. On Hugh's side the masculine kind of love and respect is shown between father and son, but the basis for it is always their affiliation to their social class.

The relationship between Hugh and Dana suffers a deep rift when the eagerly awaited baby turns out differently from what they expected. Beside the naturally demanded sexual abstinence so shortly after the child's birth, the couple's sexual attraction is dimmed by the resulting conflicts of the child's skin color. Emotionally and physically they become estranged so that even touching each other is a problem. The relationships in the novel deal with the aforementioned interpersonal conflicts, where only the results of sexual acts of the past are reported. There is no sexual or erotic scene to be found anywhere in the novel: when sex is mentioned at all, it is in a detached way. Of course, the absence of erotic scenes does not indicate that this story is not a love story, but it is not a romance in the conventional sense by which romances are defined. However, the characters' main search in their lives is the quest for love, and at best, the quest for unconditional love.

WRITING STYLE AND CODE

Although *The Family Tree* seems to be written mostly from Dana's and Hugh's perspectives, with insertions from Ellie, Eaton, and Dorothy, the impression of a heterodiegetic covert narrator telling the story is predominant, even if there are no narratorial remarks to be found. The story is more a report of what is happening to different characters: it offers few opportunities for emotional identification to the reader and with less insight into the characters and less chances to really understand the protagonists due to everyday information and reflections in the reported occurrences that are not so much musings of emotionality but contemplations of problems from different sides.

About three quarters of the novel is dialogue[63] and the characters are never alone for long with their inner thoughts to explain their real emotional situation to the reader. Longer narrative parts are used to inform the reader about settings or situations. The descriptions often focus on information about e.g. running of a shop than to thrilling emotions typical of the romance genre:

> ... the shop was abuzz.
> There was excited talk about the baby, excited talk about Dana, excited talk about the boxes. Ellie Jo wasn't sure she would have been able to concentrate enough to actually sell yarn. Fortunately, Olivia could do that. Indeed, at that very moment, she was waiting on a mother and her twenty-something daughter who were just learning to knit and wanted novelty yarns for fall scarves.
> Customers like these were good for sales; novelty yarn was expensive and quickly worked, which meant that if the customer enjoyed herself, she would soon be back for more. One scarf could lead to a hat, then a throw, then a sweater. If that sweater was cashmere at upwards of forty dollars a skein, with eight or more skeins needed, depending on the size and style, the sale could be hefty. Moreover, a year from now, this mother or her daughter might be one of those to rush to the shop ... (59)

Descriptions of situations are mostly given in this kind of report. They differ from the descriptions in romances because here the situation does not offer cause for pondering what is ailing the heroine. Readers who are used to being presented with an explanation of the meaning of the action within the description are not satisfied here:

> She made herself a cup of tea and was drinking it when Ellie Jo arrived.
> Dana immediately felt better. Her grandmother was a survivor. She was proof that bad things would pass.
> While Ellie Jo took Lizzie to her room, Dana returned to her own. Desperate for normalcy, she pulled out a pair of pre-pregnancy denim shorts. Though it took little work, the zipper went up. Cheered, she put on a hot pink cropped tee shirt, stepped into canvas slides, and brushed her hair up into a knot.

---

[63]   in Amazon readers' reviews, the dialogues are sometimes described as stiff and clumsy.

> A short time later, she was with her grandmother on the patio. Having finished their sandwiches, they were stretched out on lounges under the canopy, knitting while the baby slept in the carriage nearby. Though the late-August sun was warm on the grass, the sea breeze moderated its heat. It was in this spirit that Dana alternately knitted a row, purled a row, briskly adding inches to the moss-green sleepsack that Lizzie would need come fall. (91)

This text is an illustration of the action told in straightforward syntax. The sentences are not long, despite being mostly subordinate. Five of the twelve sentences begin with a subject, always a different one, whereas the other seven sentence beginnings range from adverbial phrases of time to adverbial phrases and restrictive adverbs. Listings here are once a listing of verbs in the past tense and two times not so obvious ones, but still a threesome of verbs (having finished, they were stretched, knitting, and knitted, purled, adding). The wording in this text seems to be everyday wording which reflects the everyday-like situation. The content does not digress much from an ordinary report.

As mentioned above, apart from the conflicts the couple experiences, sexual intercourse is excluded because of Lizzie's birth and likewise an analysis of the part how intimate sexuality is presented. Other disclosures of sexual affairs are given in a reporting style. As Dana and Hugh have to deal with feelings about each other they cannot be reconciled to their love: for a time intimacy is excluded. Even touching each other is difficult. Only in the beginning does Hugh use endearments like "sweetie" and "honey". After the baby is born they address each other with their first names.

The text on the back cover of *The Family Tree* lets the potential reader guess at a romantic content which, in a way, is misleading, because the novel's matter of concern is not so much a love story, but the problem of how people behave when confronted with snobbery and pretense, [64] although the novel's ending might send the genre's message that 'love conquers all'.

3.2.4 CONSTANTS AND CHANGES

Delinsky's work is clearly to be divided into her romance novel writing era from 1981 until 1991 and her Women's Fiction. As early as 1987 she was writing longer novels that could not be called pure romance stories, either because the plot was more complex, or because the theme was more elaborate. >From 1992 onward she

---

[64] The text at the back cover is as follows: "A loving family, a child on the way and secret that will tear their lives apart … Dana Clarke has it all – a husband, Hugh, whom she adores, a beautiful home and a baby on the way. But, when her daughter, Lizzie, is born, what should be the happiest day of her life turns out to be the moment that her world falls apart. As a family is divided by bitter mistrust, all their beliefs in each other, in their family background, are challenged. Will the birth of their first child destroy their marriage or can they overcome the repercussions of secret told years ago?"

has only written mainstream Women's Fiction, which is still rooted in romance. However, the core theme of her romance novels and her mainstream ones has remained the same: secrecy, deception and pretense.

As a native born, and life-long New Englander, Delinsky decided to rotate the setting of her stories in the New England states. *Sweet Ember* (1982) is set in Maine, *A Woman Betrayed* (1992) in Hampshire and Maine, and *The Family Tree* (2007) in Massachusetts and Maine. Descriptions of landscapes vary in degrees over the years. *Sweet Ember* contains an abundance of lengthy descriptions with interspersed, added misdirected thoughts and confused feelings on the part of the protagonist, whereas, due to a differently established emphasis on a topic, the other novels mostly use enhance longer, informative depictions of locations for characterization. They are rendered with the same accuracy as in *Sweet Ember*.

The topics have changed, and with them, Delinsky's diction. In *Sweet Ember* she writes with a pronounced eloquence, although, at times, the prose wanders off into what clearly is the formulaic, adjectively and adverbially overused language of the romance novels of the time. In *A Woman Betrayed* there are no such language slips and the novel is rendered in the style of a well composed narrative. The diction in *The Family Tree* is different again. Superfluous adjectives and adverbs as well as 'overloaded' sentences are eliminated. Instead, the chosen diction here projects the impression of a more reporting kind of narrative than an purely entertaining one equipped with a strong suspense curve. In a podcast, Delinsky admits that her new editor 'taught' her how to write better, especially how to slim down her prose thus making her "writing more efficient and sophisticated" (Writers Write). I assume that the controversial reaction of her readers to this novel is not only because of the theme, but also because of Delinsky's departure from the popular mainstream novelists' silent agreement to repeatedly explain the meanings behind behavior and incidents, this way intellectually elevating the stories.[65] Yet, for readers used to novels that end satisfyingly without the need to ponder about them afterwards, Delinsky offers reading group discussion guides included in the book itself or retrievable from the internet. These guides are proof that, with her novels, she does not intend to instantly satisfy a reader, for her novel themes are too complex to be put aside without further reflection. Here, the aspect of *docere* takes precedence over the aspect of *delectare*.

In all three novels the fictional families live in secure economic circumstances, be they due to inherited money or proficient work. In her other novels a financially secure background is also the premise on which health and emotional problems can be dealt with. The heroine in *Sweet Ember,* giving birth to a child out of

---

[65] The 114 Amazon reader reviews mirror how controversially this novel is judged. Some of the reviews even complain about missing explanations.

wedlock, does not seem to have had to endure poverty as a result, as a cliché usually demanded from a romance novel. Instead she was able to learn to become a photographer with her parents' financial support. At the time of the story, her parents are dead and she needs to work to earn her living, and is qualified to do so because she excels at the profession she was allowed to learn, despite having a child to take care of. The hero, on his part, seems to have climbed the ladder of success based on his own efforts, but he also still needs to work, albeit as president of a college, and at the summer camp as tennis instructor. Whether or not economic reasons force him to work at the summer camp is not divulged.

For a part of the Frye family in *A Woman Betrayed,* the financial situation is precarious for a short time. Jeff's 'death' restores the family's good reputation and with it, their secure economic background. Christian and Daphne have economized. This way they have some money at their disposal which they are able to lend to Laura. But all characters in the novel must work hard for their living. This effort to work hard, and the sense of thrift is alluded to as the natural basis for financial success.

In *The Family Tree*, the Clarke family is wealthy and could live from their dividends alone. Yet for them, living a life of leisure is not an option they care for. The hero's father uses this secure economic background to work according to his interests, as does the hero. Work-wise, they both benefit from their upper class social connections. Married to Hugh, Dana does not need to work either, but like her husband, she loves her chosen field of work as an interior designer, besides being a designer of knitting patterns.

The social class within which Delinsky's characters move, at least all her protagonists, are that of the educated classes and of the economically middle class to the really wealthy upper class. In her novels, books and the wealth of information they offer, besides being testimony of their owner's inquisitive mind, are mentioned as worthwhile items to indicate cultural interests. For example, seeing her ransacked house, a distressed Stephanie puts back in order "hundreds of scattered volumes which had been part of the family's diverse library" (*Sweet Ember* 179). In *A Woman Betrayed* Jeff's den is a library lined top to bottom with books. Even the diversity of topics this library contains is listed. Both, Laura and Jeff are avid readers and Christian's house is filled with art work and a collection of classical music. In *The Family Tree* the avid reading is delegated to Eaton, Hugh's father, who, in addition, is an author of historical biographies. Thus, this mark of cultural interests is consigned to the older generation, whereas the younger generation's interests and in-depth information stay within their professional inclinations.

>From the beginning of her writing career, Delinsky has portrayed strong women who love their professional work, pursue it even in their leisure time, and, with this commitment and energy beside the intelligence they put into it, they

excel in it and this way successfully cope in their working lives. The matter of equality between the sexes is not taken for granted in Delinsky's category romance novels where the heroines, even if they do lead successful professional lives, become timid creatures and are in awe of the hero when faced with his dominant behavior. Feminist ideas explain the heroines' actions, but in her Women's Fiction, equality between the sexes is never conclusive. As complicated as character constellations are, allocations of power in relationships differ and are never only one-sided. They are presented as the complex facets they are in real life. Man and woman are distinguished according to their various individual, not blatantly traditionally gender ascribed characteristics. Emancipated female characters try hard to successfully combine work, marriage, children, and the household, but cannot meet all those demands without the help of their partners, who often do not help at all. This is the exposition in many of her mainstream novels. During the unfolding story, it becomes apparent that these strong women shoulder the major part of the relationship while their husbands of many years offer no dependable support, and even undermine their efforts.

The man in her category romance novel world is taciturn, private and as such becomes a sexually attractive mystery for the heroine since she cannot fathom his behavioral inconsistencies. (Partly responsible for the presentation of enigmatic heroes is the single perspective rule of the romance publishing houses.) When two perspectives were conceded, Delinsky's heroes turned out to be the proverbial beta-heroes, still enigmatic and taciturn. They are men with a soft touch, even when they are uncompromising in their professional role. As lovers in her popular mainstream novels, they are able to permit themselves softer emotions; husbands of many years often prove to be the weaker sex. They are not faithful, or just cannot cope with being married to a strong woman.

The heroines are accorded typical feminine professions as well as androgynous ones that are also accorded to the heroes. Whether knitters or restaurant owners, lawyers or psychologists, they are portrayed as outstanding professionals who are just as successful as their male counterparts. Financial, not emotional independence, separate from that of their partners, constitutes one of the ingredients for the composition of the female characters. Delinsky likes to use certain professions repeatedly. The female protagonist in *Sweet Ember* is a photographer who teaches photography at a summer camp. Photos, although not the actual taking and developing, also play a role in *A Woman Betrayed*, albeit referred to as the heroine's hobby and not her profession. There, they serve to subconsciously connect her and her former lover, the professional photographer, whose enthusiasm influenced her so much that she has filled her house with artistic photographs. Photography as a profession, sometimes as a budding one, is attributed to many a character. The author seems to follow a rule that writers are advised to consider: to write about things they know. Having worked as a photographer for a time, she knows this matter well, just as she knows the subject of psychology well. The male protagonist in *Sweet Ember* is a teacher of psychology at a college, and the heroine's mother in *A Woman Betrayed* teaches psychology at a university. Whereas he is given this profession in name only because he does not act accordingly, she uses her knowledge by constantly analyzing her daughter, which in turn enables her daughter to provide *ad hoc* psychological answers. Psychologists also often appear in other novels. Another professional field Delinsky is familiar with is that of law. (Her husband is a lawyer.) This seems to be why many of her protagonists are successful lawyers, female or male. In *A Woman Betrayed,* the heroine's friend, a lawyer, helps as much as she can in a legal capacity, and in *The Family Tree*, besides other legal concerns of his, the male protagonist, is a lawyer whose excellence as such is exhibited in his legal campaign and win for his client. In order to portray professional, and other facts, correctly, Delinsky researches her subject matters thoroughly. Acknowledgments at the beginnings or at the end of her mainstream novels are proof of this, as are references in interviews.

For Delinsky's characters, a functioning relationship requires accomplishments on equal basic core values , different as they may be otherwise. The importance lies in the respect and trust each character professes for the other's kind of work and actions. In spite of her protagonists' sexual attraction at first sight, explicitly described sexual acts do not rank first. Strong sexual feelings develop as the protagonists become better acquainted with each other. The romances, especially those belonging to the Harlequin *Temptation* line, contain eighty percent of the story romance in the "male – female, sex-scene-driven sense".(Bookreporter). It is true that sex scenes are in the foreground in these romances, but her *modus operandi* of the physical approach is more on the tentative side, despite a strongly expressed sexual attraction, with the resulting effect that sexuality is attributed the same importance as, for instance, getting to know the person. Seen this way, sexuality plays a secondary role in the relationship. In her popular mainstream novels, sexuality is represented as one of the many aspects of life, sometimes of importance, sometimes negligible.

Taken separately from Delinsky's mainstream novels, *Sweet Ember* could pass as a typical romance novel, according to Regis' eight essential narrative elements and publishers' writing guidelines. Seen, however, in the context of her other novels, one predominantly typical Delinsky matter of concern already prevails in her category romances, including *Sweet Ember*: that of a character's innate fixation, even obsession with privacy or secretiveness, which inevitably leads to interpersonal conflicts. Initially the restricted personal configurations of romance novels encourage this trait. The isolated protagonists, be they on an island, a cabin in the woods, a summer camp, or simply characters without family ties, turn into puzzles, behave mysteriously, either because of their character's inability to communicate or because of (and this is usually the case) her/his unwillingness to reveal who s/he is beneath the person s/he shows on the outside. Often it takes about two hundred pages for the parties to be ready to talk, and thus, commit. The protagonists, especially the males, want to keep their persona secret or stay mysterious. They need to trust thoroughly before they can allow themselves to open up intimately, which they do rather quickly sexually, but not so quickly emotionally, although the levels of secretiveness differ. In *Sweet Ember,* the hero is not even willing to reveal his profession outside the camp to the heroine, the woman with whom he conceived a child, and she would rather let herself be insulted to the point where it is no longer possible to conceal the identity of the father of her daughter. The reason for this obsessive secretiveness is disclosed to the reader as an intercommunicative inability on the part of both protagonists.

In *A Woman Betrayed,* all secrets kept have reasons which are believably clarified in time. Virtually every character proves to have a different side to him/her than the one s/he publicly shows. Baring their private thoughts is difficult for each of them. In this respect, the heroine's husband leads the way. He is a reserved person, who relies only on himself, a trait which enables him to accomplish tax fraud for years and plan his disappearing act. His mother is similarly unforthcoming, capable even of taking the name of her other son's biological father to her grave. The heroine's former lover was and is able to trust a person enough to admit his personal secrets, which is a step forward to a future with the heroine, but in his youth he kept his career and life secret from his family. For over twenty years the heroine has kept her love for him to herself. Not only was her lawyer friend her husband's lover, a fact she does not divulge as long as she possibly can, but this friend also needs to keep hidden her relationship with the criminal investigator. For every concealment kept, there is a reason the reader can comprehend, even accept, as a sensible decision. Characters are endowed with more complexity by a public face versus a private one. Moreover, it is pointed out to the reader that people should never be taken at face value. (The *docere* part of the narration becomes increasingly significant.)

Inability to communicate, attempts to pass for someone other than oneself, pretense, a public face versus a private face, all these sides of the same coin seem to be a central matter of concern in Delinsky's novels. When she started out as a writer, projecting this topic in parts appeared to fit into the restricting frame of category romance novels; in time, however, the straight narrative modality of the genre, which is a basic love story that leads to a couple's sexual fulfillment and happiness, was too restrictive for the author. In addition, the one-plot publisher narrative specification became too restricting for her. With the change of her novel's format, she could now devote more pages to the problems she wanted to write about. Her covert narrator turned into an omniscient one. Writing for a mainstream audience, she inserts various extended subplots, which not only lengthen the story, but also serve her intentions in a different way from how they would be used in category romance novels. They provide her readers with varying insights into the novel's theme, acting as eye openers, while at the same time pointing out that the problems in the theme presented are not as simple as they seem to be. With her subplots, Delinsky evades black and white romance formula solutions by identifying different facets inherent to the theme. However, these novels cannot keep up the necessary suspense curve of the three act drama, so she needs to construct a different kind of suspense for her novels: some of the subplots present their own climaxes; others, closely connected with the main plot, lead to its 'main' climax. Consequently, her suspension curves are shaped by the importance of the theme in the novel, its differentiations in the subplots, and by the solutions she offers.

That Delinsky chooses "secondary characters for their ability to complement central themes in the book" (Writers Write) is seen in *A Woman Betrayed* as well as in *The Family Tree*. Pretense and concealment of states or activities is, once again, the main theme for most characters in *The Family Tree*. The big secret that gets the story rolling, the baby's great-grandmother's affair with a light-skinned Afro-American, occurred at least sixty-five years before the beginning of the story. Its materializing in the shape of a child with dark skin causes secrets to surface that characters of this novel had kept to themselves for a long time. Here it is the value people place on appearances which leads them to conceal what might alienate them from their chosen social circle, or cause them to lose power or their friends' respect. The baby's grandfather will probably disclose his Afro-American ancestor to the public: when, however, is a question of strategy. For what is obviously the first time in his and his wife's life, now that they are becoming aware of their own social arrogance, they question the privileges they were granted by the social class they were born and accepted into because of a blood-right heritage, a fact that emphasizes their political ignorance. With the heroine's help, her grandmother will be able to forever conceal her shame of having been a bigamist's wife. A customer's desperate attempt to keep up pretenses for the sake of appearances leads to her public humiliation. Hoping to build up a new respectable life somewhere else, she leaves the town, and may continue to delude herself because she craves social respectability so much. She will always carry the secret around with her. The hero's *pro bono* case shows another facet: that of a rich and influential man's struggle to maintain power and social credibility despite his morally callous behavior. Only the heroine's mother's decision to have a child out of wedlock and keep the father's name a secret differs from all the other characters' endeavors to uphold their social status. As in *Sweet Ember,* the question of giving birth out of wedlock and its socially outcast potential is benevolently overlooked.[66]

Amazon reader reviews point out that the *docere* part particularly in *The Family Tree* leads to one dimensional characterizations of the secondary characters, which are the narratological device to make the complexity of the author's matter of concern understandable since she does not offer the explanations that a reader is used to being presented with in popular fiction.

What transpires as a constant in Delinsky's novels is that
a)   the narratives are composed and well structured
b)   the plots stay linear as does the timeline
c)   the settings are restricted to the New England States
d)   reality plays a convincing part
e)   the novels are centered around the heroine and her sexuality if it is thematized
f)   the main theme is to show that everyone wears a mask and has secrets
g)   marriage and family are worth living for despite disillusionment
h)   the conviction is that a balanced relationship guarantees stability in life

What transpires as change in Delinsky's novels is that
a)   the promise of everlasting love in a romance novel is given a reality check of the 'after' of the 'Ever After' in her Women's Fiction
b)   female characters are the stronger sex when confronted with the problems of everyday life and life in general
c)   male characters don't remain charismatic and mysterious, but do have inferiority complexes when they are married to strong women, or they cheat on their wives because they can
d)   male and female characters are no longer portrayed in black and white. Each combines good and bad within his/her personality
e)   the heroine will find the right man once she knows herself and her needs better
f)   the number of perspectives increase, and with them, the characters are given more complexity
g)   serious concerns of American society are thematized (physical handicaps, illnesses, death, social snobbery etc.) and different facets of these concerns are often conveyed in the subplots
h)   to some of the mainstream novels, reading group guides are added. Obviously the elevated complexity of her novels reaches a different audience who is inclined to continue to reflect on the problem depicted in the novel.

The question whether a typical voice can be determined, can be answered as fol-

---

[66]   Giving birth out of wedlock, however, is not so benevolently overlooked in Delinsky's *Not My Daughter* of 2010

lows: from the beginnings of her writing, Delinsky has attracted attention by her educated writing style and the characterization of her private, taciturn and enigmatic heroes. Here, her consistent themes can already be perceived: the display of private versus public personalities and, closely connected to that, secrecy. In contrast to Krentz, her romances and novels are completely heroine centered. Her Women's Fiction novels acquaint the reader with different facets of the respective subject matter by way of extensive subplots. Reading groups often choose her brand of novels for discussion, and it can be supposed that it is her individual way to approach a theme which motivates readers to select her novels. Although these are identifying features and Delinsky widened the field of her narration, she remained within the scope of popular linear and explanatory narration.

In order to give a clearer overview of the synopses in the chapters 3.1.4. and 3.2.4. of this study I have tabulated them. (see annex) The tables clarify, at a short glance, each author's development toward complexity. This overview outlines the results of the analyses and the increasing length of the columns reflects the increasing degree of complexity.

PART IV

COMPARISONS IN A CROSS-SECTIONAL SURVEY OF THE SIX NOVELS

In the following sections the basic patterns of the narrative discourse will be considered, while at the same time providing further information about the subtexts and the ideas conveyed by them.

4.1 ASPECTS OF DISCOURSE

4.1.1 PLOTS

Real life differs from fiction in its messiness with regard to events and how their significance for a person's life is not instantly recognizable. Fiction, according to Andreotti, especially fiction which follows the structure of the bourgeois novel together with the assumption of a unity of the individual, the language, and the world found in the romance genre, shows a well ordered process of dramatized, inciting significant incidents, hence usually engineering an ending which is satisfying to a reader.[67] In addition, the genre offers a harmonized transparence by reducing life's complexity, emphasizing the merits of love alone. This fictional device, called plot becomes the pivot around which all the other literary aspects rotate. For all types of fiction, there are valid rules a writer needs to observe in order to become 'readable' for an audience, and if s/he wants to become successful, it is even more important to obey the rules.

If one compares the plots of these six novels, it transpires that they are structured within the conventional frame of bourgeois novels. The plots in romance novels, especially those in category romances, follow the same rules as those of a three-act drama because they are composed with one main plot. In well-developed stories, the essential idea of the narrative structure includes an identifiable beginning, middle and end. To seduce a reader into carrying on reading, however, the drama's more concise plot structure ensures this by offering an exposition in which the setting, characters and main conflicts are introduced to the reader along with a little action or emotion. What follows the introduction is the rising action

---

[67] In Delinsky's fictional world this significance shown in events, problematic or bad, is captioned with "everything happens for a reason"

or development. It comprises the major part of the novel. Here, the characters are given the chance to develop: conflicts are steadily increased and are acted out in many ways, motives are introduced, 'inciting incidents' take place, intensifying the tension, or crises occur until the tension at its highest point in the story is reached: the climax. The major conflicts erupt in some kind of final showdown such as a fight, an argument, violent or physical action, or a tense emotional moment. The events which immediately follow the climax, the falling action or denouement constitute a kind of 'cleaning up'. The point where everything ends is the resolution or conclusion. The reader may experience some sense of closure, or will be stimulated to think about what comes next. In romance novels it is the promise of a happy ending or the wedding, a reported pregnancy or the birth of a child.

As a consequence of publishers' writing guidelines for category romance novels and the required lengths of these short novels, the story is framed for one plot only and thus the observation of the three act drama's expected suspension curve becomes a necessity. Subplots, if they exist at all, are restricted to one or two pages at most. It could be worth considering whether the intended presentation of erotic intensity for a romance novel actually rules out longer subplot digressions and dramatic options for the writer. It could also be worth, considering whether the plot serves as a 'field of demonstration' for the protagonists' characterization (Andreotti 28) because the characters are focused on themselves in an all-consuming way, and readers wish for an attainment of high emotions, erotic intensity, and satisfaction alone. For this reason, a Krentz-type one plot only story is sufficient. Even if the plot is augmented by brief subplots, the timeline in such romance plots is usually linear.[68] Both authors stay within the time level of the narrative present, with subplots interwoven as parallel ones therein. Krentz likes to let a past time event take place in a prologue. Analepses, other than the one in a prologue are recounted in dialogues or, occasionally, in dreams, or in characters' pondering the implications a past event could have for the present. I recall only one novel where Delinsky inserts a second layer of time into her story by making the heroine find and read, section after section of a psychologist's report of a patient's story.[69]

Readers are used to cuts in TV soap operas that, in order to build up some

---

[68] Flusser points out that the writing system alone promotes a certain way of thinking which is specified by linearity. It is the linearity which defines the thinking process and characterizes it as consequential. He wants to show "daß sich die linearen Verhältnisse auf ganz wenige Typen (vielleicht sogar einzig und allein auf den Wenn-dann-Typus) reduzieren lassen" (Flusser 2007, 127). Accordingly it might be that the realistic novel with its linear plot is the adequate form for a general reader who by his/her cultural reading background is used to considering cause and effect only as a sequence of tenses. A literature that transgresses this 'if-then' formula of the clear straightforward plot addresses a different audience.

[69] Delinsky, *Flirting with Pete*, 2003

tension, change the place or the setting to where a part of a subplot is happening, only to return to the main plot followed by another change of place. All this takes place within the time level of a narrative present. Unlike in TV soap operas, neither authors cuts one action into pieces for tension's sake. In their novels, a reader can follow sequential actions without 'cuts'. Staying in a one-time-level with no 'hopping' between scenes, seems to make these novels 'eminently accessible' for a reader.

Pamela Regis, who derives the structure of romance novels from comedy and backs up this assertion with Northrop Frye's theory in *Anatomy*, defines 'plot' differently and only in relation to the genre. She structures romances along contentual steps. The novel as a work of prose fiction "tells the story of the courtship and betrothal of one or more heroines" (Regis 27) For her the essence of this genre is the courtship[70] whose contentual specifications have changed within the time frame of three centuries. The courtship proceeds through eight compulsory stages appearing in the narrative. (Society Defined, The Meeting, The Barrier, The Attraction, The Declaration, The Point of Ritual Death, The Recognition, The Betrothal) If a novel does not contain these eight essential narrative elements, she maintains, it cannot be called a romance novel.[71] This approach of finding a formula for the romance calls to mind structuralist Vladimir Propp's 1928 *Morphology of the Folk Tale*. While, according to Propp, folk tales always follow the sequence of 31 functions in the same order after the initial situation has been depicted, Regis restricts them to eight with the optional addition of three and, unlike Propp, for her, the order of these stages or functions is not restricted to one place within the plot.

A combination of these two aspects of plot, the structural one and the one regarding the content, might elicit an easier access to define otherwise complicated problems because the ingredients in content alone do not make a compelling story. This requires a rising action and a climax in order to arrive at the happy ending. Knowing the requirements of their genre line, editors are involved in all aspects of the author's writing, ensuring e.g. that no inconsistencies in the story occur. Plots beside complex characterizations are major considerations as well. Whether this really is their task or only a paper lie is a moot point. It only seems that the editors did or do not pay close attention to the narrative structure because the

---

[70] The old-fashioned term is used here along the following definitions: prelude to marriage; trying to gain somebody's löve; mating be havior

[71] In 1986, Helen Mae Sterk had already outlined nine basic steps in the plotline of romance novels, in this case basing her research on Silhouette genre romances. These nine steps are 1. The Cube Meeting, 2. The Complication, 3. The Circumstantial Proximity, 4. The Escalation of Attraction, 5. The Congruence, 6. The Betrayal, 7. The Crisis, 8. The Union, 9. The Coda, sometimes 10. The Epilogue. As these steps follow more or less a dramatic structure, Pamela Regis' version leaves more room for interpretation.

early novels both authors had published under their tutelage definitely show weak plots and weak characterizations: Krentz's *Stormy Challenge* does not show any development leading up to a climax which almost goes unnoticed, buried, as it is, under all the contrary dialogue, and as such is exhausting for a reader. With Delinsky's *Sweet Ember,* there is no real development toward the climax because the inciting incidents[72] are climaxes in themselves and do not heighten the final one. But both novels contain Regis' requirements for romance novels. Yet, these one plot only stories generate too much reduction of complexity.

When Krentz decided on a transition to the hybrid category romantic suspense and since 1992 only (popular) romantic suspense, she gave herself the chance to create a greater variety of plots, and, by way of a solution to a crime, she could be guaranteed at least one climax *a priori*. The other climax, leading to the couple's everlasting union, does not necessarily need to follow dramatic rules for readers. It is enough that it contains Regis' romance novel ingredients. A mystery or crime section takes up more narrative space, thus increasing the word count of the novel, but it also gives the authors opportunities to endow their characters with more complexity. Krentz's 1992 single title novel *Perfect Partners'* plot is intricate, judged from romantic suspense standards, because it contains longer subplots closely linked to the main plot. The courtship part and the crime part melt together so that the love story becomes enhanced by the crime and the characters are given a chance to display more than one character trait through the crime part.

Delinsky's plots around 1992 consist of many larger subplots linked with the main plot in a different way from those Krentz uses. (By this time Delinsky was no longer writing category romances and had turned to mainstream Women's Fiction.) Krentz adds subplots to give her characters more depth. Delinsky, who already combined topics of her concern with her one-main-plot-only category romance novels, now uses her subplots in *A Woman Betrayed* to elucidate different facets of the matters of her concern. She also uses subplots that would almost be separate stories, were they not linked with the main plot as distinguishing features of the topic. The novel does not lack the necessary tension that makes a story interesting beside content and characters. Yet, as there are multiple plotlines and each requires its own climax, the tension is divided. Of course, creating a family tableau calls for a different narrative tension structure than the one for a couple solving a crime. *The Family Tree* (2007) still shows Delinsky's preference for subplots presenting different aspects of her novel's matter of concern, and here she even adds one separate story loosely linked to the main plot making readers aware of yet another aspect of the novel's theme. It is the matter of concern that generates suspense in that story, which has to deal with only secrets that nearly every char-

---

[72]   Instead of crisis, McKee calls the tension building occurrences 'inciting incidents'.

acter has to reveal willy-nilly. The various subplots Delinsky likes to weave into her main story open up opportunities to present even secondary characters with more complex characteristics.

In 2007, Krentz chose her individual strategies in writing romantic suspense novels, letting the courtship take second place by transferring the Point of Ritual Death to the crime part of the story in *All Night Long,* and by using a plot line, which, for a romance, was intricate, albeit sequential. Still, she inserts the category romance novel requirement of explicit sex scenes. This again emphasizes that, although the love story itself takes second place, the raison d'être for the story is the couple's courtship, and not the suspense part.

Different though the authors are, they deliver plots in a linear, mostly sequential timeline with increasing tension and emotional disruptions at strategically set positions in the story.

4.1.2 FOCALIZATION

Since Henry James, the invisible narrator has become the norm in the Anglo-Saxon narrative tradition,[73] and with this tradition, the question of how perspectives are constructed led to Gérard Genette's theory of focalization in 1972. The text part in a novel where characters speak and think has become the mark that distinguishes the novel from other types of texts. Dorrit Cohn systematized the narrative rendering of consciousness in *Transparent Minds* (Cohn 1981, 61). Here the term 'psycho-narration' includes the narrative details that an invisible narrator uses to visualize states of consciousness that the character her/himself is not able to verbalize. This part of the perspective discussion distinguishes between the stream of consciousness which is like a silent monologue, and the psycho-narration which is not and which is rendered in the third-person. This third-person psycho-narrative is similar to that of the researched romance novels, although Cohn would never consider romance novels as a basis to define this kind of psycho-narration. For the purpose of narrowing down a definition for the narrative situation (Stanzel) in romance novels, a covert heterodiegetic narrator directing a homodiegetic reflector could be an expedient term.

At one time publishers forced their romance authors to tell their stories not with the help of an omniscient narrator, but by using the homodiegetic perspective or the psycho-narration of the heroine, not as first person but as third person narration.[74] In order to cope with this exclusive single perspective, romance authors needed an invisible or covert narrator. Since stories that are told in the first person perspective did and, according to publisher's writing guidelines, do not

---

[73] See J. Hillis Miller (124–135).

[74] Andreotti sees the figural narrative situation as an expression of a worldview according to which the complexity of reality, its lack of transparency, defies a meaningful reading (162).

sell well, a third person perspective, even if it is only one, offers more possibilities by the use of a covert narrator. S/he provides the necessary distancing as mediator to allow the reader to enjoy, for example, a heroine's psyche that otherwise could not be as satisfactorily explained because a heroine's ego shown in a first-person-perspective usually suggests a not so complex personality. The third-person-perspective of the heroine presents her story through thoughts, impressions, and sensations that flow through her mind. A covert narrator takes up the dialogue tags, along with the descriptive parts of events or seemingly associated ideas that could be part of the heroine's musing, but that she would never 'think of thinking'. Because it endows the characters with an emotional depth and often with a sophistication that otherwise would not emerge, publishers regard his kind of 'psycho-narration' as a more promising sale factor. Moreover the shift from authorial to figural narrative situation also transforms a reader's role because she is encouraged to give the text her own sense by a stronger identification with it.

In the 1970s, reprint houses like Harlequin were virtually myopic, clinging to established writing guideline decisions, one crucial one being the single narrative perspective only, namely that of the heroine because they assumed that their female readers, naturally, would only identify with this character. The omniscient author was losing his dominant narrative position because this heroine's perspective appeared to be more attractive, for it allowed her readers extended voyeuristic insights into her persona. (Sometimes this fictional character is not supplied with an intriguing personality so that, even if the reader is permitted access to the heroine's inner self, she will be disappointed by her apparent shallowness.) When they first started writing around 1980, both Krentz and Delinsky, were forced into the inflexible corset of their publishers' guidelines and rules to the extent that the heroine's narrative perspective in the third person excluded, for them, other narrator choices. Fortunately for them, this rule of one perspective only was soon to be suspended and, around 1985, all publishers conceded to two perspectives though still in the third person, that of the hero and the heroine. Wendell/Tan confirm this by saying: "Indeed, the most significant change in popular romance over the last thirty years is the increase in the reader's access to the thoughts and emotions of the romance hero" (2009, 4).

It seems that the use of two perspectives in romance novels forced writers to endow the rather nondescript, but always enigmatic hero with individual character traits, and that this new writing situation has also been of consequence for both authors. Before the change to the inflexible one-third-person-only viewpoint rule, the heroes as characters remained unchartered territory, although they had already been assigned the role of aggressive sexual beings by the late 1970s. Ann Barr

Snitow observes the effect this phenomenon has on the stories in a kind of romance overview:

> What is the Harlequin romance formula? The novels have no plot in the usual sense. All tension and problems arise from the fact that the Harlequin world is inhabited by two species incapable of communicating with each other, male and female. In this sense these Polyanna books have their own dreamlike truth: our culture produces a pathological experience of sex difference. The sexes have different needs and interests, certainly different experiences. They find each other utterly mystifying. Since all action in the novel is described from the female point of view, the reader identifies with the heroine's efforts to decode the erratic gesture of 'dark, tall, gravely handsome' men, all mysterious strangers or powerful bosses ...

He is the unknowable other, a sexual icon whose magic is maleness. The books are permeated by phallic worship. Male is good, male is exciting, without further points of reference. Cruelty, callousness, coldness, menace, all are equated with maleness and treated as the reader knows, whose constant reevaluation of male moods and actions make up the storyline. (Eagleton 2004 (1986), 192–193)

Krentz's heroine in *Stormy Challenge* conjectures the hero to be the 'unknowable other' and as such, he is a person so mystifying that she constantly misinterprets his words, even if they are clearly of the aggressive variety. Delinsky's heroine in *Sweet Ember* also fails to 'decode' the erratic actions of the hero, and, therefore, she is frightened and regresses into timidity.

After writers were conceded two (and later more) viewpoints in a romance novel, preferably that of the hero and heroine, they had to create a sufficiently credible decent male psyche, for the female readers now expected a narrative insight into male feelings and thinking processes. Perhaps this was an opportunity for the authors to reevaluate their own conception of masculinity. It was high time to do so, for they could not go on coupling misogynistic speech with misogynistic thoughts in their newly permitted perspectives: even for the readers who were only interested in the happy ending of a love-hate of the battle of the sexes patterned romance it would not be a pleasant reading experience to be exposed doubly to negative descriptive male dominance in this way.

Krentz toned down her hero's underlying or even open threats of violence. He might have been a physically abusive man who waited until after the wedding to reveal his true brutality, or his aggressiveness during the courtship might have mirrored male emotional helplessness that could turn into violence if his lover does not 'obey'. Once he is given his own inner perspective, duplicating his aggressiveness is counterproductive to the new romance objective from the 1990s and onward of empowering the heroine to tame the hero. So with two perspectives to deal with, as well as with feminist ideas that had already partly permeated the American society's consciousness and legal reality, besides changing romance readers value convictions, Krentz adjusted her heroes to suit the new heroines. In her later novels the hero's male attitude of dominance does not include the power to threaten, to subdue or tame the heroine. Now his only reason for dominant actions is that he wishes to protect. Krentz's writing style stays dialogical, but since the hero's speech is interfaced with his thoughts, she can no longer allow her heroine too many verbal mis-understandings. Otherwise a heroine's stupidity would become even more obvious, and stupidity is counterproductive when you want to present an open, liberal, intelligent female character who should at least show some common sense.

By turning the romance into romantic suspense novels, Krentz was able to give the heroes more complex matters to deal with other than their sexuality and jealousy. Whereas strong patriarchal attitudes were featured in Krentz's novels, and needed to be reworked, Delinsky's heroes never displayed much open aggressiveness or aggressive maleness towards their heroines. Her male characters were private, reserved, and enigmatic persons, and so just as threatening to the heroine by virtue of their superior silent treatment. Because of the one-third-person-only viewpoint rule they remained strangers, the unknown entities without an excessively displayed sexual desire, until they were allowed their own perspective. Readers then benefitted from this additional perspective. Now they were gaining access to the hero's thoughts and feelings, and thereby sometimes, becoming better acquainted with the 'private' hero than the heroine herself *(A Woman Betrayed)*. Occasionally in later novels, Delinsky readopts the single perspective of the heroine, interspersed with additional information from a covert narrator. [75]

This, however, is only a connotation of a structural aspect, explaining changes in hero characterizations and with them the turn of direction in plots. Feminists would argue that, through their efforts to enlighten women about social inequalities, the patriarchal attitude model has cracked, leaving behind a female audience which no longer enjoys reading about arrogant, dominant, possessive heroes, convinced of their patriarchal rights. Jayashree Kamble maintains that the aggressive, hyper-masculine, hyper-sexual romance hero was created in the 1970s and 1980s to help cope with fears of the threat to a heteronormal society by the gay movement and that, with the battle against AIDS, these fears subsided. Thus romance novel heroes have again become less insistent in their heterosexuality and are given more complex traits (Kamble 2008). With both authors, it seems that a combination of these arguments could explain the transformation in their characterization of the male characters.

In her 1992 apologia of the genre, Krentz and her writing colleagues empha-

---

[75] Delinsky, *Flirting With Pete*, 2003

size repeatedly that romance novels make their female readers feel 'empowered' by learning from reading in them about their powers as independent women and by being shown ways of making this possible. They are also made aware of what overpowering men are like because they are informed of diverse possible virtues in men. The splitting of perspectives is a valuable method of achieving this effect. It means the reader gets instant access to both protagonists' feelings and thought processes and can envisage herself in his or her mental situation. But it should never be forgotten that these fictional males' behavior, created by women writers possibly with the intention of a *docere*, reflect female reading preferences of their time and culture.

A different aspect is that, as a result of this perspective splitting, reader identification takes place with both hero and heroine. Who a reader should identify with lies in the narrative hands of the authors by earmarking the perspective. Once a reader can identify, reason, and fall in love with the male protagonist via his perspective, this protagonist has to become agreeable and his innate dominant traits have to turn, for example, into understandable protectiveness as an acceptable male characteristic, different from the aggressive attitude he was forced into before. Krentz's post-1986 heroes meet these identification criteria and as often as not, the reader feels alternately more connected with the hero or the heroine.[76] If one had to give a short summary of a post-1986 Krentz novel it would almost always, begin this way: "It is the story of a man courting a woman ... " For that reason there are two protagonists to contend with. Therefore, I decided to first examine the male protagonist and then the female. In Krentz's novels, both protagonists are attracted to each other, but the man begins the actual courtship and it is debatable who is actually more important, even if the writing guideline percentage allotment is 60% female and 40% male. The woman is the recipient of his sexual advances until she turns the tables within the courtship. Delinsky, however, never confuses her readers. Her stories are always about "A woman who ... " whether she uses one, two, or multiple perspectives. (Just as an aside one could consider the question of who the protagonist is. Once upon a time it was supposed to be the heroine because the reader was only offered her perspective. But now the two perspectives that divide the story between two characters are often so well balanced that it is difficult to decide who the protagonist is. To call one of them deuteragonist is counterproductive to modern romances because it is the hero's and heroine's combined life and action that makes the idea of a romance story worthwhile and rewarding for a reader. In his definition of the romance story, Cawelty places the stress on the development of the love story between two characters of equal value and thus he accords the novel two protagonists.)

---

[76] This topic is discussed in DMAW by Laura Kinsale. "The Androgynous Reader". 31–44.

4.1.3 CONTENT VERSUS LANGUAGE

Everybody seems to know that you can tell romance novels apart from 'good' literature by the language that is used in them: the so-called 'purple prose' that is formulaic with an inappropriate abundance of adjectives and adverbs, euphemistic description of feelings, particularly around sexuality, and extremely euphemistic descriptions of sexual intercourse, bordering on the ridiculous. Romances are especially criticized for this last point. As far as I can see, over the top wording of simple actions and feelings or what could be called an obviously too elaborate style for telling simple stories has not been used for a long time. Nowadays the writing style ranges from common everyday language, albeit enhanced by romance code words, to elevated good American English. At the beginning of her writing, Delinsky's narrative style evoked the impression that she was trying (too) hard to write elaborate American English. Gradually her writing style changed to a modified, more ordinary and natural tone. The same could be said about Krentz's narrative dialogical style: an abundance of explanatory dialogue tags disappeared and a modified more ordinary and natural tone prevailed.

Owing to the fact that the language employed in romance novels is criticized as being excessively rich in adjectives, other stylistic elements are disregarded, but they emphasize the differences between the voices of the authors, for instance, dialogues which Andreotti indicates as a structural particularity of popular literature (242). The dialogues I want to focus on are the conversations between the characters that are rendered in direct speech, or as Andrew Kennedy terms them the 'duologues of personal encounter' (2010, 234).

Dialogue is not a transcription from life. Of course, literary dialogues have nothing in common with how real people speak because they do not include the usual interruptions such as hesitations, false starts, repetitions, anacolutha, etc. Nevertheless, stylized as they are, they support the illusion to such an extent that they convince the reader of their being real. A dialogical narrative, particularly a romance text, shows how much power and love ensue as a result of communication. The code in which it is communicated depends on time. Our attitudes and ways of thinking are voiced in the cultural and language system. Niklas Luhmann terms this as the 'code of communication' (1994, 23).

Usually, in romance novels, dialogues are of the straightforward kind containing no subtext and no hidden meanings that have to be decoded: but for some heroines even they offer possibilities for misunderstanding, especially in the single narrative perspective category romances. If a double meaning is intended, particularly as sexual connotation, the participant of the dialogue together with the reader is usually warned by some stereotype expression like '(no) pun intended'. The dialogue part of the book serves to pace a story possibly by, for example, short conversations that speed up the reading, as do the printing conventions of dialogues which means more paragraphs that facilitate reading. Alternatively, as longer speeches are generally slower to read, particularly longer back and forth speeches, a stylistic device, which Krentz uses, is to interrupt or finish these conversations not by dialogue tags, but by a short narrative piece. With Krentz, whose writing style could be termed as being more dialogical than descriptive, the narrative sections contain about four to six sentences in which descriptions are given, usually a mixture between thoughts and activities, only to return to a dialogue that requires these descriptive parts as a narrative context. In single-narrative perspective novels the chance for other characters to become characterized comes by way of their speech contributions, supported by dialogue tags which emphasize the meaning of the speech or reactions to the speech, or by way of actions. Krentz uses dialogues with many more commenting dialogue tags in *Stormy Challenge* than in her later books. These dialogue tags, which are the covert narrator's interpretation of the dialogue, express on the one hand the protagonists' mood, and on the other hand they inform the reader of the speakers' actions. As here, the conversations disclose the protagonists' characters, they leave it entirely up to the reader to discern the implications of the dialogues behind the aggressive mood the dialogue tags display. In Krentz's later novels conversational misunderstandings make way for correct interpretations because, I argue, of the permitted change in perspective, and because hero and heroine abandon the contentual romance formula: they are attracted to each other from the start, without the need for a heated verbal exchange of underlying aggressiveness and mistrust. Now that the author no longer follows the traditionally expected love-hate narrative path of the genre, the dialogues become different, more ordinary, and natural, and dialogue tags to interpret exaggerated mood swings are no longer necessary.

Delinsky's writing style differs in so far as she delivers longer descriptive parts, as well as longer musings by the heroine in place of numerous dialogues. The protagonists in her earlier romance novels are more taciturn than conversationally adept. Misunderstandings often arise, owing to their inability to so much as mention their problems. The content or the topic in the dialogues is sometimes rendered in an ambivalent way, or the protagonists digress from what should really be talked about in order to clarify a situation for them, which is in congruence with Delinsky's characters' all-round secretiveness. But they mis-decode their conversations only at climactic points.

Instead of interrupting the linear timeline of narration, analepses often occur in dialogues. The authors use this *modus operandi*, alternating between analepses in inner musings, remembering an event, and analepses in dialogues, thus informing an interlocutor about the past. An uninterrupted timeline enables a reader to easily follow a story without having to interpret the meaning of a change of scene other than a device to propel the story forward.

Different speech styles that could classify characters do not often appear in the authors' romance novels where nearly all characters belong to the same social class. In *Perfect Partners,* Krentz gives rich Victor Copeland a distinctive lower class speech pattern that betrays his humble origins, as well as being the villain, his mental and emotional refusal to change. Having lower class people so openly shown speaking incorrect English, once there is no need to make the persona distinctly not belong to the same class, does not suit the purpose of conjuring up social equality in contemporary romance novels. It seems that class distinctions, apparent in the characters' ways of speaking, would irritate readers and, hence, in order not to irritate them, speech styles of the upper classes and lower classes are usually leveled out. Only Delinsky makes a reader aware of these speech differences by mentioning them rhetorically in her category romances and later in her mainstream ones, but not using them, and thus showing them, in speech.[77] Men and women are given speech differences, not so much in dialogues, but in thoughts where men utter tough male swearwords to themselves. In dialogues, male characters' supposedly innate speaking laziness is expressed through anacolutha, especially with Krentz heroes.

Roland Barthes disproves the notion that a text can be attributed to a single author. In his essay "Death of the Author", 1968, he argues that "it is the language which speaks, not the author" because "The text is a tissue of quotations drawn from the innumerable centers of culture" (1968/1977, 142–148). Michail Bachtin, however, adheres to the existence of a final authority, that of the author's intention that is presented in the characters or the narrator in the novel (1977, 209). In his article "Mistaking Subject Matter for Style". (1981), Gary Sloan argues that style alone, once subject matter clues are eliminated, cannot be classified. To match prose passage with author, especially with a male or female author, is only possible when subject matter clues are inserted and the passages contain more than one hundred words. What, however, is possible to establish is an epoch-related identification. The same observation can be made by analyzing the authors' prose. Once the typical romance prose, where the authors differed considerably from each other, was changed to mainstream language of an educated level, their style does not differ that much without subject matter clues. This is why an analysis of syntactic patterns, the level of diction, imagery, turns of phrases and the like can only indict reader preferences of their time. Even Argamon/Koppel/Fine/Shimoni's interdisciplinary linguistic study on "Gender, Genre, and Writing Style in Formal Written Texts". (2003) proves that depending on the theme (and thus the type of novel), such analysis does not provide a reliable means to distinguish male from

---

[77]   E.g. Delinsky, *The Carpenter's Lady* (1983) where the heroine wonders why her carpenter speaks educated English and in e.g. *The Summer I Dared* (2004) where social roots and education are a secondary theme of the novel.

female writing. This fact explains why usually an analysis of thematic content, being more promising, seems to be preferred.

When she first started writing, Krentz often repeated herself with stereotypical expressions, for example when her heroines conveyed their displeasure at the hero's behavior or when the hero demanded sexual pleasures. ("You egoistical, overbearing, arrogant creature!" (*Stormy* 68) Delinsky's brand of writing in her category romances is characterized by her use of threefold elements in her sentences, like three verbs, three nouns or three identical sentence constructions with the same beginning:

> Of the many differing sentiments she had experienced of late, only one remained constant. *It was the one* thought which had seen her successfully through eight years of building a new life, coping with its new responsibilities. *It was the one* which had eventually emerged in the aftermath of each encounters she'd had with Dough. *It was the one* which would have to give her direction now, in this latest trial, with whatever aftershocks it might bring. *It was the* vow *to never* let herself be hurt as she had once before been, *to never* let herself be manipulated as she had once before been *to never* again love in vain. (*Sweet E.*)82) (italics mine)

Her narrative style stood, and still stands out as being composed.

Publisher's writing guidelines specify to their authors how to handle descriptions in romance novels. These should be short, and also incorporate characters' emotions because, according to survey results, romance readers prefer short descriptions to long ones. Even in their later writing phases when they are no longer subjected to writing guide specifications, both authors pay attention to researched reader preferences. Since Krentz has kept writing more dialogical than descriptive texts, she still restricts the length of her descriptive insertions to short paragraphs. As readers want to ideate the story they need 'visual' information to do so. Therefore, the descriptions are restricted to the creation of generic surroundings that are almost interchangeable. Whether there are descriptions of the Oregon coast or the Washington coast, a village in the mountains or another one on a different mountain, they are similar. The descriptions themselves are short because the emphasis is put on describing settings combined with the inner feelings and emotions of her protagonists, thus characterizing them.

To begin with, Delinsky's category romance novels contained more narrative parts than dialogues, but before long, she increased the dialogue parts in order to – I am sure – pace her story differently. She offers her readers more descriptive particulars of local settings than Krentz does, not too indifferentiated, but also intermingling a character's emotion with a setting or an action. In *Sweet Ember*, the descriptions are so vivid that a reader could find her own way around the summer camp. Descriptions of locality are still detailed in her later novels though with a different objective than from pure illustration: they become a narrative device to unobtrusively characterize the characters.

What romance readers call 'purple prose' has changed with the authors over the years. An abundance of elevated adjectives and adverbs was once seen as an elaborate romance novel style. 'Nobility' in the historical romances required an elevated style in the eyes of their readers. But contemporary American romances need to be told in a different language. The authors do not have to speak the language of an imagined nobility because the setting of their romances is that of ordinary people who speak an ordinary American English.[78] In their beginnings the authors followed their predecessors in writing in an elaborate romance novel style, Krentz more so, as evidenced by her dialogue tags, and Delinsky with unusual seemingly 'romantic' wordings. They moved with the times, away from the exaggerated style to slim down their prose so that now it equates an elevated narrative level of diction. In her contemporary Arcane Society novels from 2008 onward, Krentz sometimes uses a more academic language to explain a paranormal society in her novel world as well as psychological processes and theories, albeit only superficially.

As far as I can see, the kind of language that is used in romance novels has only been researched with regard to the sexual scenes described in them, but little attention has been paid to the way it is used in other scenes. As mentioned before, romance authors have veered away from 'purple prose' for a long time, and authors have remodeled their writing style to an unobtrusive good American English that does not deserve to be denigrated. But, and this is true for both authors, even if the language is conventional, clearly composed American English, the ordinary, natural, unobtrusively good language reveals that these novels are written for 'escapist' readers who enjoy a fast-moving story and do not appreciate a poetic prose that graces the narrative with deeper insights, or with detailed descriptions that let a reader appreciate, for example, the narrative beauty of a scene. In a genre that adheres to formula, writers do not burden the reader with symbols to decipher and subtexts to decode; ambiguity or subtlety are not valued. The ideation of a more poetic, metaphoric text would hinder fast reading, as well as obfuscate the sense of an otherwise plainly explained course of action. Perhaps it is an American, rather than a British approach because whenever I discover more poetic language used in a romance story it turns out to be British.[79] I often observe that even in

---

[78] In her article "Willing Surrender" of 1997, Erica Wentworth compares critics' attitude about male and female authors by analyzing the movies "Misery" and "Romancing the Stone". The female protagonist in "Misery", a strong defender of the romance novel, pleads for 'purple prose' because there is 'nobility' in it. This opinion could also be applied to the strained 'good' language Delinsky used in her early romance novels.

[79] The British seem to enjoy a different emotionality in their mainstream romance novels.

fairly sophisticated crime fiction poetic language is used, for example, to lead the reader to understand the different moods of a character when reacting to a change of environment, which results in a better, deeper understanding of a situation or a character for a reader.[80] I mention this because romance authors like to defend their own genre by saying crime fiction is equivalent to romance fiction, as both follow a formula. But as I understand it, the formula is not as much restricted because crime fiction readers are more inclined to let themselves be guided to unknown territory. The clarity of style, devoid of unnecessary descriptive (poetic) digressions, however, seems to respond to romance readers' specifications and therefore they appear in the writing guidelines. The reason for this might be that a romance reader wants to escape her own, sometimes overwhelming, reality for a time, and complexity and poetic language that requires decoding could never quickly fulfill the craving for an ordered, transparent fictional world. It also might be that the clarity with which incidents, emotions, and characters are presented appeal to readers because, identifying with the characters, they themselves would like to act and feel in the same way.

The most delicate part of evaluating a text is analyzing the narrative part describing sexual activities. Although sexual scenes in romance stories break a taboo, because sexuality in literature generally has been associated with male writers and their male perspectives, the limitations placed on women's sexuality in American and European societies do not allow for upfront vocabulary for male and female genitals. This would insinuate that romance novels are pure pornography: apart from that, it could take out the romance of the romance. As sexuality is an inherent part of romance fiction, writers who are supposed to write sex scenes, at least for some category lines, use euphemisms, thus taking into account the complicated relationship female readers have with their own sexuality. Previously unmentionable sexual female arousal and desire required a 'shrouded' language to allow the readers to become acquainted with their right to experience sexuality without mental discomfort and reading about heroines, who enjoy as well as take an active part in sexual banter and activities legitimized their own desires to be deserved, particularly if they were, and still are encoded within heteronormality, monogamy and family. I assume that another reason for sexual euphemistic language is that obfuscating these elements in the narrative allows for romance novels to remain beneath the socially forbidding radar of American women's organizations, which explains why euphemistic descriptions of sexuality and sexual acts are termed as 'taboo deformation'.

See: Mary Stewart, Erica James, and, not so much poetic language than different emotionality, Jill Mansell

[80] See e.g.: James Church. *A Corpse in the Koryo.* 2006

The authors' euphemistic language, shrouding explicit sexual scenes, has also been toned down in keeping with the times' reading preferences: other types of media have cast off sexual inhibitions by using proper terms for genitals along with the social acceptance of the rights of females to have the same sexual needs as men. Nevertheless, since readers prefer somewhat veiled descriptions of the sexual act, as this makes them stay in the narratively created romantic mood, whereas blatantly used proper sexual terms would destroy this mood, authors comply by using such a *diegetic* language appropriate for romance. Just how embarrassing these descriptions of erotic scenes and of sexual intercourse are, or how enjoyable and arousing, depends on the reader. The authors' success would appear to indicate more enjoyment than embarrassment.

Sometimes, in accordance with her protagonists' professions, Krentz likes her characters to connect their feelings during orgasm or love scenes with job- or hobby- or mythic-imagery. So the computer expert[81] experiences mental images of fractals when he climaxes and the fern specialist[82] will treat his love with the same carefulness he would bestow on his most interesting plant specimen. The fern expert's lover even displays mythic knowledge in her imagery during the foreplay: "Images of Persephone being carried off into the underworld danced in Annie's head." (*Wildest...* 120) Delinsky's work does not contain such idiosyncratic imagery.

Names have a mythic significance and to be nameless is to have no identity. Giving characters suggestive names in order to provide a reader with hints to a character's personality is an old literary device. P.W. Nesselroth explains that name-giving in novels is important for the readers to help them identify the characters beyond their pure name-calling. As linguistic and semiotic signs, they are also important for theorists. He says:

> It is not surprising that theorists pay so much attention to naming in fiction (literature) since proper names are the nodal points through which actions and descriptions are interconnected. (133)

Both authors use this device at times, though not in all their books, Delinsky less than Krentz. They do not use it in an unsubtle simple way. An evocative name can clue in or mislead a reader. In both her novels, *Perfect Partners* and *All Night Long* she gives the criminals the name Victor, implying with this their social and financial superiority as well as divulging, in the end, how wrongly these men judged the power they wield over people's lives. These Victors do not stay victorious, but pay for their murderous sins with their own deaths. Delinsky does not give her characters such obvious names, but she also plays with name

---

[81]   Krentz. *Trust Me* 1995
[82]   Krentz. *Wildest Hearts* 1993

giving. In *Sweet Ember* the heroine's surname, Wright, implies the wrongness of her 'rightful' assumption that the hero has deceived her of his marital status. The same hidden meaning is behind the family name Frye in *A Woman Betrayed*. The family nearly becomes outlawed, 'fried', because of a newspaper campaign and the male protagonist who needs to disappear for good assumes the name Evan Walker.

4.1.4 ASPECTS OF READER'S RESPONSE CRITICISM

Although I insist on the 'author function' (Foucault), reader response aspects, however, are of importance for me because the genre is constructed with regard to its audience. One basic question when interpreting a novel is how it is constructed so that it projects itself by forming thought associations on the reader's part. Whenever literature, serious or popular, is interpreted taking into account the impact it has on a reader, it is not uncommon to cite Aristotle's Poetics and his definition of Greek tragedy. He argues that the way the story is told causes the audience to experience a pleasure of pity and fear by watching a tragedy unfold. For him the constitutive element of the technique of storytelling is that it excites emotions and the catharsis of such emotions is a purging or sweeping away of the pity and fear aroused by the tragic action; at the same time, it effects a kind of catharsis of the spectator's repressed emotions.

Aristotle stresses that without action, without the skillful arrangement of incidents that he calls plot, there cannot be tragedy. The action, however, is one part that keeps the story interesting for the audience. The other part, the one that induces fear for the protagonist as well as pity in the audience is the more important element to the plot where the character is only the object to whom things happen. The more anxiety a plot provokes, the more pleasure is derived from a satisfying ending. Aristotle applies his ideas only to tragedy. Other genres produce entertainment and pleasure by the activation of affective states such as suspense, surprise, curiosity, humor, sexual arousal, anger and irony, but the end provides a catharsis of repressed emotions as well.

In his dissertation of 1995, Peter Orton tested "the effects of perceived choice and narrative elements on an audience with regard to the interest in and the liking of a (film) story". He chose a universal story schema of information about setting and characters, initiating event, the protagonist's reaction to the initiating event, her/his attempts to solve the problem or to search for her/his quest and its achievement, and the protagonist's response to the consequence. The elements he chose were assumed to heighten the quality of a story: a high percentage of sympathy for the protagonist, a meaningful quest, time pressure, and a satisfying end. He offered his test students interactive possibilities: to alter the ending of a story, accept a different ending or no alternative at all. The test students clearly derived most pleasure from the story just as it was because the end was a satisfying one. Orton's experiment supports the conjecture that romance readers expect and prefer stories that are universally enjoyed because they follow the paradigms of such story schemas, and thus, they are well suited to mass market literature. The romance with its satisfying ending that leaves no questions open to ponder over when the story is finished concurs with the students' preference of simply watching and enjoying a film without having to decide on different outcomes. Krentz and Delinsky's romance novels follow the parameters of Orton's index, and their readers' emotional involvement in the Aristotelian sense is often expressed in reader reviews and reader blogs, where they describe the cathartic pleasure they derive from these novels. The romance heroes and heroines' quest is, however, clearly defined: to find the other half of their soul. Only Delinsky adds a search for self-knowledge as a pivotal part of the novel.

Krentz and Delinsky do not rely on a satisfying end alone. They enhance their readers' reading pleasure by dividing their novels into short chapters, usually not more than 15 pages, often less, and by providing the pages of the novels with many paragraphs, often up to eight or nine, so that the reader is not confronted with densely printed pages. Moreover, they ensure a reader's understanding of the story by offering meaningful explanations.

In 'traditional' fiction, and romance novels can be termed to be traditional, fiction is imitation, *mimesis*, in the Aristotelian sense according to which 'reality' can be reproduced in the language. Within a specific traditional novel this mimesis is mirrored in the causality of the plot, in the chronological narration, and in the coherent fictional world (Andreotti, 30–32). (Fiction, whenever it was written and whatever its theme is, always has to do with reality, reality within its fictional frame, albeit in an organized form with the understanding that a reality itself does not exist; it is only manifested by a receptor's subjective perception of 'reality'.[83]) The fictional world in romance novels, as in traditional fiction can never be totally distinct from reality in the sense of the term generally referred to, because it requires references to reality such as simply a setting with houses, cars (or better a Mercedes), telephones, computers, cameras, etc. At the same time, the world created is the author's playground where everything happens with a reason and characters act accordingly. Here she endows her characters with characteristics which, as the German author Martin Walser once said, 'show in their immoderation what we lack in reality'. A fictional world is shaped as a sphere where a reader can experience a reality in thoughts and ideation that is different from her everyday reality.

An external informative sign that a novel is not reality is the term 'novel'

---

[83]   cf. Andreotti, Luhmann 2001, Rusch, and von Glasersfeld

itself. The second sign is that in one's imagination, one can move in the world portrayed within the novel, but it is a world without the inconsistencies of reality. Celia Brayfield, a writer herself, argues that in popular novels, stories are told that circle around thoughts and ideas that are important to many people. Looked at superficially, these narratives are about verbally constructed fictional characters, fictional settings and fairy tale scenarios, but in fact they portray everyday life. They pretend to be only entertainment, but in actual fact they are about the hopes and fears of humanity. The aspects of *movere* and *delectare* are predominant so that the enjoyment that can be gained by reading fiction can be divided into four elements: the emotional, the moral, the intellectual and the symbolic. Usually a small part remains that is dedicated to the aspect of *docere* (Brayfield, 1996).

Romance novelists think of their fiction as reader-entertaining fantasy. It transmits an insight into a reality which it both imitates and virtualizes, and a reader draws her conclusions from it because she can fall back on her own repertoire of experience and her norms and values. Romance novels are affirmative literature, and, therefore, they are presented in the form of the bourgeois novel. They seem to mirror reality, especially when the reader meets moral and ethical conventions in them with which she agrees. Krentz claims that her readers are able to discern between reality and fantasy. Contrary to Krentz's conviction, Gerrig's study (1993) shows that it takes cognitive pains for a reader to distinguish between fictional and non-fictional descriptions, because in order to be adaptive to reader identification the story needs to be similar to reality. This is why the reader believes that the incidents and resolutions shown in the novels can serve as paradigms for conduct because she is familiar with the ideology. However, whether or not the reader falls into the trap of believing the written word always depends on her level of education, literary and otherwise.

4.1.5 TENSES

To begin at the beginning, for readers to feel familiar with a narrative as a reported or fictional one, it is important that the story is written in the preterite, an unmarked or invisible tense for a reader. This is an interesting point considering that the novels in question here tell contemporary stories. Suzanne Fleischman argues that in fiction the preterite loses its 'referential' meaning of signaling past time. This loss of reference for tenses, she says, has led a number of theoreticians (Hamburger 1973, Weinrich 1973, and Sternberg 1978) to declare that the use of past tense in fiction is not temporal but atemporal. For Weinrich and Hamburger the function of the past tense in fiction, the epic preterite, is that it marks events as 'fictional', hence outside of time. At the same time, the use of the past tense suggests verisimilitude (Fleischman 1990, 111–112). So, despite the use of the past tenses in a novel, the reader assumes a present time within which the story is happening and experiences a present time reality within the fictional world (Hamburger). Matias Martinez and Michael Scheffel describe this reader response as a paradox action because s/he accepts a narrative as something being open and in the present, at the same time, however, as completed and in the past: the occurrence seems to be in the past because it has been understood as an entity, as a chronological structure where the beginning has already been referred and related to the end. The reader, however, understands and follows the fictional characters' tangle of situations as occurrences happening in the present and being open (Martinez/Scheffel 2003, 119).

The function of the basic use of present or past tense in novels is currently being discussed in various blogs on the internet. There it transpires that readers are becoming increasingly aware of the differences and the different expectations that arise with the basic present tense use in popular fiction because nowadays they come across more novels that are written in the present tense.[84] The readers question the function of the use of the present tense as, for them, it suggests a greater alignment with reality, and they argue that this device seems to save an author the trouble of constructing suspense, because 'reality' is supposed to be suspenseful by nature. But in the bloggers' opinion, the resulting effect is that these stories read like a string of events without underlying meaning, although sometimes more intimacy is created than in stories told in the past tense. A final argument put forward by readers is that the story is not necessarily constructed along the 'traditional' lines of a beginning, a middle, and a meaningful ending, whereas stories told in the past tense do follow these criteria.

These preterite stories can be rendered in a linear narrative, but the string of events is carefully chosen to heighten the tension, while at the same time projecting meaning. The reader is subliminally aware of a double temporal perspective, the narrator's retrospective account of a story, which at the same time makes the events in the story unfold prospectively. She believes the narrator and because, subconsciously, for her, the past tense seems to indicate that the story really happened, she *a priori* assumes it is true. Thus stories told in the past tense send the subliminal message that they really happened, and that an author considered them worth telling. Another aspect is the reader's expectation of being presented with a constructed story to help her with interpretations of events so that she is able to understand the significance of what is really happening. For her, a story told in the present tense could be termed as 'life happens as it happens' and this can be quite

---

[84] Novels written in the present tense have a history of over one hundred years. They were the experiments of the modern novel and have nothing to do with the traditional narration of romances. The avant garde wanted to manifest the end of the novel by writing antinarratively and antifictionally in the present tense. Avanessian /Hennig's key assumption is that by using the present tense the novel is re-invented. (*Präsens. Poetik eines Tempus.* 2012)

exciting whereas the constructed story told in the past tense qualifies as 'life has a meaning'. [85] I call to mind Anita Shreve's novel *The Pilot's Wife* (1998) where she uses a present tense in the analepses while the story, itself, is told in the atemporal epic preterite. These analepses reminisce a scene of a 'life as it happens' without the sense of significance it takes on later within the story.

Both authors choose to use the preterite narrative form to insinuate the trustworthiness of their stories. The epic preterite Delinsky uses in her storytelling emphasizes her repeated narrative guarantee that 'everything happens for a reason'. Even if Krentz regards her stories as pleasurable fantasy, for her readers they convey the impression of being real. Accessible realistic elements and a structured storytelling, which also proffers a meaning behind the presented events and incidents in the authors' stories create an authenticity which might not be that easily achieved should the story be written in the present tense. They make a reader believe in the message the writers are conveying because the use of the preterite has this subliminally convincing element for her. They could support the reason why occasionally readers consider these novels as role models.

4.1.6 BLANKS

In the early 1970s Wolfgang Iser and Robert Jauß' work provided a rigorous grounding for a paradigm shift because it redirected the attention of literary theorists from author to reader. Their reader response approach states that the *intentio auctoris* loses significance because the empiric authors, being physically absent, cannot determine the readers' interpretations of their novels. Jauß focuses on the history of reader response. He worked out five patterns of reader identification with a hero that require newer empiric research in order to be conclusive for the genre: associative identification that allows for self-awareness and external experience, admiring identification for a perfect hero, sympathetic and solidarizing identification with the not so perfect hero, cathartic identification with the suffering hero and ironic identification with the anti-hero (Jauß 1977, 244–293).

Iser focuses his interest on the structure of a text. He is not interested in the meaning of the text, but in the reader's response, whoever the reader might be, an ideated one or a real one (Iser 1974). He sees the novel as manipulating the reader, but this manipulation is not controlled by the author. To what extent this 'control' is taken away from the author, Paul Auster explains in an interview (Naumann 2007), where he states that his readers are also his authors. He believes in a cooperation between author and reader because each reader inserts his/her own past into the text and his/her past experiences as a reader of other books as well. That readers can do this is a result of his writing style, because, he says, he inserts

---

[85]   I do not recall American romance stories told in the present tense, but I recall two successful British romance authors: Sophie Kinsella and Freya North.

enough blanks into his text to enable readers to put in their own fantasy, their own ideation. This means readers can literally adopt the text as their own while reading it.[86] Walter Erhart and Sigrid Nieberle, therefore, term this reader, especially the internet-reader, as 'wreader' which is an 'amalgam of writer and reader' (Erhart/Nieberle 2003, 352).

It seems to be important for the understanding of romance novels to take a closer look at the authors' supply of blanks in their novels because they may prove to be a particularity of literature designed for the mass-market. Iser who analyzes blanks in literature in his work *The Act of Reading,* postulates that "it is precisely because (fiction) is not identical to the world or reader that it is able to communicate" (Iser 1978, 181). According to him, the narrative's non-identity to reality manifests itself in degrees of indeterminacy which then condition the reader's own formulation of the text, thus decoding the norms and values that are concealed within the text. The degree of indeterminacy stimulates readers to supply in their imagination what has been withheld or left out. Filling in these blanks induces the reader to construct a more complex ideation of the fictional world than the text alone describes. Iser identifies four different kinds of blanks:

1.) Blanks that create tension and propel a reader's ideation by back cover reviews which can be exploited for aesthetic and commercial purposes.

2.) Blanks that are created by cutting techniques, such as a division in chapters or abrupt changes of settings.

3.) Blanks that mark the suspension of links between textual segments. They simultaneously form a condition for the reader's input. What it suspends propels the reader's imagination, making her supply what has been withheld or left out. Thus the reader fills in the missing links or the missing parts she needs to get a full imaginary view of a perhaps merely outlined description of a situation or a setting.

4.) Blanks that are gaps which arise from juxtaposed themes and horizons[87]. This kind of blanks needs books containing many different and controversial standpoints.

Types 1, 2 and 3 play a significant role in romance novels. Blanks of type 1 seem to be identical to what Genette terms as 'paratexts': Back cover and previews and

---

[86] This 'cooperation' is not always positively considered. Walter Erhart and Sigrid Nieberle term this problem as follows: "Die mit der Rezeptionsästhetik angebrochene Herrschaft und Befehlsgewalt des Lesers scheint sich dabei in die gänzlich grenzenlos gewordene Freiheit eines Benutzers verwandelt zu haben, dessen Sorglosigkeit und Souveränität im Umgang mit Medien und Texten heute vielleicht eine Provokation für die Rezeptionsästhetik darstellen könnte." (Erhart/Nieberle 2003, 343)

[87] "Theme and horizon structure means that each of the assumptions is to be viewed from the standpoint of another, thus becoming the theme which, in turn, becomes the horizon for what is to follow." (ibid:152)

reviews in the form of short-text excerpts make a prospective reader want to read the book. The keywords or codes that are used in them address a specific reader clientele. In the case of both authors, Krentz and Delinsky, there appear allusions to love, betrayal, emotional upheaval, etc. A prospective reader sees these allusions as the code she needs to decipher by buying and reading the book. The book cover design is a point of received controversy: category romances, particularly historical romances, still have pictures of couples fully dressed or in various states of undress, the men often displaying impressive abdominal muscles. On the internet, romance readers often complain about these covers, because they feel embarrassed when they read the books in public. But as publishing houses research reader preferences thoroughly, obviously prospective category romance readers tend to reach for the books with the colorful pictures. Single titles have less eye-catching book covers. Depending on the *Zeitgeist* these might consist of some scenery, or flowers or colorful photos with a variety of motifs.

Iser's type 2 blanks: as the analysis of these novels shows, the division of chapters often does not mark cuts in order to let a reader supply her own ideating and formulating of the text. In fact the chapter cuts in the analyzed novels serve as tension builders: they indicate a heightening of a situation, be it sexually or action oriented. This means the scene is not cut up to be finished three chapters later, but instead it is continued in the next chapter. Sometimes, when a new chapter might be expected because of a large time gap or a local setting far away from the one a paragraph before, the authors do not give this fact any consideration other than to start a new paragraph. Obviously the plot is constructed in such a way that these blanks are intended to be easily and quickly decoded. A sequential time-line helps. In *Perfect Partners* Krentz does not provide an epilogue for a two-month gap in which the lovers have married. She only offers a new paragraph in which the heroine announces her pregnancy. Delinsky juxtaposes three settings and three viewpoints in one chapter to make simultaneous actions known to the reader without the expected linking hints. These are used like the scene cuts in soap operas with which the reader is so familiar. Such narrative devices, however, are rarely used since simultaneous actions hardly ever happen in the analyzed romance novels. More often, however, are chapter divisions with emotional highs at, for example, a chapter's end; these highs are then seamlessly continued in the following chapter, without the reader's need to fill in a blank, which means without a reader's need to ideate the time passing between the end and the beginning of a new chapter. Apart from that, like in soap operas, once there are different viewpoints and settings, both authors like to finish a chapter on a concluded emotional high to then turn to a different setting and subplot, building up and concluding the emotional tension there and then returning to the first setting's new tense situation.

Iser's type 3 blanks: readers request comfortable reading material from romance and mainstream literature which means that authors provide them with the information of what, for example, a dialogue implies, or of why a character is acting this way so that they do not need to concern themselves with wordings or actions or filling in blanks, and can continue reading, being certain of the interpretation. I maintain that this *modus operandi* is the crucial point, the narrative key to understanding how romances become an 'easy read' or as Delinsky terms it, how this genre is made 'eminently accessible' to a reader: the reader is assigned the role of an omniscient reader. Her basis is her knowledge of the protagonists' characters. As her intimate access to hero and heroine through the two perspectives does not permit a withholding of information – an unreliable narrator is out of the question as a narrative device for the genre – she is given nearly *a priori* all the necessary particulars she needs to enjoy the development of the story.

Krentz and Delinsky like to offer orienteering assistance, and they serve the reader by evading ambivalence or indeterminacy. They inform the reader of, for example, a locality, but she is not supposed to become distracted from the action by a rendering of it that is too detailed. An unequivocal description spotlights the scenery for a brief moment, and having spotlighted it in her mind for an equally short moment, without needing to spend time filling in possible missing information about the locality, the reader can go on reading. The description of the male protagonist's bedroom in Krentz's *Stormy Challenge* serves as an example:

> The room was as sleek and modern and neutrally colored as the rest of the condominium. Low-profile teak furniture and cream-colored carpeting and drapes were relieved by a suitably modern abstract painting hanging over the bed. The quilt on which she lay was a fat, fluffy goose-down affair that had probably cost a fortune. Too bad it was in beige. A part of Leya insisted it would have looked much better in a vibrant red. (142)

Two and a half sentences to provide enough information to ideate a room, the purpose of which every American reader knows intimately, and, therefore, can furnish in her mind according to given hues, but she will not linger for long because the room is not mysterious in any way. The author creates a world that simulates a (contemporary) American reality of everyday life a reader can easily become acquainted with or feels familiar with because it can be filled from the repertoire of her own experience. Thus the reader is offered a blank she can fill out easily in her mind without having to read a longer description which might prove wearisome for her.

To relieve a reader from mulling over characters Krentz adds character traits to the outward description of e.g. her heroine right at the beginning of the story:

> Spectacular, haunting, amber-brown eyes lit with intelligence and shadowed with secrets; gleaming dark hair cut with precision to follow the line of her

jaw; a sleek, vital, delightfully feminine shape; sexy high-heeled boots and
a dashing black trench coat. And the lady did breakfast.

What was wrong with this picture?

He sure as hell was no fashion guru, but he trusted his instincts, Luke
thought. Right now his instincts were telling him that Irene Stenson wore
the boots and the trench and the attitude the way a man might wear a Kevlar
vest – as battle armor. (*All Night Long* 19)

Here, the reader is given *in nuce* the heroine's characteristic traits which she expects to be presented within the course of the story: secrets revealed, intelligence
displayed, attitudes and traumas explained, and physical attractiveness becoming physical delights for both hero and heroine. Characterization is usually given
more explicitly than descriptions of settings because readers have to be led to the
right conclusions without the difficulty of being compelled to interpret. Both the
authors state in detail their protagonists' individual idiosyncrasies and problems,
so that character analysis is an easy task for the reader. Citations can already offer a rounded characterization which is one of the reasons I have chosen longer
quotations in the analysis of the novels. On the other hand this way characters are
often endowed with more personality traits than the ones that are needed for and
worked with in the story. Delinsky offers an extreme example for this when she
gives an over the top characterization of a seven year old child who, in the story,
serves only as catalyst for adults and stays in the story's background:

An athletic child, she was a fine little swimmer and a promising tennis
player, even at her tender age. Additionally, she had never had trouble making friends, nor been bothered by the lack of them, all of her protestations
to the contrary notwithstanding. She was an independent soul, a loner who
went her own way whether in the company of friends or not. She was a
self-motivator, a hard worker, and a hard player, whose instinct for superiority was threatened only by an underlying distrust of people, a characteristic which her mother recognized and for which she accepted responsibility.
(*Sweet Ember* 3–4)

In her mainstream fiction, Delinsky seems to have another reason for describing
her characters in detail beside that of producing an easy read. In order to concentrate on the featured problem and not be distracted by trying to fathom a character,
detailed characteristics are given. In the third novel analyzed, *The Family Tree*,
Delinsky veers slightly away from the tried and tested device of thorough clarifi-
cation. This encourages readers to fill in blanks with the result that controversial
interpretations occur.

To cite passages in the novel to illustrate the way purposes, motivations, and
justifications of actions are explained is difficult. Nearly every page contains these
explanations, be they given in dialogues, or in a character's musing, and often they

are extensive passages. Neither author uses obvious plain explanations that the reader will notice as such; they are integrated unobtrusively, and being informed this way, a reader does not need to fill in blanks beyond the offered reasoning:

> Christian did most of the talking at the hospital, and, having decided not to fight, it was a relief to let him. It was also a relief to have him by her side the whole time, where she could lean against him for comfort. She wasn't normally a coward, and she didn't shy from physical pain, but she wasn't herself. She was weak, battered, stripped down, and frightened, so frightened. So she took what he offered. (*A Woman Betrayed* 280) The explanations the authors provide must be explanations on a level that does not insult the readers' intelligence.[88] I do not recall the authors doing this, which means that they treat their readers as partners who do not need to be instructed from an arrogant perspective.

When asked why he does not furnish his novels with matters of American everyday life, Auster answered that he does not fill in every blank because it is interesting to observe how a brain is always ready to fill in gaps or blanks. Auster as well as Iser, talks about high-brow literature, and here the difference between this and romance literature becomes obvious. The degree of mental work a reader seems to be willing to invest in e.g. Auster's intricate and often cryptic stories varies clearly from that invested by a reader of romances. Romance and popular mainstream authors do not insert blanks, which are mentally difficult to fill in (Iser's type 4 of blanks) in their books because their main component is their aspiration to tell their readers exciting escapist stories. Therefore, the surrounding fictional world is thoroughly explained. Offering interpretations and reasonings, rationalizations and explanations is the way mass-market designed literature evades Iser's type 4 of blanks that otherwise would cause the literature to be too enigmatic or mysterious for effortless escapist reading.

In novels with a contemporary American setting, the American author can rely on the American readers' knowledge of American norms and values, rites and habits, even if they may differ from state to state. A European or Asian reader might have difficulty evaluating the importance of those traditional habits, or as Naok Onishi terms them: 'table manners', for example, the formulation of the wedding vows. Another example could be swearing: in nearly every romance anyone swearing, usually a man, is reprimanded for his behavior, especially when a

---

[88] Another romance author, Judith McNaught, allows herself such an arrogance within an otherwise well written romance novel: In it the heroine announces her pregnancy to the hero by asking him to amend that part of their commitment contract saying 'Someone to Watch over Me' to 'Someone to Watch Over Us'. The author seemed to be unsure of her readers ability to grasp the significance of this change of pronoun and so she added to the heroine's comment: *"She was telling him she was pregnant*, and Michael's joy made his voice husky." (My italics) (Judith McNaught. *Someone to Watch Over Me*. 2003, 538)

child is around. These swear words are 'damn' or 'hell' or similar. In 1970 Irving M. Rosen mentioned that

> social taboos are a part of the large and still mysterious field of the folk-
> ways. Since they surround us, we are usually little aware of them as fish
> presumably are of the water in which they swim ... There has been a ten-
> dency – now diminishing – to emphasize the individual at the expense of
> attention to the forces in the total cultural milieu. One day when I inadver-
> tently said 'damn' it struck me that some of the patients were excessively
> shocked. One of them remarked that she would rather remain sick than say
> 'damn'. Another man agreed. (175)

To utter swear words like this still seems to be a social taboo in the new millennium, which is surprising to European readers. It serves for them as blanks. When
children are near the heroes are supposed to suppress swear words, but in the face
of a hero's thoughts, the reader can be exposed to many such swear words, as
she does when she is given access to the male protagonist's thoughts in Krentz's
Perfect Partners. Accounts of typical American cultural attitudes or allusions to
peculiarities only known to American culture could hinder smooth reading for
non-Americans. But, the novels were written for an American audience which
can ideate the blanks.

Hardly ever exposing the reader to the necessity of connecting crucial missing
links, or interpreting the text without an author's guiding hand serves to subconsciously influence the reader. Romance and mainstream novels' texts are what
Delinsky calls "eminently accessible" (Bookreporter 2010) because the authors
help to orient the reader. Therefore, the reader is exposed to a narrative structure of
communication that triggers acts of familiar ideation. By explaining in detail reasons and significances in their novels, the authors relieve their readers of having to
question the subject or the presented values. That is why romances are considered
to be an 'affirmative' literature. Once a reader's anticipations are met in the novel
and roughly coincide with her own norms and values, enabling her to maintain
her sense of stability, she will not take a further critical look. Romance publishing
houses benefit from this. They reissue dated novels and pretend they were written shortly before they were issued. A reader rarely verifies the date of the first
publication. When a reader likes an author who has already passed her ideological
'test', she will not compare, in her mind, differing displayed values which would
prolong text-reader interaction, but instead she will accept the implications offered within the story, especially if they are presented in a black and white moral
context or if they do not veer away too much from the agreed American moral
understanding of the respective time. Krentz stays within that frame. It is typical
that her fans might dislike some actions in, for example, *Stormy Challenge*, yet
they do not question the ideological background of 1982. In her Women's Fiction,

Delinsky shows her readers the gray moral areas, but she always conveys the reasons for morally debatable behavior in a placatory way, and makes her characters return to the commonly accepted ways of American social life.

A fifth way of looking in the direction of blanks, which is not part of Iser's listing, is the question of whose character is functioning as a projection surface for reader identification. Does a reader project herself as the acting heroine wanting to offer to the hero her loyalty and her unwavering love, or does she project herself as the hero offering the heroine his protection and his desire to boost her ego? Or does identifying with this fictional man, who is also the reader's internal construct, mean she wishes him to be a real-life man? As long as there is no empirical study on this subject the answer will have to wait. Still, readers' blogs thematize this topic. The reflections Kinsale offers in DMAW (31–44) could be a beginning.

Quintessentially, romance fiction has been characterized as escapist because it is meant to be 'just a fantasy' and nothing else, even if the mimetic parts inserted in the story background make it adaptable to ideation. If a story is concluded without leaving questions open to be answered and a contented reader is ready to move on to another satisfying story, this is proof that possible subtexts are transported on the level of the story by way of explanation, that all possible blanks have been supplied with ideation and meaning by the author or by the reader who has filled them convincingly for herself. In addition it signifies that the stories are not thought provoking and belong to escapist readings. Krentz's fiction is of this kind.

Delinsky's category romance novels were like that, although even there, she approaches serious, thought provoking problems, but since she provides a satisfying solution, they do not require further reflection. Her popular mainstream novels differ greatly, despite the fact that they still are 'eminently accessible'. As they offer an absolutely unsatisfying end, the blanks she provides the readers with are of what I would like to call an 'invisible complexity'. She increases the opportunity to selectively read with the result that only one strand of thought might be noticed by her readers and the other strand of thought is ignored,[89] hence the attached discussion guidelines. True, the topics in these novels are seemingly laid out with comprehensive explanations, but they still leave room for selective reading and possible misinterpretation although the story stays within the established plotting of popular mainstream fiction.

Another reason why popular novels are so eminently accessible is that they display a restricted world knowledge. If at all, they only offer tidbits of information that might increase a reader's knowledge. For example, when the heroine in Krentz's *Perfect Partners* is said to 'have read an article or two' – this is not a

---

[89] Qver 100 controversial reviews on *The Family Tree* at Amazon are a good example.

book, it is only an article – it is never disclosed when she has time for reading or where she gets the articles from that enable her to know exactly what to do, for example, at an unexpected home birth. The common knowledge of its being a messy affair, that babies usually come head first into the world, or that a women has contractions and in the end has to push the baby out of her body, is not increased by any additional information. Delinsky presents her readers with larger chunks of information such as the meaning of the sickle cell trait in *The Family Tree*, how angora rabbits need to be cared for in *The Summer I Dared* (2004) or how maple syrup is produced in *An Accidental Woman* (2002), making this information a part of the plot.

To give proper and convincing accounts of contemporary situations or settings or tactics, the authors need to do some research and the amount of acknowledgements in their novels are an indicator of how much they required more than common knowledge to write their books. Authors of contemporary romance novels usually do not have a need for so much research. Krentz stays within the frame of common knowledge and a little more, whereas Delinsky uses research, and this way, passes on special information to her readers in her popular mainstream novels.

4.2 CULTURAL ASPECTS

4.2.1 PSYCHOLOGIC FACETS

Seen from the point of view of Freud's psychotherapeutic literary criticism, author's and reader's unmet needs are mirrored in literature as their wish-fulfillment. Like many literary theories, depth psychology theory does not withstand criticism as a whole: however, parts of it are valuable as a means to look at literature. So the fact that romance texts are closely associated with gender and sexuality cannot be disregarded, but they do not seem to offer enough material for them to be interpreted in the restricted Freudian sense. The same applies to Jung: his theory of the 'shadow concept' serves (falsely, in my opinion) to portray the heroine's process of individuation by way of integrating in herself the hero's *animus,* or as Abby Zidle points out, that "several writers view the hero as the 'shadow self' of the heroine, complementing her characteristics – the union at the end of the book is not a marriage, but a reintegration of the psyche" (Zidle 1999, 28). I will not follow this train of thought because of implications I cannot fathom properly, as I am not a psychologist. For me this assertion seems to indicate a happy ending for the heroine in a splendid isolation that is not compatible with the promises of a life together with the hero and babies. The Jungian term 'archetype', however, has found a solid place in the interpretations of formula romances. There are eight versions of hero character archetypes and eight versions of heroine character archetypes in circulation.[90] Their deeper meaning for the stories seems negligible to me. They only emphasize that the genre revolves around a set of characters that appear often, and, as such, support the widespread belief in romantic stock characters that are beneath literary appreciation.

Whichever theory of psychology is used to interpret life and literature, the comprehensive term psychology is the common denominator. Ellen Herman argues that

> Psychological insight is the creed of our time ... More important, the progress of psychology has changed American society. Americans today are likely to measure personal and civic experience according to a calculus of mental and emotional health – 'self-esteem' in the current vernacular. We have been convinced that who we are and how we feel are more tangible, and probably also more relevant yardsticks, than whether our society lives up to its reputation of democracy and equality, ideals that appear increasingly abstract, difficult to grasp, and remote from the dilemmas of daily life ... Feelings of powerlessness against those conditions that shape the self from mind-numbing corporate depersonalization ... have nurtured forms of vehement individualism and elicited hopes that the self can be nurtured and managed at a social distance, out of harms way. (1995, 1–2)

In a way Herman's argument explains why romance novels are so successful in a world where the individual's feeling of powerlessness is overwhelming. In romances, traditional values are represented in successful individuals who instill hope against hope in the reader and make her feel optimistic about the possibilities in her own life. Krentz and Delinsky always choose themes and narrative forms that support these optimistic hopes. Their themes are the human imperfections in a world that is not very complex, without the, supposedly male, narrator's distancing position of conveying a different kind of world-knowledge, including the fact that human fate is based on politics, which would emphasize the individual's feeling of po-werlessness.

Romances provide the reader with descriptions of emotional relationships and circumstances. Cohn defines this as follows: "the landscape of popular romance is internal, the adventure psychological, and the heroine's innocence altogether a sexual innocence" (1998, 21). Authors, therefore, cannot do without a marginal understanding of psychology in order to construct a conclusive plot and convincing characters, since characters' biographical elements are expected to be psychologized and interpreted by depth psychology. Both authors seem to use

---

[90] Tami Cowden lists the following characters as 'archetypes' (1999). The hero archetypes: the Chief, the Bad Boy, the Best Friend, the Charmer, the Lost Soul, the Professor, the Swashbuckler, and the Warrior. The heroine archetypes: the Boss, the Survivor, the Spunky Kid, the Free Spirit, the Waif, the Librarian, the Crusader, and the Nurturer.

popular psychology in their novels in order to explain their characters' childhood traumata, their fears and consequently their actions. Given that the sense of self is shaped by the culture people live in, the characterizations in these contemporary American romances mirror elementary aspects of an American society that is primarily dominated by capitalism, individualism, and the apparent decline of family and community. Hidden ideal values of the protestant, white, middle class American are projected in these novels, and these are stated in the positive psychology that Martin P. Seligman defines as follows:

> The field of positive psychology at the subjective level is about valued subjective experiences: well-being, contentment, and satisfaction (in the past); hope and optimism (for the future); flow and happiness (in the present). At the individual level, it is about positive individual traits: the capacity for love and vocation, courage, interpersonal skill, aesthetic sensibility, perseverance, forgiveness, originality, future mindedness, spirituality, high talent, and wisdom. At the group level, it is about the civic virtues and the institutions that move individuals toward better citizenship: responsibility, nurturance, altruism, civility, moderation, tolerance, and work ethic. (Seligman 2005, 5)

This definition of an ideal personality could also be the basis for romance writers' characterizations of their protagonists. Seligman asserts that optimism is the most important trait people need to lead a fulfilled life in the face of all the hardship life puts in their way. This is also a significant aspect in romance novels: the underlying hope of a Happy Ever After; the underlying optimism that the love of a partner can repair or heal whatever is ailing the other; that a life with a beloved one will bring happiness and ban loneliness; the underlying expectation of a contented life if the characters live a life within a conventionally accepted frame. So what Seligman's positive psychology and romance novels have in common is that they offer a quick course on optimism. Krentz and Delinsky's novels do project optimism, even when disastrous events like the ones in *A Woman Betrayed* seem to have the power to destroy all hope and contentment which is, of course, part of a plotting in the Aristotelian sense. But, because the novels end optimistically, the seriousness and the hints of a not so radiant reality are forgotten.

Valery Parv, a successful Australian romance writer who gives advice on how to develop a well-rounded character, explains that "popular psychology books are among the most useful reference books you can have on your bookshelf" (Parv 1997, 29) Many romance novels showcase their author's psychological background knowledge. Krentz's heroines, and sometimes her heroes as well, display an unusual amount of psychological understanding, considering their alleged age and professions. Often their way of resolving problems can be seen to be achieved by common sense, but mostly the characters' actions and reactions are based on psychology. One premise of the romance novel is that emotional insecurities and disturbances are simply laid to rest by the promise of an understanding love, as occurs in *Perfect Partners* and *All Night Long*. On top of that, however, the heroines accept their heroes' psychological problems as a given and offer their help by making them talk about their difficulties, thus opening up opportunities for problem solving. Or the heroine ponders over why the hero keeps behaving in a certain way in order to come to understand the reason for it, and thus becomes able to handle his idiosyncrasies. [91] In *All Night Long,* the heroine's father, like the hero, was an ex-marine and this fact enables her to understand this male species. There are also psychologically interpreted actions that have nothing to do with the commentary on a character's seemingly irrational behavior. Thus in Krentz's *Running Hot* (2009), the psychological process of how to handle a bully is explained in detail for once. (No blanks here):

> The politically correct view of bullies was that they suffered from low self-esteem and tried to compensate by making other people their victims. As far as Luther (the hero) was concerned, that was pure bull. Guys like Flower Shirt (the bully) felt superior to others and lacked all traces of empathy. Bullies bullied not out of some unconscious desire to try to compensate for their low self-esteem. They did it because they enjoyed it. The only way to stop a bully was to scare him. The species had a strong sense of self-preservation. (27)

And three pages later:

> Fear was one of the most primitive emotions, a core survival instinct that, like all such instincts, was hardwired into the brain. That meant it was experienced across the spectrum of the senses from the normal straight into the paranormal. It was also one of the easiest emotions to trigger, if you had the knack. And once triggered, it tended to hang around for a while. Bullies comprehended fear well because they spent so much time instilling it in others. (30)

(By the way, these are texts that really should be rendered in the present tense, because they illustrate a fact that is generally valid, but such texts never are because this, according to Hamburger, is a sign of the fictionality of a text.) Krentz's protagonists often act as surrogate fathers when the real fathers are either dead or unwilling to take parental responsibility for their children.[92] These surrogate fathers

---

[91] (Krentz. *Trust Me.* 1995, 15) "Desdemona opened her mouth to respond with a crack about the goats being worth it, but at the last instant she changed her mind. It dawned on her that Stark was using the line-by-line argument over the invoice as a means of venting some of the rage and pain he must surely be feeling."

[92] *Family Man* 1992, *Grand Passion* 1994, *Trust Me* 1995, *Absolutely, Positively* 1996, *Sharp Edges* 1998

develop into psychological and pedagogical role models by letting the children take part in their lives, by participating in ritualistic manly activities like fishing or camping, and by teaching them to become responsible, honest adults. In this way readers become aware of how fathers should and could behave towards their children.

D.C. Wands reports that Delinsky "found that her background in psychology was helpful in planning the emotional entanglements of (her) characters" and claims that she has "pulled virtually every aspect of (her) background and of (her) life experience in general (in her writing)."[93] Every character in her romance novels, and even more so in her popular mainstream novels, could be analyzed with a psychotherapeutic textbook as basis. Sometimes her protagonists or secondary characters are teachers of psychology or psychotherapists who also discuss psychological processes, too. In *A Woman Betrayed,* some characters often regard their past and present behavior from a psychological viewpoint as the heroine does when she tells her mother about her new, old love, at the same time filling in a possible reader blank:

> "… I wanted to get married. Christian wasn't ready, but Jeff was, so I married him. You can analyze that all you want, Mother, but the fact is I was happy with the decision. I raised two terrific kids and had a rewarding life, and I didn't let myself dwell on what might have been wrong in my relationship with Jeff."
>
> "All along, I told you "
>
> "What was wrong, yes, you did, and I didn't listen, because you've always told me what was wrong. All my life I've heard about what I do wrong. It gets tiresome, Mom. When you never hear the good and always hear the bad, you begin to tune out, because the constant criticism is destructive. So I didn't hear what you were saying about my relationship with Jeff, and even if I'd heard it I probably wouldn't have believed it. I was too busy living my life to pick it apart piece by piece … Little by little, things became clear, things that had nothing whatsoever to do with Christian. The fundamental problem with my marriage was that I did overshadow Jeff, and he allowed it. Christian will never do that." (388)

Laura's mother, the academic psychologist, typically analyzes her daughter's behavior constantly and did so when Laura was an adolescent. This is such a typical scene to demonstrate the pedagogical aspects of *docere* in novels that are an 'easy read': readers are informed, seemingly in an aside, how adolescents react and why. If a reader is looking for advice, she can find it here. At the same time, the heroine makes clear that now she really understands why her marriage did not work.

---

[93] In *The Family Tree* Delinsky submits her hobby of knitting into the story which leads to her interest in how angora wool is gained, which information is used again in another novel.

In *The Family Tree* the readers are not informed so clearly about the psychological reasons for some of the heroine's actions like, for example, her refusal
to learn the identity of her father. Or, perhaps, because it is only explained at a
later point in the novel, this explanation is not satisfactory for the reader who is
more used to instant interpretations of the sense of actions or reactions which,
incidentally, is one of the reasons for the use of the epic preterite. The effect of
not expounding psychological reasons thoroughly and repetitively results in the
reader's resorting to her own reasoning, and in doing so she is not sure of the
'correct' interpretation, which is something that irritates her. Being accustomed to
extensive explanations and, finding herself doubting her own conclusions, she is
a little confused, and, therefore, not contented. So the guiding questions Delinsky
offers to reading groups make sense.

Another psychological aspect in Delinsky's novels, already approached in her
romance novels where identities are played out as secretive and mysterious elements in the plot, is the protagonists' questioning of how they identify themselves
and how other people see them. In *Sweet Ember,* this problem is solved in such a
way that the reader does not need to mull over it later. Self-perception and external
perception is one main theme in all of Delinsky's mainstream novels. *A Woman
Betrayed* presents at least three illusionary self-perceptions that are set straight
within the story along with explanations. *The Family Tree*'s theme is the question of identity as self-perception, illusionary self-perception and also as external perception, but despite a satisfying ending, some readers seem to be irritated
because of inconclusive facets in the novel. By contrast, Krentz's protagonists
feel comfortable with themselves. They have faults that are either their accepted
idiosyncrasies or are easily erased by a loving partner. With them, the saying 'you
get what you see' holds true.

4.2.2 SEXUAL FACETS

Sexuality is the pivotal theme in contemporary American (category) romances and
it is complex so that the different periods of time within the twenty-five years must
be surveyed.

Pamela Regis points out that romance novels of the twentieth century differ
from those of previous eras in so far as through courtship, the heroine no longer
needs to be granted "affective individualism, property rights as well as the right
to make a companionate marriage" (Regis 2003, 111). On top of that, the church
made life difficult for a young woman of earlier times. At the outset of the modern
romance novel, the heroine already has the freedom to pursue her own ends, to
possess her own property or the skill to acquire property herself, and the freedom to choose whomever she wishes to marry. In short she is in command of
her life. This means that in a contemporary romance novel of the twentieth and

twenty-first century, set in upper middle class American, the courtship focuses on emotion, that is, it focuses on the hero's and heroine's emotionality and on their relationship. A heterosexual relationship has been reduced to its emotional aspect, which, and this needs to be added for Regis ignores it, is shown primarily in sexual ways. When the main emphasis is put on the developing love story, especially the development of the white heterosexual partners' romantic attachment without the conflict of class distinctions or religious inhibition, this is no longer conceivable in a contemporary Euro-American setting without sexual connotations. Cohn agrees about the centrality of sexuality in romance novels when she says,

> The important issue about sexuality in romances is not its moral or aesthetic or political value, nor the absence of these, but its absolute centrality. Sexuality is the 'res gestae' of romance, the stuff out of which the story is made. (1998, 20)

This could also mean that American romance novels have broken the taboo that once suppressed a presentation of the female side of sexuality thanks to, if nothing else, the vast numbers of books published and sold. Both Krentz and Delinsky have been instrumental in breaking this taboo. By doing so, they stick to traditional values, set in their time, which means that their narrative premises are to portray open sexual behavior within the constraints of the conservative moral package of heterosexuality, marriage and children. However, Meryl Altman points out in her essay that second wave feminist novel authors, who are by no means romance novel authors, describe forthright hetero-sexual lovemaking from the women's point of view, demanding and professing that sexual satisfaction is important to women as well as to men. As opposed to romance novels, their quest is a search for fulfillment that is not simply a search for a happy ending in a traditional marriage. In these novels

> revelations of the existence and possibilities of female desire were bound up with a detailed unpacking of the US culture of femininity as a set of experiences of profound humiliation and shaming, with an indictment of the US educational system with its double messages and double bind. (Altman 2003, 40)

So the taboo was broken before the description of explicit sexual acts became the rule in category romances a decade later. However, the circulation of these novels was restricted whereas category romances are mass market products. Breaking taboos through these books was infinitely more effective, particularly because the contents of the novels coincide with traditional beliefs in the power of marriage and family. Altman tries to placate feminist indignation at a possible indoctrination of romance readers by stating

> that feminine manipulativeness is, and should be, a conscious feminist act
> because feminism is about Women Getting What We Want, and what we
> want is … marriage and a happy ending. (ibid 40)

and she finishes her argument by claiming that deploring mass-culture is counter-productive. This argument could nicely appease raised tempers.

The role sexuality plays in an American setting differs from its European counterpart, the reason for which can be deduced from American history. Whereas Europeans were exposed to different religious denominations and thus are open to divergent standpoints, the belief of the Pilgrim Fathers is still a dominant ideology within white US society. Specifically sexual taboos, an underlying disgust toward sex, and, thus, an anxiety about its possible dominance over people in today's American culture is evidence of this Puritan/Protestant heritage, particularly because of the increasing shift towards fundamentalism that America has undergone in the past decades.[94] It seems that female readers of romance novels, once they became aware of their own right to enjoy sexuality along with the other rights they learned from feminists, wanted and needed to be taught and to be more enlightened about what happens in other people's bedrooms in order to understand better their own sexuality. Romance novels provide the opportunity to explore, understand, and inform women of their own sexual natures with romance heroines acting as morally accepted representatives who help them to obtain background knowledge about sexuality.[95] One of the main effects these sexual scenes accomplish(ed) is/was that they help(ed) readers to understand that their bodies are not dirty and untouchable and that their own sexual satisfaction is of importance, too. As a result, the increasing sales of these novels made publishers aware of changed moral attitudes and they reacted to this by modifying their guidelines for authors. Consequently more books with sexually open scenes were published. Krentz and Delinsky played an important part as authors for the sexually explicit category romance line *Harlequin Temptation*.

---

[94] In his review of Brian Alexander's *America Unzipped* R.S. Stewart claims that Alexander was convinced that there was a large percentage of Americans who engaged in a variety of unconventional sexual practices. He found out, that this assumption still is true in spite of the fact of the increasingly fundamentalist turn America has undergone in the past decades and in spite of the country's evangelical anti-sex attitudes. In the final chapter, Alexander "onsiders what current Americans are really looking for in their pursuit of sex and implies that they "are looking for an escape from American culture, which is increasingly characterized by bewildering technology and increased loss of community, leading to a sense of personal isolation. Sex, then, provides them with a way in which they can connect with others and escape their loneliness." Review – America Unzipped – Sexuality and Sexual Problems, retrieved 8.2.10

[95] These novels, however, could and sometimes still can only be understood by a sexually enlightened woman because the 'purple prose' is obfuscating.

Sexuality has been introduced in a great number of guises in romances. In the thirty-five years since the first explicit sex-scene, a rape, was introduced in historical romances, wave after wave of different kinds of narrative situations preferred by readers have flourished. In these books, at first, heroes had to practically rape the heroines, the tempting Eves in 'Puritan' eyes. It might have been a concession to conservative morality, showing the man as the willingly or unwillingly seduced one in patriarchal clothes and the women indulging his zest.[96] Linke points out that rape aggression is a well-known female fantasy because a woman feels flattered when a man cannot control his sexual self, inspired by her attractiveness, and moreover, it empowers her for it is she who provokes his unconstrained behavior. And she cannot be blamed for the ensuing act. Thus erotic wish turns into unbridled sexual desire. She becomes his accomplice because, in spite of her resistance, she capitulates and takes part in the action, and, thus, changes the potentially criminal act (2003, 249–251). *Stormy Challenge* runs along this formula.

Tania Modleski argues that romances encourage readers "to participate in and actively desire feminine self-betrayal" (Modlesky 1982, 37) and Janet Cohn criticizes romances because "Popular romance, whatever its sexual politics, exists to provide in Frederic Jameson's terms 'imaginary or formal solutions' to unsolvable social contradictions" (1998, 12). She sees these social contradictions as inherent to women's situation in a patriarchal society that demands submission and a retrograde vision of gender relations. The imbalance of power between the hero and the heroine is accentuated by the heroine's virginity and inexperience. In addition, patriarchal convictions and attitudes prevail. Despite the heroine beginning to enjoy sex, she nevertheless still sees it as her only goal to be integrated into the man's life through marriage and having his children. *Sweet Ember* runs along this formula.

In her dissertation, Kamble argues that the excessive sexual aggressiveness of the 1970s and 1980s heroes is a result of the increasing visibility of male homosexuality that needed to be countered in romances with a strong 'alpha male' who could defuse concerns about the traditional value of family for the readers, as romance novels are imagined powerful molds of social attitudes. She maintains that romance heroes before that time were mild mannered in their courtship and nondescript for the most part. (Kamble 2008, 20) Kamble's arguments are convincing because she correlates rising and ebbing homoanxiety in American society with gays' struggle for their rights, achieved gay rights and gay acceptance. The dates she refers to coincide with the different kinds of hero characterization in romance novels.

---

[96] The book-covers of that time showed women and men embracing in a half-undressed state. These covers are called "bodice-rippers".

Feminists usually only consider the patriarchal aspect in relationships in romance novels, and argue that it does not fully justify the sexual aggressiveness
the heroes display in the books, thereby supporting Kamble's assumptions. Patriarchy plays a dominant role for many feminist scholars in their examination of
the genre. The term is linked with the notion of capitalism, a patrilineal legal system, and systematic oppression and discrimination of women. Since the 1980s,
a reduced meaning of patriarchy in contemporary American romances covers the
area of misogyny, emanations of capitalism, and a fierce sense of possessiveness.
A typical utterance of this 'retrograde vision' of patriarchal behavior can be found
in *Stormy Challenge* when a man flirting with the heroine apologizes to the hero
with "Sorry ... Didn't realize she was private property" (221). That this kind of
hero only needs to confess his love as a means to give the heroine access to his inner self and thus empower her to control him is one of the dangerous 'truths' that
circulate as strong beliefs in romance novels of the Harlequin kind, a dangerous
truth, should they really be powerful molds of social attitudes.

D. Kramer's and M. Moore's 2002 study shows to what extent patriarchal attitudes and homoanxiety continue to be mirrored in category romance novels of
today. They randomly chose one hundred romance novels from 5,000 Harlequin
titles published between 1990 and 1998. They analyzed the content thematically
with a family therapeutic approach, thus later providing therapy with a theoretical
background because they were convinced of the model forming the readers of romance novels were, and are, subjected to. They were interested in the messages
delivered by the romantic fiction genre regarding gender roles and marriage because they assumed that a causal relation exists between the patriarchal sexual
interactions depicted in romance novels and domestic abuse. The analysis showed
that 97 of these novels still portrayed extreme patriarchal ideology. In 2008 K.
Turpin documented that Harlequin Presents still sells patriarchal ideology, alongside the feminist-oriented ideology they claim to publish, and which Krentz and
her co-writers have published from 1992 onwards. Whether this is due to repeated
backlist reprints or newly written novels is not clear. But in the case of Krentz and
Delinsky these reprints really confuse a reader about the different ideology the
authors appear to present simultaneously, if she does not take the pains to look at
the copyright date. Moreover, the authors, themselves, do not want to be reminded
of their patriarchal writing phase, either because they want to promote their new
novels (Krentz) or because they have moved beyond that writing phase they do
not want to be reminded of (Delinsky).

For this project, however, I will have to go back in time. When Krentz and
Delinsky began their careers under the tutelage of Harlequin or that of other romance publishing houses in the 1980s, it is not surprising that they subscribed
to patriarchy, even aggressive patriarchy, particularly because they read the genre

type of the battle of the sexes romances of their time and wanted to be congruous with the aspired category lines. It seems that for them, the aggressive and possessive hero, learning to express gentleness and trust towards the heroine, is sufficient rationalization to idealize the relationship. Alas, sexual favors given to control a man's anger, aggression and possessive behavior are the wrong means to domesticate a man for long. According to Kramer/Moore's analysis, there were three motifs used in 97 of the 100 books: those of Cinderella, Beauty and the Beast and The Taming of the Shrew. In *Stormy Challenge* (1982), Krentz chose the most aggressive one of these three motifs, The Taming of the Shrew. The heroine's lack of submissiveness at the beginning of the story and her monetary independence allow her the freedom to act bellicosely so that the hero is challenged to subdue her. They communicate their anger which is spurred by his clumsy sexual advances, effecting no instant gratification, and her indecisive behavior: he, by pulling her braid and verbally threatening to beat her, thus demanding complete surrender, she, by throwing her wineglass at him, the alternative in other romance novels of the time to slap him in the face, and verbally demeaning him. The Krentz shrew already has an inkling of the idea that she has the right and the female power to lessen his pathological possessiveness by inducing him to confess his love which, serving as instructive material, could turn out to be disastrous in real life. Again, the sexual consummation depicts the hero's satisfaction, whereas the heroine is satisfied and happy by having provided him with satisfaction. Thus, patriarchal entitlement is showcased.

Delinsky's *Sweet Ember* of 1982 is a version of Beauty and the Beast. The heroine lets the hero behave in a beastly and distrustful manner, presenting a cold facade which makes him into the mysterious person who later needs to shed the mask. The male coldness means the heroine is utterly incapable of deciphering the man and his behavior, which in turn results in her loss of self-confidence and decisive behavior. His being a cryptogram makes him dangerous in her eyes, and, at the same time, eroticizes him for her, which is a patriarchal method par excellence. So Beauty returns to the Beast, and only after having endured passively emotional belittlement as a result of her constant awareness of her sexual feelings, she gladly accepts his physical and verbal declaration of love as this means he has shed the beastly behavior mask forever. The question of who possesses whom is not raised, but the heroine's meek submission to the hero's demands, and her capitulation, is patriarchal in its essence.

From the economic point of view, both heroines would not need to play the submissive roles of women who lose their self-worth when they fall in love. Such an emotional make-up, however, is presented as supposedly mirroring behavior expected by contemporary society with the subtext that by not giving up their financial independence, at least with the Krentz and Delinsky heroines, their instinct of self-preservation will emerge in time and act against male displays of superiority. At the same time traditional social ideals of love, monogamy, children, and heterosexuality continue to form the basis for these romance novels, although in differently structured relationships. If we can assume that Harlequin still propagates aggressive patriarchal ideology, which it did at least until 2008, and still does by reprinting backlist titles of its more prominent authors, the novels of now and then, published side by side, can easily be compared, and the difference between these two writing phases becomes blatantly obvious. Hidden homoanxiety in the Kamble sense, at least with Krentz, albeit late, is overcome when she introduces gay couples into her novels.[97]

Neither author ever refers to her 'patriarchal' phase as such, but each moves on in different directions, Krentz e.g. by gathering feminist romance authors around her who present their current ways of thinking about modern romance novel writing. Krentz and her co-authors state that in romance novels, the power of a patriarchal society is inverted because they depict the fantasy of women exerting enormous power over men. Taming their heroes (sexually) instead of being (sexually) tamed by them empowers the heroines. Implying as Radway, Thurston, Modlesky and other scholars do, that these novels serve as models or molders for reader behavior, Krentz regards her heroines' pro-active involvement in sexual matters as encouragement for her readers to work for their own happiness, thus endowing these new heroines with a substance they did not have before. However, this notion of a fully inverted patriarchy might turn out to be a self-delusion on the author's side, particularly if the heroine's power is located in her attractiveness to the hero, her sexuality and in her ability to understand the hero's emotions and also taking his name once they are married, thus changing her identity (but not being his property) and attending to her hero in the same way women of all times have handled their men. This intuitive understanding of reasons for a hero's behavior has always been a woman's means of survival in patriarchal eras, along with submitting to his sexual urges. But then, to be on the safe side, Krentz paradoxically insists in *Dangerous Men and Adventurous Women* that "the fantasies in the books have nothing to do with a woman's politics" (ibid 8).

At least from 1992 onwards, with the hero's attitude changing, the narrated kind of sex that the lovers mutually enjoyed makes the reader aware that sex can be the opposite of what inhibitory religious standpoints insinuate, although religion is anathema in these romance novels. The new heroine as agent of the narrative quest for happiness through mutual sexual enjoyment shows how sexual repression takes away the ability to enjoy physical happiness and with it intimacy. The authors define this achievement of mutual pleasure from heterosexual acts as

---

[97] Krentz, *Smoke in Mirrors* 2002, *Sizzle and Burn* 2008

love. Moreover, within their romance ideology, they make it obvious that, without sexual compatibility and action, a relationship is deprived of intimacy and thus of intimacy in every other way: this prevents characters from loving each other completely. How deprivation of intimacy leads to a couple's estrangement is demonstrated in Delinsky's *The Family Tree*.

Sexual attraction and intimacy come first in the relationship followed by a mutual cherishing of each other.[98] The explicit, aggressively open narrative address of sexual occurrences as an introduction to love is more a component of American contemporary romance novels than of their European counterparts, as far as I can see. (But I am not familiar with enough contemporary category titles to really be able to compare.) As an explanation the argument could be used that in a society where paradoxical signals about sexuality are directed at a confused audience – conservative, evangelical versus pluralistic, agnostic notions and rigid, legally enforceable behavioral norms – readers of romance novels seek answers. The structure of the romance novel contributes to an erotic potential with a different female tenor. Reading about confident and positive female sexuality (although encouraged by a male character), female sensuality, female pleasure and love heightens the reading experience and seems to provide answers. But it should never be forgotten that these heroes who provide female satisfaction for their heroines are fictive characters constructed by women who provide means of escape for women through reading. As prototypes for real life men, they are questionable, a fact that authors assume their readers are aware of, and sociologists and psychotherapists know they are not.

In all of Krentz's contemporary romance novels, from her category beginnings onward, courtship starts off with the hero's and the heroine's libido springing to life on their first meeting. The heroine, not being a virgin, is aware of her feelings as sexual ones. The male, charged with testosterone, takes the initiative, often clumsily and, in the early novels, also aggressively, but from about 1986 his female counterpart teaches him to be more sensitive and his clumsiness becomes an endearing trait. Before 1986 Krentz's heroes' sexual aggressiveness is astonishingly harsh. After 1986, a Krentz courtship goes something like this: an instant initial sexual attraction on both sides, a first half-sexual encounter that elucidates for both their readiness to go to bed with each other, without locking horns as foreplay, yet not at this moment; and then they find a way to have consensual sex,

---

[98] In an interview about *Liebe als Passion*, Luhmann talks about changes the code of love has been subjected to. There he comments that these days, wir "mehr oder weniger die Erfahrung machen, daß sich Liebe erst auf Grund von sexuellen Beziehungen entwickelt und nicht umgekehrt die Vorbedingung oder die deklarierte Eingangsformel für die Aufnahme sexueller Beziehungen sein muß" (Luhmann 2001. 147). This observation is mirrored in the romance novel plots of both authors.

described in detail, which culminates in the best orgasm that ever happened to both. The heroine usually has not had sex for a long time but, being aware of her sexual feelings and needs, she sometimes uses a vibrator which, of course, cannot compete with the real thing.[99] They go on having sexual intercourse, sometimes reported *in extenso* which can mean anything from five to ten pages, sometimes only mentioned in an aside, but always emphasizing their consensus, and the hero's efforts to control his body to give her pleasure, yet always interwoven with other facets of their getting to know each other. Although Krentz's protagonists mention how liberating it is to be able to laugh during sex, on the whole sexual acts are a rather solemn activity, emphasizing just how serious this act is for the relationship.[100]

In her Harlequin romances, Delinsky also gives extended narrative accounts of sexual acts, although her heroes and heroines, usually no virgins, do not constantly remind the reader of their aroused state. First and foremost, the protagonists' attraction for each other is shown in generally more underlying sexual vibrations, as part of a toned down love-hate romance pattern. Secrets need to be uncovered and trust issues vented before the couple can allow sexual attraction take its course. Then the explicit, though narratively veiled, sex they have culminates in the best orgasm either has ever had. An extreme example is the heroine of *Sweet Ember,* whom a simple kiss transports to 'ecstasy'.

Both Delinsky and Krentz usually have their heroes initiate the sexually connoted contacts. A heroine who is sexually aggressive would belie the romance assumption of her being chaste or not very experienced, which would be her commonly agreed way to be. The heroes, however have plenty experience. In order to counteract this male advantage, it is conceded that the heroines have feelings of sexual attraction and anticipate forthcoming pleasures. But it is up to the hero to make the initial sexual utterances and innuendos, and the initial orchestrations of sexual acts. His supposedly greater familiarity with all things sexual makes him the teacher, thus allowing him to display a dominant superiority. Although he encourages his heroine to actively take part in the sexual play – a narrative device to show his respect and acknowledgement of sexual equality along with a turning away from patriarchal behavior – he nevertheless maintains a dominant status in this respect.

Delinsky deviates from the above insofar as her heroine admittedly leaves it to the hero to take the initiative, yet her feelings are described more than his. This is why a reader receives the impression that her romance novels and her mainstream novels are more stories about women than Krentz's; the latter seems to provide

---

[99] Mentioning the use of a vibrator breaks another romance taboo as does that of a hero's masturbation.

[100] Susan Elizabeth Phillips, Linda Howard or Jennifer Crusie display fun-filled sexual activities.

a balance between the protagonists' feelings, subjecting the stories to the couple. But the first act of sexual intercourse experienced by all Krentz and Delinsky's protagonists is the foreplay to marriage, even if this only occurs years later as in *Sweet Ember*.

As times change, so do sexual connotations. A relevant shift takes place in the significance the sexual act holds for the couples. If in *Stormy Challenge* the sexual act satisfied the heroine because she felt proud to be a cherished sexual object, and if in *Sweet Ember* the hero's sexual performance indicated that a man is needed to enhance the heroine's imaginary heightened sexual feelings, both heroines' feelings relate exclusively to themselves. Their heroes' sexuality is the emanation of their, the heroines', attractiveness. In both *Perfect Partners* and *All Night Long,* complemen-tary mutuality becomes the cornerstone for the protagonists' actions and their sexuality. The sexual act culminates in them both experiencing orgasms, one way or the other. They reflect each other within the relationship insofar as both partners consider the consequences their actions will have for the other or, as both see the other's need, which they can possibly meet. The couples in Delinsky's Women's Fiction have many problems to contend with, so that the question of sexuality and its meaning for a couple becomes a question of priorities, and as such it may be relegated to the background or alternatively be given priority. Depending on the woman's frame of mind, she needs either to be the hero's cherished sexual object to boost her ego (*A Woman Betrayed),* or she needs the intimate mutually inspired and inspiring togetherness (*The Family Tree*).

In both the authors' romance stories, the protagonists' sexual encounters are a learning process in the sense that both protagonists experience a different sensuality from the one they knew before. The hero's sexual skills combined with his personality, or simply his attractiveness, which have already won her heart, make her realize that they are compatible. Sexual compatibility induces thoughts of monogamy and family. Wendel/Tan phrase it as follows: "Marriage and monogamy are never a bad choice when sex is 'that good'" (153–154). Simplistic, but seen as one part of the code for romance stories, the authors homogeneously structure their romance novels along this concept.

Rarely does a heroine take the pill. This matches the romance belief that a heroine should not be too experienced, thus giving the hero some advantage in the relationship. If the heroine took the pill in order to explore her own sexuality in a relationship that does not promise marriage, the typical romance reader would consider her to be morally reprehensible. Whether a condom is used or not, however, increases the tension in the authors' novels, allowing for some sexual plays with it if it is used, or indicating the protagonists' enormous sexual excitement when they forget to use it, or demonstrating the hero's readiness for marriage and children when he chooses to forgo it.[101] Since society was first alerted to the danger of contracting AIDS, condoms have played a role in both authors' novels.

Romance novels are dismissed as women's pornography because of their extensively depicted sex scenes designed to stimulate the reader.[102]. Romance authors try to defend their literary genre, but whatever reasoning they might give, those preconceptions are and always will be there. Yet how much impact sex scenes in romance novels have on a reader, and in what way, is shown by the results of Huei-Hsia Wu's study which states:

> that the general attitude-behavior pattern of readers of romance novels fits the Harlequin stereotype of nourishing a satisfying sex life in the context of romantic monogamous fidelity, while at the same time vicariously fulfilling sexual desires through fictitious characters in romance novels. (131)

This result could serve as justification for regarding the genre as 'female pornography'. However, just as with good or bad films, how well these scenes are written depends on an author's skill. Readers like the sex scenes, see them as indispensable, experience them as hot and stimulating, and inform other readers about their likes and dislikes in various readers' blogs. Delinsky (for her category romances) and Krentz usually receive readers' approval with regard to this part of their writing. They never seem to transgress the barriers that make a narrative sex scene embarrassing.

Today it is not only romance novels which include sex scenes to varying degrees. Umberto Eco, once asked what ingredients made a bestseller, answered approximately: "a little sex, a little money and crime, a little high society or, perhaps, a well described erection ... " That is THE formula of escapist literature per se, especially that of romance novels.

Like Kramer/Moore, only with a positive view of romance fiction, Huei-Hsia Wu's study also "argues that the content of the romance novels is at least a modestly powerful molder of the sexuality of those who read them" (WU 2006, 131–132). Sexual intercourse between the protagonists is connoted with positive life-enhancing feelings. One thing readers can learn is that you do not need a bed to have sexual intercourse. The sexual activities depicted take place in various places and various positions. Foreplay is usually an integral part of a seduction scene that includes descriptions of the sexually sensitive parts of the male and female body. This openness about the variety of possibilities people can enjoy during sex might encourage readers to experiment with their partners or with their

---

[101] Linda Howard especially likes to play with this topic.

[102] Wendel/Tan compare pornography and romance novels and decide they are not pornography because there are no anal sexual scenes there. Anal sex scenes are the taboo of the taboos in romance novels.

own sexual emotionality. There is an astonishing freedom displayed in limning these acts. Nevertheless descriptions are restricted to traditionally permitted varieties of sexual practices, whereas acts such as anal intercourse are perceived to be too close to gay activity, or sadomasochist, entertainment which is off limits. It seems that authors like Krentz and Delinsky are aware that romance novels are a kind of conventional attitude molder in the sexual area, as, for example, with the mentioning and use of condoms and situational games with them. This shows that authors know how necessary it is to remind their readers of the physical dangers of unprotected sex in the AIDS age. Since 1992 the use of condoms in romance novels' sex scenes is practically a given. Some people have even gone so far to ask whether romance novelists can be considered to be sex educators. In my opinion, the tendency to still use obfuscating 'purple prose' which is regarded as necessary for romanticizing the romance neutralizes educational intentions.

4.2.3 FACETS OF LOVE

Another integral part of both authors' romance novels is the distinction between the terms 'having sex' and 'making love'. At first, it always seems to the heroine that the hero is having sex with her, while she imagines they were making love, and in the end, both agree to make love. For a typical romance novel, this turnaround of terming the sexual act is a crucial point because now the heroine knows that his purely sexual desire has turned into an everlasting feeling of love.

With time, Krentz's hero and heroine have lost the need to differentiate between these terms because of other more pressing external problems which render this internal one obsolete. Thus, it leads to the omission of Regis' emotional Point of Ritual Death, for each protagonist is absolutely sure of the other's feelings: these feelings have to be confessed in the end, but have been there from the beginning. Another reason might be that the themes of empowerment and sexual liberation became less emphasized once these new contents were established as a norm, or the formula seemed to have been too excessively used. Delinsky's later protagonists who are not at the beginning of a courtship do not regard this distinction as relevant, but then, love between her protagonists is already missing, and for those commencing a relationship, there is no doubt about the quality of their feelings their intimacy will provide.

Facets of love can only be described by analyzing the characters' motivations and actions with regard to the emotionality seen as love. In English romance novels of the 1960s and later, like those of Mary Stewart, physical knowledge of hero and heroine will take place after the end of the book and so declarations of love imply a mutual physical attraction, which exists only as subtext. In the American romance novels of the 1980s onwards, the protagonists feel sexual attraction and have sex before their feelings for each other are interpreted as love. The anticlimax after sexual intercourse presents them with a preview of what life together could bring in physical happiness. But a good orgasm should not equate with love, which it usually seems to do in romances. Putting the aspect of sexuality aside, the question arises as to which are the decisive factors which determine love with each author.

The early Krentz heroines seem to bask in the knowledge that a man they are attracted to and trust sees them as the object of his indomitable desire, and, therefore, wants to possess them, claiming his ownership and her availability to him through his marriage proposal. They expect from their husbands love in the form of protection and everlasting appreciation: in exchange they give him their love by staying attractive for him and bearing his children.

The later Krentz heroines display an altogether different attitude. It is not the age factor which makes them different, since the early Krentz heroines are around the same age and sometimes they have also been divorced after a short marriage. It was a modification of attitude that came about as a result of feminist influence and supposed reader expectations that made Krentz create heroines who become mature partners for their mature men. Here, feelings that are identified as love are premised on adult maturity. For these women love means being able to not only trust, respect and rely on a man, but also understand, accept, and indulge his peculiarities believing they will be able to live in love together for a lifetime in spite of their personal idiosyncrasies. Beside mutual sexual fulfillment, these women know they are essential for their hero's happiness and they love him for this (*Perfect Partners* and *All Night Long*). His love for her is identified in his need for her, sexually and otherwise, because she is the source of his emotional peace, contentment and security: a haven. Being needed this way, the heroine manifests her love by taking care of him. Each loves the other's life-enhancing company. Now Krentz's heroines can combine their female abilities with those of their male counterparts, thus forming a unity that is perceived as love. The chauvinist possessiveness, defined as love in the earlier Krentz hero, matures into a protective attitude which a loving man requires to bolster his ego, an attitude supposed to emerge once his woman necessitates his male competence. A latent violence in these heroes eroticizes them for the heroine who likes to believe she can tame her 'warrior' so that he will never hurt people who belong to him, but will stay able, vigilant, and ready to defend his loved ones, a trait seen to be as a consequence of his love.

Delinsky again displays different aspects of the characteristics of love. At the beginning of her writing category romance stories, her protagonists lead a fairly content and independent life, but an intimate togetherness, as their definition of love would make their life truly happy. To this end, each party is ready to make concessions such as giving up fast-held convictions, or allowing the other to come close as happens in *Sweet Ember*. What the protagonists understand as love is at first the vague feeling of attraction that they each refuse to acknowledge, but yield to in time. They spend a period of time together, sometimes *nolens volens (The Victoria Lesser Series)*, and find out that they are well-matched and like-minded. This evolves into love and they imagine a life of togetherness in harmony with all the secrets they had carried around for so long finally revealed and the necessity for them explained.

Often in Delinsky's Women's Fiction, the story begins years after a couple's 'happy ever after' marriage vows. Now the protagonists have serious marital problems and/or are on the brink of separation. Life has eroded their love for each other. The basis of their love, the strong desire to live a life of intimate togetherness, has crumbled. What is left is the wife cherishing the illusion of love and her loving efforts to organize a life together which the husband no longer values for various reasons, be they that he no longer needed feels other than as a breadwinner, that he has affairs, or that he simply cannot cope with tragedy. When the wife realizes she has lost her husband's love for good she is able to acknowledge her futile efforts and feels relieved. As she has not lost her ability to love, she will find a new man who might be a better match.

The new men in these women's lives love differently. Whether by becoming new men in the divorced women's lives, who are able to cherish their women's love, or by becoming loving husbands, they now take on some of the nurturing and caring as an expression of their male, but self-confident emotionality and love, traits which are seen as belonging to typical romance beta-heroes. Moreover, they remain desirable and virile, exerting their leadership qualities while at the same time being warm and caring men. Sexual attraction and sexuality is also an underlying motivation for both partners' wanting to spend time and life together, but it is part of the love package that includes many more aspects: understanding the other's problems, encouraging aspirations, fulfilling yearnings or working hard to make the other happy.

In nuce, what both authors portray as love affects the loving couple's living conditions in a new way. Love means caring for the other's well-being, allowing the partner freedom to pursue his/her objectives and accepting his/her idiosyncrasies and foibles. The couple make their longing for togetherness in a loving home a reality.

Love between family and friends serves as a means to illustrate protagonists' character traits. Along with the unconditional love bestowed on children even when they behave badly or aggressively, or caring for the needy elderly, this kind of love is treated in Delinsky's Women's Fiction as an idealized womanly attitude (*A Woman Betrayed* and *The Family Tree*).

4.3 SOCIOLOGICAL ASPECTS

4.3.1 MARRIAGE AND FAMILY

Sex and love are instrumental in achieving THE romance novel goal: marriage and family. At the outset of the story the authors' heroines already live a somewhat satisfactory if solitary life. All they are lacking is a husband, because in a traditional, contemporary romance world, life without a husband and a family with him is not complete. The fact that they offer this traditional concept annoys feminists who claim these novels serve only to confirm a patriarchal world-view. Nevertheless, readers seem to hunger after these affirmative stories in which the institution of marriage and a core-family is valued above all else.

In 2001, declining sales prompted Harlequin to go urban and upscale[103] and it launched a new line with its own imprint aimed at attracting younger readers with more purchasing power (the new books cost double the price of a traditional Harlequin novel) than the typical middle-aged, married, unsophisticated, small-town, Southern American Harlequin romance readers. For *Red Dress* only one title per month was published compared with the seventy titles Harlequin otherwise issues on a monthly basis. *Red Dress* editors were trying to establish a new formula for love and romance, one that acknowledges that young women no longer see commitment and independence as mutually exclusive. They wanted to reintegrate romance into post-feminist life and sensibilities, in a way that departs from traditional marriage with its patriarchal connotations, but nevertheless satisfies the emotional need for companionship. The line was closed in 2006 because Harlequin had strayed too far from its romance roots and traditional values. Although neither Krentz nor Delinsky publishes with Harlequin anymore, this does not mean that their novels portray such drastically altered traditional core convictions about life in American society as did the *Red Dress* series. The authors value the institution of marriage and family, though each deems different aspects to be important.

No matter how emancipated the heroines have become over the years, in these novels it is nearly always the man who proposes, and the heroine adopts his family name. Weddings, as such, rarely play a role, serving only as padding for an otherwise meager plot, though sometimes being pivotal to the story. They might take place at the beginning, or in the middle: in any case, the couple's altered relationship is then questioned. If weddings are not essential for the plotline, they are either mentioned in short sentences or not mentioned at all, for what happens after the wedding is significant, be it the blissful feeling of lawful belonging, or doubts about it, or a pregnancy, or the birth of a child. So it is not that the actual wedding

---

[103] see Katherine Marsh, "Fabio gets his walking papers: can Harlequin rekindle romance in a post-feminist world?", retrieved 22.9.09

vows are important after the declaration of love: what matters is the promising future of a happy family life.

Although what readers expect from a romance novel has changed with time, along with their moral value canon, most romance category lines still uphold an ideal picture of marriage and family life beginning with the new couple's marriage. Negative experiences prior to the beginning of the story, be they the divorce of their parents when they were children, or their own divorce, have not destroyed the protagonists' ideals. Having married for the wrong reasons once, they will not repeat the same mistakes. There are two different viewpoints regarding family in the authors' text worlds: one is the role played by the hero and heroine's original family, the other is the featuring of aspects of family dynamics which the authors present to their readers as a positive role model for living a good life, thereby transmitting social values.

A common and convenient device in a category romance is to make one protagonist either an orphan, or in some way alienated from his family in order to focus solely on the courtship and the emotional ups and downs that occur there. Dealing with the family of just one of the protagonists rounds out the novel more than if no family intruded at all. Whether orphaned or alienated from their family characters are twice as happy when they are welcomed into the other's family. Being welcomed after initial reservation from the other's family makes for a good plot. Good relations with both families would create no tension for an ongoing story but, of course, a good writer can concoct a series of unexpected challenging incidents from any family constellation.

The pasts of Krentz's protagonists follows category romance novel patterns. *Stormy Challenge* features a heroine whose only living relative is a brother and a hero whose family does not appear at all, although his parents seem to be living. (This limited focus on the couple alone is an outcome of writing guidelines specifications of the time.) In *Perfect Partners* the hero is still distressed by the bleak experiences of his youth: a dying mother, a father who cannot cope with her loss, and their desperate financial situation because of inability to pay his mother's hospital bills. He has lived his life without friends and put all his energy into the successfully growing business he will own in the near future. The heroine, having grown up within a caring and emphatic family in secure financial circumstances, is aware of the life-saving importance of a network of family and friends. Realizing that the hero loves, respects, and protects the heroine, her family welcomes him. Creating his own new family within this emotionally sheltering family circle brings him complete happiness.

In *All Night Long*, family plays a similar role. Here, the heroine again has grown up in a loving family, although only until she was sixteen years old, and thus was able to develop a caring attitude that later leads to an intrinsic understanding of her lover. And she who has no family anymore gains the respect and love of his family by making the family understand him. The epilogue in which the heroine's and the hero's sister-in-law's pregnancies are announced doubly conveys that in a Krentz fictional world a marriage without children is unconceivable.

Occasionally, the illusion is projected in Krentz's novels that women are able to reconcile family rifts, to placate irritated family members, to create a friendly basis of communication between members of a family.[104] Thus, the stories suggest to a reader that a loving family, offering emotional security, is one of the most important ingredients for living a content and happy life. In one novel, an equivalent to a family made up of a close circle of friends is used in order to emphasize how necessary and important family ties are when hero and heroine have no relatives. At first getting to know this family comprising a group of friends appears strange to the fictional newcomers, but in time they come to value the invitation to join.[105]

Sometimes Krentz's protagonists have had to perform parental duties for years because their siblings and other relatives needed to be taken care of. This means, they have never been the kind of irresponsible carefree people who would be overwhelmed once they are confronted with the responsibility of taking care of their own children. The actions within the story also show that the protagonists value their family bonds so much that they take over responsibility where it is needed and do everything within their power to keep the family together.[106]

Notions about marriage and family are again divided between the ones presented in Delinsky's romance novels and those in her mainstream ones. In her romance novels, marriage occurs mostly outside the stories themselves. Usually there is a small circle of friends and some family connection in the background, but the story focuses on the courtship with a happy ending documented at least in a betrothal, supposedly a result of publishers' writing guidelines at the time. Pregnancy and babies in an epilogue that might evoke reader satisfaction are not offered. Sometimes babies or children are part of the plot, sometimes one partner is widowed and brings a child into the marriage who is accepted unhesitatingly by the new partner.[107] So marriage and the promise of family in Delinsky's romance novels is the happy genre ending with a twist. In her more mainstream Women's Fiction, marriage or remarriage are not pictured as the heaven romance novels insinuate. The life-long promise of staying together contained in the marriage vow is questioned, and the serious reasons for breaking them are thematized.[108]

---

[104] *Golden Chance,* 1990, *Absolutely, Positively* 1996

[105] e.g. *Grand Passion* 1994

[106] e.g. *Absolutely, Positively* 1996

[107] *Lilac Awakening* 1982, *Gemstone* 1983, *The Dream Comes True* 1990

[108] *Within Reach* 1986, *Commitments* 1988, *A Woman Betrayed* 1992, *Together Alone* 1995, *A Woman's Place* 1997, *The Summer I Dared* 2004

So imperfections, weaknesses, disillusion, complications, and problems wear the relationship down and turn romantic married bliss into a failing marriage. In addition, family surrounds the protagonists and their needs deflect from the couple's marriage on the rocks. In the end. however, despite all the difficulties, heartbreaks, and setbacks, the ideal of the institution of marriage (with children) remains unscathed because there, the hope is projected that marriage can succeed and the reward is the happiness of the individual. This is one reason I classify Delinsky's Women's Fiction as romances.

First marriages in romances are usually part of the past which the protagonists mention because they feel the new lover should be informed. A Krentz hero or heroine's former marriage generally ended in divorce, seldom in death. The failure of these marriages did not cause much obvious emotional distress to the characters because they were childless, and frequently both partners saw that they were simply not right for each other, and, therefore, did not stay in touch.

Although in some of Delinsky's romances death had put an end to a happy marriage, or a divorce may have undermined the heroine's self-esteem, couples remarry, hopeful that this time around it will be all right. That being so, the past is in the past and the new relationship is what the story is about. By presenting the fantasy of a promising sexual married life in their novels, marriage as a protecting haven for men and women, and a family to rely on in times of difficulties, both authors serve their readers' yearning by selling them the illusion of a successful life full of bliss within the institution of marriage. Linke comments that in romance novels, divorces provide an element of free choice for the individual person, which, she says, conforms with basic American values. But the myth of free choice clashes with the American family myth and, in romances, it is reconciled through remarriage (308).

Another question to be addressed is whose version of life will be adopted after the wedding, the hero's or the heroine's. It is convenient when the arrangement of the novel's setting's makes the protagonists live in the same town or move to the same place like the heroine does in *Perfect Partners*. Often one of Krentz's protagonists has just moved to the town where the other lives and they meet there for the first time. Where they will live together after the marriage depends on the size of the apartment or the house. If they do not live in the same town, it depends on whose job can be relocated. When the hero's professional life is – conveniently – not restricted to a special place, he can move to where the heroine lives and make his home there (*All Night Long*). Krentz's heroes are versatile in this regard. In any case, the heroines keep their businesses whether they can relocate them or not. Be that as it may: the couple will build a life together that takes both partners' professional interests into account.

Again, Delinsky's category romance novels take a different stand from her mainstream ones with regard to whose version of life will be adopted after the wedding. In her romance novels, the heroine has already gained a respected professional position and the question of who will relocate is not clear sometimes. *Sweet Ember* serves as an example. Here the reader can suppose that the heroine will live with the hero at his place. In contrast, the heroine in *Gemstone* tries to build up a branch of her business in San Francisco where her husband lives, at the same time maintaining her large business in New York. Whether she will manage to happily lead such a strenuous business life, while at the same time making a home for her husband and children, is debatable. But then, this is a nicely told fantasy, a fantasy, which in Delinsky's mainstream novels, would clearly be revealed as such.

In her mainstream novels, Delinsky's protagonists have already decided to live at a place they have chosen for heir new married life. But since the story often culminates in a separation of the married couple, one protagonist generally moves somewhere else to live there happily with a new partner. So, neither Krentz nor Delinsky disappoint their readers' expectation of a happy or satisfying ending that leaves the couple to live in a blissful union.

4.3.2 FRIENDSHIP

Friendship in Krentz and Delinsky's romances does not play a distinctive role other than sometimes surrounding the protagonists with a surrogate family consisting of friends of all ages. By the early 1980s, the traditional romance Other Woman, the antagonist, sometimes the heroine's best friend, seems to have vanished because none of the authors' novels contain this constellation of characters due, I suppose, to guidelines or editor restrictions. Genuine friendships, whether on the part of the heroine or the hero, are rare, particularly friendships between two men because of a possible underlying connotation of homosexuality (Kamble 2005). When the protagonists meet, they have no friends, that is, they have no friends who play even a tiny, but distinctive role in the story. There are good business relations, good family relations or acquaintances, or contacts required in a social setting, but no friends to spend leisure time or exchange intimate, confidential thoughts with. At least one half of the couple seems to be totally without a circle of friends, while the other has the family to rely on in a crisis. In the shorter category romances of the Harlequin brand, authors were instructed that not even a supportive member of the family should appear because the story was to concentrate solely on the lovers' emotions: as a result both authors' early category romances set supporting friends and family members unobtrusively in the background. Heroes are usually lone men, who have reached the age where one night stands have become increasingly unsatisfying. Their social lives are reduced to and focused on short sexual relationships, and work. There may be family, but there are no friends to surround them. Some heroes (and heroines) have had a short marriage that took place years before, or longer relationships that did not develop into lasting friendships nor did they turn into enmity. They just vanished. Therefore, as a rule, the heroes are free of what Germans call 'past issues', ready for a new beginning. Heroines are usually also at a crossroads in life, which is only a little more entangled, but they also lack close friends. So when hero and heroine meet, they are desperate for a close friend who turns out to be their soulmate, even if they do not consciously realize it.

Krentz's heroes are usually lone wolves who, with time, are transformed into socially more open and adept men by their heroines. But friendships outside family or surrogate family are not newly formed. For a trilogy,[109] Krentz introduced a trio of closely befriended heroines. Their friendship serves only as a loose link between the novels. The heroes are added to this friendship, but since the heroines, all three writers, now live at their husbands' homes far away from each other (because they can write anywhere), the three couples do not meet often. So the social setting Krentz arranges for her protagonists is one of family and the future core family, with no close friends other than work-related ones around them. It is more the family who takes the place of friends.

The concept of family consisting of friends, which Krentz presents in two novels, emphasizes once again a strong belief in the value of family. Moreover, she portrays a picture of close friends whose friendship relies on their commitment to a cause: in *Hidden Talents* (1993), a small community of drop-outs collectively raise an orphaned girl to become a college instructor, and act as a substitute loosely knit family for her. In *Grand Passion* (1994), a hotel owner with no family connections collects other people around her, nearly all women, without families to rely on. They all work full-time or part time at the hotel. In both novels these 'families', the term is used *expressis verbis*, take care of each other in times of need.

Delinsky's text world in her category romance novels is similar to Krentz's with regard to the relative isolation of the protagonists. But in her romances, people who could be called friends, who are more than business partners and good acquaintances, or merely family, play a role or are mentioned in an aside as being there for the hero or the heroine. These close friends might be a couple who died in a car accident and leave a child the hero wants to adopt, or an elderly widow who makes good friends separately with heroes and heroines and tries to matchmake between them,[110] but according to publishers' writing guidelines they mainly remain in the background.

---

[109] *The Pirate* 1990, *The Adventurer* 1990, *The Cowboy* 1990
[110] *Gemstone* 1983, *Moment to Moment* 1984, The Victoria Lesser Series:
    The Real Thing 1986, *Twelve Across* 1987, *A Single Rose* 1987

In Delinsky's mainstream novels, close friends surround the protagonists and their families. They play supporting roles like the heroine's friend, the lawyer, in *A Woman Betrayed* who offers successful legal help, the loose group of knitting friends in *The Family Tree* who provide a heartwarming atmosphere in the family shop, or the reading group in *Coast Road* who regularly visit the heroine who is in a coma and help the ex-husband to overcome estrangement from his ex-wife. Thus Delinsky features different networks of friends. With her discussion group guidelines she points out how valuable good friends are, and that maintaining friendship means giving as well as taking. In so doing, she strives to enlighten her readers as to how commitment works, along with other matters of her concern. Sometimes, however, since the black and white character constellations in her Women's Fiction are reduced, a close friend betrays the friendship and the solution of how to stay friends despite being aware of the betrayal portrayed in the novel is certainly thought-provoking (*A Woman Betrayed*).

4.3.3 WEALTH AND WORK ETHICS

A dominant social norm constantly referred to in the USA is the 'traditional' work ethic of job commitment and achievement, frequently termed as 'Puritan work ethic'. Its modern, secularized characteristics can be traced through Max Weber's contribution of his "Theory of the Protestant Work Ethic in America". It is still said to be the basis that explains Americans' devotion and belief in reaching worldly success via unceasing labor. These paradigm shifts, ranging from religious perspective to the secularized view of work influenced by capitalism and industrialism, have men only at the center of their meritocratic considerations. But as Applebaum notes

> the work ethic is multidimensional, a dynamic concept that changes over time, and that varies according to occupation, management, ideology, ethnic perspectives, class position, and level of income. (215)

Thus women and their work ethics have to be discussed as well. Feminist and gender research examines the connection between capitalism and patriarchy, the criticism of gender hierarchy in the work force, and the double socialization of women (family and work). Moreover it is concerned with the development of gender identity and the social construction of gender. Forty years of feminist research passing through three theoretical phases have been differentiated in various ways. Two of these phases are of interest for this project[111].

First, the equality approach: this is seen as the beginning of feminist research in the 1960s. At that time research into women was conducted by men who saw

---

[111] c.f. Gymrich 2005

women as deficient beings. As men saw themselves as the rational part of humanity, they, as the stronger sex, rightfully assigned themselves work in the business world, in politics, and jurisdiction, in contrast to the emotional human beings, women, whose given sphere of activity was nurturing the family and children. (Male self-determination is still based on the ideal of autonomy and individuality, whereas women are even today restricted to the ideal of conformity in accordance with their sex-group, which is pre-classified by men.) Now feminists hoped that, once their demands to halt gender hierarchy in the work force and to achieve equality between men and women were put into practice, women would attain proper recognition of their abilities as well as the chance of profitable work.

The second phase in the 1980s led seamlessly from the equality approach to the difference approach. It is focused on the different ways men and women lead their lives. This research is based on social structures, the pursuit of self-determination and the exercising of personal choice mediated by culture. The time was ripe for this. It is portrayed a little in Krentz's protagonists, but more so in Delinsky's. One aspect of how much feminist ideas have taken root in the novels of both authors is made manifest in the choice of work or profession the heroines are given. In her dissertation, Kamble maintains that Americanization in romance novels has brought predominantly themes of sexuality, but also capitalism and war to the reader's attention and reflects popular beliefs by confrontation.[112]

Wealth seems to be the essential ingredient without which the plot of a romance novel has no support. Romance novels are supposed to be fantasy, showing how the rich and mighty live and not mirroring reality, especially that of the lower and poorer classes. A heroine's upward mobility as motif is usually linked with patriarchal ideology. If wealth is not applied in a plot as a means to advance the heroine's societal status, it needs another justification to stay as an essential ingredient. Krentz and Delinsky's hero, with only some exceptions, is wealthier than his heroine, but her interest does not consist in accumulating worldly goods nor in improving her social status. She does it for the love of her work and nothing else and this correlates with the above-mentioned, second feminist phase. So why the need for wealth in romance novels, beside the agreed upon imaginary cushioning of the protagonists' need to sort out their conflicts peacefully, unhindered by monetary difficulties? One argument, beside the ones traditionally mentioned, is that authors who write affirmative literature combine work ethics with wealth

---

[112] According to her, the white hero's role as an entrepreneur formulates the romance plot by association with the profit that enables the hero's power. The portrayal of a wealthy protagonist shows lingering traces of his ruthlessness in business. She underlays the romance novels with a subtext by arguing that the heroine's struggle against the hero's advances is the (her) awareness of the power of global capital, which she attempts symbolically to neutralize through her struggle, an argument that, to me, seems to be rather farfetched.

in their novels, thus bearing out the American belief that the USA is the Land of Opportunity for everyone who is determined to work hard to reach his goal, as success is considered only in monetary terms. If romances are considered to be 'a powerful molder' (WU 131) this aspect, including its importance for the heroine, is subliminally inserted into them. This is valid for both authors. Thurston comments on the heroine's need for economic independence as follows:

> Today the most evolved erotic romances portray a feminine consciousness that has to do not only with sexual liberation but also with economic self-sufficiency, the cornerstone of all meaningful kinds of autonomy. (1987, 11)

Just how difficult it is to gain economic independence, however, is never questioned in a romance. When there is a financial glitch, a *deus ex machina* in the form of an inheritance or something similar helps the protagonist to overcome her/his money difficulties. Delinsky likes to use such narrative loopholes in her novels in order to secure the heroine's economic independence. Or else her protagonists simply never have to fear economic insecurities, a fact that increases romance elements in her mainstream novels.[113]

Krentz's protagonists in particular usually meet each other when at least one is sought out for his/her professional capacity. All her heroines work hard and enthusiastically in their chosen professional fields, and thereby achieve economic self-sufficiency. However, which profession is considered as appropriate for a woman, and which for a man is of interest at a time when the second feminist movement in the USA is largely perceived as having achieved at least partly equal rights in various areas, although the Equal Rights Amendment is yet to be ratified, and equal pay as well as equal professional chances are still a long way off.

Once a woman decides to become her own boss, male professional superiority does not need to be thematized. For Krentz's heroines, a woman's professional further education at university is important. College education enables them to become effective entrepreneurs like shop owners or hotel owners, accountants or writers. They are successful, but need the job to make a good living. More often than not women's jobs are inferior to those of the males, seen from a financial standpoint. (But the men's wealth is not instrumental in enhancing their sexual attractiveness for their partners as Jan Cohn sees it. For her wealth is not "an added-on value; his wealth, his property and economic power are basic attributes of his masculinity, a principle source of his virile attractiveness" (127) because "the hero's economic power ... supplies additional energy to his sexual power, as if his houses and cars ... are metaphors for or manifestations of his sexual

---

[113] *Within Reach* 186, *The Passions of Chelsea Kane* 1992, *Together Alone* 1995, *Flirting With Pete* 2003, *The Summer I Dared* 2004, etc.

allure" (154).[114]) The men's professions are similarly varied: they often work as consultants with a nearly magical knowledge of the computer and a Midas touch. They know how to make money and accordingly, they are rich and often have founded a corporation (*Perfect Partners*), but as they are interested in what they do, they go on working hard despite having accumulated enough money to last them a lifetime.[115] They do not use their money to wield unjustified power over someone else – this is the role of the rich powerful criminals. Instead they use their intelligence, skills, and knowledge to propagate the American way of life overseas by consulting firms on how to establish themselves in Europe.[116] There are the exceptions to the rule, men who have just changed their jobs and are at the beginning of a promising successful entrepreneurial future. Rarely does a protagonist have a boss to contend with. The retired military men among Krentz's heroes work as independent entrepreneurs such as private investigators or in the security business, only on a smaller financial scale.

In *Stormy Challenge,* the characters' professions only serve as décor. Whichever profession they are given does not matter because the narrative emphasis rests on their both working hard in high ranking or money making lines of entrepreneurial work. This fictional world shows the beginnings of women's professional emancipation. In later novels professions play a role as they generate part of the plot, though the mystery or murder part is given priority treatment because financial independence is the background security in the story.

All the male businesses are judged as honorable ways of accumulating money. In Krentz's futuristic paranormal novels and in the paranormal contemporary ones of the Arcane series, the protagonists are politically aware. In the 2007/8 novel *White Lies,* Krentz dares to let reality intrude by stating that in order to achieve wealth, a person needs to be ruthless because "saints didn't put together financial empires" (81). There, for the first time, as far as I can see, she causes a good, upright character in her contemporary novel to capitalize on his financial power and influence to protect his daughter, the heroine, supposedly guilty of a crime. Bad characters misuse their power constantly, but not the good characters. Until then, Krentz's fictional world has had the fairy tale quality of black and white solutions. The romance illusion of becoming rich without some shady interludes is not questioned, nor is the assumption that society can be judged from a black and white perspective: Krentz still seemingly wants to convince the reader of this in *All Night Long,* where she divides between good and evil exploitation of wealth.

Delinsky rarely chooses gender specific professions for her male protagonists. So it is an exception when, at the time of the story, some of them work in a tra-

---

[114] ctd. in Laura Vivanco. *For Love and Money.* p36
[115] *Family Man,* 1992, *Smoke in Mirrors,* 2004
[116] *Lady's Choice,* 1989

ditionally male trade like that of a carpenter or a lobsterman, but in order to have become rich, at some time in their past, they had worked in another, more sophisticated, gender-neutral job and had accumulated enough wealth to be free to choose the physical male work they feel content with.[117] Delinsky likes to equip her characters with gender-neutral professions: they are lawyers, photographers, psychologists, architects, business owners, artists, and writers, the first three more often than the rest. Some of her heroines work in female dominated lines of career such as interior designers and knitters, or cooks, and some of her heroes in male dominated ones as basket ball coach or contractor. The metier defines the characters, thus making profession and trade an integral part in a Delinsky novel. All protagonists are dedicated to their respective work, often even making it their hobby as well. The protagonists' success is measured in financial security, but also in life's enjoyment through their work/hobby. *A Woman Betrayed is an* example that emphasizes the author's departure from a black and white presentation. Here, the male protagonist decides to live a simple, not financially successful but emotionally satisfying life .

Krentz does not thematize women's rights of equality in the work force, which means she does not put her heroines into a situation where they have to choose between work and family. Her heroines' financial background will always be utopian and secure. At the end of the story the heroines seem inclined to continue working, thus continuing on their professionally chosen path, but then they are entrepreneurs and their own bosses. This signals to the reader that in order to maintain independence, it is necessary to keep on working whether one is married and has children or not.

In Delinsky's Women's Fiction, however, some of her heroines present the feminist ideal of being successful, both in their jobs, and in running a family. The problems arise when there are two full-time working parents. Nearly all her female protagonists go on working after the wedding, essentially needing their own financial security, but also because they love to work in their chosen professional fields. Difficulties are related that affect a woman's life once she decides to follow her idealized American dream of working hard, and, therefore, successfully, and to her heart's content in her chosen profession. Moreover, the fact that a working mother will always be more burdened than her husband is clearly elucidated. As this is a popular mainstream type of novel, questioning marital romance bliss is not only permitted, but also becomes the main topic because romance is more a tale rendered in a black and white presentation and popular fiction is expected to mirror gray elements of reality.

---

[117] *The Carpenter's Lady*, 1983, *The Summer I Dared*, 2004

Wealth is the financial cushion the Delinsky Women's Fiction protagonists have at their disposal when they become ill. Because of their wealth, they can go on living or existing under pleasant caring conditions.[118] To me, this is another reason, beside, that of a romantic happy ending, to maintain that her mainstream novels remain in the contemporary text worlds of romance novels although they are not romances according to the strict RWA definition: her protagonists are of the wealthy variety.

Even when they (or secondary characters) suffer from illnesses, fatal or otherwise, have physical and mental impediments, have social problems, and so on, they can always rely on sufficient wealth, which usually they themselves have accumulated or which in financially difficult situations, friends will be there to accommodate them with money so that whatever happens to them, they are financially cushioned. Wealth is the *deus ex machina* that enables them to act the way they do.

Wealth or a secure financial background for at least one protagonist is the basis on which Krentz's and Delinsky's romance novels and Women's Fiction are constructed, so that whatever problems arise during the story, they can be reduced to the emotional variety.

4.3.4 CLASSES

Americans claim to live in an egalitarian society, an ideal that has never been accomplished, where allegedly class does not matter. Pierre Bourdieu, and in his wake Paul Fussell, and others deny this vehemently. Fussell catalogues an astonishing number of signs that indicate class in America. He argues that everything in your way of life, your behavior, and your way of speaking reveals your origins, your breeding, your ancestry, and your efforts to climb the social ladder. He says:

> Actually, you reveal a great deal about your social class by the amount of annoyance or fury you feel when the subject is brought up. A tendency to get very anxious suggests that you are middle class and nervous about slipping down a rung or two. On the other hand, upper class people love the topic to come up: the more attention paid to the matter the better off they seem to be. Proletarians generally don't mind discussions of the subject because they know, they can do little to alter their class identity. (16)

Fussell also clarifies that new wealth does not guarantee class, because class is defined by much more than income. Geography is also a determinant of destiny beside what you do, say or own: all these define your class affiliation.[119]

---

[118] *Shades of Grace*, 1995, *Flirting With Pete*, 2003

[119] Geography correlated with education and social classification could also possibly distinguish the author's novels: Whereas Krentz's novels are set in the west of the USA, her protagonists seem unconcerned about their social status. Cultural indicators like e.g. the love of books or

Since both authors' protagonists are set in the middle, or upper middle class, a definition of middle class helps to understand the implications. The 2010 report of U.S: Department of Commerce, Economic and Statistics Administration defines middle class by income. The members of the upper middle class share a level of relative security against social crisis in the form of socially desired skills or wealth. This aspired security is correlated with the factors of home ownership, a car for each adult, a (private) college education for the children, health security, retirement security and family vacations. At first glance, this conventional definition covers both authors' romance novel's social settings.

In *Dangerous Men and Adventurous Women* romance authors justify their genre, beside other reasons, with the statement that their stories are intended and seen as such by their readers to be modern versions of fairy tales. Although in fairy tales that end in a high society's Happily Ever After, a characterization of a society adapted to reality is not intended, in contemporary romance novels an adjusted, time related depiction of an American society needs to be presented in order to make a story convincing and mentally accessible for a reader.

Felicia. L. Carr reports that, as early as the 1870s, the men of the lower classes were irritated by dime novels, believing that reading had a powerful impact on readers and that American middle class norms were expanded in them. The dime novel "became a site of struggle as they sought to impose middle class gender norms on the working class and to curtail new gender developments among the working class that allowed women unprecedented freedom in selecting and dating potential partners" (n.p.). The working class of today no longer needs to be irritated because they see all-class democratic values represented in the romance novels. These all-class values are displayed in the American middle to upper middle classes. College education for both genders indicate their middle class status whereas the upper middle class is "made up of professionals distinguished by exceptional high educational attainment as high economic security." Self-directed work is another criterion for the middle and upper middle classes. Reading about it in Krentz's and Delinsky's novels could be an incentive for a reader to further her own education.

Being rich is the premise to belonging to the upper middle class in American society, but new wealth is never automatically an integrative asset. In the authors' contemporary romance novels, being rich – usually it is new wealth because the stories mostly follow the rags to riches/ growing up on the wrong side of the

---

classical music or art are not displayed in her romances. In *Perfect Partners,* her heroine, a librarian, does not read 'books' only 'an article or two'. Delinsky's protagonists who live in the east of the USA, preferably near the cultural American center, Boston, live and breathe culture, so that their social awareness is different.

tracks formula – nearly always automatically gives the male protagonists a place in imagined upper social ranks, no matter whether their money is old or new.

Krentz introduces the reader to a non-defined white society as a whole because she focuses on the small social circle her characters live and act in, which is the narrative device romance authors follow in their one plot category stories. The rich never act rich so that the not-so-rich do not feel inhibited. But even in her earlier romance novels, it is conceded that social classes exist, and the way to be accepted into the wealthy class, is described by one protagonist as follows: "All I needed was an income level equivalent to theirs and the ability to talk their language." (*Test of Time* 1987, 131) This is the fantasy Krentz refers to in *Dangerous Men and Adventurous Women* because in American reality it is an uphill struggle for new money to integrate with old money.

In Krentz's novels, only when they are criminals of the upper class of the politically and financially influential wealthy, do rich people (and not necessarily old money rich people), act imperiously. So the owner of a boat yard that provides his town with secure jobs, and murderer of the hero's father, reveals himself as the proverbial self-made man through his language, which betrays working class features (*Perfect Partners*). The other murderer, who wants to protect his son's senatorial career, comes from old money with a great deal of financial influence. This son has enjoyed a privileged education and coming from old money he is accepted as the proverbial choir boy in society (*All Night Long*).

Hero and heroine might live in different social strata that should put them at odds with one another at the beginning of the story; in the end, however, they have established a level of equality where social differences are obsolete. This 'merger' has to deal with seemingly trivial stumbling blocks for a reader: for example in *Perfect Partners,* it is the heroine's academic background versus the hero's simple blue collar education – he comes from the wrong side of the tracks – which love and intuitive understanding make irrelevant. The heroine's professorial father sees the class distinction clearly when he draws her attention to the fact that the hero has a different way of thinking and approaching problems. A mitigation of possible social tension is that they both manage her inherited firm, each addressing problems in their own way, based on their social differences. Or, in *All Night Long,* the male protagonist comes from a wealthy family who considers an academic education topped by a Ph.D. appropriate for successfully managing an estate with winery. The female protagonist, who is 'only' a correspondent with a small newspaper, is quickly integrated into the different social class of his family because she makes relations with the male protagonist easier for all: intuition versus formal education. No social arrogance there. But then, in order to make this convincing Krentz provides psychological reasons: in *Perfect Partners,* it is the way the hero is inclined to listen to the heroines' intelligent suggestions, whereas her misogynistic academically bred ex-fiancé knows all and does not need to listen to different arguments; in the case of the *All Night Long* heroine, it is her having been raised by a father whose behavior and ethical code stemmed from the same military background as the male protagonist's and, in addition, as a journalist, she is able to work in all social classes.

In Delinsky's category romance novels, wealth of at least one of the protagonists is a given, but social affiliation is kept more in the background, although there are hints of class distinction. In *Gemstone* (1983), however, she points out the problems when people from different social classes marry: When a rich young man married a waitress, his mother, together with the household staff, made his young wife's life unbearable, spelling out to her that she did not belong to their social class and never will. Years later – and this is where the novel's story begins – the ex-wife, now successfully designing jewelry for wealthy people, meets her ex-husband and they can both acknowledge how much social differences were the reason for their divorce. Letting the heroine work herself successfully into the desired social stratum means that now, at last, a happy ending can occur. This time it is the romance heroine, not the hero, who 'reinvents' herself. In Delinsky's other romances the protagonists have enough inner turmoil to contend with, so that neither wealth nor a social difference between hero and heroine is significant. The protagonists do not pursue a role of importance within the social class into which they have been accepted. They have no need to, and, therefore, social involvements in the romance novels are strictly there to provide a rounded background.

Sometimes she renders an idealized version of small town social behavior which only emphasizes the fantasy a romance novel should provide. In *Sweet Ember,* for example, the heroine has a child out of wedlock and no father for the child to show for it, a situation which would still have been stigmatized in the 1970s. But in this fictional world, the fact that the unmarried mother teaches other rich people's children photography is not viewed in a negative light.[120] (This disparity between creating a fictional, unbiased romance world, and Delinsky's matters of concern that she should not present too seriously, according to publishers' advice, is reconciled in her endings that undo inflicted wrongs. In *Sweet Ember* the father of the child will marry the mother.) Astonishingly, later in her novel, which is not directed by romance rules, the same unconvincing social reaction is repeated in *The Family Tree* where the heroine's illegitimacy is morally ignored, although the novel's matter of concern is exactly that of social classification.

---

[120] In her novel *Not My Daughter* of 2010 an unwed mother has had problems to being appointed principal of a high school. This shows more social reality than the one in "Sweet Ember".

In her Women's Fiction, Delinsky widens her social focus by expanding the social contacts her protagonists live with: extended family, many good friends, a disintegrating marriage. They all feature different social aspects in a society that is still part of the background. Delinsky is mainly interested in the dynamics that arise from psychological personality problems. In her novels, facets of social misbehavior, be they a display of prejudice or social snobbery, a state intervention or legal injustice committed to socially inferiors only emphasize that her novel world is not a better escapist place to live in.

The Family Tree, however, is different. Here a social class, a dynasty in the US democracy with the power to grant success to whoever belongs to it, is presented not as background information, but as the central point of attention, although not in a political way. Some of the characters there try to stick firmly to their white, intolerant, upper class social ideology in order not to lose their sense of importance and their belief and their knowledge that they can wield power over others. The story of *The Family Tree* directs readers' attention to the role played by a biased, social elite in the USA: a social elite that is considered to be America's new aristocracy in that most democratic of democratic countries, whose members are self-proclaimed betters because they have the inherited money, and, therefore, ruling power, supported by their egos' belief in their white supremacy. The intrusion of a little color into this elite white family threatens them so much that they try to close ranks. Delinsky's mainstream novel world is not the land where people believe they will be accepted into any social class they strive for. But, on the other hand, the belief in America as the Land of Opportunity becomes apparent when vitas from rags to riches are depicted. These characters find a haven within the emotional bounds of family and love. So, like Krentz's protagonists, they feel secure in their small social circle of family and friends, at the same time learning that each social class has its own problems to contend with.

4.3.5 CRIME

The purpose of romance stories is to tell love stories. First and foremost. Accepting this as the basis means also accepting that other matters, like in-depth descriptions of living conditions, character's social environments, jobs and family dynamics, will be secondary. As such, they are not looked at more meticulously than necessary, providing, as they do, a superficial image of what things might be about. The same superficiality in descriptions is applied to the part a crime plays, although from the plot's viewpoint, crime is essential to build up the narrative tension in the course of the romantic suspense story, and also to prolong the story. In the case of white collar crimes, for example, seemingly comprehensive information is offered, but on closer inspection it remains superficial. I argue that the crimes that are introduced into the stories of both authors render a picture of current American social concerns; whether they are chosen only to make the stories more accessible for a reader or to unveil an author's concern is irrelevant.

In Krentz's romantic suspense novels, crime is presented in a wide variety of guises, ranging from industrial espionage to petty revenge and from accidental murder to a series of planned killings. During the story, one or two murders occur of which the reader is provided a blurred image, and hence, does not regard as a serious problem. Dead people are dead and quickly disposed of while the story goes on and the reader stays entertained and in suspense. In the end, the protagonists solve the criminal case, either by having the murderer handed over to the police or sent to a mental asylum – that is the women's fate – or having him killed in self-defense. Sometimes, however, Krentz's stories reveal an apparent unease about social problems. She discloses them within the crime elements of her romantic suspense. In *Golden Chance* (1990), the problem of child abuse in foster homes is thematized in an aside, in *Trust Me* (1995), the myriad possibilities of computer crimes are given voice, and again in *All Night Long* (2007), sexual child abuse within the family, is the novel's matter of concern.

Descriptions of the evil power play of the criminal rich and mighty, which I mentioned above, have got the critical undertone that Krentz's futuristic novels have already exposed earlier. Her rich protagonists, however, are cast in a different mold. Since reality would intrude too much into her romance world of fantasy, from time to time, since 1996, some of her contemporary protagonists are equipped with paranormal senses. This means the solution of the crime cases does not correlate with reality and stays purely fictive, especially with her Arcane Society series which she began writing in 2007 and which overarch her historical, contemporary and futuristic novels. The problem of self-justice is already expressed in *Perfect Partners* (1992) where the owner of a boatyard thinks he has the right to kill without legal consequences. In *All Night Long*, though, the suspense part gives way to distressed concern. Not only is there the topic of sexual child abuse, but also that of exploitation of power by the rich who take justice into their own hands. They are not depicted as a social class, but as a rich family, living apart from the people of the small town, but at the same time making some inhabitants become indebted to them by supporting them with money this way ensuring their silence about their knowledge of their crimes. In addition, the American offensive policy in the war in Afghanistan is censured here in a humanist critique of war in the backhanded fashion of subtext: the ex-military hero is troubled by Post-Traumatic Stress Disorder because of his experiences in this war, and by leaving the army, he might make a reader aware of the ethical implications of that war. Of course, this is only mentioned in an aside.

Krentz portrays crimes that need a romance hero to restore peace and happiness. Because of the dangers the heroine finds herself in, the 'warrior' hero is a necessity, but the crimes that are committed are not purely a main male domain. Even in (her) romance novels, women are capable of murder and other crimes, but not as the antagonists to the heroine of the traditional romance novel. As such, they rarely appear nowadays.

In her romance novels Delinsky's plots appear more realistic than fairy-tale fictional. Even minor crimes and, of course, betrayal that borders on the criminal occur here, although the novels are not categorized as romantic suspense romances: a pickpocket turned murderer (*Passion and Illusion* 1983), a woman with a new job and identity courtesy of the Witness Relocation Program betrayed by a friend (*Finger Prints* 1984), a threatened, not so friendly takeover of a firm (*The Forever Instinct* 1985), a kidnapping (*Heart of the Night* 1989). In her Women's Fiction all kinds of betrayals, mostly personal, take place, but also criminal acts like tax frauds, attempted murder or white collar crime. These crimes are not prominent enough in the stories for them to be labeled as mystery novels. But then, writing about problems and conflicts that are not only emotion- or illness-related means that it seems necessary to the author to also take the people's criminal nature into account.

4.3.6 ETHICS

When US American category romance authors were first given their publishers' permission to Americanize their romances, this not only meant a change of landscape descriptions, it also implied a modification of attitudes and behavior because the British way of life could not be transferred. Some romance authors, for example Nora Roberts, like to endow their protagonists with European – preferably Irish or Scottish – roots and character traits as well as hints of European attitudes and behavior, whereas both Krentz and Delinsky construct American characters whose roots are American and who embody the so-called American way of life. This means that "American values, attitudes, and sensibilities" (Regis 2003, 159) are introduced into the stories. What they are is not disclosed in detail. Presumably the authors incorporate(d) them into their settings and idealized characters, perhaps without realizing quite how American they are, and guidelines and editors ensure(d) that they are worked into the plot. Since this genre in particular is considered to be affirmative literature, it seems relevant to identify what these affirmative American 'values, attitudes and sensibilities' are like in the novels and how and where the American Dream is integrated in them.

Even if the authors writing for the category romance lines Krentz and Delinsky wrote for were forbidden to introduce religious and political issues into their romances the 'American values, attitudes and sensibilities' they incorporate in their stories might originate from manifold religious traditions. In the final analysis, various Puritan/Protestant beliefs and Puritan/Protestant morality of European origin are deeply interrelated with the American secular culture. Uhlmann claims that contemporary American attitudes in the form of judgments and actions still implicitly reflect the influence of America's Puritan heritage, linking work, for example, with divine salvation, only in a secularized form. [121] Wayne E. Baker also observes that "Protestantism is the nation's historical cultural heritance" (Baker 2005, 34). Baker argues that

> America's traditional values are path dependent. These values are incorporated in the nation's institutions and reproduced over time as they are transmitted from generation to generation.
>
> This process makes America's traditional values resistant to the changes usually associated with economic development. (Baker 2005, 53)

So in order to understand contemporary American attitudes of valuing freedom, and individual independence, which can only be achieved by a strong will and bravery, it is necessary to go back to the country's roots and recall part of the American national anthem 'The Star-Spangled Banner', which defines the states as 'the land of the free and the home of the brave', and also part of the religious aspects of the Declaration of Independence that reads as follows:

> We hold these truths to be self-evident, that all men are created equal, that they are endowed by their Creator with certain unalienable Rights, that among these are Life, Liberty, and the Pursuit of Happiness …

Why Americans of today believe in individual freedom, and consider individual control over their destinies their birthright, and why they value their nation above all and perceive that it takes an exceptional position in the world with a built-in sense of mission, [122] can be explained through their history: Some roots of these beliefs are to be found in 17th century Puritanism with the religious colonists who, in the first half of that century, emigrated to America, partly forced, partly of their own free will. These Puritans wanted to design a totally new world, which they felt to be good by virtue of not being European, while Old Europe was left to perish in its own 'morass'. Men like John Winthrop wanted to found a kind of theocracy, St. Augustin's 'City of God', that was to become a shining example for Europeans when Winthrop would return to England with the aim of reforming it. For Winthrop America, not only was a country for a new beginning, but

---

[121] Uhlman on Puritan morality: "Because Americans link both sex and work to divinity, sex and work morality should likewise be linked as part of an overarching American ethos." (Uhlmann et al. 25)

[122] See D. Yankelovich, the Pew Research Center for the People & the Press, and Baker/Campbel. Wayne E. Baker, who researched American core values, defines values that are strongly and widely held, stable over time, and shared across demographic and political lines as core values. (Baker, 2005)

also paradise on earth, a place where Puritan believers could live according to their biblical norms and values. Thus America became 'God's Own Country' and the Puritans saw themselves as the new 'Chosen People'. As the decades passed, religious and moral standards declined and people had to question their Puritan beliefs, and with it their identities. Samuel Danforth reminded the colonists of why they had originally founded the Puritan colonies in his election sermon of 1670, "A Brief Recognition of New-England's Errand into the Wilderness". At the same time he tried to determine a new definition of America and ensured the Americans of the 'promise of divine Protection and Preservation' if they renewed their efforts to live in a manner pleasing in the sight of God. The never ending search to live a pious life under changing circumstances became the driving force behind a belief in the possibility of perfection in mankind, democracy, and continuous progress. Deism and Puritan moral principles have been transferred to the civil religion[123] – not all early settlers came to America for ethical and religious reasons, but for economical reasons – which could be called the secular form of Puritanism/Protestantism combined with deistic philosophy,[124] that includes hegemonic missionary aspects, because Americans still believe they are the 'Chosen People', and that success, now individual, financial and otherwise, is the basis for the pursuit of happiness. As shown in the previous sections of this study, both Krentz and Delinsky's novels seem to adhere to such 'Chosen People' concept.

Seen from this perspective, Krentz's choice of professions for her protagonists supports this conviction of striving for individual achievement and success, which is clarified best with entrepreneurial approaches (Leya and Court in *Stormy Challenge*, Joel in *Perfect Partners*, and Luke in *All Night Long*). Entrepreneurship, together with the individual's pride in his/her work, is also showcased in Delinsky's novels. (Laura and Christian in *A Woman Betrayed*, Dana and Hugh in *The Family Tree*.)

American values of Puritan/ Protestant origin such as self-reliance, equality of opportunity, hard work and material wealth emphasize the belief in the goodness of humans (Joel and Letty in *Perfect Partners*) who inhabit the Land of Opportunity. These model American citizens, who take pride in their work and possessions

---

[123] "Born out of revolution," writes Lipset, "the United States is a country organized around an ideology which includes a set of dogmas about the nation of a good society ... As G.K. Chesterton put it: 'America is the only nation in the world that is founded on a creed. That creed is set forth with dogmatic and even theological lucidity in the Declaration of Independence ... for now the important point is that the imagined community of the United States is based on a set of ideas and values with as much legitimating and integrating force as religion." (Baker 2005, 11–12)

[124] Hochgeschwender points out that what is usually referred to as Puritan or Protestant influence still valid in the American society in fact survived through evangelical revival movements and the effective English Victorian moral ideology in them. (77–117)

and acknowledge responsibility for themselves and their family, do not want the government to play more than a minimal role in their private lives. People are supposed to fend for themselves – there is no guaranteed access to health care for the American population –, and in the case of illness, they should have a financial bolster. This view comes across clearly in some of Delinsky's stories, and, at the same time, it emphasizes how much even her Women' Fiction is rooted in romance telling tradition. In her mainstream novels, the American conviction that everybody is responsible for him/herself could lead to a reader's conviction that self-made wealth, being thrifty and saving money is the way to live: wealth will offer protection from the hazards of life and times. This is seen in the portrayal of successful entrepreneurs who do not need a state's financial intervention when they require round the clock day care or weeks or months' care at the hospital, for example. Thus wealth provides a reassuring backup for the storylines because modest living circumstances might create a plot that is too overladen, which would be counterproductive to the story, which is already complex.[125]

The American virtue of being inventive, smart and seizing the initiative to take charge of one's own destiny is what Krentz's heroines endeavor to do within the story (Letty in *Perfect Partners*) or plan to in the future (Leya in *Stormy Challenge*), while the heroes are already set in their entrepreneurial ways before the story begins. Disabling illnesses, as an obstacle, are never taken into consideration. It is always other people who have been mortally ill that are conveniently placed at a point in the past, preferably when one of the protagonists was young. This illness or death, and the description of one of the protagonists' grappling with it, economically and/or psychologically, is the only reference that individual control over one's own destiny could encounter a stumbling block in the form of physical ailments (Joel in *Perfect Partners*). Only one hero in Krentz's contemporary novels had a crippling accident that forced him to use a cane for the rest of his life; otherwise he is of sound mind, and rich thanks to hard, clever work (Max in *Grand Passion* 1994). Thus he is a shining example of the Land of Opportunity, as is the hero in *Perfect Partners*. In Delinsky's category romance novels, the heroines meet death, illness, and physical handicaps in their heroes[126] and in their families, but, as mentioned before, the characters have lived the American dream, and as a result, are economically secure enough to cope.

As questions of hierarchy and class within Krentz's text world do not play a role, her novels display the American ideal that all men are equal, as stated in the Declaration of Independence. But this equality displayed is that of the middle

---

[125] *Shades of Grace*, 1995, (Alzheimer), *Coast Road*, 1998 and *Flirting with Pete*, 2003 and *While My Sister Sleeps*, 2008 (Coma), *Lake News*. 1999 (Stuttering), *An Accidental Woman*, 2003 (Paraplegia)

[126] *Lilac Awakening* 1982, *Moment to Moment*, 1984, *The Dream Comes True*, 1990

classes, where only personal differences are of importance. Delinsky's romance novels already reveal a text world different from that in Krentz's novels. They portray less fantasy and more ordinary reality (*Sweet Ember*), and class differences within a supposedly classless American society are critically addressed (*The Family Tree*).

Predominantly, American values are presented for readers' identification in the characterization of hero and heroine and the values and norms they display. The first instance that comes to mind is the description of their outward appearances, which is an obvious recognition of their success, their accomplishments and their belief to demonstrate a kind of perfection. It is not only the demands of a social class that makes the authors construct such characters. Robert N. Bellah describes in *The Broken Convenant* (1975) the reason for the cult of youth as follows:

> The American ideal, as it increasingly came to be stated in the 19th century as a tensionless harmony of moral and religious idealism and the quest for economic success, required a peculiarly innocent conception of human life. In order to keep this harmonious ideal intact Americans have had to brush aside the darker moral ambiguities of life, the tragic dimension of human existence, and maintain a stalwart optimism and "positive thinking". But the middle years of life treat no man kindly and forever sow the seeds of cynicism and despair. For the last century or more one of the great tactics for keeping the ideal of shining innocence alive even in later years is to concentrate it on the young ... it is not youth as such but our ideal of youth we demand in them. To save our fading illusions and defend us from our deepening cynicism they must be trim, fair haired, clean in mind and body, ambitious ... In other words they must be all that we want to be and fear we are not. (chapter 3.8)

According to this American ideal, romance heroines, although no longer young, as they usually are around thirty years of age, have retained their 'innocence', thereby showing they are not disillusioned, but optimistic, and thus, serve as good American fantasy material.

A male American romance character has to be tall, virile, and of superb and healthy physique because he is proof for the latin adage of mens *sana in corpore sano*. This healthy man does his utmost to stay fit in order to maintain the optimism of staying forever young. Both Krentz's and Delinsky's heroes, aged between thirty-five and forty-five, prevent their bodies from becoming flabby by doing sports. Many of Krentz's male protagonists run, have black belts in karate or practice a similar kind of martial arts. Delinsky's male romance protagonists simply maintain their bodies in perfect shape, as do most of her heroes in her mainstream novels, but there, as often as not, their job requires hard physical effort and they do not need a gym to keep in form. Signs of fitness and being in shape epitomize the protagonists' personal American ideals coupled with professional successes.

An essential requirement for American romance heroes and heroines is intelligence – not intellectuality – maturity and rightful self-confidence. The intelligence displayed in both authors' heroes is reduced to its use in the professional area, and in everyday situations that are met with common sense (Joel in *Perfect Partners* or Hugh in *The Family Tree*). Specific intelligence is required in order to financially prosper when there is neither a good educational background nor parental wealth to fall back on (Joel). Intelligence and the moral virtues Eric Erikson observed in his study on American adolescents of 1940 correspond with the authors' heroes:

> The outstanding characteristics of these tall, slim, muscular boys, mostly Anglo-Saxon ... were autonomy, efficiency, and decent. They had personalities well geared to enter the American occupational sphere and attain a modest success. Autonomous, efficient, and decent young men are obviously not something any society needs to apologize for. The enormous productive achievements of just such men have made America the richest and most powerful nation in the world. (Bellah Chapter 3.8)

However, the authors' heroes (Doug in *Sweet Ember* or Joel in *Perfect Partners*) display the same foibles that worried Ericson: They do not want to talk or think too much, but feel more comfortable in action, in sports or work. He says,

> Our boy is anti-intellectual. Anybody who thinks or feels too much seems "queer" to him. This objection to feeling and thinking is, to some extent derived from an early mistrust of sensuality ... And what worried Erikson the most and seems today the most ironic, was that these young men seemed incapable of rebellion, incapable of questioning anything basic about their own society. (Bellah Chapter 3.8)

Sixty years later the trend of anti-intellectuality is still in vogue. The myth of simple folk wisdom continues. President George W. Bush's admission of his lack of intellectual inquisitiveness, demonstrated by his not wanting to read newspapers himself, did not deter people from electing him.[127] You can find an astonishing amount of criticism of American anti-intellectualism on the internet and the book market. I suppose this American distrust of intellectualism is the reason the romance novel protagonists do not display this trait, despite the majority of their protagonists being college educated. Again, Delinsky's protagonists are the exception to the rule. They seem to be fairly intellectual judging from the thematic variety of the many books that are reported to be in the different households, as well as from some conversations and reported actions in the novels.

---

[127] "USA: Dumb Is the New Cool", Hofi Enterprises. 2008, retrieved 05. 02. 2010, see also: Susan Jacoby, 2008, *The Age of American Unreason,* New York

As both authors' heroes are no longer young, often having been married before and being successful in their chosen professions, they display a sound self-confidence and mature adult behavior. The ideal American moral character traits like loyalty, honesty, decency, responsibility, protectiveness of one's family, and courage are the basic requirements in their romance hero for both authors. Their additional gender behavioral allotment is dominance. Krentz's post-1986 heroes are kind, highly intelligent men, but never intellectual, a trait that is reserved, if at all, for secondary characters. They never fail their women because of their innate sense of loyalty, honesty and decency (Joel and Luke), which is put to test in the stories, even with patriarchal heroes. Of course, these alpha men do not lack courage and the readiness to protect their women in this dangerous world. They can serve as American dream men but are also global ideals.

Actually the important alterations that have taken place in the authors' text worlds over the years are that now the women are equipped with virtues which used to be connoted as male. Female American ideal character traits mirrored in romance novels differ from male ones only where typical demands are added that make the woman responsible for her family. So first and foremost, a woman is supposed to be caring and compassionate as well as intelligent, loyal, honest, decent and courageous, which are character traits women of all times have needed to survive in patriarchal and not so patriarchal times (Letty in *Perfect Partners* or Laura in *A Woman Betrayed*). Krentz and Delinsky design their heroines as entrepreneurs with typical skilled female leadership qualities (Leya in *Stormy Challenge* or Laura in *A Woman Betrayed*). Intruding into the male domain, they strengthen their position by hard work, which the males do as well, but – and here they differ from males – they add empathy and a caring consciousness, which causes their co-workers to identify with them. All these fictitious character traits, however, reflect wishful feminist ideas.

Delinsky's American category romance novel heroines have no impressive character traits other than those of good, decent and intelligent persons. Being emotionally too much involved with their own problems, their various character traits get little chance to be featured. Delinsky's popular mainstream novel heroines, however, are provided with enough opportunities of action and situations to show off their various American moral facets, often explained to the reader from a psychological point of view, Laura, for example. Partly they have the makings of the picture perfect woman an American society might wish for. Loyalty, faithfulness, dedication to their jobs and also to their husbands and children are the basis of their moral standard. Life, however disappoints them and shows them the different American reality underneath the American moral code they themselves, but not necessarily their partners, follow because they have accepted it as a societal constant.

Equality of opportunity, if only for men, is seen as a central value of the American system. The romance protagonists, belonging to white middle and upper middle class societies, are the idealized representatives. Their inventiveness, entrepreneurship, and hard work end successfully in material wealth. Here the Puritan/Protestant ethics that proclaim that hard work is morally good, character building, with the reward of producing material wealth, translate into a fictional reality. Hero, and now also heroine, are successful in no matter what they do and they regard work as the essential part of their life. With Krentz, professional work, whatever it is, does not create problems between the lovers because they are both described as having strong personalities (Joel and Letty). The heroes can even relocate their jobs to the place where the heroine lives without losing face (Luke). As a couple, they live on terms of equality and their self-respect remains unaffected. Delinsky, whose mainstream fictional couples have already spent years together at the beginning of the novel, makes some of her heroes, as the morally weaker half of the relationship, experience minority complexes. Heroes as the morally and otherwise weaker gender is a diametral reversal of the convention in romance novels. There, an ambivalence in the characters, male or female, is illustrated, as well as a demonstration of American ordinary reality, the difficulties people face, even strong characters, in conforming to ideal American values. As work essentially determines human lives in reality there does not seem to be a novel where a protagonist's work is not part of their characterization. It is always work and its success that defines these American characters, or causes trouble.

According to a 2007 survey of national cultural values, the last part of which was devoted to the nation's convictions about sexual morals, it transpires that only 68% consider sex between unmarried adults acceptable (The National Cultural Values Survey 22). Therefore, if an author is in tune with demographic surveys of this kind, and both authors are, she will not write romance stories that contradict conventional beliefs and might, therefore, hinder successful sales. So in their romances both authors allow their adult protagonists to have unmarried sex with the expectation of a later marriage. Only Delinsky presents the range of sexual alternatives like adultery in various[128] forms, or high-school sex, or rape as a problem within the plotline of her popular mainstream novels. In order to not to seem too pessimistic, however, she also offers the promise of a Happily Ever After. Being aware of their readership's expectations, the authors do not discuss alternatives to marriage for their protagonists. In their fictional worlds, they cling to the conservative notion of an American core family life that regards (heterosexual) matrimony as the only basis for a truly successful life, never accepting the

---

[128] E.g. in *Together Alone* (1995) the husband has a second secret family, in *The Summer I Dared* (2004) the husband has a string of affairs, in *Within Reach* (1986) the husband is a secret homosexual.

unconventional alternatives that, to a high degree, are already part of American reality.

4.3.7 IMPLICATIONS

This analysis demonstrates that marketing strategies, *Zeitgeist* and individual writer's developments influence the implications[129] or messages both romance novelists send to their readers, intentionally or unintentionally. If, as Huei-Hsia Wu proves in her study, "the content of the romance novel is at least a powerful molder of the sexuality of those who read them" it can also be assumed that other aspects displayed in the stories could be similarly influential, for instance when readers sometimes use romances as a background to find help for problems other than sexuality. This is why, since women began writing novels and women were able to read them, men have worried that these novels could influence their wives' and daughters', who had up to that point been docile, and make them disobedient. Janice Radway remarks that "all popular romance fiction originates in the failure of patriarchal culture to satisfy its female members" (Radway 1984, 151). These novels, then as now, function like a drug, and like drugs they clarify that desire, in the Lacanian sense, is never fulfilled which can be equated to seeking answers in books to life's problems. The myth of the romance, however, is that the desire can be fulfilled and it is for the very moment when readers read about the fulfilled desire. When, at the time both authors began writing their novels, the divorce rate in the USA was 50%, it is not surprising that readers find some kind of consolation through reading about relationships and marriages that succeed. When, by the 1990s, the institution of marriage was no longer regarded necessary to raise children, readers still required stories within the confines of heteronormativity, marriage, and family. They found their particular authors who served their desire. When, in the new millennium, women began relying again on the man as breadwinner, it was gratifying for women who needed to work to read about married women in the work force, thus defining having a job as an important part of one's identity and also of gaining more social respect (all these statements Coontz, 262–267).

The main interest in romance novels, however, is to lead a couple to a heterosexual marriage, which is still one sound value despite the variety that couples can choose from when setting up in life. In the USA of today, marriage still has a privileged status that enjoys more than a thousand legal and tax benefits. "And for most Americans, marriage is the highest expression of commitment they can imagine" (Coontz 278). (In order to boost marriage rates, President George W. Bush even committed 1.5 billion dollars in federal funds in 2003 (ibid 287).)

---

[129] The term 'implication' entails both cultural and spiritual worlds which a potential reader might actualize for herself.

Hence, both authors present a value system within their culture's comfort zone, although, as forty-three percent of all first marriages in America end in divorce within fifteen years, they paint an illusionary picture in their novels, even if the hero and/or heroine might have been married for a short time and divorced before the romance story begins. When in Delinsky's differing Women's Fiction critical but narratively softened matters of concern are portrayed, it makes a reader hopefully assume that the couple she is reading about will be the exception to the divorce rule, whether it is a first or a second marriage.

It is necessary to pay regard to the historic reality behind the fictional illusion in respective contemporary romances, for otherwise the messages both authors are sending to their readers do not become transparent. When Krentz and Delinsky caused their heroines to submit to male aggressiveness and possessive behavior in 1982, this reflected traditional moral convictions of their time that correlated, though only partly, with right-wing activists who organized campaigns against changes in gender roles and sexual norms that had already been set in motion. With Krentz, the reader gradually becomes familiar with the notions of gender equality in two ways: the first being that the traditional gender roles of the man as breadwinner and the woman as homemaker need to be redefined because, in the novel, she is already an independent professional and wants to stay that way after her marriage. The second is only rhetorical, for the time being: decision making as a mutual act and enjoying sexuality as a mutual experience. Around 1984 Krentz was still constructing strong patriarchal relationships, where even financially independent women, once they marry, become the husband's emotional, though not financial, property, and have to submit to their husbands' rules, which they do gladly after some resisting interludes. The heroines accept that their fiancés have the right to 'discipline' them for negligible acts that displease them. Sexually satisfying their heroes makes these heroines happy. The underlying message Krentz points out to her readers is that men have the right to be dominant and because a woman loves her husband she should better submit to his demands. She is not given an opportunity to actually bypass her hero's attempts to dominate her, which other authors, like for example, Linda Howard, make their heroines do at around the same time.

Delinsky's heroines circa 1982 also meekly concede the superior role in the relationship to the men, despite being financially independent. If there is an underlying message Delinsky wanted to send to her readers, it could be to show how important communication and negotiations are for a good relationship.

The mid-1980s saw a transformation in women's attitudes regarding feminine self-esteem and the desire for gender equality in their reading preferences. The contraceptive revolution of the 1960s, together with the fundamental changes in women's work roles[130] caused men to reconsider their contributions to a relationship in American society. No longer the family breadwinner, his right of dominance and possessive monopoly was questioned, and as women were legally allowed to decide whether they wanted to earn their own money and stay financially independent, even when they were married, he was forced to reconsider his patriarchal attitude.[131] Now he was supposed to offer his future wife emotional dependability as well as earning an income at least equal to hers in order to make the union worthwhile for her.

It took over twenty years for the second feminist movement[132] to arrive in romanceland. The reader was presented with a different kind of male protagonist and she approved of his fictional male turn-around-behavior. In later years both Krentz and Delinsky worked their special, feminist but traditional American value system into their characters as explained through the scenarios in the plot they created and in the character traits they depicted, so that a reader was and, is given a clear picture of how ideal Americans should be and how they should act. Thus they presented the reader with a new role model to compare.

Both the contraceptive as well as the sexual revolution have passed romance novels by. Coontz mentions that sexual standards of the 1950s viewed premarital sex "as acceptable for men under most conditions, and for women if they were in love" (252). As mentioned before, the Survey of National Cultural Values shows that this standard was still relatively confirmed in 2007. Again, the authors' messages meet this accepted attitude through the construction of hero's and heroine's behavior.

As a sexual expert after a morally accepted promiscuous life, the hero needs to make the first sexual encounter impressive for the heroine and then continue to impress her so that she falls in love with him. Thus, romance authors draw their readers' attention to the options that women can expect, and demand a sexually skillful husband who, in addition, has to prove his worthiness for them by being faithful which they are, of course, but also by opening up emotionally and by developing a pleasing sensibility beside his professional success. Fictional heroes gladly submit to these demands and readers could learn to notice and decide which

---

[130] Coontz: "In 1975 it became illegal to require a married woman to have her husband's written permission to get a loan or a credit card" (255).

[131] There is this desperate male outcry trying to recover lost territory. Coontz: "In 1998 the sixteen-million member Southern Baptist Church approved a code for marital conduct that harks right back to the 1950s. The code says a husband should "provide for, protect, and lead his family." A wife is to "submit herself graciously" to her husband's leadership and "serve as his helper in managing their household," (298)

[132] The exact years of the movement are difficult to pinpoint. Usually Betty Friedan's *The Feminine Mystique* of 1963 is seen as the cornerstone of its beginning. The movement is said to have ended in the 1990s.

of the virtues portrayed that are depicted in a husband they regard as essential and non-negotiable.

The heroine's quest for equality turns demands on the hero into a message of underlying subtle misandry, replacing the previous misogynistic attitude of before. This is done by degrading the fictional man as a sexual object who has to perform spectacularly, and also by insisting that it is only he who has to be taught how to be sensitive or to be honorable etc., while the heroine is perfect in spite of her little flaws. The way of thinking presented in these novels leads a reader to understand that now the man is inferior in many ways. And she feels good about reading how her sex can turn around male dominance. Krentz's heroes from 1986 onward need their heroines in order to be taught emotionality and to be 'tamed' for their part, so that life can be lived in harmony. Like the heroes they are allowed protectiveness as their domain besides providing excellent sex. As the heroines, and this is the message, are paragons, women should attempt to mold men to be adaptable to their, the women's, needs. They, themselves, have strong-minded personas, which can force the men to submit under the pretext of love.

In all of Krentz's novels the following convictions are emphasized:
1.) Men and women need each other to lead a fulfilled sexual love life, but the hero, being a man, requires his heroine to allow himself emotions other than the superficial sexual ones.
2.) Living alone is all right for a time but later it means loneliness; being married means having an emotional home – usually this is more important to the hero – where one is loved.
3.) In order to make a marriage work for life, financial independence on both sides, love, trust and the knowledge of the other's moral decency are essential.
4.) Children make that union complete.

Delinsky does not portray a black and white fictional world. She does not place her heroines on a pedestal, although many of her male protagonists are depicted as the weaker sex. The heroines have their own deficiencies, which are different from those of the heroes and often not as grave. As her messages are openly of the didactic kind, her readers could derive the following visualizations for their life:
1.) Whatever happens in their lives, 'happens for a reason', as senseless as it may seem when it happens.
2.) Delinsky balances happiness and progress with a sense of realism, informing the reader that relationships are always difficult, they require work, but they, the readers, are equally up to the task as are the protagonists.
3.) The first thing you have to do before you deal with a problem is to look at yourself and your own deficiencies. That will help you to realistically assess your options of how to solve the problem.
4.) Discussing specific problems in reading groups will naturally lead to dis-

cussing the group members' own problems and conflicts, and perhaps even help to solve them.

5.) Delinsky nearly always assures her readers that every problem can be solved, albeit in a different way than might have been expected. That she provides solutions with a 'satisfying ending', though not all-round happy ones, but ones with a romantic promise, might give readers hope that they can solve their own problems as well.

Since Krentz's and Delinsky's novels have become bestsellers and each is recognized in her own right for her individual voice, it is obvious that they fill a cultural need. In these novels readers do not like to see conventions violated, but have nothing against some subversive 'new' suggestions such as womanly enjoyment of premarital sex once it is blessed with the promise of marriage.

PART V

ON MYTHS

At the beginning of this study the focus was laid on the analysis of the six novels and the romance publishing houses' writing guidelines the authors were obliged to take into consideration. There the objective was to present in detail the authors' literary changes within a time frame of twenty-five years and to establish whether the authors have an individual voice within the restrictive frame of popular romance fiction. A second objective was to research subtexts, underlying structure, and inherent American values and convictions that might appear in these novels. Obvious and inherent messages within the novels are the key for a further perusal of the meaning which romances have for such an enormous audience. (As mentioned above, Donna Hayes, CEO of Harlequin, the largest publisher of romance novels, claimed in 2009 that the publishing house publishes 130 million copies annually. Harlequin is only the largest romance publishing house with not quite as large houses beside it. In order to provide a comparison figure, the Harry Potter series is said to have published a total number of 325 million copies in 2012.) Although this genre's main topics love, sexuality and partnership combined with a happy ending of the stories told in the novels account for only a segment of the reality of life, the reason for such a high acceptance of the genre needs an explanation. In consequence, a third question arises, which has evolved from some aspects of the analysis of the novels and their underlying cultural positioning, the question of why romance novels connect and resonate to such a high degree with their readers.

I assume that Erika Fischer-Lichte's theory of performativity combined with myths will be applicable to explain the immense popularity of the genre. Fischer-Lichte examines the performativity of literary texts. In opposition to John L. Austin she starts with Jonathan Culler's thesis of 'literature as act' and Wolfgang Iser who is interested in the interaction between text and reader which he terms the 'act of reading'. Culler describes the performative of a novel as follows:

> If a novel happens, it does so because, in its singularity, it inspires a passion that gives life to these forms, in acts of reading and recollection, repeating its inflection of the conventions of the novel and, perhaps, effecting an alteration in the norms or the forms through which readers go on to confront the world. A poem may well disappear without a trace, but it may also trace

itself in memories and give rise to acts of repetition. Its performativity, then, is less a singular act, accomplished once and for all than a repetition that gives life to forms that it repeats. (Fischer-Lichte 137)

Fischer-Lichte deduces from the quotation above that 'acts of reading' are the premises that literary texts accomplish something in a reader or a reading subject. (Incidentally, sometimes she terms her reader as feminine. But she does not seem to distinguish between male and female readers and their possible different approach to probable male/female acts of reading.) As premises for the study of performativity of texts, these acts of reading novels are interpreted in two respects: 1) Reading is performed as an act of incorporation of what is read and in this sense it is to be comprehended as a process of incorporation. 2) The immersion into the world of what is read silently sends the reading subject into a liminal state, which allows for different transformations. In order to study the interaction between the appellative structure (Appellstruktur) of a text and the respective subjectivity of a reader, a differentiation between *structural* and *functional performativity* was introduced. Bernd Häsner et al. define these two aspects of performativity as follows:

> Während die Frage nach struktureller Performativität darauf fokussiert, wie der Text das *macht*, wovon er spricht, oder gegebenenfalls etwas anderes macht, als er behauptet, zielt der Begriff der funktionalen Performativität auf das ab, was er *auslöst*. Funktionale Performativität bezeichnet zunächst die Wirkungen und Dynamiken, die ein Text an der Schnittstelle mit seinem Rezipienten entfaltet. ... Des Weiteren zielt der Begriff der funktionalen Performativität auf die gesellschaftliche Zirkulation von Texten, durch die Produkte der schriftlichen Kultur in performative Kulturpraktiken eingebunden werden. (Fischer-Lichte 139)

Structural performativity differentiates clearly from actions of cultural performance described in novels. It relates to the process of reading which initiates unpredictable imaginations and associations which the text itself does not insinuate, but which the reading subject produces due to his/her own experience. As the text cannot determine the reading process this process is open to ambivalences, a fact that clarifies the connection between structural performativity and functional performativity. Effects of reading depend on cultural contexts as well as on a reader's or many readers' particular dealing with textual structures and there the transformative power of the performative manifests. Reading as a performative act does not mean narrowing the search for a uniform interpretation which an author might have had in mind, but it indicates a complex cognitive, imaginative, affective, and energetic occurrence in a liminal situation which provides the reading subject with new means to feel, to think, behave, and act possibly with a lasting effect. To translate these aspects into action will also be of consequence for the social reality (Fischer-Lichte, 135–145).

When Fischer-Lichte draws attention to the aspect that the act of reading alters readers' behavior or provides new means to view the real world it correlates with the results in this study particularly when the effects are empirically substantiated by how the depiction of sexual behavior is transported into readers' lives. Moreover, I assume that the appeal of romance novels may be based on the fact that romance stories hark back to myths, that is to say romance novels contain archaic elements which have always fascinated and appealed to audiences.[133] Maybe the following hypothesis is bold, but I believe it to be corroborated by all the facts I have unearthed. I argue that romances are contemporary myths and that, by reading romances, readers follow or perform the ritual that reenacts the myth.

Studies have been carried out into romances with regard to possible mythical elements which explain human conditions. Radway reads romances as a reenactment of the girl's Oedipal drama with a happy ending; Zidl considers the hero's role as the Jungian 'shadow-self' of the heroine and she duplicates this interpretation by referring to Lacan's 'mirror stage' where the heroine recognizes herself in the hero. Roach understands the romance as narrative eschatology. As far as I can see, the biblical myth of Eve's being created from a part of Adam's body has never been used to explain the human craving to become one again. All the interpretative readings of romances seem to be based on Plato's myth of the androgynous spherical creature that, once it has been cut in two, longs for its own other half and this pursuit of wholeness is called 'love'. Love is forever frustrated because, despite the impulse toward union and wholeness, lovers are inherently and essentially separate.

Longing for the other half of a couple is the basis for narrating a romance story. Romances provide this human craving of the sexes for an everlasting union with the promise that it can be achieved in the form of marriage and, to show that the union is successful, in the formation of a family. In Krentz and Delinsky's novels, the platonic myth finds its imaginary time-related realization within the context of a conventional American value system. In addition, with Delinsky the extended complex and social spheres make the reader aware of other cravings, too. Nevertheless, the hope that the search for the forlorn mythical union of man and woman will succeed continues to be a strong motif in Delinsky's novels, for beside the social dilemmas she speaks of, she always provides a satisfying ending that promises a couple's everlasting union. *Ipso facto* she broadens and amplifies the romance pattern, but in the end she remains within it.

---

[133] According to the Oxford Dictionaries a mythos in literature is "a traditional or recurrent narrative theme or plot structure" and "a set of beliefs or assumptions about something".

It is debatable whether the platonic mythical context is related to the American way of viewing history. A mythical positioning in the biblical tradition of creation seems to be more closely related, together with God's love for Israel which is depicted in the biblical book Song of Solomon and has often been considered to be a romantically phrased metaphor of the love between God and his people (Weiser 264) despite the lack of religious reference and its being laically read as a love song. Modern theologians interpret the Song of Solomon as a parable in which God is conversing with the Jewish people, his allegorical and future bride (Hulst 428–431). (In Jeremiah 31:32, God even refers to himself as Israel's husband.) No other explicit depiction of sexual pleasure with positive connotations is to be found in the Bible. All the other, often crude, references are connected with the House of Israel's breaking the covenant with God. Later, the Christian context offers the faithful hope of an all-embracing kingdom of heaven. Understood from a mythical point of view, the kingdom of heaven is the epitome of the fulfillment of all wishes and yearnings of the material and (physical?) life.

This hope, considered as a fulfilled love in the world to come, is transformed into a contemporary myth within the world of romance fiction. By existing in this world, even the most promising happy relationship and marriage exposed to a mundane ordinariness is doomed to failure. Thus no love can be as perfect as the simile of a love in the world to come, though in the contemporary mythic form of the romance fiction, it is suggested, and therefore, the stories are read abundantly. In order to evade the dilemma of presenting a secular happiness that is not so perfect and of keeping up the idea of an ideal love, the romance ends at a point that implies the fulfillment of a love that has become true. But it is precisely this ending which reveals a mythological subtext as its core.

To me, however, an older mythic model, that of the Sacred Marriage, seems to explain even more profoundly the underlying reasons for women's yearnings to read these romance novels, particularly because these secular novels do not refer to Christian ideas, although, in this study, I have shown how many Puritan convictions still seem to be valid in the romance fictional world.

The mythic model of the Sacred Marriage, which is older than the biblical myths, does not exclude sexuality. Here, explicit sexuality between man and woman is even considered as the prerequisite for the 'creation of the world'. One purpose of the ensuing ritual act of sexual intercourse is believed to show heaven and earth how to cooperate in order to grant fertility of the land.

If the objective of life is marriage and family, with a wedding at its beginning, which means fertility and order, it may be a viable idea to look for role models other than focusing on the topic of the longing of the sexes. Mircea Eliade states that the function of myth is to establish models for behavior (*Das Heilige und das Profane* 86) and, I would like to add, models that might possibly ensure a romance reader of their social trustworthiness, because to affirm or establish models for behavior is also a function that could be described as being part of romances. In view of this fact, the mytheme of the Sacred Marriage is an essential point of reference for an interpretation of the basic structure of (contemporary category) romances. Here, I mainly refer to Mirjam and Ruben Zimmermann's essay which is a structural analysis of the Sacred Marriage: "'Heilige Hochzeit' der Götter-söhne und Menschentöchter?" In order to explain the scientific starting point for their structural analysis they state:

> Die neuere Mythosforschung hat den Mythos aus dem Vorurteil des naiven Märchens und der Reduktion auf archaische Göttergeschichten (H. Gunkel) befreit und seine authentische Leistungsart im Erfassen und der Reflex-ion von Wirklichkeitserfahrungen herausgearbeitet. Bereits E. Cassirer hatte den Mythos als sinnstiftendes Prinzip und zwar vor allem als "symbo-lische Form" von Kultur gewürdigt. Es war dann aber der französische Ethnologe Claude Lévi-Strauss, der in noch grundsätzlicherer Weise den Mythos als Ausdruck eines Reflexionsprozesses beschrieben hat, indem er in der Tiefenstruktur des Mythos eine Antwort auf bestimmte Aporieer-fahrungen des Menschen gesehen hat. (331) (annotations and quotations in the essay)

The term Sacred Marriage, the *hieros gamos*, stands for 'joining the separated', a myth that, according to classical Greek literature was ritually performed between Zeus and Hera, is originally primordial and was enacted in many other cultures with minor modifications in meaning. Ancient oriental scholars claim that the Sacred Marriage was originally performed by the two deities Inanna, the dominant female, and Dumuzi, the male, the reproductive power and that later, this rite was used in the Ishtar-cult. M. and R. Zimmermann comment that the term Sacred Marriage should not only refer to ancient Greece, but should be extended to term alliances between other deities, or deities and humans, particularly when they are marked by ritual. They understand the Sacred Marriage as an umbrella term for phenomena of religious studies. For the reasoning of my argument, I want to focus solely on the mytheme of Innana and Dumuzi, their sexual union and the purpose of the ensuing rite, bearing in mind that evidence for this is meagre: a number of poems and some terracotta. In Sumeric texts the ritual of the cultic reenactment of the marriage between Inanna and Dumuzi is particularized at great length. According to the oldest text, the king of Ur as Dumuzi's proxi went to Uruk, the town of the goddess Inanna, to present her with sacrificial offerings in order to unite with the goddess in sexual intercourse. (It is assumed that the goddess was incarnated by a priestess.) As a result of the ceremony, the king, now the consort of a goddess, could confirm his kingship.

Moreover, this sexual consummation was a fertility act. The objective of this rite was to ensure life, fertility of the land, a good fate supporting and validating a social order by forcing chaos to retreat. A reenactment of the rite was possibly performed annually. The consumption of the sexual act, in whichever region and whichever time period it took place, was not that important, but its underlying meaning, its purpose and its result were significant. Performing the Sacred Marriage connotes a) what religious scholars term as 're-creation of the world' and b) a safeguarding of life and its continued existence guaranteed in a reliable and ordered social form. As chaos is bound to be on the rise, the Sacred Marriage requires that it be reenacted, so that the cosmos can be united again. Hereby, according to the mythical paradigma, the original state of paradise is visualized and through the union of man and woman, is intended to be reestablished. Though the ritual of the Sacred Marriage is performed by humans, de facto heaven (the divine) and earth (the human) meet here symbolically and thus transcendence and immanence are united. Seen from the mythological standpoint, the union of the human and divine brings forth the respective individual qualities of men and women. If, removed from mythos and religion, these qualities are not mythologically identified. They require secular sociological, psychological, pedagogical, and biological explanatory interpretation, some of which I applied in this study.

M. and R. Zimmermann state the basic dimensions of the mythos of the Sacred Marriage as follows:

> Nach C. Lévi-Strauss erschöpft sich der Mythos nicht in dem je konkreten mythischen Text (parole) sondern kann als eine dem Sprachsystem (langue) vergleichbare sekundäre Abstraktion bestimmter Sinnstrukturen verstanden werden. Jenseits der jeweiligen historischen Manifestation zeichnet einen Mythos als Reflexionsmodell eine bestimmte wiederkehrende Struktur aus, die sich gewissermaßen wie ein 'Signifikat' höherer Ordnung zum 'Signifikanten' des Mythischen Textes verhält. Um diese Mythenstruktur darzustellen, hat C. Lévi-Strauss vorgeschlagen, wiederkehrende 'Mytheme' bezw. 'Codes' durch synchrones Vergleichen unterschiedlicher Mythenvorkommnisse zu suchen. (338)

Consequently M. and R. Zimmermann elaborated a concise structural survey of the Sacred Marriage, to which immense and varying interpretive versions this mytheme was subjected. (Their interest, however, was to prove a connection to the biblical Gen 6:1–4.) They mapped out four basic characteristics from this collectively present myth, the narrative of Sumeric-Babylonian origin, which is passed on in the Old Testament in Gen. 6:1–4, in addition to the myths associated with cults such as Isis and Osiris, Kybele and Attis, Aphrodite and Adonis, and Persephone and Hades. They say that in general, the myth of the Sacred Marriage tells of two heterosexual protagonists who withstand the conflicts of life, and by doing so, come together and are united in order to create fertility and new life. The four characteristics are:

1.) The cosmic-transcendental dimension, that describes the union of heaven and earth as a union of two essentially incompatible areas. This union is also semiotically transferred to focus attention on the union of the sexes as an essential symbol of the unification of the separated.

2.) The cosmic-genealogical dimension which explains the origin of the world and that of the humans.

3.) The dimension of fertility and sexuality which comprises husbandry, fertility, and the interval of time between birth and death.

4.) The political-legitimizing dimension which comprises the area of political power.

M. and R. Zimmermann's four characteristics of the Sacred Marriage led me to consider basic characteristics for romances which might support the assumption of romances as contemporary myths. Pamela Regis defined eight essential components that determine a romance in her structural analysis of romances. (1. Society Defined, 2. The Meeting, 3. The Barrier, 4. The Attraction, 5. The Declaration, 6. The Point of Ritual Death, 7. The Recognition, 8. The Betrothal.) Actually these components which can appear in any order, require an addition for a definition of modern contemporary romances, that of 9.) Sexuality, which has become relevant there. For a comparison of the four characteristics of myths, however, the following essential components for romances could present equivalents: 1.) The Core, the Union of the Sexes 2.) The Meeting and Commitment 3.) The Barriers and Sexuality 4.) Society Defined 5.) Reader Participation.

The following structural comparison of myth and romance will show their similarities and divergences:

1.) The Core, the Union of the Sexes: myths are narrations, as are romances. They tell the story of the Sacred Marriage as a contemporary love story. The myth of the Sacred Marriage is a postulated myth of origin with manifold variants all over the world. Its general tenor is its being a rite that creates some order as a means to evade a life in chaos (Eliade. *Das Heilige und das Profane* 18). Romances come in manifold variants and they are available all over the world. Myth and romance have to do with a heterosexual, and, as such, with an intrinsically separated couple, their controversies and their separation, and their battle to achieve an indivisible entity.

2.) The Meeting and Commitment: there is no obvious parallel to the mythological cosmogonic-genealogical dimension. In romances, however, the couples create their own world and cause chaos to retreat by embarking on order through marriage, thus, offering a prospective child stability when growing up.

3.) The Barriers and Sexuality: the focal points in romance stories are different from those in myths. It may be true that romances portray fundamental themes of life and death, of sexuality and validation of a social order; and that the sexual sphere in romances can be regarded as the place of fulfillment in the union, together with a wish for the creation of a family as the symbol of fertility as well as the continuation of the human race. Gail Sheehy even argues, that "in our secular culture sexuality often replaces religion as a means of pursuing the meaning of life" (328–9). The Sacred Marriage, however, contains sexual desire and the act of sexual consummation, but love in the romantic sense is not there, only the basic dependence of the sexes on each other. In romance novels, the rather 'young' notion of 'romantic love' is first portrayed as sexual desire, followed by sexual consummation which meets the mythic requirement of basic needs being fulfilled and of obvious dependence of the sexes on each other. In addition, and this transcends the myth, the sexual scenes in romances depict a high degree of physical intimacy and scenes portraying modern human needs of emotional intimacy other than a sexual one, and make this 'marriage' valuable. Thus, the reason for and the ensuing possible result of inducing order to the emotional chaos are of importance as it is with the performance of the rite. (As Fischer-Lichte claims, because the texts may induce physical reader reactions, this confirms the idea of a performance of the rite.)

In both, myth and romance, repetition of the sexual act is important whether it is annual as in the myth or repeated more often within the story of the romance. But in the romance, intensity of emotion is paramount and the core of the story is the search for and the finding of the right partner; mythologically speaking this means that the chaotic state of the world becomes ordered by the 'finding'. It leads to a future that will ensure an ordered life within the social order of marriage and in the broadest sense, within an 'ordered' society, and here the promise of an 'eternal' love refers to mythic dimensions. (According to Fischer-Lichte these depictions may influence reader convictions as a consequence.)

4.) Society Defined: the political-legitimizing dimension in myths offers a parallel shown in the structure of power in romances. Power is not justified and legitimized by divine entitlement, but being completely secularized, power is granted to individuals because of their highly successful achievements on the job. This way they obtain social respect and appreciation. In older contemporary romance novels, men, equipped with such power, were justified the domination of their women.

5.) Reader Participation: the mythic core, the public participation in the rite is mirrored twofold in romances: a reenactment of the love story takes place when romances are read, the reader immerses herself in another world, and identifies herself with one of the protagonists; while the text is visualized, its performative actualization is generated by the reader's physical and emotional reactions: immersion in the story causes an emotional effect and empathy in the reader; reading romances also leads to physical reaction like a racing pulse, which is a process that involves a person completely. While reading, the reader's own feelings of irritation and frustration are calmed through a satisfying ending of the story. The reading of romances seems to generate such a high degree of emotion in readers which they communicate on the internet, be it pleasure or frustration, be it advice to change the outcome of a story or a character's characterization, or be it a plea for a sequel of a novel. This reader reaction closely resembles a participation in a ritual act, as it invokes elemental feelings within the recipient that, compared with a mythical ritual kind of view, are even more intense than those of the Babylonian participants. Thus, the act of reading romance can be understood to some extent as a ritual act the reader performs.

Mirroring realities and basic experiences of life as it does, the myth is structured in such a way that even after consummation of a marriage, chaos will return. Therefore, the rite of the Sacred Marriage needed to be reenacted and this, it is believed, was performed as a New Year celebration. In a similar way, a reader experiences a waning of her energy with a tendency of chaos returning in her life. To halt this feeling of inadequacy, she goes for the next romance in order to connect again with the act of meeting and committing, this way re-experiencing excitement and satisfaction. So the mythic core of the genre incites the reader to continue reading romance after romance in order to find an imaginary, ordered structure within fiction which cannot be achieved in real life, a fact which resembles the reenactment of the rite. Unconsciously the reader is aware that in romances basic human needs and longings which are anthropologically typical, and, therefore, individually present, are thematized: provided that, in identifying with these human needs and longings and by taking part in the ritual act of reading, the reader feels she is involved and as such becomes part of a 'community', as reader, as learner, and as like-minded peer on the internet.

(A survey of this comparison of myth and romance can be found in the annex.)

PART VI

CONCLUSION

The purpose of this study was to explore the narrative and ideological development in the contemporary romance novels of the authors Jayne Ann Krentz and Barbara Delinsky in the context of the conditions of production and reader reception within a time frame of twenty-five years. Based on the analysis of three novels from the years 1982, 1892 and 2007 by each author I wanted to find answers to the following questions:

1.) whether the authors remained within the same narrative pattern predetermined by the modern industrial romances based on publisher's writing guidelines

2.) whether the authors had an individual voice from the beginning of their writing and if this remained the same over the years

3.) as the romances are erotic narratives, which degree of explicitness in descriptions of sexual acts and which language is used, and what sexual morals are revealed in the novels

4.) what narrative devices make the novels so eminently accessible

5.) whether these contemporary American novels mirrored and continue to mirror US American concerns, values and ideology and what they are and what the social settings are

6.) whether these authors send messages to their readers, consciously or unconsciously and what they are

7.) whether there is an anthropological pattern that could explain the enormous popularity of the genre and its perpetual popularity on the book market

The results are as follows:

1.) When they began writing around 1980, both authors wrote industrial category romance novels that abided by publishers' guidelines and sales figures. The guidelines contained regulating literary premises that both authors had to follow in order to be published.

When the narrative restrictions were partly removed, Krentz turned to writing romantic suspense novels. These follow the romance formula defined by Pamela Regis and, furthermore, that of the traditional three-act drama with suspense and climaxes. Both authors still abide by the guidelines of the romance novel industry, although they adapt them to their own concerns and their own voices. Delinsky moved into a different, though related field of writing, Women's Fiction, that allowed more complex plots and the portrayal of family dynamics as well as social concerns which remain in what is assumed to be a female writer's domain. The main plot is no longer the love story, and her plotlines are too complex to follow the suspense curve of a three-act drama.

2.) From the outset, the authors had their individual voices, always within the parameters of popular contemporary romance fiction, which showed divergent writing styles as well as greatly differing characterizations in their first novels I analyzed. In time, however, they adopted a way of story telling that is rendered in good, unobtrusive American English, with Krentz still using a more dialogical than descriptive writing style and Delinsky now applying more dialogues into her texts, but still using longer descriptive parts in her writing. The authors clearly have their own voices. Krentz has an understated humor that often appears in special scenes and likes to insert the literary device of a 'falcon' in the Boccaccian sense. From 1986 onward, the characterizations of her protagonists portray a particularly unwavering set of moral and ethical values. Delinsky's writing style in some of her romance novels is over-conscientiously elaborate with an abundance of adjectives and adverbs and threefold adjective – adverbial – and sentence constructions. Later, her descriptions still stand out strikingly. Her characterizations vary greatly. In her romance novels, the heroes remain mysterious and the heroines offer a comprehensive picture of themselves. In her Women's Fiction, the men are often portrayed as the (morally) weaker sex in a relationship of many years and are sometimes 'disposed of' by divorce, whereas the women are capable of fulfilling responsibilities and braving adversities. Later in their lives, these women meet equally strong men. Delinsky's subplots always elucidate her main plot by rendering different aspects to the matter of concern in question. Her constant matter of concern in different guises is the personas her protagonists present to the world and their private ones.

3.) Both authors offered, and Krentz continues to offer longer, explicit sex scenes of up to eight pages in length that include long sexual foreplay. Krentz usually has about three explicit sexual scenes in a novel. In her romance novels, Delinsky also depicts longer sex scenes, but in her popular mainstream novels, the sex scenes, though they are there and explicit, do not occupy the same prominent position as they do in her pure romance stories. The language used in these scenes in both authors' novels is 'purple' and euphemistic; in time, however, more concrete sexual terms are used.

4.) It is difficult to really pinpoint what makes these novels so eminently accessible for so many readers beside the assured happy ending. The stories are fast-paced, linear, stringent and cohesive, the narrative style is a not elaborate

American English, and, with regard to the understanding of the story, there is no second layer or much subtext to consider. Blanks the authors insert in the short narrative parts between dialogues are easily filled in the reader's imagination because they are schemata that do not need elaborate explanations. There are no longer descriptions that invite the characters, and with them the reader, to linger. The reason for descriptions of scenes or landscapes is always a psychological situation a character dwells on. Longer descriptive paragraphs in which additional ideas could veer away from the topic of the developing love story are not included in this specified genre. Delinsky does not follow publishers' parameters about short descriptions in her romance novels. In her Women's Fiction she leads a reader to pause to make her ideate what she is narratively shown. Moreover, the author(s) interpret every act and every scene for the reader so that in the end she is satisfied because all questions are answered for her. Reading such a text provides escapist pleasure just because it is not necessary to make a huge effort to decode the text.

Another aspect that makes reading so accessible is that readers living in a reality that is still dominated by men can escape into the fictional worlds of Krentz and Delinsky where a balanced relationship between the sexes is portrayed (Krentz) or balanced relationships are strived for (Delinsky). For a reader this means that, here, a reversal of power is narratively offered and women, not men, are at the center of the plot, which fills her with a sense of satisfaction.

5.) At their beginnings of their writing careers both authors portrayed patriarchal behavior on different levels in their heroes and submissive behavior in their heroines. Around 1986, Krentz developed new, non-patriarchal characteristics for her male protagonists, which she has maintained to the present day. The submissive heroine disappeared. Krentz endows her heroines with a good dose of empathy they need to stay on a par with the heroes. Over ten years, Delinsky has continued to write romance stories with protagonists whose behavior is directed by their wanting to keep personal information or secrets hidden. This remained a prime concern when, in 1992, she moved away from category romances to Women's Fiction, although her protagonists' secretiveness still unfolds as a display of complex identities to which she adds more comprehensively new topics of women's concerns, such as coping with everyday life and broken dreams, illnesses or social dilemmas.

The authors' US American social settings mirror values consistent with US social middle class concerns and beliefs. Regardless of their differences in writing and their individual fictional worlds, their norms and values do not differ. They portray white, heterosexual middle class American ideal values in their characters, and they are strong defenders of the institutions of marriage and family. Because of these conventional convictions, a reader can be sure that these authors do not describe sexual libertinage when they portray explicit sexual acts, but instead use these descriptions to demonstrate that premarital sexual acts should necessarily lead to marriage and family life. As explicitly mentioned, religion and politics are anathema, essential concerns of American society can be ignored and furthermore, the image of a society can be depicted where evil is positioned in individuals, and, therefore, can be removed by an individual. This proffered notion of an intact American society stabilizes the belief in the worthiness of its *status quo*. Socially and financially speaking, nearly all Krentz and Delinsky's protagonists belong to the middle middle or upper middle classes. Krentz often portrays protagonists who are social climbers through professional inventiveness and prudent money-management. These characters do not crave to be a part of their new social class to boost their egos. They remain 'normal' in their attitudes and display their wealth unobtrusively. Delinsky's protagonists are concerned with their social status. In her mainstream novels social roles are thematized.

6.) Each author has chosen her individual fictional cosmos: Krentz one that stays firmly in the black and white fictional realm, often highlighted by the paranormal abilities of her protagonists, thus offering her readers the fantasy of a successful relationship and love, although some crimes in her romantic suspense novels disclose a disturbing reality. Delinsky's fictional world is closer to reality because of its greater complexity which has increased over the years. She thematizes contemporary problems that depart from romantic ones, yet they mirror mainly womanly concerns and remain in the private realm. As she writes longer, complex popular mainstream novels that can only be called romances in the broadest sense of the term for her stories usually end with a couple in love, thus, offering a kind of happy ending, she has had to find a new audience for herself, whereas Krentz has been able to hold on to her romance novel audience owing to the fact that she has remained within the romantic suspense novel category, albeit with single titles or longer narratives and different publishing houses. In spite of the differences in their text worlds, the authors send messages to their readers, whether they are conscious of them as in Krentz's case, or didactic as in Delinsky's case (Women's Fiction). For her readers, Krentz portrays ideal American characters that are part of the Land of Opportunity and determined to live a good and decent American life. She demonstrates to her readers the ingredients that are necessary to achieve this. Delinsky makes her readers aware of the difference between the public and the private personas of her characters and different aspects of American womanly matters of concern and she encourages them to consider them, and also reflect on their own problems from different viewpoints to find a solution, because in fiction as in real life 'everything happens for a reason'. For that she offers reading group discussion guides.

7.) As an additional point which initially was not part of my study's objectives, but which has evolved from some aspects of the analysis of the novels and their underlying cultural positioning I suggest the hypothesis that reading romances can be considered as taking part in the reenactment of the mythical commemoration of the ritual of the Sacred Marriage. Marriage, family, worldly goods, and happiness are considered as the desirable permanent circumstances in life, a belief that is based on seemingly typically American values as well as on the objective of regaining the lost paradise. Thus, reading romance novels celebrates a secular myth of the Sacred Marriage, the annual reenactment of its ritual being mirrored in the romance novel readers' repeated search for the next story of consummation; not, as the ritual, which is repeated annually, is supposed to regain order and hinder chaos to control the world, but to achieve an emotional balance within the reader. For, as the intense effect of this myth only holds for a short time, a new story will also recreate an imaginative paradise for only a short time.

When I decided to portray these two authors who have written and partly still write romance fiction, I wanted to demonstrate that even category romances which are restricted by publishers' writing guidelines are not written in an undistinguishable style, and that plots, settings, characterizations, morals, and ethical values are dependent on their author's individuality and (changing) preferences as well as on the *Zeitgeist*. I think the texts analyzed demonstrate this difference, but they also show the authors' individual art in creating their own different plausible text worlds which brings their dedicated readers enjoyment, shrouded in myths, as well as a means of escaping the trivialities of everyday life.

ANNEX

WRITING GUIDELINES

The guidelines of the 1980s are retrieved from romancewiki, Professor Gabriele Linke sent me the1990s guidelines and I was able to retrieve the Harlequin writing guidelines for the new millennium from the internet.

GALLEN BOOKS GUIDELINES CIRCA 1980

(These guidelines suggest a freer, more open sexual environment than those suggested by imprints such as Silhouette Romance. This particular set of guidelines is particularly interesting for its acknowledgment of the Rape Fantasy that seems to be largely misunderstood in romance fiction. On a funnier note, it is interesting to note that the profession of matador was "already used" and presumably discouraged by the publisher, while the heroine was allowed to be a plastic surgeon ... as long as she worked at a Swiss clinic.

Richard Gallen was a book packager whose romances were published by Pocket Books.)

GALLEN BOOKS – CONTEMPORARY ROMANCES

HEROINE: Since she is the focus of the story, we prefer the first chapter to center on her activities. Her age ranges between 18 to 30. She is beautiful. Though not necessarily obvious to everyone, her beauty is recognized by the hero. Instinctively, she knows how to dress well, can carry off almost any fashion. She may choose to wear very casual clothes, but descriptions of pretty clothes are important. The heroine is a spirited, intelligent woman, often more initiating the story's action than simply reacting to it. She must be likable, though she may also have some personal problems. These she recognizes and eventually overcomes. Such problems should be easily recognized as things which the readers have experienced themselves, or have seen others affected by. Examples: selfishness, jealousy, sibling rivalry, difficulties with parents, stubbornness, imagined figure problems, fear of handling money.

She should have a career in a glamorous industry or want one. On-the-job problems can be integrated into the story. The author must be able to speak authoritatively on the profession so that the reader feels she is provided with the inside picture.

She need not be a virgin, though her sexual encounters with the hero are likely the best she has ever had. Tension with the hero is a must; however, relaxed and/or humorous moments are also encouraged. In the end they will decide to marry, and their basic differences will be resolved if only to acknowledge they will always exist.

If the heroine is interested in some other men, there should be no more than two.

The heroine's parents may be living, but, if so, are not capable of giving her the full support she needs.

HERO: He is older than the heroine but not by more than 15 years. He is in a position of authority or on his way to being so. He is self-confident, strong, passionate, tender, and understanding. Naturally he is handsome; no specific type is required. His attire and body should be described. Though not currently married, he may have been in the past.

SECONDARY CHARACTERS: With these the author may exercise more creativity, though they should never steal the show from the main characters.

If there is another woman, the hero should not be fooled by her deviousness. He is too perceptive for that, but may be pretending to be as a means to a positive end.

Other men cannot quite measure up to the hero.

Sub-plots are needed. These should parallel, contrast, or otherwise be connected to the major plot of what happens to the heroine and hero.

PLOT: The major theme is a love story between two dynamic people. The narrative moves the story forward, though there may be some flashbacks. Good plotting and character development, as well as fast paced action are all essential. Obvious padding will not be permitted.

LOVE SCENES: These should be frequent, with the accent on the romantic. Hopefully, the first sex will appear within the first 50 manuscript pages. If not, at least some passionate embraces. Love scenes can be dynamic or gentle. We want to see foreplay, during play, and after play. Though these scenes are explicit, euphemisms [sic] must be used, particularly when referring to below the waist. Varied positions and locales (not just the bed) are suggested.

Rape scenes are not recommended. If the author is compelled to do so, only one will be permitted with the following limitations. Between the heroine and hero, such an act should never be initiated with the violent motivation that exists in reality. A woman's fantasy is to lose control and this distinction must be kept. Should a true rape occur, it must move the story forward. Preferably the heroine is rescued in the nick of time, or it happens to another female character.

SETTING: Beautiful and/or exciting places. A limited number of locations per book is requested.

WRITING: All incidents and characters must be important to the overall telling of the story. Descriptions of clothing, people, body language, nature, and interiors should be included. Lengthy passages of background information should be broken up with demonstrations of character interactions. Dialect, slang, obscenities, etc. should be kept to a minimum and within character. Foreign words should be underlined and translated if not in common usage. Proper English is required.

POSSIBLE PROFESSIONS FOR CONTEMPORARY ROMANCE HEROINES: Computer Expert – Silicone Valley, Auctioneer at Sotheby-Parke-Bernet type place, Police officer, Detective on art fraud squad. Las Vegas card dealer, Scientist, Country & Western singer, Disc Jockey, Advertising, Plastic surgeon (Swiss clinic), Fashion co-ordinator for men, Securities broker, Wall Street, Government service (Foreign Service, State Department, Agency for International Development, etc.), Real Estate, Tennis, skiing, other sports, Interior decorator, Personnel [sic] Agency, Model Agency, Radio news reporter, Bartender.

PROFESSIONS ALREADY USED: Matador, Photographer, Novelist, Magazine reporter, Marathon runner, Artists' manager, Cosmetics tycoon, Lawyer, TV Anchor woman, Owner of horse farm/stable, Fashion designer, Story editor, films, Actress, Owner of party service business (plans and executes parties), Editor, publishing company.

CANDLELIGHT ECSTASY ROMANCE GUIDELINES CIRCA 1980

(Candlelight was an imprint of Dell, publishing the Ecstasy imprint.)

SPECIAL LETTER FROM THE EDITORS

TO WHOM IT MAY CONCERN:

Thank you for your interest in the Dell Candlelight Ecstasy Romance line. Though there are no hard and fast rules for our line in regard to plot, characterization etc., there are a few things to keep in mind if you're submitting a manuscript for our consideration.

Most Ecstasy heroines are between the ages of 25 and 35, most are established in an interesting career. Avoid the use of formula plot devices such as a marriage of convenience between the protagonists, or amnesia. These romances are essentially sensuous, realistic contemporary stories set **in the United States**. We prefer that writers focus on developing the relationship between the hero and heroine and that conflicts in the story arise out of this relationship (i.e.: career vs. marriage, unresolved feelings regarding a prior relationship, etc.). Love scenes should be tastefully handled without being pornographic, or overly explicit.

We will consider completed manuscripts of 50,000 to 60,000 words (approximately 200 to 225 typewritten, double-spaced pages) or partials of 50 to 70 pages in length, containing a detailed synopsis and outline.

Good luck in your writing. We hope to hear from you soon!

SILHOUETTE ROMANCE GUIDELINES CIRCA 1980

(Guidelines are issued by publishers of genre fiction, particular romance, to ensure that submissions to specific lines meet the imprint requirements. These guidelines were sent to prospective romance authors (who obtained them courtesy of a stamped, self-addressed envelope) in approximately 1980. They are particularly notable for the sexual and language requirements still in effect long after the Feminist Revolution.)

SILHOUETTE BOOKS

RE: LOVE SCENES

It is all right for the hero and heroine to go to bed together, although if they actually make love before they are married, a wedding should follow almost immediately. Bringing them to the brink of consummation and then forcing them to retreat either because of an interruption or because one or both of the lovers suffer from doubt or shame is an appropriate Silhouette device. Descriptions of lovemaking should be sensuous with some details. They cannot be limited to "he kissed her passionately." However, there are limits to what and how it can be described. In general, nudity above the waist is fine and almost anything goes, as long as the tone remains titillating. Below the waist things become trickier. Veiled references to our heroine's "hidden" or "secret" places are OK; our hero's "hard male strength" also gets by the stern Silhouette censor. Nudity is permissible, depending on context, but should not be too graphic. Of course, references to pain and blood are out. The only pain permitted is the sweet pain of fulfilled (or unfulfilled) desire. Above all, Silhouette love scenes should be romantic – our readers should be as in love with the hero as is the heroine.

EXAMPLES

She might have been looking at the face of a man who had suffered the agonies of hell itself and emerged covered with scars. Every feature had changed, the mouth was sensuous still, but thinned by lines of ruthlessness and even cruelty; the nostrils were wide, flaring; the eyes, dark as the pitchblende to which she had previously likened them, were black pools of hate. Deeply ingrained lines ran down each side of his mouth and across his forehead. It was the face of a pagan, primitively ruthless and cruel. She shivered and the surging wave of fear that swept through her body was more than mental. A pallor stole into her cheeks, and the palms of her hands felt damp ...

She had expected him to kiss her, and as she wanted him to, it was in a state of pleasant expectancy that she stood in the circle of his arm her sweet young face lifted, her eyes aglow in the light from a full moon which created a fairyland around the sacred building above them ... His mouth came down, gentle, as she had known it would be, and in the sudden eagerness that came to her unbidden, she reciprocated in a way that set his pagan instincts on fire. Without warming she was swept away into the vortex of primitive, nerve-firing passion, her protesting body crushed against his virility as his loins melded with hers. Her lips parted at the moist insistence and mastery of his sensuous mouth, and with a stifled little gasp of disbelief she felt his tongue enter and probe. Instinctively she began to use her own tongue to expel it, an action that proved to be her undoing, for the contact and movement of her tongue against his only served to add fuel to the flame of his passion and for a long moment she was the victim of her own awakened desires, drawn irrevocably into a conflagration of pagan lovemaking against which any resistance on her part could not possibly survive. He slid his hand beneath her evening blouse and as, after unclipping her bra, he took one firm small breast into his hand she truly believed her virginity must surely be nearing its end. For as he caressed the nipple, raising it to the hardness of sense-shattering desire, spasm after spasm of sheer undiluted ecstasy throbbed with violent intensity through her whole body. "Remain single," he was to say later, in very different circumstances after she had refused his offer of marriage. "You're made for love, Sarah, and I've proved it to you – No, don't blush. It was natural and beautiful – it could have been more beautiful if we had lain together in the gardens, beneath the moon, and made real love. Let me show you," he pleaded. "When we're married I'll make love to you in romantic places ... beneath the palms, on the beach of my island, or maybe in the warm water when we've been swimming in the sea. There are places where the rocks can shelter us ... "

A LOVE SCENE: This pair ARE MARRIED.

As she quivered against him the pressure of his warm lips softened into a tantalizing caress, his tongue gently probing her lips apart. Her resistance ebbed away, dissolved by his ardent exploration.

Sensing her capitulation, Drew swung her up in his arms and carried her through the bedroom never allowing her to establish her defenses by continuing his seductive stroking of her breast with the tips of his calloused fingers and teasing the bare skin of her shoulder and throat with titillating kisses.

He set her on her feet for an instant while he threw back the bed covers and then he was lowering her to the bed pushing her back onto the soft cotton sheets and covering her body with his.

The buttons of his shirt pressed into her tender skin, but, after kissing her for another moment he uttered a muffled groan, rolled off the bed, and stood jerking his shirt from the waistband as he unfastened it. Quickly he shrugged out of the sleeves as Stacy watched transfixed as he continued to undress.

Any niggling doubts were overpowered by the love that welled up inside her. She knew that this was the moment that she had been craving. It was right for him to possess her completely.

Instinctively, with a naturally seductive movement, she raised her arms to him as he stepped out of his clothes. He melted his powerful body against her and her nostrils caught his distinctively masculine scent. His hardening muscles mutely proclaimed his desire. Gently teasing her with his hands and mouth, he patiently continued to arouse her with infinite care until she reached a fevered pitch. She felt as though she'd go crazy unless he filled the gnawing void within her. Sensing her readiness, he rained fervent kisses on her mouth. Caught up in a vortex of sensual delight, Stacy arched her back to meet his movements until all her senses exploded with ultimate fulfillment.

Spring Fires Of Love by Cynthia C. Richardson (Possibly published as Spring Fires by Leigh Richards)

THE HEROINE: Though the point of view of a SILHOUETTE BOOK is usually omniscient i.e. the author can get in anyone's head, she chooses to remain almost completely in the heroine's. These books are seldom told from the "I" point of view, though, in fact, they are always primarily about one person – the heroine. She is always young, (under 25) and capable of being beautiful, though this is not always immediately apparent. She is basically an ingenue, and wears modest make-up, clothes, etc. Her figure is always perfectly in proportion, usually petite, and slight of build. Of course, when she dresses up, she is stunning. Her outfits are described in detail, as is her physical appearance. In spite of her often fragile appearance, she is independent, high-spirited, and not too subservient. She should not be mousey or weepy. Though she wants to work, and often plans to after marriage, often in some sort of business with her husband, her home and children would always come first. She is almost always a virgin; her occasional sexual interlude is just before the assured wedding with her lover and in no circumstances that could in any way be called promiscuous. She is usually without parents or a "protective" relationship. Sometimes she has lived with an elderly female relative, but she breaks away to lead a life of her own. A brother is permissible, but she is often in the position of caring for him, rather than vice versa – he may be weak, crippled, or uncertain as to his morals or future. He can in no way suggest the kind of character that is our hero's prerogative.

THE HERO: Older, arrogant, self-assured, masterful, hot-tempered, he is capable of violence, passion, and tenderness. He is often mysteriously moody. Heathcliff

(WUTHERING HEIGHTS) is a rougher version; Darcey [sic], (PRIDE AND PREJUDICE) a more refined one. He is always older than the heroine, usually in his early or mid 30's, rich successful in the vocation of his choice. He is always tall, muscular, (but not muscle-bound) with craggy features. He is not necessarily handsome; he is above all virile. He is usually dark, though we have seen some great Nordic types, and, recently, we have been introduced to a stunning redhead. Here, as for the heroine, physical description and clothes are important.

THE OTHER WOMAN: Usually mean, over-sophisticated, well groomed. She NEVER gets our hero.

THE OTHER MAN: Appealing, but not assertive, egotistical in some cases. Occasionally, (very occasionally) a bad type. He cannot ever take the limelight from the hero. He is not as rounded as the hero, and is often off stage throughout most of the book.

OTHER CHARACTERS: Stock, easily recognized, cameos; the Scotch housekeeper, the overbearing aunt, the aristocratic mother of the hero. A good writer can give them individuality, but they must not take the focus off the hero and heroine. They are always periphery.

PLOT: The action should primarily concern the relationship between the lovers. The only flashbacks should be memories – mostly in the heroine's head. The narrative is sequential, straightforward. As a SILHOUETTE is primarily a romance, it should not be a Gothic, a novel of suspense or adventure. Murder, gunplay, spies, and nurse-hospital novels are out. –

SETTING: Preferably exotic or lush. In certain circumstances a familiar setting works, depending on the author's ability to romanticize [sic] them. The setting should transport the reader out of her ordinary, humdrum life.

WRITING: No long-winded descriptions, rather extremely sensuous details – sense, taste, smell, touch, all important. The love scenes should be suggestive, titillating, not graphic.

SPECIAL EDITION GUIDELINES CIRCA 1980

(Special Edition was launched as Silhouette's sophisticated, modern imprint. These guidelines reflect a more sexually aware heroine and more vulnerable hero. Especially notable (for the era) is the express note that the story can, when appropriate, reflect the hero's point-of-view in the text.)

Silhouette Special Edition

Silhouette Special Editions are longer, more sophisticated romances, featuring realistic plots and well developed characters. As with the Silhouette Romances, these books are built around romantic tension.

THE HEROINE: A Special Edition is always written in the third person, but it is the heroine's point-of-view which shapes the novel. The heroine is generally 23–32 and she is intelligent and mature. Independent and accomplished, she supports herself successfully in her chosen profession and is never clinging or weepy. The heroine need not be a virgin. She accepts sex as a natural part of any loving relationship. She should be single when the book opens, bur she may have been married in the past. If she is divorced, it must be clear that the divorce was not her fault.

THE HERO: The hero, older than the heroine, is a dynamic, virile, supremely masculine man, one any woman could imagine herself falling in love with. Though he is self-confident, he also has a gentler, more vulnerable side, and may even admit to an occasional human weakness. He is never brutal or gratuitously cruel. Like the heroine, he may be a widower or divorced, but he is usually single when they meet. The narrative may sometimes include the hero's point-of-view in order to more fully develop his character and the plot.

SUBSIDIARY CHARACTERS: Subsidiary characters never overshadow the hero and the heroine. They must be realistic, not stereotypical, and they often bring out aspects of the hero and heroine that aren't evident in their relationship with each other.

THE PLOT: In keeping with the sophistication of these books, the plots must be complex and believable. The plot centers on the developing relationship between the hero and heroine and the problems they must overcome on their way to a happy ending. The tension comes from a real problem that has to be solved and not merely from misunderstandings. This problem should be a realistic one, and deep enough to sustain the length of the book. It's crucial that the reader feels she is being presented with real people solving real problems, yet the story should never slip from the romantic to the mundane.

These books incorporate subplots that either complement the action or play against it in some way. The subplots, an integral part of the book, should hold the reader's attention without overwhelming the romance. Silhouette Special Editions are contemporary romances. Elements of mystery, suspense and the occult are inappropriate. These books are not Gothics, nurse-doctor romances or thrillers.

Silhouette Special Edition, as of April 2011: Harlequin Special Edition

Length: 55,000–60,000

Sophisticated, substantial and packed with emotion, Special Edition demands writers eager to probe characters deeply, to explore issues that heighten the drama of living and loving, to create compelling romantic plots. Whether the sensuality is sizzling or subtle, whether the plot is wildly innovative or satisfyingly traditional, the novel's emotional vividness, its depth and dimension, should clearly label it a very special contemporary romance. Subplots are welcome, but must further or parallel the developing romantic relationship in a meaningful way.

Silhouette Desire Guidelines Circa 1982

(The guidelines from Silhouette written for the Silhouette Desire imprint reflect a wish for innovative, unique stories – elements that had been largely ignored by category romance up to that point. Authors were encouraged to write fresh characters and plots.)

Silhouette Desire

The Heroine: The Desire heroine is a mature, capable woman of 25–32 who has a strong sense of her own individuality and an unshakable resolve to be happy no matter what obstacles she encounters. She need not be a virgin and is definitely not a naive young girl. Rather, she is a vulnerable, sensitive woman looking for a partner to share to the fullest the joys and challenges of life.

The Hero: The hero must be a realistic, believable modern man, one any woman could imagine herself falling in love with. He should be strong, caring, sexy, and warm. He will tend to be in his mid to late thirties.

The Setting: Both international and American locales are encouraged, providing the setting is presented in a romantic and appealing way.

Writing Style: The writing should be extremely sensuous, providing vivid, evocative descriptions of lovemaking and concentrating on the characters' reactions to each other and the sexual tension between them.

The Plot: A Desire book centers on the developing relationship between the hero and heroine. The book should open with their meeting or the events leading up to it and end with their decision to make a lifetime commitment to one another. The tension and excitement in the book stem from the fact that neither protagonist is certain of the other's love until the end. Each scene must contribute to the process of discovery they're going through. The plot should not consist of a series of chance encounters, coincidences or filler scenes in which nothing substantial happens.

EMPHASIS : Desire books will emphasize innovative, unique plots, exploring realistic relationships which have been ignored up to now in other romance lines. They should depict the fears, doubts and problems, as well as the exhilarating wonder of falling in love. Because Desire intends to mirror the real lives of modern women, marriages of convenience and similarly contrived situations are inappropriate for this line. For the same reason, realistic and detailed love scenes will be possible, providing they are tastefully handled. Sexual encounters – which may include nudity and lovemaking even when the protagonists are not married – should concentrate on the highly erotic sensations aroused by the hero's kisses and caresses rather than the mechanics of sex. A celebration of the physical pleasures of love, as well as its emotional side, should be an important part of these books.

LENGTH: 53,000–56,000 words

SILHOUETTE SUPER DESIRE GUIDELINES (NO DATE GIVEN)

(Silhouette Super Desire appeared to be the publisher's attempt at capturing the audience who gravitated toward authors such as Judith Krantz. The guidelines suggest a flashier, high society approach to the storylines, though the actual length of the books was much shorter than the single-title novels published by authors such as Krantz. These novels contrasted with traditional Silhouette Desire titles by adding additional layers of sophistication to the story elements.)

SUPER DESIRE TIP SHEET

The Super Desire line is designed to appeal to readers looking for a heightened feeling of romance and fantasy in a category novel. The Super Desire novel ought to sweep the reader away into a special world where everyday cares are forgotten in the thrill of passions which are frankly larger than life.

HEROINE: The romantic heroine is the reader's entrée to the story. The events of a Super Desire are seen primarily through her eyes, so it is essential that she be a sympathetic character. Independent, intelligent and strong-willed, she should also be emotionally vulnerable. Though she may find herself in circumstances unfamiliar to most readers, she reacts to them in a familiar and believable way. The reader should experience her fears and joys as though at first hand.

HERO: The Super Desire hero is not the average boy next door. He should be a uniquely charismatic character, a man who has unusual presence and emotional strength. He may have overcome tremendous obstacles to rise to his present position; he has always lived life to the fullest. He feels at home in situations, professions and life styles which the average person rarely experiences. In short, he is the man every woman dreams about in her most exciting fantasies.

SETTING: The setting of a Super Desire may be foreign or American, but it should seem exotic and different. The story should introduce the reader to a new world. This may be accomplished by using a glamorous, high society background, an unusual locale, or by giving the hero and/or heroine offbeat jobs.

LOVE SCENES: The level of sensuality should be high throughout the story. Sexual tension between hero and heroine will build until they actually make love – probably about halfway through the book. Several detailed love scenes – between the hero and the heroine only – should be included. There must be evidence of emotional commitment before they actually go to bed together.

PLOT: The Super Desire plot centers on the romance between hero and heroine, but it may incorporate elements of adventure, suspense or melodrama. These elements must never overshadow the romance; instead, they should be used to heighten the emotional highs and lows of the developing relationship between hero and heroine. The Super Desire will be more action-oriented than the average romance, often dealing with life and death situations and always featuring an emotionally moving, dramatic climax. Ideally, it will elicit a few tears along the way, as well as a buoyant [sic] feeling when we learn that the two lovers will, indeed, live happily ever after.

LENGTH: 80,000- 85,000 words.

SILHOUETTE DESIRE, AS OF APRIL 2011: HARLEQUIN DESIRE

LENGTH: 50,000–55,000 words

A powerful, passionate and provocative read ... guaranteed!

At 50,000–55,000 words, Desire books are filled to the brim with strong, intense storylines. These sensual love stories immediately involve the reader in a romantic, emotional conflict and the quest for a happily-ever-after resolution. The novels should be fresh, fast-paced, modern and present the hero and heroine's conflicts by the end of chapter one. Readers need to understand immediately what obstacles will impact the characters throughout the novel.

The desire hero should be powerful and wealthy – an alpha male with a sense of entitlement, and sometimes arrogance. While he may be harsh or direct, he is never physically cruel. Beneath his alpha exterior, he displays some vulnerability, and he is capable of being saved. It's up to the heroine to get him there. The Texan hero should own the ranch, not work on it, and the urban hero should be someone in charge, not a handyman. The desire hero often has fewer scenes from his perspective, but in many ways, he owns the story. Readers should want to fall in love with and rescue the Desire hero themselves!

The Desire heroine is complex and flawed. She is strong-willed and smart, though capable of making mistakes when it comes to the matters of the heart.

The heroine is equally as important as the hero, if not more so. There is room for both protagonists' perspective, but desire novels are usually 60% heroine and 40% hero.

The conflict should be dramatic and original. Unexpected and new takes on classic plot lines, such as secret pregnancies, marriages of convenience and reunion romances, are welcome. Plots that focus on suspense or paranormal are best directed elsewhere. The story can be set anywhere in the world, but the tone should be true to the author's voice.

Desire novels are sensual reads and a love scene or scenes are needed, but there is no set number. Rather, the level of sensuality must be appropriate to the storyline. Above all, every Desire novel must fulfill the promise of a powerful, passionate and provocative read

SILHOUETTE ROMANTIC SUSPENSE, AS OF APRIL 2011: HARLEQUIN ROMANTIC SUSPENSE

Sparked by Danger; Fuelled by Passion.

LENGTH: 55,000–60,000

Silhouette Romantic Suspense books offer an escape read where true-to-life heroines find themselves in the throes of extraordinary circumstances … and in the arms of powerful heroes. These books combine all the classic elements of category novels with the excitement of romantic suspense, creating big, sweeping romances amid dangerous and suspenseful settings. A strong, compelling romance should dominate the book, but there must be a suspense plot. Silhouette Romantic Suspense romances are fuelled by the romance and not the suspense.

When Romantic Suspense characters come together they create sparks that make for an unforgettable story. The hero should be a force to contend with. He may be harsh and direct, but never cruel. Though formidable and heroic, he is capable of being saved, and it is up to the heroine to get him there. Our heroines should be complex, strong and smart. As independent as the heroine may be, she is often in jeopardy and needs the hero's help to overcome obstacles. Because this is primarily the heroine's story, we ask that roughly 60% of the point of view be hers, and 40% the hero's.

The hero and the heroine's conflicts need to be presented as soon as possible and carried throughout the novel. The conflicts should be dramatic and compelling. Romantic Suspense books revolve around classic plotlines that are tried and true in category romance: revenge, women in jeopardy, espionage, law enforcement and military, reunion romances, secret babies and others. We are not looking for plots that focus entirely on the suspense. The romance must always be at the heart of these books, and gratuitous violence or graphic details must be avoided. These are universal stories and can be set anywhere in the world, but the tone should remain true to the author's voice. Romantic Suspense stories will be consistently high on sensuality, as well as romantic and sexual tension. At this time, we're not looking for paranormal stories.

If you have written a romance that meets the above guidelines, we would love to hear from you! Please submit a query letter with a detailed synopsis, or a synopsis and three chapters with a SASE (self-addressed stamped envelope) large enough to hold the entirety of your work. We do not accept submissions via e-mail. If a previous editorial relationship with the company has been established that can be continued – or feel free to submit directly to one of the editors above.

MILLS&BOON TEMPTATION (no date given, but clearly before 1991)

(Submissions were to be directed to the same senior editor, Birgit Davis-Todd, in Ontario, Canada, as were the submissions for the Harlequin Temptation of 1991.)

In every woman's life there comes a moment when her heart must choose her destiny. This series of contemporary love stories exemplifies this theme, blending the decisions that must be faced in every day life with the questions only the heart can answer. This is not a line moving into heavy realism, but one based on believable fantasy. People perennially want happy ending. Women read these contemporary books and yearn to believe that such things could really happen to them.

LENGTH: 60,000–65,000 words (approximately 240 manuscript pages)

HEROINE: The heroine is a capable, mature American woman in her twenties and thirties, established in an interesting career. She has a strong sense of her own individuality and an unshakeable resolve to survive and be happy, no matter what the obstacles. While not weak, she may nevertheless be a vulnerable and sensitive woman looking for a partner to share to the fullest the joys and challenges of life. She has already experienced and is aware of her own sexuality. She is attractive, but not necessarily ravishing.

HERO: The hero is usually older than the heroine; his age tends to be mid- to late thirties. He may or may not be American. He is not necessarily fabulously wealthy, but is certainly successful at what he does. He is a realistic, believable modern man – strong, sympathetic, caring and warm. A man, with whom any woman could imagine herself falling in love.

PLOT: The momentum of the plot should be generated by the conflicts, yearnings, doubts and possible alternate paths that confront the protagonists during their growing relationship. At an early stage in the story the heroine should be faced with a conflict that arises from some facet of her personality or background or an external situation. But problems, though contemporary ones, should not be so strongly realistic that they overshadow the romance. The story should always leave the reader with an uplifting feeling of fulfillment, and though twists of the plot should aim for originality and freshness, the romance should remain the prime focus. Most importantly, the story should be a good, fast-paced and exciting read. The book should conclude with the couple making a mutual decision to a lifetime commitment and marriage. While the story remains the heroine's, the hero could have a voice when the plot demands it.

SETTING: The stories are written from an American viewpoint and in an American context, but may take place anywhere in the world. A feeling for the setting should be subtly evoked without overwhelming the romance.

SEX: Because this series mirrors the lives of contemporary women, realistic descriptions of love scenes should be included, provided they are tastefully handled. Each book should sustain a high level of sexual tension throughout, balanced by a strong storyline. Sensuous encounters should concentrate on passion and the emotional sensations rather than the mechanics of the love-making act. Of course, the couple have to be obviously in love, with emphasis put on all that being in love entails. They should definitely consummate their relationship before the end of the story, at whatever point this fits naturally in the plot. The love scenes may be frequent, but not overwhelmingly so, and should never be gratuitously included.

HARLEQUIN TEMPTATION, 1991

Sensuous, bold, sometimes controversial, Harlequin Temptation stories focus on contemporary relationships between adults. These fast-paced books may be humorous, topical, adventurous or glitzy, but at heart, they are pure romantic fantasy.

HEROINE: She is an attractive North American woman aged 23 or older, who may be single, divorced or married. A contemporary woman of the Nineties, the heroine is involved with a career she cares about and has a strong sense of her own individuality. She'd like to meet the right partner in order to fulfill herself emotionally and sexually and to make a lifetime commitment.

HERO: He is compatible in age to the heroine and may or may not be North American. Handsome, successful at his job, he's sexier than any man has a right to be! The Temptation hero should be strong, compelling and larger-than-life and play an active role in the story. Beyond that, he may be characterized as the more self-assured, strong-willed, new alpha man, the unpredictable, rough-edged bad boy or the highly appealing and sometimes humorous Nineties man.

PLOT: In a Harlequin Temptation novel, the plot is the developing romance between hero and heroine. The plot must be fresh, original, complex enough to sustain 60,000 words and action-oriented rather than introspective. A good blend of sparkling dialogue and minimal narrative is important. Strong believable conflicts are essential in a Temptation. Secondary characters and minor subplots may be included to enrich the plot. Temptation books cover a range of plots: humorous, fantasy (both romantic and sexual fantasy), topical, adventurous, emotional, glitz and glamour. Truly innovative stories may be designated "Editor's Choice."

SEX: Temptation is Harlequin's boldest, most sensuous series, mirroring the lives of contemporary women. A high level of sexual tension is required throughout the story in order to maintain the necessary edge and arousing feel. The hero and heroine should have several sensuous encounters and should consummate their relationship at a point appropriate to the plot. Love scenes should be highly erotic, realistic and fun, but above all, emotional. Let your imagination be your guide!

SETTING: The stories are written from a North American viewpoint, but may take place anywhere in the world. A feeling for the setting should be subtly evoked.

LENGTH: 60,000 words or approximately 235 manuscript pages.

HARLEQUIN BLAZE, 2011

(Harlequin Blaze is the successor of Harlequin Temptation that was last printed in 2005. When the line was launched in 2005 Birgit Davis-Todd was still the senior editor, but by 2011 was no longer in the post, although the text of the guideline remains the same.)

LENGTH: 55,000–60,000 words
     The Blaze line of red-hot reads is changing the face of Harlequin and creating a continual buzz with readers. The series features sensuous, highly romantic, in-novative stories that are sexy in premise and execution. The tone of the books can run from fun and flirtatious to dark and sensual. Writers can push the boundaries in terms of characterization, plot and explicitness. Submissions should have a very contemporary feel – what it's like to be young and single today. Heroes and hero-ines should be in their early 20's and up. We want to see an emphasis on the physical relationship developing between the couple: fully described love scenes along with a high level of fantasy, playfulness and eroticism are needed. And don't forget, secondary characters and subplots contribute to the richness of story and plot action we look for in a successful Blaze novel.
     Are you a *Cosmo Girl* at heart? A fan of *Sex and the City* or *Red Shoe Diaries*? Or may be you just have an adventurous spirit. If so, then Blaze is the series for you!

THE FAMILY TREE: READING GROUP DISCUSSION GUIDE (DELINSKY)

1.) One of the major themes of FAMILY TREE is the discrepancy between the face we show to the public and the one we see in the mirror each day – the difference between who we say we are and who we really are. This arises in different contexts in FAMILY TREE. What contexts can you identify? Is this dichotomy one that you have seen in your own life or in those around you?

2.) Eaton's personality was shaped in part by who he feared he was. Identify and discuss these different aspects of the man.

3.) Shakespeare wrote in *Hamlet*, "The lady doth protest too much." The same can be said for various characters in FAMILY TREE. Who are they, and in what ways do they overcompensate?

4.) Dana lost her mother at the age of five. How did this event shape her personality? In what regards is she more needy? In what regards is she stronger? How did this early unexpected event prepare her for the surprise of Lizzie's birth?

5.) In FAMILY TREE the term 'passing' can be applied to different characters in different ways. Who are these different characters, and in what ways have they 'passed'?

6.) Have you known someone who has 'passed' either racially, religiously, or economically? Is this a common phenomenon? Prior to reading FAMILY TREE, were you aware of the 'one-drop rule'? Have you ever seen evidence of that sort of discrimination?

7.) Halfway through the book, Dana says of her marriage, "I thought it was perfect. Well, it's not, and maybe it never was, maybe that was an illusion … " Do you think that the perfect marriage exists? The perfect relationship? What role does illusion play in the relationship we foster? Is illusion determined by our own needs?

8.) Dana hypothesizes that Hugh would never have married her if she'd had brown skin, because as open he claims to be, an inbred elitism would have surfaced back then. Do you agree with her assessment? Do you think it is possible to change beliefs that have been ingrained since childhood? Can you cite examples from your own life in which you or the others around you have 'reverted' in some ways as you have grown older?

9.) When Ellie Jo breaks her ankle, Dana finds herself challenged to do more than a new mother should be doing. Undaunted, perhaps bull-headed, she thinks, "She could do anything herself, if she wanted to badly enough – could do anything herself, if she had to." Is this a mother thing? A woman thing?

Can you site examples from your own life where you or someone else has felt this way?

10.) Though Hugh remains close to his former client, Yunus El-Sabwi, he understands that, like other Arab males, Yunus has trouble talking about personal family matters, and that keeping silence and a stiff upper lip is a matter of honor among such men. But is it only Arab men who feel this? What about Western men? Are they more forthcoming about personal matters? And if not, why not? Honor? Pride? Stubbornness? Competitive instincts?

11.) When Dana and Hugh arrive in Albany, Dana insists on carrying the baby herself. She considers Lizzie her security, proof that she is loved. Given the circumstances, is she justified in feeling this way? What dangers are involved in this? Do you know people who have unhealthy ties to their children?

12.) When Dana meets John Jack Kettyle, he says that he simply stopped thinking about Liz Joseph when she left school. He explains it as follows: "The choice was between pining forever over a relationship that wasn't to be, or moving on. Putting Liz behind me was the only way I could survive." Is this attitude cold and calculated? Is it compatible with the idea of a priest who cares for all people? Are there other characters in FAMILY TREE who have experienced variations on this theme? Is there a lesson in his words for Dana?

13.) On the day Ellie Jo has her stroke, Hugh makes the analogy of life as a chronological chain of change, whereby each distinct link alters the direction, however slightly, of a person's future. Do you agree with this analogy? What other links might Hugh have had in mind, beside the one of Ellie Jo's impairment? What are some of the links in your own life?

14.) Eaton accuses his brother Brad of suggesting Hugh's marriage is shaky to compensate for Brad's own daughter's divorce. Likewise, Ellie Jo accuses her cousin Emma of starting rumors about Ellie Jo's Earl to compensate for Emma's lack of any husband at all. Do you think these accusations are valid? Do you see jealousy as a major problem in families? Among friends? Have you had personal experience with this?

15.) With the results of the sickle-cell test, Dana suddenly sees Hugh as "more human". Do you? How do you define 'human'? If you were to pick one word to describe Hugh prior to getting the results of this test, what would it be?

SYNOPTIC ANALYSIS OF KRENTZ'S THREE NOVELS

aspects	Stormy Challenge, 1982	Perfect Partners 1992	All Night Long, 2007
Genre	contemporary category romance	contemporary romantic suspense	contemporary romantic suspense
length	250 pages, 22 chapters	372 pages, 20 chapters	321 pages, prolog, 50 chapters, epilogue
plot	one plot, no subplot, next to no tension	main plot, 2 small subplots with their own climaxes, well placed turning points creating suspense on two levels: the love story and the crime part	main plot extended by reports of the past, one on video, one short subplot, well placed turning points to ensure tension
Local Setting	USA, Oregon, Northern California	USA, Seattle, Washington State	USA, Northern California
Social Setting	upper middle class	upper middle class, academic world versus business world, no societal affiliation	middle and upper middle class, possibly upper class, no societal affiliation
Time-frame	4 weeks	4 weeks	14 days, prologue: 17 years before, epilogue: some months later
Focali-zation	the heroine's perspective, no auctorial remarks	the protagonists' perspectives, no auctorial remarks	8 perspectives, the protagonists' ones in the majority, no auctorial remarks
Narrative Style	chronological time-line, dialogical writing style with many dialogue tags, very short descriptive parts, no complexity in characterization	chronological time-line, dialogical writing style, good inconspicuous American English, short descriptive parts, rather complex characterization with typical romance elements	chronological time-line, dialogical writing style with some longer descriptions, unobtrusive good American English, fairly complex characterization

aspects	Stormy Challenge, 1982	Perfect Partners 1992	All Night Long, 2007
Male Protagonist	around 35, athletic physique, consultant, sexually aggressive with strong patriarchal attitude, primed to marry	37, with a sad past, physique of a runner, successful self-made businessman, a 'lone wolf', decent, reliable, protective, craving a family	nearly 40, athletic physique, Ex-Marine, Ph.D. in philosophy, financially independent, divorced, no children, owner of a run-down lodge, decent, protective, introverted, but not commitment-shy, PTSD shown in nightmares
Female Protagonist	28, attractive, college educated, owner of bookshop, adolescent emotional behavior, psyched up to marry	29, ex-librarian at a college, comely, wearing glasses, intelligent, insightful, emphatic, exudes emotional warmth	32, attractive, divorced, no children, journalist, intelligent, insightful, PTSD shown in fear of darkness, in wearing black clothes
Secondary Characters	a younger brother who needs a consultant to run the inherited firm	heroine's academic parents, father daughters adviser, and family's protector, stepmother, pregnant serving to characterize heroine, as do hero's former girlfriend and her husband; to characterize hero, heroine's ex-fiancé and hero's former employer and murderer of his father	heroine's dead girlfriend serving as catalyst for many murders, the girlfriend's father, senator and childabuser, the girlfriend's grandfather who murdered at least six people, two within storyline; the hero's family becoming the new family for the heroine
Theme	love story	definition of love as understanding the other's needs and problems; revenge reverted	sexual child-abuse, misuse of political power, definition of love as understanding the other's needs and problems

aspects	Stormy Challenge, 1982	Perfect Partners 1992	All Night Long, 2007
Prota-gonists' Conflicts	deception	external: how to deal decently with inher-itance, internal: her sexuality, his being guilt-ridden	overcoming PTSD
Relation-ship and Erotic Scenes	a constant back and forth of the hero-ine's indecision to trust and love, the hero's heavy handed despotic courting leading to interrupted sexual encounters and blissful consumma-tion	instant attraction and trust, explicit sexual scenes meaningfully connoted	instant attraction and trust, emotionally binding dangerous events, explicit sex scenes serving as affirmation of the rightness of the union

SYNOPTIC ANALYSIS OF DELINSKY'S THREE NOVELS

aspects	Sweet Ember, 1982	A Woman betrayed 1992	The Family Tree, 2007
Genre	contemporary category romance	Women's Fiction (mainstream)	Women's Fiction (mainstream)
Length	233 pages, 9 chapters	470 pages, 31 chapters	329 pages, 30 chapters
Plot	one plot, identifiable turning points, not much tension	main plot, 2 subplots closely woven into main plot, 2 subplots connected to the main plot, each subplot with its own climax, chapter endings at a high point, clearly constructed complex plotting with strategically set turning points to create tension	main plot, 4 subplots, three closely connected to main plot, one separated from main plot, all with their own partially not high climaxes, clearly constructed complex plotting with strategically set turning points to create tension.
Local Setting	USA, a summer camp in Maine, a house in Cambridge, Ogunquit	USA, 5 places in Northampton, Hampshire, a house in Vermont, a cabin and a diner at the Maine coast, a place in Tahiti	USA, 3 places in Newport, Rhode Island, a place south of Boston, a rectory in Albany, New York State
Social Setting	heroine: cultured middle class, hero: middle class, both employed	middle class, societal dynamics noted in the margin	hero belongs to the super rich American 'aristocracy', heroine: illegitimate, middle class
Time-frame	8 weeks	about 4 months	4 weeks
Focalization	the heroine's perspective, auctorial remarks	4 perspectives, auctorial remarks	5 perspectives, predominantly the protagonists', no auctorial remarks despite the impression of a covert narrator

aspects	Sweet Ember, 1982	A Woman betrayed 1992	The Family Tree, 2007
Narrative Style	chronological timeline, around one fifth of text dialogues, language on an elaborate level, often stilted, genre typical use of adjectives, longer detailed descriptions of rooms and landscapes, no complexity in characterization	chronological and simultaneous timeline, balanced dialogic and descriptive writing, unobtrusive good American English, complex, but rather short sentences, complex characterizations	chronological timeline, three quarters of the text dialogical, some longer descriptive parts often given in a reporting way, often no explanation of the meaning of an action, unobtrusive good American English, not very long, not very complex sentences, fairly complex characterization.
Male Protagonist	38, tall, superb physique, at the camp head of the tennis department, off camp psychology teacher and president of a college, is said to be communicatively adept, but is not ready to talk or impart information about himself	there are 2 protagonists: Jeff, 42, heroine's husband, handsome, well kept, an avid reader, intelligent, punctual, reliable, a very private person, is an accountant with his own firm, with low self-esteem he tries to upgrade through successful tax-fraud. He planned his disappearing act well. In his new neighborhood he finds a simple and content way to live. Christian, 48, his half-brother and his opposite, a photographer and house-builder, is communicative, successful, responsible, decent, a strong character, apt as romance hero	40, handsome, married to heroine, new father, partner in a multi-racial lawyer firm, independently wealthy, privileged because belongs to that rich upper class community that partly molded his character, values decency, honor and fairness, has a compulsive need to find explanations, is capable of loving

aspects	Sweet Ember, 1982	A Woman betrayed 1992	The Family Tree, 2007
Female Protagonist	28, beautiful, un-wed mother of hero's daughter, photographer at the camp and off camp, has continuous love–hate feelings, no self-confidence, cowers at hero's moods	38, wife of 20 years, attractive, mother of 2 children, successful entrepreneur, warm, compassionate, energetic, dominant, thinks she has created a perfect life for her family, defends her non-academic life against her mother's academic one	34, illegitimate, married to hero, new mother, designer and obsessive knitter, needs her grandmother's yarn-shop as emotional haven, deeply fears rejection, craves the unconditional love she gives her daughter, is impervious to bigotry, loves and trusts and understands her husband
Secondary Characters	the 7 year old daughter, providing 3 turning points, other characters play minimal roles	a daughter, 16, rebelling against her mother, a son, 19, being wrongly accused of rape, the heroine's best friend and lawyer, 40, who had an affair with Jeff, begins one with the investigator of Jeff's tax-fraud while helping with the legal problems and defending the son at court, the investigator, 32, who wants to marry this friend, the heroine's mother, whose cowardice is drawing attention to people's blinders, the trusting retarded girl, 30, who is Jeff's starting point for a new relational network	the other characters serve to elucidate different kinds of deception; on the heroines side: the grandmother, her dead mother, a professor of psychology, the reason for her daughter's non-academic life, the brother's mother her father who turns out to be a caring person, a poor customer at the shop, on the hero's side: his father who is proud of his white ancestry, his mother who begins to see her social class' intolerance, the hero's pro bono case involving a senator and his illegitimate child, and the couple's black

aspects	Sweet Ember, 1982	A Woman betrayed 1992	The Family Tree, 2007
			neighbor's daughter's problem coping with her skin color
Theme	if there is a theme at all, it is 'communicative difficulties'	self-deception, Janus-headed personas	different kinds of deception and self-deception, upper class biased racial attitude
Protagonists' Conflicts	secretiveness on both sides, inability to communicate	strong versus weak characters, public defamation, rebellion against parental rules, decency versus emotional basic needs, efforts to gain respect and love, need to be needed	a daughter's deep fear of being rejected by her father, an obsessive need to find explanations, a threatened loss of credence, different facets of fears losing face
Relationship and Erotic Scenes	a one night stand of 8 years before as basis of the relationship that results in an on-off emotional closeness and heroine's sexual arousal with genre-typical interrupted sex scenes as well as rather short consummated ones	typical family relationship problematic dynamics; everybody is given a sexual side to his/her persona; 2 couples' physical love is presented: heroine and Christian renewing their love in an explicit sex scene serving as committing act; the investigator and heroine's friend are given one page of explicit sex serving to put an end to loneliness; erotic scenes do not go with constant reminders characters' sexual arousal	as the story time comprises one month after the child's birth, erotic and sexual scenes are nonexistent, because relationship issues become predominant, such as trust and love in a non-sexual sense

This chart illustrates the authors' narrative changes over the time frame of 25 years via the increasing complexity of the narrative aspects.

STRUCTURAL ANALYTIC COMPARISON OF MYTH AND ROMANCE

The Structure of Myths	The Structure of Romances
The cosmic-transcendental dimension that describes the union of heaven and earth and the union of the sexes as an essential symbol of the unification of the separated	**The core, the Union of the sexes:** the core of romantic stories is the union of the sexes and the inherent belief that love will hold 'eternally', thus insinuating a union of heaven and earth
The cosmogonic-genealogical dimension which explains the origin of the world and that of the humans	**The Meeting and Commitment:** hero and heroine create their own cosmos by living out their emotions and being sealed off from the world around them
The dimension of fertility and sexuality which comprises husbandry, fertility, and the interval between birth and death	**The Barriers and Sexuality:** hero and heroine meet, unite (sexually), and overcome problems and hardship. They always die a ritual death before they commit for a life-time
The political-legitimizing dimension which justifies the king's king-ship	**Society Defined:** the social structure of marriage legitimizes sexual intercourse, and with marriage as an objective, justifies premarital sexual intercourse. Sexual intercourse must be connected with love in order to grant a prospective child to grow up well. In older contemporary romance novels, the man can regard the woman as his property once she is married with him
The public reenactment of the rite takes place once a year	**Reader Participation** is imperative. Narration without reader participation is ineffective. The reading act becomes a ritual act a reader performs. Public participation can be seen when a reader becomes part of the reader-community

BIBLIOGRAPHY

PRIMARY LITERATURE

JAYNE ANN KRENTZ
NOVELS CITED
CURTAIN SERIES

2. *Amaryllis* (1996). New York: Pocket Books, 1996. Print.
3. *Zinnia* (1997). New York: Pocket Books, 1997. Print.
4. *Orchid* (1998). New York: Pocket Books, 1997. Print.

CATEGORY ROMANCE

Stormy Challenge (1982). New York: Harlequin, 2004. Print.
Uneasy Alliance (1984). New York: Harlequin, 2009. Print.

STAND-ALONE NOVELS

Golden Chance (1990). New York: Pocket Star, 1990. Print.
Family Man (1992). New York: Pocket, 1992. Print.
Perfect Partners (1992). New York: Mandarin Paperbacks, 1995. Print.
Hidden Talents (1993). New York: Pocket, 1993. Print.
Wildest Hearts (1993). New York: Pocket Books, 1993. Print.
Grand Passion (1994). New York: Pocket Books, 1994. Print.
Absolutely, Positively (1996). New York: Pocket Books, 1996. Print.
Smoke in Mirrors (2002). New York: Jove, 2002. Print.
All Night Long (2007). New York: Jove, 2007. Print.
White Lies (2007). New York: Jove, 2007. Print.

BARBARA DELINSKY
NOVELS CITED

Sweet Ember (1981). New York: Harper Paperbacks, 1997. Print.
Lilac Awakening (1982). New York: Harper Torch, 1982. Print.
Gemstone (1983). New York: Harper Torch, 1993. Print.
Moment to Moment (1984). New York: Harper Torch, 2004. Print.
The Carpenter's Lady (1983). New York: Avon, 1999. Print.
Within Reach (1986). New York: Harper Torch, 2004. Print.
Commitments (1988). New York: Grand Central Publishing, 2009. Print.
A Woman Betrayed (1991). New York: Harper Paperbacks, 1991. Print.
The Passions of Chelsea Kane (1992). New York: Harper Torch, 2004. Print.
Together Alone (1995). New York: William Morrow Paperbacks, 2009. Print.
Shades of Grace (1995). New York: Avon, 2009. Print.
A Woman's Place (1997). New York: Avon, 1997. Print.
Coast Road (1998). London: Headline, 1998. Print.
Flirting with Pete (2003). New York: Pocket Books, 2003. Print.
The Summer I Dared (2004). New York: Pocket Books, 2011. Print.
Family Tree (2007). New York: Harper Collins, 2007. Print.

VICTORIA LESSER SERIES

1. *The Real Thing* (1986). New York: Silhouette Books, 1994. Print. 2. *Twelve Across* (1987). New York: Silhouette Books, 1994. Print. 3. *A Single Rose* (1987). New York: Silhouette Books, 1994. Print.

THE DREAM: CROSSLYN RISE SERIES

1. *The Dream* (1990). New York: Harlequin, 1999. Print. 2. *The Dream Unfolds* (1990). New York: Harlequin, 1999. Print. 3. *The Dream Comes True* (1990). New York: Harlequin, 1999. Print.

Anita Shreve. The Pilot's Wife. London: Abacus, 1995. Print.

SECONDARY LITERATURE

Adorno, Theodor W. *Gesammelte Schriften: Aesthetische Theorie.* Ed. Adorno, Gretel, and Rolf Tiedemann. Bd. 7. Frankfurt a.M. 1997. 351. Print.

Agamon; Koppl; Fine, Shimoni. "Gender Genre, and Writing Style in Formal Written Texts." *Texts.* 23(3), August 2003

Alberts, J.K. "The role of couples' conversations in relational development: A content analysis of courtship talk in harlequin romance novels." *Communication Quarterly.* 1986. 34(2). 127–142. Print.

Altman, Meryl. "Beyond Trashiness: The Sexual Language of the 1970s Feminist Fiction." *Journal of International Women's Studies.* Vol.4. 2003. Print.

Andeotti, Mario. *Die Struktur der modernen Literatur.* 4th ed. Stuttgart: Haupt UTB, 2009. Print.

Anz, Thomas. *Literatur und Lust, Glück und Unglück beim Lesen.* München: C.H. Beck, 1998. Print.

Applebaum, Herbert (Hg). *The American Work Ethic and the Changing Work Force: An Historical Perspective.* Westport CT: Greenwood Press, 1998. Print.

Applebaum, Herbert. "A Feminine Genre: Romance and Women". Retrieved 02.08.2009. http://fds.oup.com/www.oup.co.uk/pdf/0-19-924984-9.pdf

Aristotle. *Aristotle's Poetics,* Translated by S.H. Butcher, Hill and Wand. New York, 1961. Print.

Arnold, Heinz Ludwig, and Heinrich Detering. *Grundzüge der Literaturwissenschaft.* 8th ed. München: Deutscher Taschenbuch Verlag, 2008. Print.

Augustinus, Aurelius. *Die Bekenntnisschriften des heiligen Augustinus,* übersetzt von Otto F. Lachmann, Leipzig: Reclam Nr. 2791, 1888. Print.

Avanessian, Armen and Hennig, Anke. *Präsens. Poetik eines Tempus.* Zürich: diaphanes, 2012. Print.

Bachtin, Michail M. *Probleme der Poetik Dostojewskis.* München, 1971. Print.

Baker, Wayne E. *America's Crisis of Values: Reality and Perception.* New Jersey: Princeton University Press, 2005. Print.

Baker, Wayne and Campbel, Gayle. "American Values: Are We Really Divided?" http://www.everydaysociologyblog.com/2011/03/american-values-are-we-really-divided.html 21.03.2011. Retrieved 15.03.2013

Barlow, Linda, and Jayne Ann Krentz. "Beneath the Surface." *Dangerous Men and Adventurous Women.* University of Pennsylvania Press, 1992. Print.

Barthes, Roland. "The Death of the Author." *Image Music Text*. London: Fontana, 1968/1977. 142–148. Print.

Barthes, Roland, and Lionel Duisit. "An Introduction to the Structural Analysis of Narrative." *New Literary History*. Vol.6, No.2. *On Narrative and Narratives*. (Winter 1975). The John Hopkins University Press. 237–272. Print.

Barthes, Roland. *Mythen des Alltags*. Frankfurt a.M.: edition suhrkamp 92, 1964. Print.

Bayertz, Kurt (Hg). *Warum moralisch sein*, 2. Auflg. Paderborn: C.H. Beck, 2006. Print.

Beauvoir, Simone de. *Das andere Geschlecht, Sitte und Sexus der Frau*. Hamburg: Rowohlt, 1986. Print.

Bein, Thomas. "Zum 'Autor' im mittelalterlichen Literaturbetrieb und im Diskurs der germanistischen Mediävistik." Jannidis et al.(Hg). *Rückkehr des Autors. Zur Erneuerung eines umstrittenen Begriffs*. Tübingen: Niemeyer, 1999. Print.

Bellah, Robert N. *The Broken Convenant: American Civil Religion in Time of Trial*, New York: Seabury Press, 1975. Print.

Blair-Loy, Mary. "Moral Dimensions of the Work-Family Nexus." NSF Morality Conference. June 2009, http://www.google.com/search?client=safari\&rls=en\&q=BLAIR-LOY$++$MORAL$+$DIMENSIONS$+$NEXUS$+$NSF$+$MORALITY\&ie=UTF-8\&oe=UTF-8

"Bookreporter.com – Author Profile: Barbara Delinsky." interview 2010. Retrieved 25.03.2010. http://www.google.com/search?

Booth, Wayne C. *The Rhetoric of Fiction*. The University of Chicago Press, 1983(2). Print.

Booth, Wayne C. *The Company we Keep: An Ethics of Fiction*. Berkely: The University of California Press, 1988. Print.

Botts, Amber. "Cavewoman Impulses: The Jungian Shadow, Archetype in Popular Romantic Fiction." *Romantic Conventions*. Bowling Green State University Popular Press, 1999. 62–74. Print.

Bourdieu, Pierre. *Die feinen Unterschiede*. Frankfurt a.M.: suhrkamp, 1987. Print.

Bourdieu, Pierre. *Die männliche Herrschaft*. Frankfurt a.M.: suhrkamp, 1998. Print.

Bourdieu, Pierre. *Distinctions. A Social Critique of the Judgement of Taste*. translated by Richard Nice. Harvard University Press, 1984. Print.

Brayfield, Celia. *Bestseller Secrets of Successful Writing*. London: Fourth Estate, 1996. Print.

Brayman Hackel, Heidi, "Boasting of Silence: women readers in a patriarchal state." *Reading, Society, and Politics In Early Modern England*. Ed. Sharpe, Kevin, and Steven N. Zwicker. Cambridge University Press, 2003. 101–121. Print.

Brayman Hackel, Heidi, and Catherine E. Kelly. "Reading Women: Literacy, Authorship, and Culture." *The Atlantic World, 1500–1800*. University of Pennsilvania Press, 2008. Print.

Bun, Jennifer, C. "The Effects of Romance Novel Readership on Relationship Beliefs, Romantic Ideals, and Relational Satisfaction." An Honors Thesis Directed by Prof. Jonathan M. Booman. Boston, 2007. Retrieved 27.04.2010. http://www.bc.edu/content/dam/files/schools/cas_sites/communication/pdf/thesis07.bun.pdf.

Cawelti, John G. *Adventure, Mystery, and Romance: Formula Story as Art and Popular Culture*. University of Chicago Press paperback edition, 1977. Print.

Camacho, Kristie. "Author Profile – Jayne Ann Krentz." Suite 101.com, http://suite101.com/article/author-profile-jayne-ann-krentz-a116531, retrieved 30.05.2009.

Carr, Felicia L. "American Women's Dime Novel Project." http://chnm.gmu.edu/dimenovels/the-american-womens-dime-novel, retrieved 25.08.2009.

Chatman, Seymour, *Story and Discourse. Narrative Structure in Fiction and Film.* Cornell University Press, 1980. Print.

Chen, Li-Fen. *Fictionality and Reality in Narrative Discours, A Reading of Four Contemporary Taiwanese Writers.* Diss. University of Washington, 2000. Print.

Cohn, Dorrit. *Transparent Minds. Narrating Modes for Presenting Consciousness in Fiction.* Princeton University Press, 1978/1981. Print.

Cohn, Janet. *Romance and the Erotics of Property, Massmarket Fiction for Women.* Duke University Press, 1998. Print.

Coontz, Stephanie. *Marriage, a History.* New York: Penguin, 2005. Print.

Crusie, Jennifer, Essays: "Romancing Reality: The Power of Romance Fiction to Reinforce and Re-Vision the Real." 1998. Retrieved 29.05.2009 http://www.jennycrusie.com/for-writers/essays/romancing-reality-the-power-of-romance-fiction-to-reinforce-and-re-vision-the-real/
"Defeating the Critics: What We Can Do About the Anti-Romance." 1998. Retrieved 29.05.2009. http://www.jennycrusie.com/for-writers/essays/romancing-reality-the-power-of-romance-fiction-to-reinforce-and-re-vision-the-real/
"Let Us Now Praise Scribbling Women." 1998. Retrieved 29.05.2009. http://www.jennycrusie.com/for-writers/essays/romancing-reality-the-power-of-romance-fiction-to-reinforce-and-re-vision-the-real/
"So, Bill, I Hear You Write Those Little Poems: A Plea For Category Romance." 1998. Retrieved 29.05.2009. http://www.jennycrusie.com/for-writers/essays/romancing-reality-the-power-of-romance-fiction-to-reinforce-and-re-vision-the-real/
"This Is Not Your Mother's Cinderella: The Romance Novel as Feminist Fairy Tale." 1998. Retrieved 29.05.2009. http://www.jennycrusie.com/for-writers/essays/romancing-reality-the-power-of-romance-fiction-to-reinforce-and-re-vision-the-real/
"I Know it When I Read It: Defining the Romance," 2000. Retrieved 29.5.2009. http://www.jennycrusie.com/for-writers/essays/romancing-reality-the-power-of-romance-fiction-to-reinforce-and-re-vision-the-real/

Danford, Samuel. "A Brief Recognition Into the Wilderness." An electronic text edition, no date. 24. Retrieved 28.10.2009. http://digitalcommons.unl.edu/libraryscience/35/

Danto, Arthur C. *The Transfiguration of the Commonplace. A Philosophy of Art.* Cambridge, Mass.: Harvard University Press, 1982. Print.

Davidson, Cathyy N., and Linda Wagner-Martin (ed.). *The Oxford Companion To Woman's Writing in The United States New York.* Oxford University Press, 1995. Print.

Davis, Sara N. "Romance Readers: Bridging the Gap Between Readers and Scholars." IGEL Conference, August 2004. Retrieved 05.09.2009. http://www.arts.ualberta.ca/igel/igel2004/Proceedings/Davis.pdf

Davis, Sara N. *Values and the Romance Novel,* New York: Kluwert Academic, 2005. Print.

Dixon, j. *The Romance of Mills & Boon 1909–1990.* London: Routledge, 1999. Print.

DMAW = Krentz, Jayne Ann (ed.). *Dangerous Men and Adventurous Women.* 1992.

Dowling, Colette. *Der Cinderella Complex. Die heimliche Angst der Frauen vor der Un- abhängigkeit*. Frankfurt: Fischer, 1984. Print.

Downey, Kristin. *Irony, Ideology, and Resistance: The Amazing Double Life of Harlequin Presents*. Diss. McMaster University Hamilton, Ontario, 2005. Print.

Dubino, Jeanne "The Cinderella Complex: Romance Fiction, Patriarchy, and Capitalism." *Journal of Popular Culture* 27:3. 1993. 103–118, retrieved 16.03.2010. http://jlcoady. net/papers/cinderellas-historical-character

Duerr, Hans Peter. *Der erotische Leib, Der Mythos vom Zivilisationsprozess*. Bd. 4. Frank- furt a. M.: suhrkamp, 1997. Print.

Eco, Umberto. *Zeichen*. Frankfurt a.M.: suhrkamp, 1977. Print.

Edelstein, Wolfgang and Gertrud Nunner-Winkler (Hg). *Zur Bestimmung der Moral*. Frankfurt a.M.: suhrkamp, 1986. Print.

Eder, Jens Jannidis, Fotis and Schneider, Ralf. *Characters in Fictional Worlds*. Berlin/New York: de Gruyter, 2010. Print.

Egleton, Mary (Ed,). *Feminist Literary Theory. A Reader*. USA: Blackwell Publishing, 2004 (1986) Print.

Eisenstein, Elizabeth L. *The Printing Revolution in Early Modern Europe*. Cambridge University Press, 1983. Print.

Eliade, Mircea. *Geschichte der religiösn Ideen*. Bd. 1. Freiburg: Herder, 1978. Print.

Eliade, Mircea. *Das Heilige und das Profane*. Hamburg: Rowohlt, 1957. Print.

Equal Rights Amendment, The, http://www.equalrightsamendment.org/ updated on 06/26/2012.

Fester, Richard, et al. *Weib und Macht*. Frankfurt a.M.: Fischer, 1984. Print.

Fischer-Lichte, Erika. *Performativität Eine Einführung*. Bielefeld: transcript Verlag, 2012. Print.

Fishkin, Shelley Fisher. "Crossroads of Cultures: The Transnational Turn in American Studies." *American Quarterly* 57. Baltimore: John Hopkins University Press, 2005. 17–57.

Fleischman, Suzanne. *Tense and Narrativity: from medieval performance to modern fic- tion*. University Press of Texas, 1990. Print.

Fletcher, Lisa. *Historical Romance Fiction: Heterosexuality and Performativity*. Burling- ton: Ashgate, VT, 2008. Print.

Flusser, Vilem, "Kriterien, Krise, Kritik.", 5. Fotosymposium 1984, *Denkprozesse der Fotographie*. Deppner/Jäger (Hg.). Bielefeld: Kerber Verlag, 2009. 78–86. Print.

Fontane, Theodor. "Rezension über Gustav Freitags *Soll und Haben* (1855)." Hartmut Steinecke (Hg.). *Romanpoetik in Deutschland: Von Hegel bis Fontane*, Tübingen: Narr, 1984

Friday, Nancy. *Die sexuellen Phantasien der Frauen*. München: Scherz, 1978. Print.

Frizzoni, Brigitte. "Adonis revisited: Erotic Representations of the Male Body in Women's Crime Fiction", *Electronic Journal of Folklore*, no.43. 2009. 27–42. Re- trieved 05.01.2010. http://www.folklore.ee/folklore/vol43/frizzoni.pdf

Frye, Northrup. *Anatomy of Criticism: Four Essays*, Princeton: UP, 1957. Print.

Frye, Northrup. *The Archetypes of Literature Forming Fours and Expanding Eyes, Jun- gian Literary Criticism*. Northwestern University Press, 1992. 21–37. Print.

Gelder, Ken. *Popular Fiction, The Logics and Practices of a Literary Field*. London: Routledge, 2004. Print.

Genette, Gerard. *Narrative Discourse*. translated: Lewin, Jane. Oxford: Blackwell, 1972/1980. Print.

Gerrig, Richard. *Experiencing Narrative Worlds. On the Psychological Activities of Reading*. London: Westview, 1993. Print.

Gianoulis, Tina. "Harlequin Romances." *James Encyclopedia of Pop Culture*. 2002. http: //findarticles.com/p/articles/mi_g1epc/ai_2419100567/, retrieved 25.08.08.

Gildemeister, Robert. "Im Spannungsfeld von Rationalisierungen der Arbeitswelt und 'postindustriellem Haushaltssektor':Vergeschlechtlichung, Neutralisierung und Revergeschlechtlichung." Brandes and Roernheld (Hg). *Männernormen und Frauenrollen, Geschlechterverhältnisse in der sozialen Arbeit*, Leipzig: Evangelische Verlagsanstalt, 1993. 37–50. Print.

Glasersfeld, Ernst von. "Siegener Gespräche über radikalen Konstruktivismus." Siegfried J. Schmidt (Hg). *Der Diskurs des Radikalen*. 4. Aufl. Frankfurt a.M.: suhrkamp, 1991. Print.

Grescoe, Paul. *The Merchants of Venus, Inside Harlequin and the Empire of Romance*. Vancouver, B.C. 1996. Print.

Gymnich, Marion. "Gender in der Literatur seit den 1960er Jahren." Nünning, Vera (Hg). *Kulturgeschichte der englischen Literatur Von der Renaissance bis zur Gegenwart*. Tübingen: UTB, 2005. Print:

Haefner, Colon, Lizardo. *Chipping Away at Patriarchy One Romance Novel at a Time*. Chicago: North Park University, 2008. Print.

Hamburger, Käte. *Die Logik der Dichtung*. Stuttgart: Klett Verlag, 1957. Print.

Harlequin Writing Guidelines: Harlequin Presents, 2009, retrieved 05.06.2009. Harlequin.com |Writing Guidelines

Hart, Alison and Barbara Keller. "Romance Fiction as a Feminist Issue." *The Romance Reader Forum Page*. 2001. Retrieved 14.07.2010. http://www.theromancereader.com/forum24.html,

Hartling, Florian. *Der Digitale Autor, Autorschaft im Zeitalter des Internets*. Bielefeld: transcript Verlag, 2009. Print.

Hawthorn, Jeremy. *Grundbegriffe moderner Literaturtheorie*. Tübingen: Unitaschenbücher Nr. 1756, 1994. Print.

Hebel, Udo, J. *Einführung in die Amerikanistik, American Studies*. Stuttgart: Metzler, 2008. Print.

Heidbrink, Henriette. "Fictional Characters in Literary and Media Studies. A Survey of the Research." Eder, Jens/ Jannidis, Fotis/ Schneider, Ralf. *Characters in Fictional Worlds. Understanding Imaginary Beings in Literature, Film and Other Media*. Berlin, New York: de Gryter, 2010. Print.

Hemmungs-Wirten, Eva. "Global Infatuation: Explorations in Transnational Publishing and Texts. The Case of Harlequin and Sweden." *Section for Sociology of Literature at the Department of Literature*. no.38. Uppsala University, 1998. Print.

Herlinghaus, Hermann. "Populär/volkstümlich/Popularkultur." Barck, Karlheinz et al. *Ästhetische Grundbegriffe*. Bd. 4. Stuttgart: Metzler, 2002/2010. Print.

Herman, Ellen. *The Romance of American Psychology. Political Culture in the Age of Experts.* University of California Press, 1995. Print.

Hesse, Carla. "Reading Signatures: Female Authorship and Revolutionary Law in France, 1750–1850." *Eighteenth Century Studies,* Vol.22, No.3. Special Issue: *The French Revolution in Culture.* Spring 1989. 469–487. Print.

Heyse, Paul. "Einleitung." *Deutscher Novellenschatz,* Vol.1. ed. Paul Heyse und Hermann Kurz. München: Oldenburg, 1881. Print.

Hochgeschwender, Michael. *Amerikanische Religion. Evangelikalismus, Pfingstlertum und Fundamentalismus.* Frankfurt a.M.: Insel Verlag, Verlag der Weltreligionen, 2007. Print.

Hoggart, Richard. *The Uses of Literacy.* New York, 1970. Print.

Hühn, Peter, and Wulf Künne. *Englische triviale Frauenliteratur: Fallstudien zu ihrer Rezeption bei Schülern und Studenten.* Königstein/Ts: Athenäum, 1978. Print.

Huntigton, Samuel P., and Lawrence E. Harrison. *Streit um Werte.* München: Goldmann, 2004. Print.

Ingrassia, Catherine. "Fashioning Female Authorship in Eliza Haywood's 'The Tea Table.'" *The Journal of Narrative Technique.* Vol.28, No.3 (Fall, 1998). 287–304. Print.

Iser, Wolfgang. *The Implied Reader.* Baltimore: John Hopkins University Press, 1978. Print.

Iser, Wolfgang. *The Act of Reading, A Theory of Aesthetic Response.* London, 1974. Print.

Jahn, Manfred, *Narratology; A Guide to the Theory of Narrative*, English Department, University of Cologne, 2005. version 1.8, http://www.uni-koeln.de/~ame02/pppn. htm. Print.

Jannidis, Fotis. *Figur und Person. Beitrag zu einer historischen Narratologie.* Berlin, New York: de Gryter, 2004. Print.

Jannidis, Fotis, et al.(Hgg.). *Rückkehr des Autors.* Tübingen: Niemeyer, 1999. Print.

Jannidis, Fotis, et al. (Hgg.) *Texte zur Theorie der Autorschaft.* Stuttgart: Reclam, 2000. Print.

Jauß, Hans Robert. *Literaturgeschichte als Provokation der Literaturwissenschaft*, Konstanz: Unversitätsverlag, 1967. Print.

Kaler, and Johnson-Kurek (ed), *Romantic Conventions,* Bowling Green State University Popular Press, 1999. Print.

Kamble, Jayashree. *Uncovering and Recovering the Popular Romance Novel*, Diss 2008. University of Minnesota, 2008. Print.

Kinsale, Laura. "The Androgynous Reader, Point of View in the Romance." *Dangerous Men and Adventurous Women.* Ed. Jayne Ann Krentz. University of Pennsylvania Press, 1992. Print.

Knopf. J. "Roman." *Historisches Wörterbuch der Philosophie.* Bd. 8. Basel, 1992. 1070–1076. Print.

Konzal, Kornelia. "Wen kümmert's, wer spricht? Autor-Diskurs-Tabu(bruch)." 2005. Retrieved 20.8.2010. http://www.johannes-angermueller.de/deutsch/ADFA/konczal.pdf

Koschorke, Albrecht. *Wahrheit und Erfindung. Grundzüge einer allgemeinen Erzähltheorie.* Frankfurt a.M.: S. Fischer Verlag, 2012. Print.

Kramer, Daniela, and Michael Moore. "Gender Roles, Romantic Fiction and Family Ther-

apy." *Psycology* 12, (024). 2002. Retrieved 02.08.2009. http://www.cogsci.ecs.soton.
ac.uk/cgi/psyc/newpsy?12.024

Kraus, Wolfgang. "Identität als Narration: Die narrative Konstruktion von Identitätsprojekten." retrieved 25.6.2012. http://web.fu-berlin.de/postmoderne-psych/berichte3/
kraus.htm,

Krentz, Jayne Ann (ed). *Dangerous Men and Adventurous Women*, University of Pennsylvania Press, 1992. Print.

Kristeva, Julia. "Probleme der Textstrukturation." *Strukturalismus in der Literaturwissenschaft.* Hrsg. Heinz Blumensath. Köln, 1972. 243–262. Print.

Lafont, Christina. *Sprache und Welterschließung.* Frankfurt a.m.: suhrkamp, 1997. Print.

Lapinkivi, Pirjo. *The Sumerian Sacred Marriage in the Light of Comparative Evidence.*
Helsinki: University of Helsinki, 2004. Print.

Laquer, Thomas. *Auf den Leib geschrieben.* München: dtv, 1996. Print.

Lieske, Stefan. "Strukturalismus, amerikanischer, französischer, genetischer." *Metzler
Lexikon Literatur- und Kulturtheorie*, 2nd ed. Ed. Ansgar Nünning. Stuttgart: Metzler, 2001. 610–613. Print.

Lindhoff, Lena, *Einführung in die feministische Literaturtheorie*, Stuttgart: Sammlung
Metzler Bd. 285, 1995. Print.

Linke, Gabriele. *Populärliteratur als kulturelles Gedächtnis: eine vergleichende Studie zu
zeitgenössischen britischen und amerikanischen popular romances der Verlagsgruppe
Harlequin-Mills and Boons.* Heidelberg: Universitätsverlag Winter, 2003. Print.

Livingston, Paisley. *Art and Intention: A Philosophical Study.* New York: Oxford University Press, 2005. Print.

Long, Bridget. *Women's Romance Novel Readership: Motivations, Expectations, and
Reader Satisfaction.* Chicago, 2007. Print. Retrieved 28.10.2010. http://citation.
allacademic.com/meta/p_mla_apa_research_citation/

Lotmann, Juriij, M. *Die Struktur literarischer Texte.* 4. Auflg. München: UTB Nr. 103,
1972/1993. Print.

Luhmann, Niklas. *Die Gesellschaft der Gesellschaft.* Bd. 2. Frankfurt a.M.: suhrkamp,
1997. Print.

Luhmann, Niklas. *Liebe als Passion.* 13. Aufl. Frankfurt a.M.: suhrkamp, 1994. Print.

Luhmann, Niklas. "Was ist Kommunikation?" and "Darum Liebe." *Short Cuts.* Frankfurt
a.M.: Zweitausendeins, 2001. Print.

Lutz, Deborah. *Heidegger, the Erotics of Ontology and the Mass Market Romance.* Purdue
University Press, 2003. Print.

Marsh, Katherine. "Fabio Gets His Walking-Papers: Can Harlequin Rekindle Romance
in a Post-Feminine World?" *Free Online Library.* retrieved 22.09.09. http://www.unz.
org/Pub/WashingtonMonthly-2002jan-00039

McKee, Robert. *Story: Substance, Structure, Style, and the Principles of Screenwriting.*
New York: Harper-Collins, 1997. Print.

Mead, Margaret. *Mann und Weib.* Hamburg: Rowohlt, 1958. Print.

Merten, Kai. *Antike Mythe – Mythos Antike.* München: Finck, 2004. Print.

Middle Class in America, Report prepared by the US Department of Commerce, Economic and Statistics Administration, January 2010. Retrieved 3.08.2010.

Miller, J. Hillis. "Henry James and 'Focalization' or Why James Loves Gyp." *A Compan-*

ion to Narrative Theory. Eds. James Phelan and Peter J. Rabinowitz. Oxford: Blackwell Publishing, 2008. Print.

Modleski, Tania. "The Disappearing Act: A Study of Harlequin Romances." *Journal of Women in Culture and Society*, vol.5. No 3, 1980. 435–448. Print.

Modleski, Tania. *Loving with a Vengence: Mass-Produced Fantasies for Women.* New York: Methuen, 1982. Print.

Morgan, Robin. *Anatomie der Freiheit.* München, 1985. Print.

Morrissey, Katherine E. *Fanning the Flame of Romance. An Exploration of Fan Fiction and the Romance Novel.* Washington. D.C. 2008. Print.

Mussell, Kay, *Women's Gothic and Romantic Fiction: A Reference Guide*, Westport, CT: Greenwood, 1981. Print.

Mussell, Kay. *Fantasy and Reconciliation: Contemporary Formulas of Women's Romance Fiction.* Greenwood Press, 1984. Print.

Mussell, Kay. "All About Romance Novels: Quickie with Kay Mussell: Are Feminism and Romance Novels Mutually Exclusive?" 1997. Retrieved 25.06.2009. http://www.likesbooks.com/mussell.html

Naison, Mark, "The McCain Palin Ticket Appeals to a Powerful Strain of Anti-Intellectualism in American Society." *History News Network*, 09.06.2008. Retrieved 31.05.2010. http://hnn.us/roundup/entries/54182.html

Nathason, Paul, and Katherine Young. *Legalizing Misandry: From Public Shame to Systemic Discrimination against Men.* McGill-Queens University Press, 2006. Print.

National Cultural Values Survey, The, a special report of the Culture and Media Institute, 2007. Retrieved 28.06.2009. http://www.freerepublic.com/focus/f-news/1796999/posts

Naumann, Michael. "Paul Auster." *Die Zeit*, Nr. 6, 2007.

Neitzel, Sönke, and Harald Welzer. *Soldaten, Protokolle vom Kämpfen, Töten und Sterben.* 5. Aufl. Frankfurt: Fischer, 2011. Print.

Nesselroth, P.W. "Naming names in telling tales." *Fiction Updated Theories of Fictionality, Narratology, and Poetics.* Eds. Mihailescu, C., and Haranarneh, University of Toronto Press, 1997. 133–143. Print.

Nünning, Vera, and Ansgar Nünning (Hgs.). *Erzähltextanalyse und Gender Studies*, Stuttgart: Klett, 2004. Print.

Nünning, Vera (Hg). *Kulturgeschichte der englischen Literatur.* Tübingen: Francke, 2005. Print.

Nünning, Vera, and Ansgar Nünning. *An Introduction to the Study of English and American Literature.* Stuttgart: Klett, 2008. Print.

Océ case study *retrieved 22.04.2013*

Orton, Peter. *Effects of Perceived Choice and Narrative Elements on Interest in and Liking of Story.* Diss. Stanford University. 1955. Print.

Owens Malek, Doreen. "Mad, Bad, and Dangerous to Know: The Hero as Challenge." *Dangerous Men and Adventurous Women.* Ed. Jayne Ann Krentz. University of Pennsylvania Press, 1992. 73–80. Print.

Owens, Malek, Doreen. "Loved I Not Honor More: The Virginal Heroine in the Romance." *Dangerous Men and Adventurous Women.* Ed. Jayne Ann Krentz. University of Pennsylvania Press, 1992. 115–120. Print.

Parv, Valerie. *The Art of Romance Writing*. St Leonards NSW, Australia: Allan&Unwin, 1997. Print.

Pearce, Lynne. *Romance Writing*. Cambridge: Polity, 2007. Print.

Petz, Annette. *Chick Lit, Genrekonstituierende Untersuchungen unter anglo-amerikanischem Einfluss*. Diss. Mainz, 2009. Print.

Pew research Center for the People & the Press. "Partisan Polarisation Surges in Bush, Obama Years. Trends in American Values: 1987–2012." 04.06.2012. http://www.people-press.org/2012/06/04/partisan-polarization-surges-in-bush-obama-years/ retrieved 15.03.2013. Print.

Phelan, James and Peter Rabinowitz (eds). *A Companion to Narrative Theory*. Oxford UK: Blackwell Publishing, 2005. Print.

Platon. "Die Rede des Aristophanes." *Das Gastmahl* übers. von Franz Susemihl. Bonn, 1949. 189c–193e. Print.

Pratt, Annis. *Archetypal Patterns in Women's Fiction*. Indiana University Press, 1981. Print.

Propp, Vladimir. *Morphology of the Folk Tale*. Austin: University of Texas Press, 1928/1979. Print.

Pusch, Luise F. (Hg.). *Feminismus*. Frankfurt a. M.: suhrkamp, 1983. Print.

Radway, Janice A. *Reading the Romance, Women, Patriarchy, and Popular Literature*. University of North Carolina Press, 1984. Print.

Radway, Janice A. *A feeling for books: The Book-of-the-Month Club, literary taste, and middle-class desire*. Chapel Hill: University of North Carolina Press. 1997. Print.

Raeithel, Gerd. *Geschichte der Nordamerikanischen Kultur*. Bd. 1

Raeithel, Gerd. *Geschichte der Nordamerikanischen Kultur*. Bd. 3 (1930–1988). Weinheim: Parkland, 1989. Print.

Regis, Pamela. *A Natural History of the Romance Novel*. Philadelphia: University of Pennsylvania Press, 2003. Print.

Rholetter, Wylene. "Romance Novels." in: *St. James Encyclopedia of Pop Culture*. 2002. Retrieved 5.6.2008. http://findarticles.com/p/articles/mi_g1epc/is_tov/ai_2419101042/

Roach, Catherine. "Getting a Good Man to Love: Popular Fiction and the Problem of Patriarchy." *Internet Journal of Popular Romance Studies*. Issue 1.1.2010. Retrieved 5.07.2011. http://jprstudies.org/2010/08/getting-a-good-man-to-love-popular-romance-fiction-and-the-problem-of-patriarchy-by-catherine-roach/

Romance Writers of America / industry statistics/2004 romstat report Romance Writers of America readership statistics, retrieved 02.06.2009. http://www.ebookoverlord.com/2004-romstat-report-home---romance-writers-of-america

Rosen, Irving M. "Social Taboos and Emotional Problems." *Journal of Religion and Health*. vol.11, No.2. 1972. Print.

Routledge Encyclopedia of Narrative Theory. Eds. Hermann, Jahn, Ryan. London: Routledge, 2008. Print.

Rusch, Gebhard. "Autopoiesis, Literatur und Wissenschaft." Siegfried Schmidt (Hg). *Der Diskurs des Radikalen Konstruktivismus*. Frankfurt a.M.: suhrkamp, 1987. 374–400. Print.

Russell, Bertrand. *The Conquest of Happiness*. New York: Liveright, repr. 1977/1996. Print.

Schabert, Ina. *Englische Literaturgeschichte aus der Sicht der Geschlechterforschung*. Stuttgart: Kröner, 1997. Print.

Schabert, Ina. *Englische Literaturgeschichte des 20. Jahrhunderts, eine neue Darstellung aus der Sicht der Geschlechterforschung*. Stuttgart: Kröner, 2006. Print.

Schmidt, Siegfried J. ed. *Der Diskurs des Radikalen Konstruktivismus*. Frankfurt a.M.: suhrkamp, 1987. Print.

Schneider-Mayerson, Matthew. "Popular Fiction Studies: The Advantage of a New Field." *Studies in Popular Culture*. 33.1. University of Minnesota, Fall 2010. 21–36. Print.

Schöbert, Jörg. "Author." Eds. Hühn et al. *The Living Handbook of Narratology*. Hamburg: University Press and internet, 2011. Print.

Schutte, Jürgen. *Einführung in die Literaturinterpretation*. 4. akt. Auflg. Stuttgart: Metzler, 1997. Print.

Seligman, Martin E.P. and Mihaly Csikszentmihalyi. "Positive Psychology." 2000. Retrieved 25.08.2010. http://psycnet.apa.org/index.cfm?fa=buy.optionToBuy&id=2000-13324-001

Sheehy, Gail. *New Passages*. London: Ballantine Books, 1996. Print.

Simonis, Anette. "Mythentheorie und -kritik." *Metzler Lexikon Literatur- und Kulturtheorie*. 2nd ed. Ed. Ansgar Nünning. Stuttgart: Metzler, 2001. 461–463. Print.

Sloan, Gary. "Mistaking Subject Matter for Style." *College English*. vol.43, No.5. 1981. 502–507. Print.

Snitow, Ann Barr. "Mass Market Romance: Pornography for Women Is Different." *Radical History Review*. no.20. 1979. 141–161. Print.

Stanzel, Franz K. *Theorie des Erzählens*. 2nd ed. Göttingen: Vandenhoek, 1982. Print.

Stein, Sol. *Über das Schreiben*. Frankfurt: zweitausendeins, 2009. Print.

Sterk, Helen Mae. *Functioning Fictions: the adjustment rethoric of Silhouette romance novels*. PhD thesis, University Press of Iowa, 1986. Print.

Sunita. "When we defend romance reading as escapism. the critics win." http://dearauthor.com/features/letters-of-opinion/when-we-defend-romance-reading-as-escapism-the-critics-win/

Thurer, Shari. *Mythos Mutterschaft*. München: Droemer Knaur, 1995. Print.

Thurston, Carol. *The Romance Revolution: Erotic Novels for Women and the Quest for a New Sexual Identity*. Urbana, Il: University of Illinois Press, 1987. Print.

Trent, Caroline Jamie. "Culture of Sex. Sexual Linguistics and Discourse of *Cosmopolitan* Editions in the United States, France and India". Thesis presented to the Faculty of the Graduate School University of Missouri-Columbia. 2009. 41–45. Retrieved 25.6.2012. https://mospace.umsystem.edu/xmlui/bitstream/handle/10355/5373/research.pdf?sequence=3

Turpin, Kelley. "Holding Out for a Hero. A Duel Method Analysis of the Damsel in Distress in Harlequin Presents." paper presented at the American Sociological Association Annual Meeting, Boston 2008. Retrieved 12.10.09.

Uhlmann, Poelman, Bargh. "American Moral Exceptionalism." *Social and Psychological Bases of Ideology and System Justification*. Oxford, 2009. 27–53. Print.

Volli, Ugo. *Semiotik*. Tübingen: UTB Nr. 2318, 2002. Print.

Vivanco, Laura and Kyra Kramer. "There Are Six Bodies in this Relationship: An Anthropological Approach to the Romance Genre." *Internet Journal of Popular Romance Studies*, Issue 1.1.2010. Retrieved 8.5.2010. http://independent.academia.edu/LauraVivanco/Papers/1100936/

Vivanco, Laura. *For Love and Money: the Literary Art of The Harlequin Mills&Boon Romance.* Humanities – Ebooks, 2011. Print.

Walsh, Richard. "The Pragmatics of Narrative Fiction" Eds. James Phelan and Peter J. Rabinowitz. *A Companion to Narrative Theory.* Blackwell Publishing, 2008. Print.

Watt, Ian. *The Rise of the Novel, Studies in Defoe, Richardson and Fielding.* London: Chatto and Windus, Ltd, 1957. Print.

Weber, Max. *The Protestant Ethic and the Spirit of Capitalism,* New York: Dover, 2003. Print.

Webster, Dan. "spokesman review. com, Jayne Ann Krentz." 01.07.2004. Retrieved 25.05.2009. http://www.spokesmanreview.com/interactive/bookclub/interviews/interview.asp?IntID=17,

Weiser, Artur. *Einführung in das Alte Testament.* 5th ed. Göttingen: Vandenhoek-&Ruprecht, 1963. Print.

Welsch, Wolfgang. *Unsere postmoderne Moderne.* Berlin: Akademie Verlag, 2002. Print.

Wendell, Sarah and Candy Tan. *Beyond Heaving Bosoms. The Smart Bitches Guide to Romance Novels.* New York: Simon and Schuster. 2009. Print.

Wentworth, Erica. "Willing Surrender; The Politics of Writing Romance." 1997. Retrieved 02.08.2009. http://www.romancewiki.com/Academic_Online_Essays_(not_published_in_academic_journals_or_volumes)

Willand, Markus. *Autorfunktionsanalyse in literaturwissenschaftlicher Theorie und Praxis anhand verschiedener Interpretationen des Dramas 'Die Soldaten' von J.M.R. Lenz.* Berlin: Humboldt-Universität, Magisterarbeit. 2008.

Williams, Susan S. *Reclaiming Authorship: Literary Women in America, 1850–1900.* University of Pennsilvania Press, 2006. Print.

Winkle, Sally, *Women as Bourgeois Ideal: A Study of Sophie von La Roche's Geschichte des Fräuleins von Sternheim und Goethe's Werther.* Berlin: Peter Lang Verlag. Studies in Modern German Literature, 16. 1988.

White, Claire E. "A conversation with Barbara Delinsky, Writers write." The IWY, retrieved 31.08.2009. http://www.writerswrite.com/journal/jun00/delinsky.htm,

Winko, Simone. "Autorfunktionen: Zur argumentativen Verwendung von Autorkonzepten in der gegenwärtigen literaturwissenschaftlichen Interpretationspraxis.", *Autorschaft, Positionen und Revisionen.* Detering, Heinrich (Hg.). Stuttgart: Metzler, 2002. Print.

Winthrop-Young, and Maresch. "Die Zeit der Kulturkriege ist vorbei." retrieved 11.05.10. http://www.heise.de/tp/artikel/22/22430/1.html

Wood, Peter. "Reading at Risk" *National Review Online*, July 19, 2004. Retrieved 2.10.2011. http://old.nationalreview.com/comment/wood200407190842.asp,

Wu, Huei-Hsia. "Gender, Romance Novels, and Plastic Sexuality in the USA." *Journal of International Women's Studies.* vol.8. Bridgewater, Nov. 2006. Print.

Wyckhoff, Donna. *Romancing Reality: Newsstand Novels and Social Morality.* Baskent University, 1999. Print.

Zapf, Hubert: *Kurze Geschichte der anglo-amerikanischen Literaturtheorie.* München: Fink, 1991. Print.

Zidl, Abby. "From Bodice-Ripper to Baby-Sitter: The New Hero in Mass-Market Romance." *Romantic Conventions.* Eds. Kahler, and Kurek. Bowling Green State: University Popular Press, 1999. 23–34. Print.

Zimmermann, Miriam and Reuben Zimmermann. "'Heilige Hochzeit' der Göttersöhne und Menschentöchter? Spuren des Mythos in Gen. 6,1–4." *Zeitschrift für die alttestamentlichwe Wissenschaft.* Hans-Christian Schmitt and Gunther Wanke (Hrsg). Bd. 111. Berlin, 1999. 327–352. Print.

Zipfel, Frank. *Fiktion, Fiktivität, Fiktionalität. Analysen zur Fiktion in der Literatur und zum Fiktionsbegriff in der Literaturwissenschaft.* Berlin: Erich Schmidt Verlag, 2001. Print.

Zizek, Slavoj. *Lacan, Eine Einführung.* Frankfurt: Fischer, 2008. Print.

Yankelovich, Daniel. "How Changes In The Economy Are Reshaping American Values." https://www.msu.edu/~mandrews/global/Changingvalues.pdf retrieved 14.03.2013. Print.